Productivity Growth and Economic Performance

P.J. Verdoorn

Productivity Growth and Economic Performance

Essays on Verdoorn's Law

Edited by

John McCombie
Fellow in Economics
Downing College, Cambridge
UK

Maurizio Pugno
Professor of Economics
University of Trento
Italy

and

Bruno Soro
Associate Professor of Economic Policy
University of Genoa
Italy

palgrave
macmillan

First published 2002 by
PALGRAVE MACMILLAN
Houndmills, Basingstoke, Hampshire RG21 6XS and
175 Fifth Avenue, New York, N. Y. 10010
Companies and representatives throughout the world

PALGRAVE MACMILLAN is the global academic imprint of the Palgrave Macmillan division of St. Martin's Press, LLC and of Palgrave Macmillan Ltd. Macmillan® is a registered trademark in the United States, United Kingdom and other countries. Palgrave is a registered trademark in the European Union and other countries.

ISBN 0–333–96877–8 hardback

This book is printed on paper suitable for recycling and made from fully managed and sustained forest sources.

A catalogue record for this book is available from the British Library.

Library of Congress Cataloging-in-Publication Data
Productivity growth and economic performance: essays on Verdoorn's law/edited by John McCombie, Maurizio Pugno, and Bruno Soro.
p. cm.
Includes bibliographical references and index.
ISBN 0–333–96877–8
1. Labor productivity. 2. Industrial productivity. 3. Division of labor. 4. Economic development. I. McCombie, J.S.L. II. Pugno, Maurizio. III. Soro, Bruno, 1945–

HC79.L3 P743 2003
338.9'001–dc21

2002029400

10 9 8 7 6 5 4 3 2 1
11 10 09 08 07 06 05 04 03 02

Printed and bound in Great Britain by
Antony Rowe Ltd, Chippenham and Eastbourne

Contents

List of Tables

Notes on the Contributors

Carluccio Bianchi is Professor of Economic Policy at the University of Pavia, Italy. He was awarded a BA (Hons) in Economics from Cambridge University in 1974. His research work has been concerned with input–output theory and applications, monetary theory and policy, macroeconomic analysis, and several empirical issues, with particular reference to the Italian experience.

Sergio Destefanis is Associate Professor of Economics at the University of Salerno, Italy. He took his PhD at Cambridge, and was awarded the Tarantelli Prize for the best paper given at the 1995 meeting of the Italian Association of Labour Economics. His research interests include wage and price determination, growth in dualistic economies and the quantitative analysis of productive processes.

Miguel A. León-Ledesma is a Lecturer in Economics at the Department of Economics of the University of Kent, UK. He has a PhD in Economics from the University of La Laguna, Spain, and his main research interests are in the areas of economic growth and international economics. His research has focused on demand-led models of economic growth and the analysis of the relation between trade and growth. Some recent publications include 'Economic Growth and the Verdoorn Law in the Spanish Regions' (*International Review of Applied Economics*, 2000) and 'Accumulation, Innovation and Catching-up: an Extended Cumulative Growth Model' (*Cambridge Journal of Economics*, 2002).

John McCombie is Fellow in Economics at Downing College and a member of the University of Cambridge. His main research interests are economic growth, Keynesian economics and regional economics. He is currently working on a critique of the neoclassical aggregate production function and its associated measure of technical progress. He is the author (with A.P. Thirlwall) of *Economic Growth and the Balance-of-Payments Constraint* (1994).

Maurizio Pugno is Professor of Economics at the University of Trento, Italy and was awarded an MPhil in Economics, Cambridge, UK, in 1980. He has published several articles, both theoretical and empirical, on economic growth, structural change and trade cycle, and a book on Harrod. Two contributions have appeared in *Economic Dynamics, Trade and Growth: Essays on Harrodian Themes* (G. Rampa, L. Stella and A.P. Thirlwall, eds, 1998).

Giorgio Rampa is Professor of Economics at the University of Genoa, Italy. His research work has focused mainly on input–output theory and applications, general economic equilibrium, economic dynamics, rationality and learning theory. He edited (together with L. Stella and A.P. Thirlwall) the book *Economic Dynamics, Trade and Growth: Essays on Harrodian Themes* (1998).

Mark Roberts is a Fellow in Economics at New Hall, Cambridge University, UK. He is also a College Lecturer at Girton College, Cambridge University. He received his BA (Hons) in Economics from Cambridge University in 1996 and his MSc in Economics from Warwick University, UK, in 1997. He was awarded his PhD from the University of Cambridge in 2002 for his thesis entitled *Essays in Cumulative Causation.*

Bruno Soro is Associate Professor of Economic Policy at the University of Genoa, Italy. His main research interests are on the areas of applied economics, growth and development, regional and international economics. He took part in the Research Unit ISTAT-University of Genoa that reconstructed the annual series of the Input–Output tables for the Italian economy 1980–95.

Foreword

John Maynard Keynes once said that there are very few incontrovertible laws in economics, and he is right, but one contender for the status of law might be the empirical regularity, first established by the Dutch economist P.J. Verdoorn in 1949, between the growth of output and labour productivity in manufacturing industry based on Adam Smith's principle of the division of labour. As Verdoorn says himself in the original article : 'in fact one could have expected *a priori* to find a correlation between labour productivity and output, given that the division of labour only comes about through increases in the volume of production ; therefore the expansion of production creates the possibility of further rationalisation which has the same effect as mechanisation.' Verdoorn was too modest a man to elevate his findings to the status of a law, but others did – notably Nicholas Kaldor in his Cambridge Inaugural Lecture in 1966. Up to then, Verdoorn's 1949 paper had hardly been recognised; not surprisingly, perhaps, since it appeared in the relatively obscure Italian journal *L'Industria*, and written in the language of Dante. Only two economists had made reference to Verdoorn before Kaldor: Colin Clark in the third edition of his *Conditions of Economic Progress* published in 1957, and Kenneth Arrow in his classic 1962 paper 'The Economic Implications of Learning by Doing'. Maybe Verdoorn's findings would have surfaced sooner if Kaldor had been interested in the applied economics of growth earlier in his career, since Verdoorn and Kaldor were colleagues in the Research and Planning Division of the Economic Commission for Europe in Geneva when the article was first published, and Kaldor would have known about it.

By the late 1960s/early 1970s, many economists were using and quoting Verdoorn's Law, but I guessed that very few had read the actual article. In Christmas 1973, with the help of an Italian wife and ensconced in a hotel room in Trieste, I decided to translate the article into English and to circulate it privately, with the intention of eventual publication. I wrote to Verdoorn in early 1974 saying 'if you like the translation, would you be averse to its appearance, say, in *International Economic Papers*? I think that the English version of the paper ought to be circulated widely. After all, everybody uses Verdoorn's Law but I bet not many people have read the original!' One of the first persons I circulated it to was Colin Clark whose interest in Verdoorn's Law at this time was in order to support his view that rapid population growth brings scale economies, and therefore confers a blessing on mankind (although in evaluating Clark's views on population growth it should be remembered that he was a Catholic with nine children!). Clark then circulated the translation to Julian Simon at the

University of Illinois, also a population growth optimist, who was editor of *Research in Population and Economics* and wanted to publish the translation in his journal. Out of courtesy, I asked Verdoorn for permission, but he declined on the grounds that he now believed that his so-called 'law' only held in the steady state and that publication of the original article in English would only serve to set people on the wrong track again. My own view was exactly the opposite – that scholarship was not being served by ignorance of the original article – but I respected his wishes. After Verdoorn's death, however, I took the liberty of finally publishing the translation as an appendix to a paper on 'Population Growth and Economic Development' in a book of essays in honour of Colin Clark published in 1988. Verdoorn's Law has generated an enormous secondary literature, both theoretical and applied. The theoretical literature, quite rightly, has been concerned with the underlying production relations by which manufacturing output growth induces labour productivity growth because the estimated 'Verdoorn coefficient' is essentially a reduced-form 'black box'. Verdoorn himself thought of the relation as a learning function based on the division of labour improving the dexterity of workers. In the original article the coefficient is composed of the rate at which capital is growing relative to labour and the parameters of the (static) neoclassical production function. There is no technical progress. Empirically, Verdoorn found the coefficient to range between 0.41 and 0.57, and realistic values applied to his theoretical model produce a value of 0.5. Nowadays, most economists like to think of the Verdoorn relationship in more 'dynamic' terms related to the extent to which capital accumulation is induced by output growth and technical progress is embodied in capital (as well as 'learning by doing') in the spirit of Kaldor's technical progress function. As an aside, I might add that there are strong affinities between Verdoorn's Law, Kaldor's technical progress function and 'new' endogenous growth theory, which has yet to be fully recognised in the literature.

The only way knowledge can progress in the social sciences is by repeated experiments. Whatever the laws of production underlying the relation between output growth and induced productivity growth in manufacturing (and some sections of the service sector too), the extensive empirical evidence overwhelmingly supports such a relationship. Cross-section studies across countries, across regions within countries, and industry studies, all produce a central estimate of the Verdoorn coefficient close to 0.5.

The importance of Verdoorn's Law for our understanding of growth and development is that it is the lynchpin of models of circular and cumulative causation which were first articulated in a rigorous way by Gunnar Myrdal and Albert Hirschman in the 1950s. The law therefore presents a challenge to equilibrium theory which predicts that growth and living standards between regions and countries will converge because the underlying assumption of orthodox theory is that production is subject to constant (not increasing) returns, with diminishing returns to individual factors of production. The contrary view has profound implications for the way the growth and development process should be viewed. Structure matters for economic growth. I leave it to readers to decide what sort of world they think they live in: a world in which economic processes lead to regions and countries converging to a stable equilibrium, or a world in which cumulative forces based on increasing returns in selected activities leads to perpetual divergence.

The editors of this book have done a magnificent job in bringing together a selection of papers that were presented at the conference held in the University of Genoa in 1999 to celebrate the fiftieth anniversary of the publication of Verdoorn's original article, and I feel privileged and honoured to have been asked to write this Foreword.

A.P. THIRLWALL

1
Introduction

John McCombie, Maurizio Pugno and Bruno Soro

Empirical economic laws, viewed as statistical relationships between economic variables that are robust with respect to different data sets and time periods, have often fascinated economists. This may be because they suggest that economics is a science, with a methodology analogous to physics, although without the benefit of controlled experiments. However, these laws have also given rise to lively debates concerning both their empirical validity and their economic interpretation – consider, for example, the original Phillips curve. 'Verdoorn's Law' is no exception to this.

Verdoorn's Law, in its simplest form, refers to a statistical relationship between the long-run rate of growth of labour productivity and the rate of growth of output, usually for the industrial sector. The term 'Verdoorn coefficient' denotes the regression coefficient between the two variables. Around fifty years ago, the Dutch economist P.J. Verdoorn was amongst the first to discover this empirical regularity (Verdoorn, 1949, and chapter 2). Since then the law has been investigated in a large number of studies, using a wide variety of data sets and employing different econometric methods. This may be seen from the Appendix to this Introduction, which provides a concise summary of the methodology and empirical results of the various empirical studies of Verdoorn's Law. The importance of the law is that it provides evidence that industry is subject to substantial increasing returns to scale, defined broadly to include both those that are internal and external to the firm and an industry and those that are dynamic as well as those that are static.

On the whole, the law appears to be largely substantiated in these studies, although, as is the case for most statistical economic relationships, the estimates sometimes need to be qualified. Indeed, in certain circumstances, the law still needs further work to solve a number of econometric problems. However, it is fair to say that Verdoorn's Law should be regarded as something more than just a 'stylised fact'.

This book has a number of objectives. It shows how Verdoorn's Law was originally conceived, and how it has become well known largely through its restatement and interpretation by the late Lord Kaldor, particularly in his famous inaugural lecture at Cambridge in 1966. The chapters in this volume also evaluate a number of important empirical and methodological issues underlying the estimation of the law, as well as discussing the various theoretical rationales that have been advanced to explain it. Finally, the application of the law to other growth models is considered and this leads to some suggestions about possible new areas for research.

In 1945 Verdoorn was appointed by Jan Tinbergen (who was Director of the Netherlands Central Planning Bureau and Verdoorn's supervisor for his PhD dissertation) to run the Central Planning Bureau's 'Labour Issues' department. In this capacity, Verdoorn started to collect data on production and employment for the limited number of countries for which these were available. Working with these statistics, he quickly came to realise that for several manufacturing industries the growth of output per worker, over long periods of time, was closely related to the growth of production. In 1948, Verdoorn joined the team of economists and statisticians of the Research and Planning Division of the Economic Commission for Europe based in Geneva, which was led by Nicholas Kaldor. The following year he published the results of his research into productivity and output growth in the now famous article, written in Italian and entitled 'Fattori che regolano lo sviluppo della produttività del lavoro' – an English translation of which appears as chapter 2 of this volume. This article was published in the Italian journal *L'Industria* and, perhaps as a result of this, for many years its importance went largely unrecognised. The same results were also presented in the following year at the Annual Meeting of the Econometric Society, which was held in Varese, Italy, in September 1950.

The importance of the discovery of such a relation did not escape Kaldor's attention. Indeed, it was Kaldor (1966), who meanwhile had returned to Cambridge University, who coined the term 'Verdoorn's Law' and ensured that it received general recognition. It was one of the two empirical regularities by which he tried, in his famous inaugural lecture held in Cambridge on 2 November 1966, to explain the causes of the United Kingdom's slow rate of economic growth. (The other 'law' put forward by Kaldor was the close relationship between the growth of the industrial sector and GDP growth.) In the mid-1960s, there was great concern in the United Kingdom about the country's slow rate of growth compared with the other advanced countries (with the exception of the United States). In his inaugural lecture, Kaldor placed Verdoorn's Law at the heart of his explanation. A fast rate of productivity growth is induced by a rapid growth of output. In most of the other advanced countries, the growth of industrial output was not constrained by the growth of the labour supply. This was either because there was disguised unemployment in the often large agricultural sectors or because these countries had access to temporary labour or 'guest' workers. By contrast, the United Kingdom had a small, highly productive agricultural sector by this time and so the growth of industrial output was constrained by the growth of the labour supply. Through Verdoorn's Law this led to a slower rate of growth of industrial productivity. Kaldor (1975a) subsequently changed his mind on this in the light of other empirical evidence and concluded that the growth of industry in the United Kingdom had not been limited by the supply side, but rather by balance-of-payments problems. However, even in this later analysis Verdoorn's Law still remained central to his explanation of the United Kingdom's slow growth rate. John McCombie (chapter 4) discusses the interpretation of the law from a Kaldorian viewpoint.

It is since the mid-1960s that Verdoorn's Law, which in the ensuing debate was often restyled the 'Verdoorn–Kaldor Law', or Kaldor's 'Second Law' has attracted the greatest attention. However, ironically, Verdoorn himself did not like the status to which his empirical regularity had been raised. This is best shown by an exchange of letters with A.P. Thirlwall, in which Verdoorn prohibited the publication by Thirwall of an English translation of his original work. Moreover, Verdoorn did not take part in the debate over the 'Verdoorn–Kaldor Law' controversy until he published a short note in 1980, when he cast doubt on his own discovery. In a comment on Rowthorn's (1979) interpretation of his law, he concluded that, '(t)he "law" that has been given my name appears therefore to be much less generally valid than I was led to believe in 1949'. The background to the law is discussed further by Bruno Soro in chapter 3.

Nevertheless, since Kaldor's inaugural lecture, there have been a large number of studies that have generally, although not always, provided estimates confirming Verdoorn's Law. As may be seen from the Appendix to this Introduction, the studies fall into three groups: those that use cross-country or cross-region data, those that use inter-industry data and those that use time-series data for individual countries and regions.[1] The first of these groups includes estimates for the United States, the United Kingdom, the European Union and China. Cross-industry estimates have been undertaken for, inter alia, the United States and the United Kingdom at varying levels of industrial aggregation. Estimates for individual countries have been carried out for a number of countries, including Italy (Carluccio Bianchi, chapter 5). Some of the studies even use statistics dating back to the nineteenth century.

A variety of econometric techniques have been used for estimating Verdoorn's Law including OLS, two-stage least squares and instrumental variable techniques, and more recently, time-series, error correction models and cointegration methods. For spatial data, appropriate methods to test for and, correct, spatial autocorrelation are now more or less routine. One promising alternative way of estimating the law using non-parametric frontier analysis is undertaken by Sergio Destefanis in chapter 6 (see also Førsund, 1996b).

Unfortunately, the earlier studies encountered a number of statistical and econometric problems. Verdoorn's Law suffers from the potential problem of bias due to simultaneity and questions have also arisen over the direction of causality. While more recent studies explicitly address these problems, this was not always the case in the past. There is, furthermore, the danger of a spurious Verdoorn's Law occurring with the use of cross-country data to the extent that the less advanced countries may have a faster growth of 'exogenous' productivity (due to the phenomenon of technological catch-up) as well as a faster growth of output. The latter may be due to the feedback effect from a faster growth of productivity to a faster growth of output through the resulting improved price competitiveness. Hence there is a clear question about the direction of causality. In such cases Verdoorn's Law will be misspecified, although some recent studies have attempted to take account of this by including various proxies for the level of technological development. The use of regional data will generally avoid this problem to the extent that it is unlikely that regions of a single country greatly differ in terms of their level of technology.

There is also a problem with the use of time-series, in that the relationship may capture Okun's, rather than Verdoorn's Law. Okun's Law arises from the observation that in the downturn of an economy, employment does not fall as fast as output, because labour is hoarded. It is costly to sack labour and then re-hire it and if this is done firm-specific skills may be lost. In the upturn, output therefore increases at a faster rate than employment, and this generates a Verdoorn-type relationship between productivity and output growth. However, this has nothing to do with increasing returns or 'learning by doing'. Attempts to circumvent this problem have been undertaken by introducing a lag structure into the relationship and adjusting the inputs for changes in their intensity of use. (Estimates of the capital stock calculated by the perpetual inventory method make no allowance for the changes in the rate of utilisation of the stock.) However, more research needs to be undertaken on this issue, particularly given the problems involved in using time-series (see Carluccio Bianchi, chapter 5).

The original Verdoorn's Law suffers from the problem that no allowance is made for the growth of productivity being determined by increased capital deepening. Sometimes inferences are drawn about the degree of returns to scale on the assumption that the growth of capital is roughly equal to the growth of output – one of Kaldor's 'stylised facts' of economic growth. Most recent estimations of the law explicitly include the growth of the capital stock, although the problem of estimating an underlying identity now arises – a matter that has not yet been fully examined in the literature. By contrast, a lively debate has arisen around the paradox of finding different results when passing from the dynamic specification of the productivity – output relationship to the static one, and this raises the question as to whether or not Verdoorn's Law is simply a conventional production function expressed in growth rate form. This is important because the specification of Verdoorn's Law in growth rates generally finds evidence of substantial increasing returns to scale, whereas this is not the case when log-levels of the variables are used (John McCombie, chapter 4, and Sergio Destefanis, chapter 6).

The story of the theoretical explanations of Verdoorn's Law is even more complicated, and far more open to debate. In his various writings, Verdoorn himself proposed two different approaches, one based on a fixed-coefficient production technology (the 'complementary approach') and the other on the Cobb-Douglas production function, which has an elasticity of substitution of unity between labour and capital. He also suggested a specific mechanism that could give rise to Verdoorn's Law – namely the phenomenon of 'learning by doing'. However, this explanation was not developed in his later works.

It can be inferred that Verdoorn abandoned the complementary approach from his correspondence with A.P. Thirlwall. In a letter to Thirlwall (29 October 1973) Verdoorn wrote: 'On the whole I think that the suggested "law" only holds as an asymptotic case of long term equilibrium development. Compare my "The role of capital in long-range projection", *Cahiers Economiques de Bruxelles*, 5, Oct. 1959, p. 59–69 ... and also: "Méthodes de prévision etc." in *Informations Statistiques de l'Office Statistiques des Communautés Européennes*, 1960, 6 (Nov./Dec.), pp. 561–70'. Moreover in this last Report, in which it is not possible to distinguish his own contribution, Verdoorn *did use* the complementary approach. This might be because he convinced himself of the superiority of the alternative 'substitutability approach' – and the related steady-state solution – when engaged in the correspondence with Thirlwall in the early 1970s, due to the latter's request to publish an English translation of 'Fattori'. In a subsequent letter (11 February 1974) Verdoorn declined to give permission its publication, giving the reason 'that I happen to have shown myself that, theoretically, the "law" holds only in a very special case and that practical implications of this have been discussed and illustrated at length in the *Informations Statistiques* of 1960. Publication in English, therefore, would serve only to set people on the *wrong* track again' (our emphasis). Ending his letter he concluded: 'I hope that you agree that it would be rather foolish to consent to the publication of one's earlier views that one has abandoned, for valid reasons, *already years ago*' (our emphasis). When Thirlwall replied to him (22 February 1974) saying he was 'interested to know what this special case', Verdoorn answered (22 May 1974) that: 'the special case is – presupposing substitutability – the limit case for $t \to \infty$ with the growth of the labour-force, technical progress and the rate of saving being kept constant, i.e. under conditions of steady state growth'. In the same letter he added a summary with the relevant equations.

In the 1950s and 1960s, mainstream growth theory did not adequately explain the determinants of the rate of technical progress. In fact, the usual assumptions adopted were those of exogenous technical progress, full employment, and steady-state growth. In the mid-1960s, Kaldor revitalised Verdoorn's Law by placing particular emphasis on the role of the demand side and the division of labour in economic growth. The latter approach was very much in the tradition of Adam Smith and Allyn Young. However, in the following quarter of a century this approach was neglected by the neoclassical strand of research. One reason for this lies in the microeconomic underpinning of Verdoorn's Law – namely, the existence of increasing returns, broadly defined. It is probable that the Hicksian (1939) dictum on the necessity of perfect competition in order for general equilibrium to exist constrained the research on increasing returns, and, more specifically, on endogenising technical progress.

The renaissance of economic growth theory since the mid-1980s has largely arisen from the availability of new internationally comparable data, dissatisfaction with the assumption of constant returns to scale, and from the recognition of the multitude of disparate growth patterns. This latter factor was especially important because the evidence initially suggested that for the world as a whole there was no necessary tendency for there to be a convergence in international productivity levels – a result which is at variance with the predictions of the Solow–Swan model of economic growth. (This finding was subsequently qualified to a certain extent by the finding that once factors such as the savings rate and human capital were controlled for, there was evidence of conditional beta convergence.) Romer (1986) proposed, as is well known, a model of economic growth with increasing returns and endogenous technical progress. This, with Lucas's (1988) growth model, gave rise to a new line of research in modelling economic growth. As a result, Verdoorn's Law has become of interest to a wider audience. The endogenous growth models have stressed the importance of increasing returns to scale and hence Verdoorn's Law has become particularly relevant for the recent developments in orthodox growth theory. It provides empirical evidence that increasing returns is an issue that any satisfactory growth model has to address, and also that technical progress has an endogenous component.

Consequently, the law is an important piece of empirical evidence with respect to the causes of differences in productivity growth rates. This is because it has implications for research on the determinants of productivity growth and technical progress, on the macroeconomic role of increasing returns, and on the interplay between demand and supply factors in economic growth.

There are, broadly speaking, two competing types of explanations for Verdoorn's Law: one is based on the demand side, the other on the supply side. But it is interesting to note that both Kaldor and Romer argue that

that the same mechanisms are important for understanding economic growth – namely, 'learning by doing' and the increased specialisation of firms and production processes as growth occurs.

Verdoorn's Law is an important piece of analysis, as it can effectively help explain the process of economic divergence among countries and regions, both within a Kaldorian perspective and within the endogenous growth framework. In most of the work to date on the law, the former approach has been followed to a greater extent. In one of his later publications, Kaldor himself gave an indication of how to proceed. First, 'on account of economies of scale, internal and external', he argued that industrial activities give rise to a circular and cumulative process of growth. Secondly, he considered that international trade is a key ingredient for explaining economic growth, as each region (or country) 'is dependent on other regions both for satisfying some of its needs and for providing a market for its products'. A further unavoidable issue in macroeconomic modelling, according to Kaldor, is 'how prices are determined in the oligopolistic conditions prevailing in industry' (Kaldor, 1986, pp. 20–3). Thus, as a result of these suggestions, a number of 'cumulative causation models' have been developed, following the canonical formalisation of Dixon and Thirlwall (1975), with Verdoorn's Law as an important element (Mark Roberts, chapter 7, and León-Ledesma, chapter 8).

The connection between Verdoorn's Law and the 'endogenous growth' models is, as we have noted, partly through the learning function. This had been originally observed for a single production process and is the positive relationship between the level of labour productivity and the level of cumulative output, with the later acting as a proxy for experience gained through simply undertaking production. Moreover, decreasing returns to learning has been also been found so that eventually the benefits from learning become exhausted for any given production process (Hirsch, 1952). Verdoorn (1956) accepted Hirsch's intuition, and generalised the learning function to both individual sectors and to the macroeconomy. This provided an alternative explanation for his Law. Arrow's (1962) 'learning-by-doing' model drew on both Hirsch's and Verdoorn's work, and has inspired both Romer (1986) and Lucas (1988, 1993).

The research concerning Verdoorn's Law can be further developed in new directions, as it appears to be a reduced form of various mechanisms that are still only partly understood. In the search for microeconomic foundations of Verdoorn's Law, one can go back to the Verdoorn's original 1949 article for a consideration of the application of the law to the industrial sectors and even to individual production lines. Several familiar issues thus arise, but in a new light. 'Learning by doing' and increased specialisation become interacting explanations. In fact, 'learning by doing' resulting from producing a single product tends to exhaust itself , thus weakening the Verdoorn relationship. (It is for this reason that Arrow (1962) proxied experience by cumulated gross investment, rather than cumulated output.) When the effect declines, it paves the way for specialisation in new products. Furthermore, in analysing the development of the production techniques of one product, the demand side needs to be considered because it determines whether providing new capacity for a particular product is worth undertaking. Therefore, learning on the part of users becomes important in order to explain growing demand, and to revive the Verdoorn relationship (Giorgio Rampa, chapter 9, and Maurizio Pugno, chapter 10).

The chapters in this volume show that even after more than fifty years, Verdoorn's Law still has much to say about 'why growth rates differ' and also that there are still issues to be explored that will further enhance our understanding about the economic growth process.

Finally, we should like to thank the DIGITA and DISEFIN Departments of the University of Genoa and the Department of Economics of the University of Trento for making this book possible by jointly organising and sponsoring a conference commemorating the fiftieth anniversary of the publication of Verdoorn's seminal paper. We also are indebted to Luciano Boggio, Luca De Benedictis, Fabio Fiorillo and Alessandro Vaglio for having discussed the papers. The chapters of this book have benefited also from the helpful comments of two anonymous referees.

Appendix – Empirical evidence on Verdoorn's Law

Legend

AC	Across countries
ABIC	Across branches of industry within a single country
ABICS	Across branches of industries across countries
ABIRS	Across branches of industries across regions
ARC	Across regions within a country
CEM	Cointegration estimation method
GE	Growth of (sectoral) employment
GO	Growth of (sectoral) output (value added)
GME	Growth of manufacturing employment
GMO	Growth of manufacturing output (manufacturing value added at constant prices)
GMOW	Growth of manufacturing output per worker
GMOWH	Growth of manufacturing output per worked-hour
GRC	Growth rates of capital
GRCOWH	Growth rates of capital per worked-hour
MVCEM	Multivariate cointegration estimation method
OLS	Ordinary least squares
RGDP	Real GDP
RGDPW	Real GDP per worker

SE	Single equation
SEIVT	Single equation instrumental variables technique
SEM	Simultaneous equation model
TFI	Growth of total factor inputs
TWH	Total worked hours
TS	Time series data from a single country
2SLS	Two-stage least squares
3SLS	Three-stage least squares

Empirical evidence

Author(s): VERDOORN, P.J. (1949) 'Fattori che regolano lo sviluppo della produttività del lavoro', *L'Industria,* vol. 1, 3–10. Reprinted as chapter 2 of this volume.

Method and data: GMOW on GMO (Verdoorn's specification), AC for 14 countries; interwar period.

Findings: For industry as a whole, a fairly constant relationship between the rate of growth of labour productivity and output was found. No statistical tests were provided.

Author(s): KALDOR, N. (1966) *Causes of the Slow Rate of Economic Growth of the United Kingdom. An Inaugural Lecture,* Cambridge: Cambridge University Press, reprinted in his *Further Essays on Economic Theory*, London: Duckworth.

Method and data: GMOW on GMO (Verdoorn's specification), and GME on GMO (Kaldor's specification), AC for 12 OECD countries; period from 1953/54 to 1963/64.

Findings: Regression coefficients significantly less than one were found in both specifications. This is interpreted by Kaldor as showing substantial dynamic and static increasing returns to scale.

Author(s): KATZ, J. (1968) 'Verdoorn Effect, Returns to Scale, and Elasticity of Factor Substitution', *Oxford Economic Papers*, vol. 20, 342–52.

Method and data: Production function approach, ABIC for nine industrial branches for Argentina. The elasticity of substitution, returns to scale, and the 'true' Verdoorn coefficient are estimated using a CES production function over the period from 1954 to 1961.

Findings: Seven out of nine industries exhibit increasing returns to scale. In almost all cases, the rate of neutral technical progress is significantly different from zero. In five industries out of nine the elasticity of factor substitution is significantly different from zero and less than one. It is argued that there is a systematic bias in the way in which Verdoorn's coefficient has normally been estimated.

Author(s): VACIAGO, G. (1968) 'Sviluppo della produttività e legge di Verdoorn nell'economia italiana', *Moneta e Credito,* vol. 83, 326–43.

Method and data: Verdoorn's Law using his original data was re-estimated; GMOW on GMO (Verdoorn's specification), AC, ABIC for UK, Italy, yearly and quarterly data were used from 1951 to 1965.

Findings: Short-term effects are relevant in explaining the rate of growth of labour productivity.

Author(s): PALMERIO, G. (1969) 'Economie di scala e progresso tecnico incorporato nel settore industriale in Italia nel periodo 1951–1965', *L'Industria*, vol. 3, 316–46.

Method and data: GMOW on GMO, ABIC for 42 manufacturing industries of the Italian economy; period from 1951 to 1961.

Findings: The Verdoorn coefficient was found to be highly significant for most of the 42 manufacturing industries of the Italian economy. The growth of production played an important role in explaining productivity growth rates.

Author(s): KENNEDY, K.A. (1971) *Productivity and Industrial Growth: the Irish Experience,* Oxford: Clarendon Press.

Method and data: OLS, GMOW and GMOWH on GMO (Verdoorn's specification) and GME on GMO (Kaldor's specification), ABIC for Ireland for 44 individual manufacturing industries; period from 1953 to 1968.

Findings: A high positive correlation emerges between the growth rates of productivity and output, and the results are very close to the figures found by Verdoorn.

Author(s): GOMULKA, S. (1971) *Inventive Activity, Diffusion, and the Stages of Economic Growth,* Aarhus: University of Aarhus.

Method and data: GMOW on GME, AC, for 42 countries; period from 1958 to 1968.

Findings: As long as the diffusion of innovations is significant, the very long-run dependence of growth of labour productivity on the rate of growth of employment is disturbed. For 39 countries out of 42, the rate of growth of labour productivity of manufacturing (or total industry) was found to be independent of the rate of growth of employment (that is, using Rowthorn's specification).

Author(s): CRIPPS, T.F., AND TARLING, R.J. (1973) *Growth in Advanced Capitalist Economies 1950–70,* Cambridge: Cambridge University Press.

Method and data: OLS, GMOW on GME, AC for 12 OECD countries; period from 1951 to 1970; subperiods.

Findings: When regressing the growth of labour productivity on employment, instead of output, growth (the authors' interpretation of Verdoorn's Law), the law only holds in the period from 1951 to 1965. In the last subperiod considered, 1965–70, it broke down in that there was no statistically significant relationship between the growth of productivity and employment.

Author(s): BOGGIO, L. (1974) *Crescita e specializzazione produttiva in un'economia aperta*, Milano: Vita e Pensiero.

Method and data: OLS, GMOW on GMO (Verdoorn's specification), GME on GMO (Kaldor's specification), and an 'extended' Verdoorn's specification (an investment per worker variable was included),

ABIC for 42 manufacturing branches of the Italian economy; AC for each of nine manufacturing industries in a sample of 22 countries; period from 1951 to 1967; subperiods.

Findings: The Verdoorn coefficient was found to be significantly less than one, showing the existence of increasing returns in manufacturing industries, and there were no significant differences in the value of the coefficient between branches.

Author(s): Vaciago, G. (1975) 'Increasing Returns and Growth in Advanced Economies: Re-evaluation', *Oxford Economic Papers,* vol. 27, 232–9.

Method and data: GMOW on GMO (Verdoorn's specification), AC for 18 OECD countries, including some (at that time) developing countries like Greece, Portugal, Spain and Yugoslavia; a semi-logarithmic form of Verdoorn's Law was estimated from 1950–2 to 1967–9.

Findings: Evidence of 'decreasing' increasing returns was found, the role of the latter being smaller in the less advanced economies and in the relatively fast-growing ones.

Author(s): Rowthorn, R.E. (1975) 'What Remains of Kaldor's Law?', *Economic Journal,* vol. 85, 10–19.

Method and data: OLS, GMOW on GME (Rowthorn's specification), AC from 1958 to 1968 using data from Gomulka (1971), and from 1951 to 1965 using Cripps and Tarling's (1973) data.

Findings: When regressing GMOW on GME (Rowthorn's preferred specification of Verdoorn's Law) instead of GMOW on GMO (Verdoorn's specification), the estimate of returns to scale is found to depend on whether or not Japan is included in the sample of advanced countries. If it is excluded, regressing productivity growth on that of employment suggests constant returns to scale.

Author(s): Conti, V., and Filosa, R. (1975) 'Produzione, occupazione e produttività nel settore industriale', *Rivista Internazionale di Scienze Sociali,* vol. 83, 490–519.

Method and data: OLS, GOMH on GMO, TWH on GMO, ABIC for 12 Italian manufacturing branches; extended to capital per labour hour worked; period from 1951 to 1972; subperiods.

Findings: A highly significant (but unstable between subperiods) Verdoorn's coefficient was found for the manufacturing branches.

Author(s): Cornwall, J. (1976) 'Diffusion, Convergence and Kaldor's Laws', *Economic Journal,* vol. 86, 307–14.

Method and data: AC, GMO on GME (extended to include the reciprocal of per capita income and the investment ratio in manufacturing), for 12 OECD countries; period from 1951 to 1965; Cripps and Tarling's (1973) data.

Findings: When the size of technological gap faced by each country was considered, the estimates proved to be sensitive to the inclusion of Japan in the sample, although not nearly as acutely as in earlier studies. The results were not sensitive to the inclusion or exclusion of countries, other than Japan.

Author(s): Cornwall, J. (1977) *Modern Capitalism: its Growth and Transformation,* London: Martin Robertson.

Method and data: GMOW on GMO (Verdoorn's specification), and GME on GMO (Kaldor's specification), AC for 12 OECD countries; period from 1951 to 1965; Cripps and Tarling's (1973) data were used.

Findings: When using the Verdoorn–Kaldor specification, the value of the estimates did not depend on whether or not Japan was excluded from the country sample.

Author(s): Unece (1977) *Structure and Change in European Industry,* New York, 1977.

Method and data: GMOW on GMO, for each of 10 European countries across 18 branches, and for each of 18 branches across 10 countries; period from 1958–60 to 1968–70; subperiods.

Findings: With the exception of Yugoslavia, the relationship between productivity growth and output growth for branches, as well as for individual manufacturing branches estimated using cross-country data, are all significant and positive.

Author(s): Valcamonici, R. (1977) 'Struttura di mercato, accumulazione e produttività del lavoro nell'industria manifatturiera italiana 1951–71', in G. Carli, *Sviluppo economico e strutture finanziarie in Italia,* Bologna: Il Mulino, 157–237.

Method and data: GMOWH on GMO, ABIC, between 12 manufacturing branches in the Italian economy; extended by including capital per labour hour worked, and industrial concentration; period from 1951 to 1971; subperiods.

Findings: Increasing returns to scale were found to be more significant in the 1960s. The growth of capital per labour hour worked was found to be highly significant for the whole period.

Author(s): Parikh, A. (1978) 'Differences in Growth Rates and Kaldor's Laws', *Economica,* Vol. 45, 83–91.

Method and data: 2SLS, simultaneous equation framework; Cripps and Tarling's (1973) data, extended to include other variables such as the growth of exports. Pooled cross-section subperiod growth rates were used.

Findings: Rowthorn's version of Verdoorn's Law is not supported. Demand seems to be relevant in explaining the slow growth of the manufacturing sector.

Author(s): Stoneman, P. (1979) 'Kaldor's Laws and British Economic Growth: 1800–1970', *Applied Economics,* vol. 11, 309–19.

Method and data: TS for Agricultural and Manufacturing in UK, using GMOW on GMO (Verdoorn's specification) and GMOW on GME (Rowthorn's specification); period from peak to peak over 1800–1969.

Findings: The results for manufacturing support the Kaldor hypothesis, but using Rowthorn's specification, the Verdoorn Law does not hold. The data on British economic growth for the period considered are not inconsistent with Kaldor's hypothesis, but neither are they such as to give strong support to it.

Author(s): Chen, E.K.Y. (1979) 'Kaldor's Law and the Developing Countries: an Empirical Study', *Rivista Internazionale di Scienze Economiche e Commerciali*, vol. 26, 274–85.
Method and data: GMOW on GME (Rowthorn's specification of Verdoorn's Law) for 15 developing countries; period from 1963 to 1971.
Findings: Rowthorn's specification of Verdoorn's Law does not hold.

Author(s): Panas, E.E. (1980) 'The Simple and True Verdoorn Coefficient for Greek Manufacturing Industries', *Rivista Internazionale di Scienze Economiche,* vol. 4, 341–57.
Method and data: Production function approach, ABIC for 17 industrial branches, for the Greek economy; period from 1958 to 1971.
Findings: The estimations of the 'true' Verdoorn coefficient, as derived from a CES production function, show that, in developing countries and at branch level, its value differs from 0.5.

Author(s): Rayment, P.B.W. (1981) 'Structural Change in Manufacturing Industry and the Stability of the Verdoorn Law', *Economia Internazionale*, vol. 34, 105–23.
Method and data: GMOW on GMO (Verdoorn's specification), AC on Manufacturing for 18 countries, ABIC for UK and France; period from 1950/52 to 1967/69, subperiods.
Findings: There is some suggestion that Verdoorn's Law may have weakened in the 1960s, but on the whole it was confirmed as a relatively robust relationship.

Author(s): Boyer, R., and Petit, P. (1981) 'Progrès technique croissance et emploi: un modèle d'inspiration Kaldorienne pour six industries Européennes', *Revue Économique*, vol. 32, 1113–53.
Method and data: GMOW on GMO, AC, 11 OECD countries; TS for USA, Canada, Japan Sweden; period from 1950 to 1977, subperiods.
Findings: The Verdoorn coefficient was found to vary considerably between countries.

Author(s): McCombie, J.S.L. (1981) 'What Still Remains of Kaldor's Laws?', *Economic Journal*, vol. 91, 206–16.
Method and data: GME on GMO (Kaldor's specification), AC for 12 OECD countries; period from 1950 to 1970; subperiods.
Findings: Examines whether the Verdoorn Law might be subject to bias due to measurement errors. IV estimation did not resolve the differences in the degree of returns to scale found using Rowthorn's and Kaldor's specifications.

Author(s): Chatterji, M., and Wickens, M.R. (1981) 'Verdoorn's Law – The Externalities Hypothesis and Economic Growth in the UK', in

Currie, D., Nobay, R., and Peel, D. (eds), *Macroeconomic Analysis*, Croom Helm.

Method and data: TS, OLS, GMOW on GME (Rowthorn's specification) and GMOW on GMO (Verdoorn's specification), for UK manufacturing and non-manufacturing sector including agriculture and services; quarterly time-series data, period 1961.2 to 1977.2, seasonally adjusted.

Findings: When using Rowthorn's specification, Verdoorn's Law does not hold for UK manufacturing industry in the long run. Evidence is found for the presence of increasing returns in manufacturing only in the short run, when Verdoorn's Law is analogous to Okun's Law.

Author(s): Felli, E. (1981) 'Produttività del lavoro, rendimenti di scala e accumulazione di capitale nell'industria manifatturiera italiana (1954–78)', *Rivista di Politica Economica*, vol. 71, 279–327.

Method and data: TS, GMOWH on GMO for manufacturing; ABICS for 12 manufacturing branches for the Italian economy; period from 1954 to 1977; subperiods.

Findings: Time-series analysis produced a better fit than cross-section estimates. Other variables were considered: gross investment in manufacturing; hours worked; the capital–labour hours worked ratio.

Author(s): Chatterji, M., and Wickens M.R. (1982) 'Productivity, Factor Transfer and Economic Growth in the UK', *Economica*, vol. 49, 21–38.

Method and data: TS, OLS, GMOW on GME (Rowthorn's specification); period from 1961 to 1977.

Findings: Viewed as a structural relationship, Verdoorn's Law, estimated using Rowthorn's specification, does not hold for UK manufacturing industries in the long run.

Author(s): McCombie, J.S.L. (1982a) 'Economic Growth, Kaldor's Laws and the Static–Dynamic Verdoorn Law Paradox', *Applied Economics*, vol. 14, 279–94.

Method and data: GME on GMO (Kaldor's specification), AC for 12 OECD countries, SEIVT; period from 1950 to 1973; subperiods.

Findings: The existence of a paradox between the 'static' and 'dynamic' specification of Verdoorn's Law was pointed out. The static specification uses logarithms of the levels, and finds constant returns, and the dynamic specification uses growth rates and finds substantial increasing returns to scale.

Author(s): McCombie, J.S.L. (1982b) 'How Important is the Spatial Diffusion of Innovations in Explaining Regional Growth Disparities?', *Urban Studies*, vol. 19, 377–82.

Method and data: GME on GMO (Kaldor's specification), and GMOW on GME (Rowthorn's specification); GRC, and a proxy for spatial diffusion of innovations were considered; period from 1963 to 1973; USA manufacturing sector.

Findings: The technological gap played a negligible role in explaining disparities in the postwar regional growth rates of the United States.

Author(s): RANCI, P., AND SAMEK, M. (1982), 'La crescita industriale negli anni dell'inflazione', *L'Industria*, n.s, vol. 2, 201–32.

Method and data: GMOWH on GMO, ABIC for 9 branches of the Italian manufacturing industries; period from 1960 to 1979, subperiods.

Findings: A highly significant (but unstable) Verdoorn's coefficient was found in manufacturing branches in the medium to long run.

Author(s): CHATTERJI, M., AND WICKENS, M.R. (1983) 'Verdoorn's Law and Kaldor's Law: a Revisionist Interpretation?', *Journal of Post Keynesian Economics*, vol. 5, 397–414.

Method and data: GMOW on GME, extended for capital growth and the rate of growth of hours. A generalised dynamic model was estimated. TS for six OECD countries (Canada, West Germany, Italy, Japan, the UK and the USA); period from 1960 to 1980.

Findings: The generalised dynamic versions of both Verdoorn's Law and Kaldor's Law have a role to play in understanding the growth process of capitalist countries.

Author(s): MCCOMBIE, J.S.L., AND DE RIDDER, J.R. (1983) 'Increasing Returns, Productivity, and Output Growth: the Case of the United States', *Journal of Post Keynesian Economics*, vol. 5, 373–88.

Method and data: GME on GMO and GMO on GME, ARC for US state data, using the full sample and the 20 largest states; TS for manufacturing sector; AC using Cripps and Tarling (1973) data; period for US State Data from 1947 to 1963; for international data from 1950 to 1970; for time-series data from 1953 to 1978.

Findings: The estimates largely confirm the cross-country results. Services provide a good fit with a Verdoorn coefficient that does not significantly differ from unity; time-series data for manufacturing also provides a good fit for both Rowthorn's and Kaldor's specifications of Verdoorn's Law, but cast doubts on whether this is capturing increasing returns to scale, as distinct from the short-run Okun's Law.

Author(s): METCALFE, J.S., AND HALL, P.H. (1983) 'The Verdoorn Law and the Salter Mechanism: a Note on Australian Manufacturing Industry', *Australian Economic Papers*, vol. 12, 364–73.

Method and data: GMOW on GMO (Verdoorn's specification), ABIC for Australian manufacturing industries; two separate data sets; period from 1950–51 to 1967–68 for 62 individual industries, and from 1968–69 to 1973–74 for 127 industries (at the ASIC four-digit level); subperiods.

Findings: The Verdoorn relationship is strongest for the period 1950–51 to 1964–65 – a period of rapid expansion in Australian manufacturing.

Author(s): GOMULKA, S. (1983) 'Industrialisation and the Rate of Growth: Eastern Europe, 1955–75', *Journal of Post Keynesian Economics*, vol. 5, 388–96.

Method and data: GMOW on GMO (Verdoorn's specification), ABIC for seven East European countries; period from 1961 to 1975, subperiods.
Findings: Industrial output growth in Eastern Europe is positively related to industrial labour productivity growth. It was also found that productivity growth in neither the material services nor in the agricultural sector was positively related to industrial growth.

Author(s): Turner, R.E. (1983) 'A Re-examination of Verdoorn's Law and its Application to Manufacturing Industries of the UK, West Germany and the USA', *European Economic Review*, vol. 23, 141–8.
Method and data: OLS, GMOW on GMO (Verdoorn's specification), for the manufacturing industries of UK, West Germany and the USA; using a model based on a Cobb–Douglas production function, long-term and short-term contributions to productivity growth have been estimated; period from 1955 to 1979.
Findings: For all countries the dominant contribution to long-term productivity growth came from technical change and investment (a minor contribution was due to returns to scale). The short-term effect on productivity growth of the 'stickiness' of the labour market played a major role for UK.

Author(s): Sylos Labini, P. (1983–84) 'Factors Affecting Changes in Productivity', *Journal of Post Keynesian Economics*, vol. 84, 161–79.
Method and data: OLS, TS, GMOWH on GMO for the manufacturing sector for Italy and the USA. The ratio between the wage rate and a price index of capital goods, and investment are also considered; period from 1962 to 1980 for Italy, and from 1950 to 1981 for the USA, subperiods for the USA.
Findings: The estimates show that the Verdoorn coefficient is important in explaining changes in productivity, more for the Italian manufacturing sector (with a Verdoorn's coefficient around 0.5), than for the USA (where the Verdoorn's coefficient is around 0.2).

Author(s): Casetti, E. (1984a) 'Verdoorn's Law and the Components of Manufacturing Productivity Growth: a Theoretical Model and an Analysis of US Regional Data', in Anderson, A.E., Isard, W., and Puu, T. (eds), *Regional and Industrial Development Theory: Models and Empirical Evidence, Studies in Regional Sciences and Urban Economics Series*, vol. 11, Amsterdam: North Holland, 295–308.
Method and data: Production function approach, ARC for the 51 states of the US; period from 1967 to 1976.
Findings: The empirical analyses show a positive and significant relation between productivity growth and growth of output for the US and for the Sunbelt, but not for the Snowbelt.

Author(s): Casetti, E. (1984b) 'Manufacturing Productivity and Snowbelt–Sunbelt Shifts', *Economic Geography*, vol. 10, 313–24.
Method and data: Production function approach, ARC for the USA and four census regions; period from 1958 to 1976, subperiods.
Findings: The empirical analyses show that the productivity response to output growth was greater in the Snowbelt in the earlier

subperiods but became greater in the Sunbelt in the more recent subperiods. This can be explained in terms of (i) spatial and tem poral variations of the elasticities of manufacturing output with respect to labour and capital; (ii) tendency for the marginal productivity of factors to decrease in mature regions and (iii) in the existence of differential spatial distribution of social welfare costs.

Author(s): Dormont, B. (1984) 'Productivité-croissance. quelle relation a moyen-long term? Un rapprochement des modèles de Brechling et de Kaldor–Verdoorn', *Revue Economique*, vol. 3, 447–78.

Method and data: GMOW on GMO using data for a sample of firms for France and Germany. A Brechling employment function was estimated and compared with the Kaldor–Verdoorn relationship; a sample of 124 French firms for the period 1967–75 and a sample of 128 German firms for the period 1967–77.

Findings: A positive relationship between productivity and output growth rates was found. The estimated parameters were very similar to those obtained by Boyer and Petit (1981).

Author(s): McCombie, J.S.L., and de Ridder, J.R. (1984) 'The Verdoorn Law Controversy: Some New Empirical Evidence Using US State Data', *Oxford Economic Papers*, vol. 36, 268–84.

Method and data: GME on GMO (Kaldor's specification); GMO on GME (Rowthorn's specification), and TFI on GMO, ARC for the 49 states of the USA (excluding Alaska and Hawaii); period from 1963 to 1973.

Findings: Estimates of the growth of the capital stock were constructed and included in the regressions. Substantial increasing returns to scale were found using both Kaldor's and Rowthorn's specification of the Verdoorn Law.

Author(s): Heimler, A., and Milana, C. (1984) *Prezzi relativi, ristrutturazione e produttività. Le trasformazioni dell'industria italiana*, Bologna: Il Mulino.

Method and data: TS, production function approach for 12 manufacturing branches of the Italian economy; period from 1955 to 1982.

Findings: The elasticity between labour productivity and output were estimated for each of the 12 manufacturing branches using time-series data. The Verdoorn coefficient was found to be positive and generally smaller than unity.

Author(s): Ghosh, D., and Mizuno, Y. (1985) 'Causes of Growth in the Japanese Economy from a Kaldorian Point of View', *Pakistan Economic and Social Review*, vol. 23, 151–63.

Method and data: GMOW on GMO (Verdoorn's method), TS, for Japan, 1965–1981.

Findings: The Verdoorn coefficient is found to take a value of 0.712 and is statistically significant.

Author(s): Bianchi, C. (1985) 'Crescita, produttività e occupazione in una analisi dinamica. Prospettive e proposte per l'economia italiana nel prossimo decennio', *Economia e Politica Industriale*, vol. 48, 37–58.

Method and data: OLS, TS, GME on GMO for the US, Germany, UK, France and Italy; for Italy an extended version was estimated, taking into account the ratio between the wage rate and a price index of capital goods, and investment; quarterly data, period from 1970. 1 to 1983.4.

Findings: Values of 0.83 and 0.22 for the employment–output elasticities were found for the US and for the Italian economy, respectively. The value of the employment–output elasticity for the Italian economy decreases when other variables were included.

Author(s): Michl, T.R. (1985) 'International Comparisons of Productivity Growth: Verdoorn's Law Revisited', *Journal of Post Keynesian Economics*, vol. 7, 474–92.

Method and data: GMOW on GMO (Verdoorn's specification), AC for 12 countries, an augmented technical progress function (i.e. including the growth of the capital–labour ratio) was estimated for eight countries; period from 1950 to 80, subperiods.

Findings: The augmented technical progress function explains more of the variation in productivity growth rates than the simple Verdoorn Law. The estimates suggest substantial increasing returns to scale.

Author(s): McCombie, J.S.L. (1985) 'Increasing Returns and the Manufacturing Industries: Some Empirical Issues', *The Manchester School*, vol. 53, 55–75.

Method and data: OLS, TFP on GMO, and production function approach for 17 manufacturing industries for the USA; period from 1958 to 1965 and from 1963 to 1972.

Findings: Using the same data set, contradictory results are obtained depending on the specification chosen. Increasing returns to scale are found when the Verdoorn Law is estimated but not when Rowthorn's specification is.

Author(s): Soro, B. (1985) 'Crescita regionale a tassi differenziati: possibilità e limiti di applicazione di uno schema analitico kaldoriano', *Economia e Politica Industriale*, vol. 45, 85–107.

Method and data: GMOW on GMO (Verdoorn's specification); and GME on GMO (Kaldor's specification), ARC for 20 Italian regions; period from 1970–71 to 1979–80.

Findings: Regression (Verdoorn) coefficients that were significantly less than one were found for the Italian regions in both specifications.

Author(s): McCombie, J.S.L. (1986) 'On Some Interpretations of the Relationship Between Productivity and Output Growth', *Applied Economics*, vol. 18, 1215–25.

Method and data: TFI on GMO, for nine advanced countries; period from 1955 to 1979; subperiods.

Findings: Using 3SLS and OLS techniques, a simultaneous equation model was estimated which included a labour supply function and the Verdoorn Law (which included the growth of the gross capital stock). The model performed very badly using 3SLS. Using OLS, the Verdoorn coefficient was significant for 1955–65, but not for 1965–79. Using the growth of total factor productivity as the regressand, the Verdoorn coefficient was statistically significant for both periods and indicated the presence of substantial increasing returns.

Author(s): Soro, B. (1986) 'Crescita della produttività, dell'occupazione e della produzione manifatturiera nell'esperienza regionale italiana', in Camagni, R., and Malfi, L., (a cura di), *Innovazione e Sviluppo nelle regioni mature*, Milano: Angeli.

Method and data: GMOW on GMO (Verdoorn's specification), ABIRS, 13 manufacturing branches for each region and 20 regions for each manufacturing branch of the Italian economy; period from 1973–74 to 1980–81.

Findings: Significant differences between regions have been found in the autonomous productivity growth rate, and the hypothesis of the existence of a unique Verdoorn relationship between Italian regions was rejected.

Author(s): Bairam, E.I. (1986) 'Returns to Scale, Technical Progress and Output Growth in Branches of Industry: the Case of Eastern Europe and the USSR, 1961–75', *Keio Economic Studies*, vol. 23, 63–78.

Method and data: Cobb-Douglas production function, ABICS for Eastern Europe and the USSR; period from 1961 to 1975.

Findings: The Cobb–Douglas specification (with the growth of inputs as the regressors) gives either constant or decreasing returns to scale. The Verdoorn Law shows increasing returns to scale, although for some industries the standard errors of the coefficients are large.

Author(s): Bairam, E.I. (1987b) 'Returns to Scale, Technical Progress and Output Growth in Branches of Industry: the Case of Soviet Republics, 1962–74', *Scottish Journal of Political Economy*, vol. 34, 249–66.

Method and data: Cobb–Douglas production function approach, ABICS, for nine branches of the Soviet Socialist Republic and for five major European COMECON; period from 1962–65 to 1971–74, subperiods.

Findings: The rate of technical progress and the degree of returns to scale were estimated with inputs, and not output, as the regressors. The hypothesis of increasing returns to scale is refuted.

Author(s): Pigliaru, F. (1987) 'The Performance of the Mezzogiorno's Indigenous Manufacturing Sector, 1951–70: a Discussion on Graziani's Effect and the Cumulative Causation Hypothesis', *Studi Economici*, vol. 33, 3–40.

Method and data: TS, GMOW on GMO (Verdoorn's specification), for South and Centre-North of Italy; period from 1951 to 1970; subperiods.

Findings: There is a good fit to the Verdoorn Law for the Mezzogiorno and the Centre-North.

Author(s): STAVRINOS, V.G. (1987) 'The Intertemporal Stability of Kaldor's First and Second Growth Laws in the UK', *Applied Economics*, vol. 19, 1201–09.

Method and data: TS, GMOW on GMO (Verdoorn's specification) for manufacturing in the UK, using instrumental variables to deal with the problems of capacity utilisation for the estimates of the degree of returns to scale; quarterly data from 1960.1 to 1984.2.

Findings: The results detected a considerable weakening of the degree of correlation between productivity growth and output growth in the manufacturing sector, with two statistically significant structural slowdowns during 1974.2 and 1979.4.

Author(s): WHITEMAN, J.L. (1987) 'Productivity and Growth in Australian Manufacturing Industry', *Journal of Post Keynesian Economics*, vol. 9, 576–92.

Method and data: Cobb–Douglas production function approach for the Australian manufacturing industries; period from 1954–55 to 1981–82.

Findings: A Tinbergen/Verdoorn general equilibrium model and a Kaldor/Young moving equilibrium model were compared. It was found that in the Kaldor/Young theoretical framework the Verdoorn coefficient is not asymptotically constant, but continuously changes in response to market growth.

Author(s): BAIRAM, E.I. (1988) *Technical Progress and Industrial Growth in the USSR and Eastern Europe: an Empirical Study, 1961–75,* Aldershot: Avebury.

Method and data: AR, GME on GMO, and TFI on GMO; pooled data from 1961–65 to 1971–75 for the URSS and Poland, and from 1966–70 and 1971–75 for GDR.

Findings: For the European COMECON economies, the Verdoorn Law estimates (particularly at the aggregate industry level) do not suggest substantial and statistically significant economies of scale.

Author(s): FASE, M.M.G., AND VAN DEN HEUVEL, P.J. (1988) 'Productivity and Growth: Verdoorn's Law Revisited', *Economics Letters*, vol. 28, 135–9.

Method and data: CEM and Granger-causality, GMOW and GMOWH on GMO; quarterly data for the Netherlands; period from 1968 to 1987.

Findings: Statistical causality analysis with the bivariate time-series model does not support Verdoorn's Law formulated in growth rates. However, the application of the Granger test with a modified specification leads to a confirmation of the causality implied by Verdoorn's Law. The direction of causality in the Verdoorn Law is confirmed as running from output growth to productivity growth.

Author(s): BOYER, R., AND PETIT, P. (1988) 'The Cumulative Growth Model Revisited', *Political Economy*, vol. 4, 23–43.

Method and data: GMOW on GMO (Verdoorn's specification), pooled cross-section and time-series data, for 16 OECD countries; period from 1960 to 1985, subperiods.

Findings: The estimates display some upward shift in Verdoorn's Law, occurring at the same time as a weakening of the relationship.

Author(s): Hildreth, A. (1988–89) 'The Ambiguity of Verdoorn's Law: a Case Study of the British Regions', *Journal of Post Keynesian Economics*, vol. 11, 279–94.

Method and data: GMOW on GMO (Verdoorn's specification) and GMOW on GME (Rowthorn's specification), ARC for British regional data; period from 1970 to 1983.

Findings: The estimation was divided into the short and the long run. The expected value for the Verdoorn coefficient was found in the long-run estimates only. The growth of the capital stock per employee was included, but the estimates were insignificant and took the wrong sign.

Author(s): Jefferson, G.H. (1988) 'The Aggregate Production Function and Productivity Growth: Verdoorn's Law Revisited', *Oxford Economic Papers*, vol. 40, 671–91.

Method and data: 2SLS, TS, GMOW on GMO (Verdoorn's specification), an extended version (1) that incorporates various determinants of short-run productivity growth; and an extended version (2) that incorporates the effects of plant-level scale economies, economies of agglomeration and 'learning by doing'; period from 1949 to 1981.

Findings: The Verdoorn specification suffers from a failure to specify the economic process through which growth affects productivity.

Author(s): Bairam, E.I. (1990) 'Verdoorn's Original Model and the Verdoorn Law Controversy: Some New Empirical Evidence Using the Australian Manufacturing Data', *Australian Economic Papers*, vol. 30, 107–12.

Method and data: SEM, 2SLSE, using annual total manufacturing data for Australia; period from 1955 to 1982.

Findings: The empirical evidence obtained from a simultaneous two-equation model suggests that the Verdoorn coefficient is determined by technological parameters only. Rowthorn's interpretation is refuted.

Author(s): Heyndels, B., and Vuchlen, J. (1990) 'Verdoorn's and Kaldor's Law in Tax Administration: An International Analysis', *Applied Economics*, vol. 22, 529–37.

Method and data: Static and dynamic version of both GMOW on GMO (Verdoorn's specification), and GME on GMO (Kaldor's specification), AC for 10 OECD countries; four different points in time (1966, 1970, 1980 and 1984);

Findings: The estimation of the Verdoorn–Kaldor static law confirms the existence of economies of scale in tax collection. No dynamic relation could be found between the growth in tax revenue and the changes in productivity.

Author(s): Mohammadi, H., and Ram, R. (1990) 'Manufacturing Output and Labour Productivity. Further Evidence for the United States', *Economics Letters*, vol. 32, 221–4.

Method and data: CEM and Granger-causality, GMOW and GMOVH on GIMO, quarterly data for the US; period from 1950 to 1988.

Findings: The direction of causality in the Verdoorn Law from output to productivity growth is not confirmed.

Author(s): Bairam, E. (1991) 'Economic Growth and Kaldor's Law: the Case of Turkey, 1925–78', *Applied Economics*, vol. 23, 1277–80.

Method and data: TS, OLS, SEIVT, GMOH on GMO for the Turkish manufacturing sector; the rank instrumental variable method was used; period from 1925 to 1978.

Findings: Regardless of the estimation technique used, the coefficients that relate productivity growth and industrial production growth are all statistically different from zero at the conventional significance levels. Verdoorn's Law is confirmed.

Author(s): Drakopoulos, S.A., and Theodossiou, I. (1991) 'Kaldorian Approach to Greek Economic Growth', *Applied Economics*, vol. 23, 1683–9.

Method and data: TS, GMOH on GMO for the Greek manufacturing sector; a capacity utilisation index was used to take into account the cyclical effects of output growth; period from 1967 to 1988.

Findings: Productivity growth and production growth in manufacturing show a positive and highly significant relationship. Verdoorn's Law is confirmed.

Author(s): Wulwick, N.J. (1991) 'Did Verdoorn's Law hang on Japan?', *Eastern Economic Journal*, vol. 17, no. 1, 15–20.

Method and data: OLS and 2LSE, GMOW on GMO (Verdoorn's specification) and GMOW on GME (Rowthorn's interpretation of Verdoorn's Law), AC for 12 OECD countries (Kaldor's sample); period from 1953/54 to 1963/64 (Kaldor's data).

Findings: Kaldor's and Rowthorn's specifications of Verdoorn's Law were re-estimated using Kaldor's data. When estimating the Verdoorn Law by least squares, using the Kaldor's equation and without the Japanese data, the Verdoorn hypothesis is confirmed. Taking the alternative approach of two-stage least squares, and assuming that output is demand-led, it transpires that the Verdoorn law expressed by Rowthorn's equation does not depend on the presence of the Japanese data in Kaldor's sample.

Author(s): Casetti, E., and Tanaka, K. (1992) 'The Spatial Dynamics of Japanese Manufacturing Productivity: an Empirical Analysis by Expanded Verdoorn Equations', *Papers in Regional Science*, vol. 71, 1–13.

Method and data: OLS and quasi-Bayesian mixed estimation for maunfacturing output.

Findings: Estimates the expanded Verdoorn Law, which includes functions of population density and per capita income in a manner analogous to dummy variables, finds Verdoorn coefficients of around 0.4 to 0.6, confirming the law.

Author(s): ATESOGLU, H.S. (1993) 'Manufacturing and Economic Growth in the United States', *Applied Economics*, vol. 25, 67–9.

Method and data: OLS, TS, GME on GMO for the US manufacturing output; period from 1965 to 1988.

Findings: The findings in favour of Kaldor's specification of Verdoorn's Law, obtained by using time-series data for the US manufacturing output, are compatible with earlier cross-section state data reported by McCombie and de Ridder (1983).

Author(s): BOUGRINE, H. (1994) 'Capital Accumulation, Output Growth and Disparities in Labour Productivity Among Canadian Regions', *International Review of Applied Economics*, vol. 8, 283–90.

Method and data Production function approach, OLS with annual data for six Canadian regions; period from 1961 to 1991.

Findings: Manufacturing productivity growth in all six Canadian regions appears to be strongly influenced by the Verdoorn effect, and the impact of capital accumulation, although small, is not insignificant.

Author(s): MCCOMBIE, J.S.L. AND THIRLWALL, A.P. (1994) *Economic Growth and the Balance-of-Payments Constraint,* London: Macmillan, 155–231.

Method and data: Original Verdoorn's data, pooled data from Cripps and Tarling (1973) and from Michl (1985) were re-estimated; Michl's augmented technical progress function and the production function approach used by McCombie and de Ridder (1984) were compared; period from 1955 to 1987.

Findings: When considering pooled data, confirmation of the simple Verdoorn Law was found; when the contribution of the growth of capital is considered, multicollinearity problems arise; when the magnitude of the returns to scale were estimated using a total factor productivity approach, the results suggest a value of the returns to scale of around 1.5.

Author(s): HAMALAINEN, K., AND PEHKONEN, J. (1995) 'Verdoorn's Law in the Multivariate Context', *Economic Notes*, vol. 24, 175–86.

Method and data: MVCEM, GMOWH on GMO, for data from four Nordic countries (Denmark, Finland, Norway and Sweden); period from 1960 to 1990.

Findings: Two main results were obtained: the dynamic form of Verdoorn's Law was confirmed, as in other previous analyses using international data. However, the static form of the law appeared not to be particularly well-identified.

Author(s): PUGNO, M. (1995) 'On Competing Theories of Economic Growth: Cross-country Evidence', *International Review of Applied Economics*, vol. 9, 249–74.

Method and data: OLS, 2SLS, 3SLS, SER, GMOW on GMO and investment share (extended Verdoorn's specification,) and GMOW on GME and investment share (extended Rowthorn's specification); AC for a 58-country sample; period from 1960 to 1988, subperiods.

Findings: The Verdoorn coefficient was found to be highly significant, of the expected sign, significantly smaller than one and stable over the subperiods.

Author(s): Hansen, J.D., and Zhang, J. (1996) 'A Kaldorian Approach to Regional Economic Growth in China', *Applied Economics*, vol. 28, 679–85.
Method and data: GMOW on GMO, ACR for 28 regions in China; period from 1985 to 1991.
Findings: The estimated relation reveals strong productivity effects of industrial growth in the industry sector. The Verdoorn Law is confirmed.

Author(s): Bernat, G.A. (1996) 'Does Manufacturing Matter? A Spatial Econometric View of Kaldor's Laws', *Journal of Regional Science*, vol. 36, 463–77.
Method and data: OLS, spatial autocorrelation models were estimated, ARC for the 49 states of the USA; period from 1977 to 1990.
Findings: The most important finding is the presence of significant spatial autocorrelation: the spatial correlation coefficient is not only highly significant, but is of roughly the same magnitude as the coefficients of the other explanatory variables. A significant Verdoorn Law is found, confirming McCombie and de Ridder (1984).

Author(s): Førsund, F. (1996b) 'Productivity of Norwegian Establishments: a Malmquist Index Approach', in Mayes, D.G. (ed.), *Sources of Productivity Growth*, Cambridge: Cambridge University Press.
Method and data: A non-parametric frontier analysis was performed, using establishment data (twelve 4–5 digit ISIC sectors), for Norway, period from 1976 to 1988.
Findings: Verdoorn's Law, originally formulated at the macro level, was supported at the micro level: productivity and output growth are positively correlated.

Author(s): Kie, C. (1997) *The Effects of Flexible Manufacturing Contexts: Geographical Patterns in Labour Productivity Impact of Output Growth. Studies on Industrial Productivity*, London: Garland.
Method and data: Production function approach, three industries (electronics/instruments, machinery, and apparel) for the US manufacturing sector were considered; period from 1977 to 1987.
Findings: An augmented Verdoorn model including the effect of capital deepening was estimated. Parameter values for individual states were estimated in order to examine the inter-regional pattern of the Verdoorn coefficient and the variability of the effect of capital deepening. The results suggests that Verdoorn's Law is confirmed.

Author(s): Ofria, F. (1997) 'Una verifica empirica della legge di Verdoorn per il Centro-Nord e il Mezzogiorno (anni 1951–1992)', *Rivista economica del Mezzogiorno*, vol. 11, 497–518.

Method and data: TS, OLS, instrumental variables, GMOWH on GMO; ARC, for North-Centre, South of Italian economy; period from 1951 to 1992, subperiods.

Findings: Better estimates for Verdoorn's Law were found for manufacturing and service sectors in the North-Centre of Italy.

Author(s): TARGETTI, F., AND FOTI, A. (1997) 'Growth and Productivity: a Model of Cumulative Growth and Catching Up', *Cambridge Journal of Economics,* vol. 21, 27–43.

Method and data: 3SLS, GMOWH on GMO, extended for an index of the technological gap-index and the investment–output ratio; AC for a selected OECD country-sample; a selected Latin American country-sample; a selected East Asian country-sample; period from 1950 to 1988 (for the OECD country-sample); from 1960 to 1988 (for the Latin American and East Asian country-sample).

Findings: Different values for the Verdoorn coefficients among economic areas and in different periods were found.

Author(s): FINGLETON, B., AND MCCOMBIE, J.S.L. (1998) 'Increasing Returns and Economic Growth: Some Evidence from the European Union Regions', *Oxford Economic Papers,* vol. 50, 89–195. Correction, ibid., vol. 51, 574–5.

Method and data: Production function approach, using growth rates of manufacturing of the various European Union regions; period from 1979 to 1989.

Findings: The results obtained using a static version of the Verdoorn Law suggests very much smaller increasing returns to scale than those given by the dynamic version, and both are very similar to those found using international data for advanced countries (see McCombie, 1982).

Author(s): HARRIS, R.I.D., AND LAU, E. (1998) 'Verdoorn's Law and Increasing Returns to Scale in the UK Regions, 1968–91: Some New Estimates Based on the Cointegration Approach', *Oxford Economic Papers,* vol. 50, 201–19.

Method and data: Johansen's approach for estimating long-run cointegration vectors is used for 16 industries using UK regional data; period from 1968 to 1991.

Findings: There is substantial evidence that large increasing returns are the norm for the majority of manufacturing industries in British regions.

Author(s): LEÓN-LEDESMA, M.A. (1999) 'Increasing Returns and Verdoorn's Law: an Empirical Analysis of the Spanish Regions', *Applied Economic Letters,* vol. 6, 373–6.

Method and data: GME on GMO (Kaldor's specification), extended for capital growth; GMO on GME (Rowthorn's specification), extended for capital growth, TFI on GMO; GIMO in TFI; ARC for the 17 Spanish regions, for manufacturing. Method used: panel data with fixed and random effects; period from 1962 to 1991, subperiods.

Findings: Strong support for the hypothesis of increasing returns for all the specifications. Larger estimates of increasing returns using Kaldor's, rather than Rowthorn's, specification.

Author(s): HARRIS, R.I.D., AND LIU, A. (1999) 'Verdoorn's Law and Increasing Returns to Scale', *Applied Economic Letters*, vol. 6, 29–34.
Method and data: MVCEM, RGDPW on RGDP; annual data for 62 countries; period from 1965 to 1990.
Findings: The Johansen approach and the inclusion of the capital stock variable show increasing returns to scale for most countries.

Author(s): LEÓN-LEDESMA, M.A. (2000) 'Economic Growth and Verdoorn's Law in the Spanish Regions, 1962–1991', *International Review of Applied Economics*, vol. 14, 55–69.
Method and data: GME on GMO (Kaldor's specification), extended for capital growth; GMO on GME (Rowthorn's specification), extended for capital growth, TFI on GMO; GMO in TFI; ARC for the 17 Spanish regions, for manufacturing and non-manufacturing sectors; period from 1962 to 1991, subperiods.
Findings: The hypothesis of increasing returns to scale in the manufacturing sector is supported; some degree of increasing returns to scale are found for the service sector. A test of the static-dynamic paradox suggests that Verdoorn's Law should not be derived from a Cobb–Douglas production function.

Author(s): PIEPER, U. (2000) 'Sectoral Regularities of Productivity Growth in Developing Countries. A Kaldorian Interpretation', MERIT, November, mimeo, 1–31.
Method and data: TS, GME on GMO (Kaldor's specification); time-series data for nine main sectors were pooled from 30 countries for the period from 1975 to 1993.
Findings: When linear estimations were performed substantial evidence was found that patterns of productivity growth varied across sectors. This underscores the usefulness of analysing growth at levels of aggregations lower than the whole economy, industry and total manufacturing. When non-linear estimations were performed, the local regression curves exhibited a regular non-linear pattern of positive relationships between employment growth and output growth for all nine sectors. Strong evidence for increasing returns to scale was found at the sectoral level.

Author(s): TIMMER, M.P., and SZIRMAI, A. (2000) 'Productivity Growth in Asian Manufacturing: the Structural Bonus Hypothesis Examined', *Structural Change and Economic Dynamics*, vol. 11, 371–92.
Method and data: OLS, TFI on GMO; for 13 manufacturing branches; four Asian countries (India, Indonesia, South Korea, Taiwan); period from 1963 to 1993.
Findings: Highly significant values for the Verdoorn coefficient were found. When taking the highest value for the Verdoorn coefficient of 0.53 (for machinery and transport equipment

branch) as the base for comparison, only three branches (namely the metal, the non-metallic mineral products and the electrical machinery) had estimates that were significantly different.

Author(s): BIANCHI, C. (2001) 'A Reappraisal of Verdoorn's Law for the Italian Economy: 1951–1997', chapter 5, this volume.

Method and data: OLS, GE on GO for different sectors of the Italian economy; an extended version including capital growth, and a partial adjusted model were estimated; annual data period from 1951–97; subperiods.

Findings: Estimates of the traditional Verdoorn's Law suggest that there are increasing returns to scale both for the whole economy and for all its sectors, although the size of returns to scale turned out to be decreasing over time. The use of a partial adjustment model confirmed the presence of increasing returns to scale. Estimates of the more appropriate specification that explicitly includes capital growth confirm that the industrial sector exhibits increasing returns to scale over the whole sample period.

Author(s): DESTEFANIS, S. (2001) 'The Vendoorn Law: Some Evidence from Non-Parametric Frontier Analysis', chapter 6, this volume.

Method and data: A non-parametric frontier analysis for a sample of 52 countries was performed, using Penn World Table data, period from 1965–92; subperiods.

Findings: The results obtained in the present application point to the pervasive existence of increasing returns to scale across developed and developing countries, in sharp contrast with traditional parametric estimates obtained using the same data set.

Notes

1. The relationship between productivity and output growth using inter-industry data is sometimes called one of Fabricant's Laws (Fabricant, 1942). Although this relationship has also been interpreted as providing evidence of increasing returns to scale, the issues involved are somewhat different from the law estimated using regional or national data. Fabricant's Laws are not discussed in this volume, although this is not to say that they do not provide insights into the determinants of productivity growth.

2

Factors that Determine the Growth of Labour Productivity

P.J. Verdoorn

[Translated by A.P. Thirlwall from the original 1949 article in Italian.[1]]

1. One of the difficulties in long-term planning is to estimate the future level of labour productivity. Unless this is known, one does not know the relation between output and employment.

Since it cannot be assumed that the annual rate of growth of labour productivity will be constant, and the production function cannot be used, an alternative method of estimating the future level of labour productivity is suggested.

2. The statistics available for the periods 1870 to 1914 and 1914 to 1930 for various countries suggest the existence of a fairly constant relation over a long period between the growth of labour productivity and the volume of industrial production.

From analysing the historical series for industry as a whole (Table 2.1) and for individual industrial sectors, for the two time periods, it is found that the average value of the elasticity of productivity with respect to output is approximately 0.45 (with limits of 0.41 and 0.57). This means that over the long period a change in the volume of production, say of about 10 per cent, tends to be associated with an average increase in labour productivity of 4.5 per cent.

3. In fact, one could have expected *a priori* to find a correlation between labour productivity and output, given that the division of labour only comes about through increases in the volume of production; therefore the expansion of production creates the possibility of further rationalisation which has the same effects as mechanisation.

This interdependence of a purely theoretical character does not by itself imply that the elasticity will be constant because in practice it will be influenced by various economic factors; none the less, it can be demonstrated (see the Appendix) that under the normal assumptions of long-period analysis the elasticity assumes a mathematical form that tends to make it – within reasonable limits – fairly independent of variations in such economic factors.

Moreover, it is found that when the economic conditions of the various countries and different periods of time are taken into account, the values of

Table 2.1 Annual increases in volume of production and labour productivity in industry

Period	*Country*	*Annual change*			
		Production %	*Labour productivity* %		*Elasticity*
1913–1930	Switzerland	2.40	1.03	0.43	
1841–1907	UK	2.40	0.98	0.41	0.43
1907–1930		1.28	0.605	0.47	
1869–1899	USA	5.61	2.31	0.42	0.42
1899–1939		3.35	1.91	0.57	
1882–1907	Germany	4.38	2.14	0.49	(1859–1939)
		Period between the wars			
1924–1938	Switzerland	5.0	5.3	1.06	
1926–1938	Japan	6.7	3.4	0.51	
1924–1938	Finland	5.1	3.2	0.63	
1927–1938	Hungary	3.4	2.8	0.82	
1924–1938	Holland	2.3	2.6	1.13	Regression
1924–1938	Norway	2.6	2.5	0.96	equation
1924–1938	Denmark	3.5	1.9	0.54	$d \log \frac{x}{a} =$
1927–1938	Poland	1.6	1.9	1.18	0.573 d log, x
1924–1938	UK	1.4	1.5	1.07	+ 0.00239
1924–1939	USA	0.6	1.0	1.67	
1924–1938	Canada	1.6	1.0	0.63	
1924–1938	Czechoslovakia	0.4	0.7	—	
1927–1938	Estonia	0.8	0.4	0.50	
1924–1938	Italy	0.8	0.2	0.25	

the elasticities calculated theoretically are of the same size as those found empirically.

4. While the hypothesis of constant elasticity is not in practice very suitable for making forecasts, it can nevertheless be used profitably as one criterion for making a judgement, on the basis of past experience, about the realisation of long-term plans.

(a) If in a plan we have the data available on labour requirements and the data on production, and the value of the elasticity falls within the limits that have been found empirically, then we can say that the plan under study, from the point of view of labour productivity alone, is technically possible and economically plausible.

(b) If instead data are only available on labour productivity, labour requirements can be forecast on the basis of historical values of the elasticity,

Table 2.2 Comparison of the productivity elasticities based on the Monnet and Saraceno plans and their historical values

Industrial sector	*Italy (Saraceno)*	*France (Monnet)*	*Historical value of the elasticity* *Value*	*Country*	*Period*
1. Automobiles	—	0.65	0.70	USA	1919–1929
2. Rubber	0.52	—	0.60	Holland	1922–1939
3. Food	0.51	—	0.51	USA	1899–1937
4. Wood	0.52	—	0.46	USA	1899–1937
5. Construction Material	0.42	0.32	—	—	—
6. Paper	0.35	—	0.44	USA	1899–1937
7. Chemicals	0.35	—	0.29	USA	1899–1937
8. Public Utilities	0.11	—	—	—	—
9. Metals	0.29	0.60	0.52	France	1890/94–1924/29
Blast Furnaces	—	—	1.52	USA	1899–1937
Iron Products	—	—	0.31	USA	1899–1937
10. Textiles	0.77	0.45	0.44	USA	1899–1937
Cotton	—	—	0.46	France	1873/79–1926/36
	—	—	0.51	USA	1899–1937
Artificial Silk	—	—	0.68	USA	1899–1937
	—	—	0.87	Holland	1922–1939
11. Clothing	0.42	—	—	—	—
Average	0.52*	0.51	0.57	USA	1899–1937

Note:
*Including mining.
Sources: Italy: *Elementi per un piano* ecc., September 1947 (n. 7) p. 125.
France: *Premier plan de Modernisation* ecc., November 1946–January 1947, p. 78.

and the soundness of the plan can be judged on the basis of the availability of labour.

(c) On the other hand, in the cases in which a plan does not exist, the value of the elasticity of productivity gives a rough idea of how much industrial production must expand to absorb a certain availability of labour.

5. Finally, this method allows us to make separate calculations for individual industrial sectors. If the historical elasticities are calculated for sectors instead of for industry as a whole, one takes into account differences in technical and economic conditions existing between industries (for example, differences in the production function and in the elasticity of labour supply).

6. Until now[2] only the Monnet and Saraceno Plans have given data relating to both labour and production. In Table 2.2 a comparison is made between

the value of the elasticity calculated on the basis of these two plans and some historical values.

In this table it is evident that on the whole there exists a rather close relation between the three series of values; considerable divergencies are found in the case of textiles and metallurgy, but here a more detailed subdivision of the data of the plans would be necessary because of the heterogeneity of the technical production relations employed in the same principal branches of the two industrial sectors (rayon in comparison with cotton, blast furnaces in comparison with rolling mills).

The lack of precise data on investment does not allow us to establish how much of the divergencies found in these two sectors, and other smaller divergencies, have been influenced by differences in investment policy.

7. As a general rule to follow, if new plans are available in the future, it is suggested that the years 1937 or 1938 should be taken as a starting point for analysis rather than 1947 or 1948. These latter years are still influenced by the consequences of the war. If 1952/53 or 1960 are the final years of the plan the important characteristics of the period of reconstruction can be considered to have disappeared.

In comparing 1938 with 1952/53 normal conditions can be considered to prevail, bearing in mind permanent changes due to the war.

If a close correspondence is found to exist in each individual industry in the three[3] countries between the increase in production and capital and labour requirements, it is possible to obtain a number of normal [elasticity] values for the different industries.

In the case of wide divergencies an analysis of a more general character is suggested. Taking into account other variables (such as the development of production techniques; the amount of unused capacity in 1938; the relation between total labour and capital requirements and so on) an attempt can be made to find some less rigid relations between labour and capital requirements in the industries under examination; for this purpose a method is outlined in the Appendix which, although it cannot be applied in practice, serves to establish some starting points for research along these lines.

The choice of the most efficient and practical method will depend on the quality and quantity of the statistical material available. However, leaving aside the method that may be chosen it is clear that, proceeding in this way, concrete and quantitative criteria can be obtained to judge the compatibility of the labour market compared with other aspects of the plan.

Appendix

1. Conditions for a stable relation between labour productivity and output. If we let:
   a be the quantity of labour[4]
   $\dot{a}$ be the first derivative with respect to time
   x be the volume of production

$\dot{x}$ be the first derivative with respect to time
the elasticity of labour productivity with respect to output can be written:

$$K = \frac{\frac{d}{dt}\left(\frac{x}{a}\right)}{\frac{x}{a}} \bigg/ \frac{\dot{x}}{x} = \frac{a}{\dot{x}} \cdot \frac{a\dot{x} - x\dot{a}}{a^2}$$

or

$$\dot{K} = 1 - \frac{\dot{a}/a}{\dot{x}/x}$$

Assuming the production function is Cobb–Douglas[5]:

$x = a^{\alpha} b^{\beta}$ (*b* is capital)

and differentiating with respect to time:

$$\begin{aligned} \dot{x} &= \alpha a^{\alpha-1} b^{\beta} \dot{a} + \beta b^{\beta-1} a^{\alpha} \dot{b} \\ &= \alpha x \frac{\dot{a}}{a} + \beta x \frac{\dot{b}}{b} \end{aligned}$$

one obtains:

$$\frac{\dot{x}}{x} = \alpha \frac{\dot{a}}{a} + \beta \frac{\dot{b}}{b}$$

$$\frac{\dot{x}/x}{\dot{a}/a} = \alpha + \beta\left(\frac{\dot{b}/b}{\dot{a}/a}\right)$$

from which:

$$K = 1 - \frac{1}{\alpha + \beta\left(\frac{\dot{b}/b}{\dot{a}/a}\right)}. \qquad \text{(I)}$$

If α and β are assumed to be constant, the constancy of *K* evidently depends on the constancy of the relation $\dot{b}/b : \dot{a}/a$.

2. The constancy of the elasticity of capital with respect to labour can be proved using a system of equations similar to that developed by Tinbergen.[6]

For our purposes the following equations will be sufficient:

3. – I: *System of equations*

Production equation: $x = a^{\alpha} b^{\beta}$ (1)

Labour demand: $$v = \alpha \cdot \frac{x}{a} \tag{2}$$

Labour supply: $$v = \alpha\left(\frac{a}{p}\right)^{\rho} e^{\lambda t} \tag{3}$$

Capital supply: $$\dot{b} = \gamma x \tag{4}$$

Population: $$p = e^{\pi t} \tag{5}$$

In equation (2): the demand for labour: the average wage (v) is equal to the marginal product of labour.

In equation (3): the supply of labour: this equation can also be written:

$$\frac{a}{p} = \left(\frac{v}{\ell}\right)^{\rho 1} \text{ where,}$$

a is the number of people employed in industry,
p is the total active population,
ℓ is average wage in non-industrial production,
ρ^1 is essentially an elasticity of competition: in fact the percentage of labour supply in industry is determined by the relation between the average wage in industry and that in other branches of production. In equation (3) it is assumed that the average wage increases at the constant annual rate e^{λ}. According to Tinbergen, the factor $e^{\lambda t}$ in equation (3) may be considered as indicating the increased demands of trade unions for higher wages.

If for the initial value ($t = 0$) of a, p and b we assume the number 1, the constant in equation (3) is α.

In equation (4): γ is the average propensity to invest.

In equation (5): a constant annual increase is assumed (e^{π}).

3. – II: $\dot{a}/a$.

From equations (3) and (5):

$$\begin{aligned} v &= \alpha\left(\frac{a}{p}\right)^{\rho} e^{\lambda t} \\ &= \alpha \cdot a^{\rho} \cdot e^{-\pi t p} \cdot e^{\lambda t} \\ &= \alpha a^{\rho} e^{(\lambda - \pi p)^t} \\ &= \alpha \cdot a^{\rho} e^{\mu t} \end{aligned}$$

(where $\mu = \lambda - \pi p$).

From equation (6) and (2) we have:

$$\alpha a^{\rho} e^{\mu t} = \alpha \frac{x}{a}$$

but from equation (1) $x = a^{\alpha} \cdot b^{\beta}$, therefore:

$$a^{\rho} e^{\mu t} = \frac{a^{\alpha} b^{\beta}}{a}. \tag{6}$$

It follows that:

$$a^{\rho} e^{\mu t} = a^{\alpha-1} b^{\beta}, \text{ from which}$$
$$a = b^{\beta/w} e^{-\mu t/w} \tag{7}$$
$$(\text{where } w = 1 + \rho - \alpha).$$

Differentiating equation (7) with respect to time gives:

$$\dot{a} = \frac{\beta}{w} \cdot b^{\frac{\beta}{w}-1} e^{-\frac{\mu}{w}t} \dot{b} - \frac{\mu}{w} b^{\beta/w} e^{-\mu t/w}, \text{ and therefore}$$
$$\frac{\dot{a}}{a} = \frac{\beta}{w} \cdot \frac{\dot{b}}{b} - \frac{\mu}{w}.$$

Equation (11) gives a relation between $\dot{a}/a$ and $\dot{b}/b$. However, it only considers the equations (1) (2) and (3) of 3. – I and therefore neglects the dependence of b on the other variables in the system as given by equation (4).

3. – III: $\dot{b}/b$

From equation (4) we can write: $\frac{\dot{b}}{b} = \gamma \frac{x}{b}$ (8)

Since we can choose freely the instant for which $t = 0$, we take $t = 0$ for the year for which the elasticity is to be calculated. However, in such a case, we are tied by the initial values for the variables considered, as assumed in 3. – I; for example:

$$a_0 = b_0 = p_0 = 1: \; v_0 = \alpha.$$

Therefore, it follows from equation (1) that $x_0 = 1$, and from equation (8):

$$\frac{\dot{b}_0}{b} = \gamma \frac{x_0}{b_0} = \gamma.$$

Dividing equation (II) by $\frac{\dot{b}_0}{b_0}$, we find:

$$\frac{\dot{a}_0}{a} \Bigg/ \frac{\dot{b}_0}{b_0} = \frac{\beta}{w} - \frac{\mu}{\gamma w}. \tag{III}$$

3. – IV: K

Substituting equation (III) into (I) we find:

$$K = 1 - \cfrac{1}{\alpha + \cfrac{\beta}{\cfrac{\beta}{w} - \cfrac{\mu}{\gamma w}}}$$

$$= 1 - \cfrac{1}{\alpha + \cfrac{w}{1 - \cfrac{\mu}{\beta\gamma}}}$$

From which, letting $\mu = \lambda - \pi\rho$

$w = 1 + \rho - \alpha,$

$$K = 1 - \cfrac{1 - \cfrac{\mu}{\beta\gamma}}{\alpha - \cfrac{\alpha\mu}{\gamma\beta} + 1 + \rho - \alpha}$$

$$= \cfrac{\rho + (1-\alpha)\cfrac{\mu}{\beta\gamma}}{\rho + 1 - \cfrac{\alpha\mu}{\beta\gamma}}$$

and finally:

$$K = \frac{\rho\left(1 - \frac{1-\alpha}{\beta} \cdot \frac{\pi}{\gamma}\right) + \frac{1-\alpha}{\beta} \cdot \frac{\lambda}{\gamma}}{\rho\left(1 + \frac{\alpha}{\beta} \cdot \frac{\pi}{\gamma}\right) + 1 - \frac{\alpha}{\beta} \cdot \frac{\lambda}{\gamma}} \tag{IV}$$

The stability of K can easily be seen taking different combinations of π and λ (taking as given α, β and γ). It appears therefore that quite considerable modifications would be necessary for K to lie outside certain limits, for example ± 0.15 around an initial value of 0.45.[7] Analogous conclusions would be reached if variations in α, β and γ were taken for fixed values of π and λ.

Notes

1. 'Fattori che Regolano lo Sviluppo della Produttività del Lavoro', *L'Industria*, 1949. This paper is the origin of 'Verdoorn's Law'. Verdoorn died in 1985 and the translation was not authorised by the author prior to his death.
2. *i.e.* up to August 1948.
3. *Translator's note*: it is not clear what three countries the author has in mind.
4. *Translator's note*: Verdoorn defines a as labour productivity. This is clearly a mistake.
5. The Cobb–Douglas production function has been chosen to represent the relation between production, capital and labour because it has been used a long time as a theoretical device. However, it can be proved that also using a more general formulation of the production function the same formula can be obtained as those described below.
6. *Weltwirtschaftliches Archiv*, May 1942, p. 530.
7. *Translator's note*: Letting $\alpha = 0.7$; $\beta = 0.3$; $\rho = 1$; $\pi = 0.01$; $\gamma = 4$; $\lambda = 0.01$ gives $K = 0.5$.

3
'Fattori che regolano lo sviluppo della produttività del lavoro' Fifty Years On

Bruno Soro

Dr. Verdoorn, in this field, may prove to have played much the same role as Pareto in the field of income distribution. (Colin Clark, 1957)

The 'law' that has been given my name appears therefore to be much less generally valid than I was led to believe in 1949. (P.J. Verdoorn, 1980)

Some introductory notes on 'Fattori che regolano lo sviluppo della produttività del lavoro'

'Fattori che regolano lo sviluppo della produttività del lavoro' (henceforth simply referred to as 'Fattori') is an article which, although much quoted, has been, perhaps, seldom read. The fact that it was originally written in Italian certainly did not help it to achieve widespread recognition.[1] Indeed, over time, the increasing fame of this paper stands in marked contrast to the lack of knowledge generally available about the author's personal life.

In chronological terms the very first citation of 'Fattori' is actually a self-quotation: Verdoorn (1956a),[2] in his 'Complementary and Long-Range Projection', recalled the existence of the 'rule' (introduced in his original paper), according to which, over the long period, a fairly constant relation was to be expected between output per worker and the level of production. He pointed out that this relation also implied a constant elasticity of productivity with respect to output, the value of which, as emerged from the examination conducted in 'Fattori', seemed to change 'from industry to industry in different countries between 0.45 and 0.6' (Verdoorn, 1956a, p. 434). Verdoorn himself suggested that the most adequate theoretical justification for this rule was to be found in the literature on the 'manufacturing progress function': namely, in the mechanism whereby an increase in cumulated output gave scope for a greater division of labour. This, in turn, would help to develop, on the one hand, (static) internal economies of scale, and, on the other hand, (dynamic) external economies of scale – namely, a better skilled labour force and new technological discoveries (Verdoorn, 1956a, p. 434).

The second citation of 'Fattori' is contained in the third edition (published in 1957) of *The Conditions of Economic Progress* by Colin Clark.[3] Apart from a minor error (namely, that Verdoorn's original paper was not written in English, as Clark stated, but in Italian),[4] Verdoorn's views were very accurately summarised by this author. Indeed, Clark was able to correctly identify that the theoretical structure on which Verdoorn's relation is based was the 'learning curve'. In addition, he empirically attempted to confirm Verdoorn's value of the elasticity (for the first time since Verdoorn's own estimates). The outcome of this verification was actually to question the value of Verdoorn's coefficient of 0.5 and its stability over time. Nevertheless, Clark judged Verdoorn's discovery to be as important as Pareto's law on income distribution (Clark, 1957, p. 359).

A few years later, Clark (1962) himself (in a study with H. Frankel and L. Moore) quoted the article 'Fattori' again. In a chapter discussing the low growth rate in the United Kingdom – which anticipated the issue developed by Kaldor (1966) in his famous Inaugural Lecture[5] by four years – Clark gave an explanation of the low growth rate of output per worker in British industries. In doing so, he assigned an important role to what he repeatedly referred to as 'Verdoorn's Principle' – namely the rule whereby 'whenever an industry's scale of production is enlarged, productivity per man-hour of labour also improves by a factor equal approximately to the square root of the factor by which production has been increased' (Clark, 1962, p. 39).

The next (and perhaps most authoritative) citation of 'Fattori' is that by Kenneth J. Arrow (1962). In his paper 'The Economic Implications of Learning by Doing', he noted that Verdoorn, in an essay published in *Econometrica* in 1956, had applied 'the principle of the learning curve to national outputs' (Arrow, 1962, p. 156). Arrow further pointed out that for the empirical basis of the 'principle' and also for its interpretation 'in terms of increasing capital–labour ratios', Verdoorn had made reference to another of his papers published in 1949.

From that time onwards, and especially after the unexpected fame acquired through the explicit reference made by Kaldor (1966) to 'Verdoorn's Law', 'Fattori' has been cited widely. From our own incomplete research, we have found over one hundred references to the paper. However, it was only in 1988 (that is, 39 years from the publication of the original work and six years after the death of its author), that the first English translation by Thirlwall was published (although it had not been authorised by Verdoorn while he was alive).[6] (It is reproduced as chapter 2 of this volume.) The same version was published five years later in the second of the two books entitled *Italian Economic Papers*, edited by Luigi Pasinetti (1993).[7]

Therefore, unsurprisingly, the lively debate which started at the beginning of the 1980s on the interpretation made by Rowthorn (1979) of Verdoorn's Law, mainly focused on the mathematical appendix to the 'Fattori', which made for more straightforward reading than the rest of the paper. Indeed, it was almost as if the article itself were a sort of appendix to the actual Appendix. Actually, as we will explain below, Verdoorn aimed in this appendix to provide a theoretical justification for the assumption that elasticity remains constant over time: an assumption which soon turned out to be invalid.[8]

Finally, a footnote contained in 'Fattori' states the following: 'This article presents the preliminary outcome of an investigation carried out by the Author. A more comprehensive presentation of the technique employed and the meaning of its conclusions is to be published in English' (Verdoorn, 1949, p. 45n1). This, most probably, refers to the work conducted by Verdoorn as a member of the Research and Planning Division, a team of 25 economists and statisticians (including Verdoorn himself) co-ordinated and led by Kaldor, and in charge of producing reports for the *Economic Surveys of Europe* of the Economic Commission for Europe (ECE) (Kaldor, 1986, p. 14; Thirlwall, 1987, pp. 104–5). However, there is no trace of the report presented by Verdoorn at the European Meeting of the Econometric Society held in Varese in September 1950.[9] Only its abstract has survived – this was published the following year in volume 19 of *Econometrica*.

Some events of the private life of the author of 'Fattori' also stimulate our curiosity. Professor Verdoorn's scientific works were mostly written in Dutch and, as such, have remained the exclusive preserve of scholars who are familiar with this language. It is also true, however, that some of his works – written in English and which prove very useful in clarifying some of the theoretical foundations of Verdoorn's Law – have practically been ignored in most of the literature that has blossomed around the law. Furthermore, the lack of available information (obviously in English) on his personal life has made it difficult exactly to determine even the date of his death.[10]

In summary, the questions raised by the debate around Verdoorn's Law are the following: (i) What is the right interpretation of the existing empirical relation – both at a sectoral level and also between countries or regions – between the growth of output per worker and the growth of production? (ii) What are the difficulties raised by an econometric evaluation of this relation? (iii) To what extent, if any, does the productivity/output elasticity identify increasing returns to scale? (iv) Finally, how should this relationship be applied to (endogenous) growth modelling? The first three questions are so closely interconnected that they could be grouped together to form just one main problem: namely, the identification of the theoretical structure underlying Verdoorn's Law.

We are convinced that by considering an idea abstracted from the context (and the related evolution) of an author's thought, one runs the risk of making an arbitrary interpretation of its meaning. Consequently, through a careful re-reading of 'Fattori' and of some other more neglected writings by Verdoorn on the same theme, we have tried to capture the meaning which he intended to attach to his 'rule'. From this re-reading, it is clear that Verdoorn was well aware of the need to base this rule on a sound theoretical foundation. The two theoretical interpretations that Verdoorn himself put on this rule also becomes clearer. The first (and never disclaimed) interpretation was based on the assumed 'complementarity' between factors of production (having in mind a fixed-coefficients technology), and the second was based on the hypothesis of a 'perfect' substitutability of factors of production (having in mind here the Cobb–Douglas substitutability of one between labour and capital).

However, the debate which followed the interpretation of Verdoorn's Law made by Kaldor (1966), and which accounts for the majority of the literature on this topic, has subsequently led to several other interpretations – from a post-Keynesian one, to an interpretation that we could consider as 'technological'. Each of these interpretations come up against the same difficulty (which is shared by all theories on growth) – namely, how to conceptualise technological progress and how to measure its impact on productivity growth.

These are the issues that we are going to briefly deal with in the following paragraphs. This discussion will be preceded by some biographical notes on Verdoorn and his bibliography, and followed by some final remarks.

On the life and works of Petrus Johannes Verdoorn (1911–82)

Petrus Johannes Verdoorn was born in Amsterdam on 21 March 1911. After taking a degree in Economics at the Municipal University of Amsterdam, he started work with the Dutch railways. The first known paper of Verdoorn is an article published in 1939, and written in collaboration with Professor Jan Tinbergen, about the demand for passenger traffic by rail. In 1942, after attending the Netherlands School of Economics in Rotterdam, he successfully presented his PhD thesis, written under the supervision of Professor Tinbergen. In his doctoral dissertation on the growing rigidity of production costs he questioned the thesis by Schamatenbach on the increase of fixed costs relative to total cost (Verdoorn, 1949, p. 45 of the original Italian version).

Verdoorn dealt with many aspects of economic research, including the theory of growth, international economics, statistics and econometrics, and marketing and business economics. The editors of *liber amicorum* –

published to celebrate the 25th anniversary of the lecture given by Verdoorn when appointed Professor of Economics at the Netherlands School of Economics at Rotterdam – summed up this diversity as follows:

> Verdoorn showed a great versatility in all the fields in which he worked. Without exaggeration he may be characterised as one of the most many-sided economists in the Netherlands. However, much the subjects he studied may have varied, the methods he applied show persistent characteristics: theories are formulated to yield testable hypotheses which, when they can be maintained, are operational for policy purposes. (van Bochove et al., 1977, Preface)

In Appendix I of this chapter, we have reconstructed a brief chronology of the events of Verdoorn's life, using the sparse amount of information available in English.[11] Moreover, simply to highlight the wide range of scientific interests of Professor Verdoorn, we have listed some of his most important works in a Selected Bibliography. (See Appendix II, which, as was noted above, includes all the references to Verdoorn made in this chapter.) His bibliography has indeed been divided into two discrete parts. The first section includes works written by Verdoorn in Dutch, from the 1940s to the 1950s, which were listed in the bibliography (with just the title translation in English) published in volume 22 of *Econometrica* of 1954, when Verdoorn was elected a Fellow of the Econometric Society.[12] The second section includes Verdoorn's works published directly in English (some of them written in collaboration with others), which, apart from some few additions by us, are all listed in the 'Selected Bibliography of Professor Dr. P.J. Verdoorn' annexed to the volume of essays written in his honour.

Professor Verdoorn's scientific work has two main strands: one focuses on economic issues, and the other on the development of statistical-econometric techniques for economic analysis and market surveys. The first line of research dates from the time when Verdoorn worked with the Central Planning Bureau (CPB).[13] The second line arose largely from his experience as a lecturer at the Netherlands School of Economics in Rotterdam. For example, the manual written by Verdoorn (in collaboration with R. Ferber) is part of this second type of research. It deals with the methods and techniques employed in both economic and business analysis and is addressed to graduate or senior undergraduate classes. It is designed to meet the research requirements necessary for the preparation of Master's or PhD dissertations (Ferber and Verdoorn, 1962, Preface, p. vi).

Verdoorn's writings on strictly economic topics can be grouped into three different areas of interest: (a) labour market problems; (b) the planning and development of the Dutch economy; and, finally, (c) the economic consequences of European integration in general – and, in particular, its impact on the Dutch economy.

The works published by Verdoorn while he was in charge of CPB's Labour Market Unit (from 1945 to 1947) centre on this first area of interest, as do those he produced during the two years when he was member of the above-mentioned working group of the Economic Commission for Europe (ECE) based in Geneva (from 1948 to 1949). A monograph on the links between welfare, labour productivity, and hours worked (Verdoorn, 1947a)[14] and the 'Fattori' are among his most outstanding works of this period.

All of the works written by Verdoorn after becoming director of CPB's Division for Structural Problems and focused on the analysis of planning problems and the development of the Dutch economy belong to the second area of interest. Several essays on the development of a growth model belong to this line of research. This growth model, which follows the example of the much more popular one developed by Domar (1946), was also applied to an assessment of the economic prospects for the Netherlands.[15] In developing this model, Verdoorn conducted an in-depth analysis of the 'complementarity' between factors of production – considered to be a more suitable approach for long-term forecasting (Verdoorn, 1956a), as well as of the 'perfect' substitutability of production factors (Verdoorn, 1959a and 1959b). There are also some works, still belonging to this line of research, dealing with techniques to forecast production capacity and the final demand for goods and services (Verdoorn, 1960, 1964a, 1964b).

Finally, the third area of interest includes all his works published over a twenty-year period which analyse the economic effects of European integration in general and, more particularly, its impact on the Dutch economy. In this third group there are a few works that are worth mentioning, which were still in progress at the time of publication of the abovementioned *liber amicorum* (Van Eijk, 1977, p. 5). These are (i) a survey (the first one) on the effects for the Dutch industrial system of an economic union between western European countries (Verdoorn, 1952c);[16] (ii) the analysis of the effects on Benelux intra-bloc trade of the formation of a customs union (Verdoorn, 1960); (iii) a review of the techniques employed for measuring the effects of economic integration (Verdoorn and van Bochove, 1972b); and, finally, (iv) the application of two of these techniques[17] to the analysis of the effects of intra-bloc trade on EEC and European Free Trade Association (EFTA) countries (Verdoorn and Schwartz, 1972a).

As reported by his biographer, in addition to his strictly scientific work, Verdoorn was also very active as a consultant and took part in many working groups and committees, which were set up to tackle specific economic and social issues. He had been a long-time member of the Dutch Social Economic Council, a member of the government committee for the study of political, development and demographic problems in his country, as well as Senior Economic Advisor with the United Nations' Economic Commission for Europe (Van Eijk, 1977, p. 7).

During the 1960s, Verdoorn spent some time carrying out research work in the United States. Initially, he was Visiting Professor of Economics at the University of California at Berkeley, before becoming Senior Fellow at the Centre for Advanced Studies of Wesleyan University. In 1975, back in Holland, he was appointed Full Professor of Macroeconomic Policy at the Netherlands School of Economics at Rotterdam. Awarded numerous and important honorary titles, Petrus Johannes Verdoorn died in 1982 at the age of 71.

Verdoorn's 'rule' and its meaning

When, in 1945, Verdoorn was appointed head of the Labour Market Unit of the Central Planning Bureau, and started to deal with long-term planning issues, postwar reconstruction was the main problem to be faced. In a manner similar to that occuring in other European countries – in France with the first Monnet Plan and in Italy with Piano Saraceno – the CPB was producing the first documents of economic planning. The gathering and processing of data on industrial production and employment, to which Verdoorn made his own contribution,[18] was an important step in the preparation of these documents. In the following phase, namely in the actual application of these data to forecasting activities, the main obstacle seemed to be the fact that figures for productivity were generally unavailable. 'Unless this is known' – wrote Verdoorn in 'Fattori' – 'one does not know the relation between output and employment' (Verdoorn, 1949, p. 199).[19] Furthermore, since 'it cannot be assumed that the annual rate of growth of labour productivity will be constant, *and the production function cannot be used*' (Verdoorn, 1949, p. 199, our emphasis), he was looking for an alternative solution. In other words, Verdoorn was looking for a rule which would allow him to determine the level of output per worker as a function of some other variables or, to use more modern terminology, which would make the level of output per worker endogenous.

It is most likely that Verdoorn conceived the idea of a likely relation between the growth rates of industrial production and output per worker in 1947, while he was working on his first monograph, which dealt with the relations between welfare, productivity and hours worked (Van Eijk, 1977, p. 1). He must then have obtained confirmation of this idea in the summer of 1948.[20] While starting to write 'Fattori', he realised the following. The historical values of the elasticity of output per worker with respect to industrial production volume (obtained by calculating the ratio between their growth rates) in a certain number of industrial sectors,[21] ranged on average between 0.51 (for four industrial sectors identified in the Monnet Plan for France) and 0.57 (for 14 industrial sectors, mainly in the United States). Similarly, the analysis of data referred to a certain number of countries and for long periods of time (both before the first World War and in the interwar period)[22] seemed to confirm that the elasticity was actually around 0.5.[23] On the basis of these, although limited, data he thought that he was justified in claiming that 'over the long period a change in the volume of production, say of about 10 per cent, tends to be associated with an average increase in labour productivity of 4.5 per cent' (Verdoorn, 1949, p. 199).[24]

In looking for an economic mechanism that would give rise to such a rule, he invoked Adam Smith's idea according to which market expansion would favour a greater division of labour. Indeed, in 'Fattori', he wrote that

> one could have expected *a priori* to find a correlation between labour productivity and output, given that the division of labour only comes about through increases in the volume of production; therefore the expansion of production creates the possibility of further rationalisation which has the same effects as mechanisation (Verdoorn, 1949, p. 46).

Finally, in order to apply this rule for the benefit of long-term planning – namely, in order to assess whether a plan is plausible, employment requirements foreseeable, and the plan itself feasible in terms of labour availability and the growth rate of industrial production required to absorb the available labour – *the elasticity has to remain stable over time*.[25] Therefore, in his famous mathematical appendix, Verdoorn tried to give an in-depth analysis of the conditions 'for a stable relation between labour productivity and output' (Verdoorn, 1949, p. 203). For this purpose, first of all, he used a Cobb–Douglas production function (without technical progress) in order to derive an analytical expression for the output per worker/production elasticity. In this way, the value of the elasticity would depend on the parameters of the Cobb–Douglas production function (the partial elasticities of the factors of production), together with the growth of the labour–capital ratio. Then, by using a model which, although devised by Tinbergen in 1942, remained almost unknown until 1959 (when it was published again, this time in English),[26] he tried to demonstrate that 'under the normal assumptions of long-period analysis', the elasticity would, within certain limits, acquire a value which could be expressed as a combination of the parameters of the model and, as such, would remain constant over time (Verdoorn, 1949, p. 199).

However, Verdoorn failed to realise then that the expression of its elasticity, intended exclusively as ratio of the growth of output per worker to that of production, was indeed a *total* elasticity. Actually, the elasticity of the output per worker with respect to production would be constant only if the (growth of) production were the only cause of the (growth) of output per worker.[27]

The presentation of his discovery at the European Meeting of the Econometric Society – held in Varese in September of the year following the publication of 'Fattori' – must have created quite an impression on the audience. Indeed, the author of the summary of the paper presented by Verdoorn which, quite significantly, was entitled 'On an Empirical Law Governing the Productivity of Labour'[28] wrote that

> (t)he statistician impressed by this apparent dependency of the development of the productivity of labour on the growth of production, may feel inclined to formulate his findings in the form of an empirical law, in the same manner as Pareto sixty years ago formulated his famous law of the distribution of income.

After pointing out that this 'law' was to be interpreted in the sense that 'productivity as a rule has been increased as the square root of the volume of output', and as if he wanted to mitigate its impact, he drew attention to the fact that 'a law of this type describes only the behaviour pattern of the industrial entrepreneur and therefore cannot even be regarded as one of J.S. Mill's axiomata media, unless per chance a satisfactory explanation by means of technical conditions or the more general economic laws becomes feasible' (see *Econometrica*, 1951, p. 210).

Finally, considering that, as also pointed out by the author of the report, a 'rigidly constant relation between the rates of increase of productivity and output *appears not to be a necessary consequence of the model*' (*Econometrica*, 1951, p. 211, our emphasis), the real problem of this rule was – and still is – to identify the theoretical structure (namely the 'technical conditions') whereby the rule may acquire the status of 'Law'.

Verdoorn's Law and the approach based on the 'complementarity' between factors of production

Verdoorn himself suggested recourse to the literature on the manufacturing progress function in order to identify the technical conditions underlying Verdoorn's Law. In an article on the possible use of long-term planning in the approach based on the complementarity between the factors of production (henceforth simply referred to as the 'complementarity' approach), he clearly outlines the learning function as the theoretical structure required to explain his law (Verdoorn, 1956a).

This article was written while he was the head of the Division for Structural Problems – the CPB's operational unit in charge of analysing the planning and development problems of the Dutch economy.[29] In our opinion, this is quite a significant article, as it allows us to understand the exact meaning Verdoorn intended to attach to the rule identified in 'Fattori'.

By analysing the features and limits of the 'complementarity' approach, Verdoorn became convinced that such an assumption was actually leading to a rather 'strange world'.[30] Nevertheless, he thought that 'since perfect substitutability tends to exaggerate the possibilities of adjustment, the complementarity approach should perhaps be preferred from a purely pragmatic point of view when making long-term projections' (Verdoorn, 1956a, p. 443). When he then asked himself which analytical expression could define, in such a 'strange world', the demand for production factors, he thought that the multiplicative exponential function was 'the best suited to allow for changes in factor productivity as output increases' (Verdoorn, 1956a, p. 433). It was actually the same function, already mentioned before, from which Verdoorn had derived the regression equation used in 'Fattori'.[31] The only difference was the fact that the volume of output per worker was in this case held to be solely dependent on the volume of production – that is to say, by means of a constant total elasticity.[32]

With this in mind, the literature on manufacturing progress functions that had flourished in the United States at the end of the 1930s suggested to Verdoorn the lines of thought along which it would be possible to identify the technical conditions that he needed to provide the foundations of the law. Those studies had indeed indicated that 'the unit cost of labour and hence productivity are uniquely related to the *cumulated* volume of output' (Verdoorn, 1956a, p. 433, our emphasis). Therefore, in the expression in which he had formulated his rule, he just had to replace the *level* of output with its *cumulated* volume.[33] Also, legitimately assuming that, as part of a long-term planning approach, production would grow at a constant trend rate, it would thus be possible to obtain a new expression of his rule which was formally equivalent (in terms of growth rates) to the one formulated in Verdoorn's Law.[34]

After referring to 'Fattori' for the statistical verification of that relation, Verdoorn could state that 'a rather stable long-run relation between (the level of) productivity and the *level* of national product' was to be expected (Verdoorn, 1956a, p. 434, our emphasis). He was also convinced that the economic mechanism explaining the rule still needed a more adequate illustration. Therefore, with the help of a simple graph, he illustrated the likely links between the level of output and the division of labour and also between the latter and internal economies of scale (factors such as increased specialisation) on the one hand, and external economies of scale (such as the development of skilled labour and new technologies), on the other. Finally, according to Verdoorn, that same mechanism could justify the use of a similar expression 'also in the case of the capital stock', although only for certain industries (Verdoorn, 1956a, p. 434).

Therefore, there is no doubt that, simply with regard to that 'strange world' represented by the assumption of strict 'complementarity', Verdoorn successfully outlined the technical conditions required to provide his law with a strong theoretical foundation – namely, the learning function.

This interpretation is undoubtedly quite fascinating. The parameters of the linear relation estimated between the growth rates of output per worker and industrial production become easy to interpret. The regression slope coefficient indicates the contribution of the learning process to the growth of output per worker, while the regression constant indicates the contribution attributable to the other elements (the autonomous part).[35]

However, this interpretation, even without considering the aggregation problems involved (McCombie, 1982a, p. 290; Vaglio, 1990, pp. 157–8), can be easily challenged. On the one hand – as also made clear in earlier criticisms by Colin Clark (1957) – the range of variation in the value of the elasticity proved to be much wider than originally expected by Verdoorn. On the other hand, the contribution attributable to the 'learning by doing' process, apart from not being stable over time, has diminished in importance compared with the autonomous component.[36] In other words, the effect attributable to production growth alone, which, according to 'Fattori', was to be the (only) main cause of the growth of output per worker, over time and, more importantly, with the increasing mechanisation of production, now has only a secondary significance.[37]

This interpretation of the law is being thoroughly re-examined in the light of the issues recently raised by endogenous growth theories, partly following the lines recently presented by Arrow (1994).

The interpretation of Verdoorn's Law from the point of view of 'perfect' substitutability of the factors of production

The interpretation of Verdoorn's Law from the point of view of 'perfect' substitutability of the factors of production is presented in the well-known Appendix annexed to 'Fattori'. Actually, Verdoorn himself confirmed that this was the approach he preferred. When taking part in the debate raised by Rowthorn (1979) concerning the possible interpretations of his law, he expressed his satisfaction that the discussion was devoted to 'a critical discussion of the theoretical appendix of my 1949 article in *L'Industria*, whereas most authors simply discard it when discussing my so-called "law"' (Verdoorn, 1980, p. 382).

The first thing that we want to highlight here, quite curiously again, is that in this intervention (actually his only one on this issue), Verdoorn did not refer to his previous interpretation in terms of a learning function. In addition, he remarked that 'Fattori' had to be interpreted as a 'progress report': 'With the hindsight of my 1959 publication, its main shortcoming, from the operational point of view', wrote Verdoorn, 'was that it insufficiently emphasised that rigid constancy *over time* of the productivity–output elasticity is only to be expected in the steady-state' (Verdoorn, 1980, p. 383, italics in the original).

Only after the publication of the work on the role of capital in long-term forecasting, 'with a follow-up in the 1960 Report by a group of experts of the European Community', did Verdoorn develop the approach of 'perfect' substitutability of the factors of production (Verdoorn, 1959a; and Office Statistique des Communautés Européennes, 1960). He became convinced that apart from in the steady state, i.e., that situation where 'the neo-classical model degenerates into quasi-complementarity' (Verdoorn, 1980, p. 383), the value of elasticity would be subject to significant variations over time. He thus reached a conclusion which sounds like an epitaph to Verdoorn's Law. 'The "law" that has been given my name appears therefore to be much less generally valid than I was led to believe in 1949' (Verdoorn, 1980, p. 385).

What happened after this intervention has nothing more to do with Verdoorn's interpretation of Verdoorn's Law. From then on, apart from some lingering 'tails' of debate by de Vries (1980) and Thirlwall (1980), and a few other rare exceptions, the discussion concentrated on Kaldor's interpretation of Verdoorn's Law.[38]

Before discussing Kaldor's interpretation, it is useful to briefly refer to the possible reasons that led Verdoorn to include the much discussed Appendix in the 'Fattori'. Verdoorn wrote:

> This interdependency of a purely theoretical character ... does not by itself imply that the elasticity will be constant because in practice it will be influenced by various economic factors; none the less, it can be demonstrated (see the Appendix) that under the normal assumptions of long-period analysis, the elasticity assumes a mathematical form that tends to make it – within reasonable limits – fairly independent of variations in such economic factors (Verdoorn, 1949, p. 199).

Therefore, according to Verdoorn, this elasticity was undoubtedly to be considered not as a *parameter*, but rather as a *variable*. Furthermore, from the point of view of a 'perfect' substitutability of the factors of production, as pointed out by Arrow (1962), the conditions for a stable relation between labour productivity and output, had to be looked for 'in terms of increasing capital–labour ratio'.

The fact is, however, that in the Appendix to 'Fattori', Verdoorn proceeded in three distinct steps. He first derived an analytical expression for the elasticity, the value of which is definitionally equal to the ratio between the logarithm of productivity and the logarithm of output or, in terms of growth rates, to one minus the ratio of the growth of employment to that of output. Then, disavowing his initial intention not to use any production function as providing the technical conditions, he assumed a Cobb–Douglas production function (in a static form and with no first-degree homogeneity constraint imposed on the degree of returns to scale). In this way, he could express the values of that elasticity as a function of the growth of the capital–labour ratio (namely, in Verdoorn's own terminology, the elasticity of capital with respect to labour).[39] Finally, he proceeded with the construction of a model borrowed from Tinbergen, in order to analyse the conditions that would guarantee the stability over time of the so-defined elasticity.[40]

As also remarked by Thirlwall (1980, p. 387), the technical conditions do not necessarily have to be expressed in the first step. Hence, the elasticity will depend on the assumptions made concerning the existing relation between employment and production growth rates. Therefore, everything depends on the view held about the production process. In other words, the elasticity will depend on which approach is being adopted (that is, whether it is assumed that there is 'complementarity' or 'perfect' substitutability of factors of production); whether employment is considered as exogenous or endogenous; and the concept of technical progress adopted (whether it is exogenous/endogenous, embodied/disembodied, neutral/non-neutral), as well as on the method employed to measure its effects on the productivity growth rate.

By adopting the 'perfect' substitutability approach, just like both Verdoorn (in the Appendix to 'Fattori' and in his paper of 1980), and de Vries (1980), and by using the model developed by Tinbergen, it can be shown that the elasticity will remain constant, provided growth is in a steady-state condition. Following this approach, the easiest and most effective *test* to check the validity of 'Verdoorn's Law', as suggested to Verdoorn by de Vries himself, is to empirically verify whether a steady-state condition exists, namely whether capital and production growth rates are the same[41] (Verdoorn, 1980, p. 384; de Vries, 1980, p. 276).

Now, let us return to the debate following Rowthorn's interpretation of 'Verdoorn's Law'. Sparking off that debate, Rowthorn intended to question Kaldor's, rather than Verdoorn's, position. He pointed out two distinct formulations of that law coexisting in the model illustrated in the Appendix to 'Fattori'. The first one, which was independent of technology, failed to solve the problem of the technical conditions underlying the law itself, while the second formulation, which referred to investment and technology parameters, was not capable of giving 'an accurate indication of returns to scale' (Rowthorn, 1979, p. 132). Finally, after noting that technical progress had been left out of that model, Rowthorn reached the following conclusions. First, the returns to scale, even if accurately measured, were exclusively of a static nature. Secondly, that there was no learning by doing in the model 'nor any of the other "dynamic economies of scale" upon which later authors have laid so much stress' (Rowthorn, 1979, p. 133).

Actually, as we can infer from our reconstruction of Verdoorn's thought, this latter conclusion is correct only if we solely refer to the model outlined in the Appendix to the 'Fattori'. It is, instead, wrong, if the full Appendix to Verdoorn's original text is taken into consideration, together with his own interpretation based on the 'complementarity' approach. As a matter of fact, any learning by doing or any other dynamic economies of scale depend on the type of technical conditions that are assumed in order to provide a theoretical justification to Verdoorn's Law.

Thirlwall (1980, p. 387), contrary to what Rowthorn maintained in his interpretation of Verdoorn's Law, also pointed out later that, on the basis of the analytical expression for the elasticity obtained from the Appendix to 'Fattori', Verdoorn's coefficient depended on the degree of (static) returns to scale (as measured by the *total* elasticity of the production function) *and* on the ratio between capital growth of labour growth. Furthermore, without technical change, and if (and only if) the growth of the capital and labour are equal, Verdoorn's coefficient would exactly equal one minus the reciprocal of the degree of homogeneity of the production function.[42] Moreover, since in this formulation, Verdoorn's coefficient is free of any steady state condition,[43] this would explain why 'the Verdoorn relation may have broken down in the turbulent years since 1966 (if it has broken down)' (Thirlwall, 1980, p. 388).

Finally, Turner (1983), in a paper which, in a sense, was to put an end to the debate, pointed out that all hypotheses were assuming a total elasticity of the output per worker with respect to output (that is, the absence of a constant term in the Verdoorn's Law). By getting away from this assumption, he reached an interesting conclusion. With reference to Verdoorn's Law in growth rates (derived from a Cobb–Douglas production function, with exogenous technical change), and assuming that capital increased at a constant (exogenous) rate, the growth in labour productivity would arise 'from three sources: returns to scale of labour which depends upon output growth, a constant term which depends upon technical change, and the returns to scale of capital parameters [with] [t]his latter term ... multiplied by the constant growth of capital stock' (Turner, 1983, p. 143).

Therefore, Verdoorn's Law, in the usual formulation employed in empirical analysis, is perfectly compatible with both points of view – namely, with the one envisaging 'complementarity' and the one based on the 'perfect' substitutability of the factors of production. This conclusion is identical to the one which, in measuring the effects of technical progress on the productivity growth rate, considers the two opposite approaches. These are one based on the production function and the other one centred on Kaldor's 'technical progress function' (in its linear formulation). At an empirical level, it is impossible to discriminate between the two interpretations.

Kaldor's and Kaldorian interpretations of 'Verdoorn's Law'

Kaldor's interpretation of Verdoorn's Law is presented in his 1966 inaugural lecture on the *Causes of the Slow Rate of Economic Growth of the UK*. It reflects the complexity of Kaldor's views of the growth process, and it is too well known to be reviewed in detail in this chapter. However, since

Kaldor's views have significantly affected the debate on Verdoorn's Law – to the extent that it is often referred to as the Verdoorn–Kaldor Law – it is useful to present a brief synoptic review at this point.

Trying to summarise the thought of an economist like Kaldor, and especially on such a limited and, to a certain extent, secondary issue, is extremely difficult. As his biographers have correctly pointed out, questions of methods and value judgements are inextricably intertwined in the theories of this author (Targetti, 1988; Thirlwall, 1987).

Kaldor's criticisms of the approach based on the 'perfect' substitutability of production factors, and especially 'with regard to the model of general competitive equilibrium, perfect information and completed markets' (Vaglio, 1990, p. 149), do not only question the theoretical, but also the realism of the assumptions. According to Kaldor, the limitations of this approach are to be found in its failure to consider increasing returns to scale (with their various forms and implications); the constraints to growth determined by the demand side; and the essentially endogenous nature of technical progress. In his opinion, these shortcomings are so severe that the associated theory is of no practical use in understanding the development of modern industrial economies.

As is well known, 1965 is a turning point in Kaldor's thought and in the method with which he tackled issues like economic development and growth theories (Kaldor, 1986, p. 20). By moving from a deductive to an essentially inductive approach, he intended to identify 'what kind of regularities can be detected in empirically observed phenomena and then try to discover what particular testable hypotheses would be capable of explaining the association' (Kaldor, 1978a, p. xvii). While searching for an explanation of 'why growth rates differ', Kaldor came across 'an extraordinarily close correlation between the rate of growth of manufacturing output and the rate of growth of GDP – relationship of a kind which suggested that the rate of economic growth will depend on how much faster its manufacturing output grows than the rest of the economy' (Kaldor, 1978a, p. xviii).

Having been the director of the ECE Research and Planning Division, of which Verdoorn had been a staff member, Kaldor knew that the latter had identified an empirical relationship between the rate of growth of productivity and the rate of growth of production. It was Kaldor who coined the term 'Verdoorn's Law', 'in recognition of P.J. Verdoorn's early investigations, published in 1949' (Kaldor, 1966, p. 106). The point is, however, that Kaldor's own interpretation of that relationship was not precisely the same as Verdoorn's. According to Kaldor, 'owing to increasing returns to scale', in the manufacturing sector (which were not prevalent in the other sectors of the economy), 'the marginal product of labour is likely to be considerably *above* the average product (approximately twice as high)' (Kaldor, 1978a, p. xix, italics in the original).[44] As a consequence, a value of the regression (Verdoorn's) coefficient of 0.5 when the growth of productivity is regressed on the growth of output was interpreted as providing evidence of increasing returns to scale in that particular sector (Kaldor, 1975a). (Kaldor's preferred specification was to regress employment on output growth, but a regression coefficient of 0.5 in this case also implies increasing returns to scale.) Since this hypothesis had been confirmed by a number of empirical studies, Kaldor began to think that not all sectors play the same role in determining economic growth. Finally, since the growth of the manufacturing industry was determined 'by the growth of the exogenous components of demand originating outside the sector' (Kaldor, 1978a, p. xxii), this was indeed the (only) really 'Keynesian' sector. Hence, economic growth as a whole is thus *demand*-constrained rather than resource-constrained.

Kaldor, in his interpretation, thus ignored Verdoorn's rule. By focusing on Verdoorn's Law defined as the linear relationship using growth rates, Kaldor argued that if such a law exists, it is evidence that economies of scale are significant in manufacturing at the macroeconomic level.[45]

Notwithstanding all the problems related to the empirical validation of Verdoorn's Law, Kaldor's interpretation of such a law is undoubtedly nearer to Verdoorn's first, rather than his second, view of it. This may be seen by noting Kaldor's constantly voiced dislike of the approach based on the 'perfect' substitutability of factors of production; his insistence on the importance of the role played by increasing returns in his explanation of regional (international) differences in growth rates; the importance attached to the 'stylised fact' that sectoral growth rates are not equal (as evidenced by the fact that manufacturing industry and exports generally grow at higher rates than income) and Kaldor's concept of technical progress as an endogenous and embodied phenomenon.

In their 'attempt to formalise the (Kaldorian) model in order to clarify its structure', Dixon and Thirlwall (1975) gave an interesting (and original) interpretation 'on Kaldorian lines' of Verdoorn's Law. According to their interpretation, the linear relation between productivity and output growth rates is obtained by means of a Kaldorian 'technical progress function'. Similar to the other two previously examined approaches – namely those involving 'complementarity' and 'perfect' substitutability of production factors – this latter approach too, while Kaldorian in spirit, allows an unambiguous interpretation of the linear statistical relationship between productivity and output growth. Verdoorn's coefficient thus indicates 'the rate of induced disembodied technical progress, the degree to which capital accumulation is induced by growth and the extent to which technical progress is embodied in capital accumulation'. The intercept term indicates 'the autonomous rate of disembodied progress, the autonomous rate of capital accumulation per worker, and the extent to which technical progress is embodied in capital accumulation' (Dixon and Thirlwall, 1975, p. 209).

Therefore if we consider Verdoorn's Law merely as the simple linear relationship between growth rates, we have three different, equally legitimate, interpretations: two of them suggested by Verdoorn himself, and one by Kaldor. Which of the three is to be preferred depends, generally speaking, on one's view of the production process. In other words, assuming that Verdoorn's 'law' is not just 'a simple statistical mirage' – to use Kaldor's words (1975a, p. 891)[46] – everything depends on how one intends to proceed to solve the problem identified already by Verdoorn himself in 'Fattori' – namely, what is the theoretical structure underlying the 'law'?

Conclusion: what remains of 'Verdoorn's Law'?

The reason why we decided to re-read 'Fattori' more than fifty years after its publication, was our impression that this rightly celebrated article has been frequently quoted, but, actually, not often read. We also had the impression that readings of it were mainly confined to its mathematical appendix (and then not even to all of that). Consequently, some interpretations of Verdoorn's Law seem to have been derived from a partial reading of this work or, in any case, from a reading that failed to consider Verdoorn's thought as a whole. We have therefore tried to reconstruct the logical pathway that led Verdoorn to believe, first of all, that he had made an exciting discovery and, thirty years later, to question the general validity of his own finding.

Our reconstruction has shown that there are two distinct interpretations of this law. The first one, considered in terms of a learning function, refers to the approach of 'complementarity' between production factors. The second, conversely, based on the use of a production function, is inspired by the hypothesis of the 'perfect' substitutability of the factors of production. Both interpretations derive from the need to provide the rule – identified in 'Fattori' – with a theoretical basis. According to this rule, the level of output per worker changes (by a constant elasticity) depending on the volume of production. Both interpretations have been accredited by Verdoorn himself, although in different times and with a different importance attributed to each of them.

Finally, there is the third, and most famous interpretation – that of Kaldor. It belongs to the attempts made by this author to construct a 'two-sector model', the most important basic features of which, unfortunately, have remained, as Kaldor himself put it, '"on the drawing board", unpublished' (Kaldor, 1978a, p. xxii). See Targetti (1985) and Thirlwall (1986) for growth models along these lines.

Each of these three interpretations possess some merit, but they all have a number of limitations. Furthermore, they are equivalent in their 'dynamic' formulation, namely the relationship between the growth of output per worker and production. In other words, by starting from the simple linear relation between the growth rates of these variables, it is impossible to establish which of the three interpretations is the most convincing. Everything, indeed, depends on the theoretical framework under which the law finds its justification.

This is the outlook emerging from our brief literature review on Verdoorn's Law. However, it should also be added that, under each reference framework, there are several interesting research opportunities to try and address the still unsolved issues. We shall now attempt to identify some of them, although without claiming to be exhaustive.

By sticking to the problems underlying Verdoorn's Law, in both the interpretations made by Verdoorn, the easy assumption according to which production growth is the only cause of the growth of output per worker should be discarded. In other words, we should examine in greater depth what would happen to the law if the elasticity defined by Verdoorn were *not* a total elasticity. Also, in the wake of some recent work on the limits to the production function and its form (Bairam, 1994; McCombie, 1998), the hypotheses on the constant nature of partial elasticities of the factors of production and the homogeneous nature of the production function should be dropped. Finally, owing to the multiple forms of technical progress, the analytically very convenient assumption whereby innovations are considered to be exogenous and ubiquitous should be considered obsolete. From this point of view, the work by Lenderink and Siebrand (1977) is interesting. In trying to analyse the long-run relationship between employment and production embodied in the Verdoorn Law, these authors have shown that 'much of the empirical work with regard to the relations between employment and production becomes more or less interpretable if vintage production models are combined with disequilibrium theory' (Lenderink and Siebrand, 1977, p. 113).

Vaglio (1990) drew attention to the so-called innovation economy, a school of thought taking inspiration from the comprehensive and articulated technological-evolutionary approach grafted on *catching-up* theories, and, more generally, on the problem of convergence. These research lines have recently been picked up by Nelson (1998) and Archibugi and Michie (1998). Furthermore, as also pointed out in the debate on endogenous growth theories, the assumed homogeneity of initial conditions in cross-country comparisons must be removed, especially when considering the presence (and the importance) of the so-called human capital, as well as of learning.

Finally, as part of the Kaldorian tradition, some models of export-led growth, in which Verdoorn's Law plays a crucial role, have recently attempted to extend Kaldor's notion of cumulative growth. Work on this idea, which, perhaps, has been overshadowed by the theory on international growth rate differences based on Harrod's dynamic foreign trade multiplier, has been resumed. Attention is drawn to international competition, and to both international and sectoral specialisation in the process of economic growth (see, inter alia, Boggio, 1996; Pugno, 1996a, 1998; De Benedictis, 1998; Setterfield, 1998).

Appendix I: Chronology

1911 Born in Amsterdam on 21 March.

1939 Joined the Economics Department of the Posts, Telegraphs and Telephones. He published an article on passenger traffic by rail in co-operation with Professor Jan Tinbergen.

1943 Received a PhD degree from the Netherlands School of Economics in Rotterdam, for which he wrote a doctoral thesis under the supervision of Professor Jan Tinbergen.

1945 Appointed a staff member of the Central Planning Bureau, of which Professor Tinbergen was the first director, he became head of the section considering labour problems.

1948 Appointed a staff member of the Research and Planning Division of the Economic Commission for Europe in Geneva (of which Lord Kaldor was the director).

1949 His research work at the Research and Planning Division in Geneva continued. He published in *L'Industria* the article, entitled 'Fattori che regolano lo sviluppo della produttività del lavoro'.

1950 Became head of the division for structural problems of the Central Planning Bureau. He presented his report 'On an Empirical Law Governing the Productivity of Labour' at the European Meeting of the Econometric Society held in Varese.

1952 Appointed part-time Professor of Business Statistics, Market Research and Marketing at the Netherlands School of Economics at Rotterdam, he gave his Inaugural Lecture. The same year he presented a paper at the annual meeting of the Dutch Economic Association on the economic consequences for the Netherlands of its economic integration with the other Western European countries. From 1952 to 1969 he was a member of the Editorial Board of the book series 'Contributions to Economic Analysis'.

1953 Elected Fellow of the Econometric Society.

1955 Appointed Deputy Director of the Central Planning Bureau. Under his guidance, the construction of an econometric model was started, based on the Harrod – Domar growth model. The CPB used this model for its long-term 1955–70 economic forecasts of the Dutch economy. This research work led to the publication of *An Exploration of the Economic Perspective of the Netherlands, 1950–70* (only available in Dutch). He played a leading role in the construction of a macro model of the Dutch economy, set up in the so-called 'Econometric Analysis' project.

1958 Was a staff member of the High Authority of the European Community for Coal and Steel (CECA).

1961 Visiting Professor of Economics at the University of California, Berkeley.

1968 Spent two years (1968–9) as Senior Fellow at the Centre for Advanced Studies at Wesleyan University.

1969 He left his position as part-time Professor of Business Statistics, Market Research and Marketing at the Netherlands School of Economics in Rotterdam which he had been held since 1952.

1971 Was awarded the Royal-Shell prize for his entire scientific work by the 'Hollandsche Maatschappij der Wetenschappen'.

1975 He left CPB and moved to The Hague. He became Full-Time Professor of Macroeconomic Policy.

1982 Died at The Hague, at the age of 71.

Appendix II: Selected bibliography of the works of Professor P.J. Verdoorn

Publications in Dutch

VERDOORN, P.J. (1939) (with J. Tinbergen), *De vraag naar het personenvervoer per spoor* (The demand for passenger transportation by railways), Nederlandsche Conjunctuur, Mei, 79–89.

VERDOORN, P.J. (1943a) *De verstarring der produktiekosten* (The growing rigidity of production costs; PhD thesis), Netherlands Economic Institute no. 33, Haarlem, Erven F. Bohn N.V., pp. XVI, 164.

VERDOORN, P.J. (1943b) *De ontwikkeling en druk der constante kosten* (The historical development of constant costs), Netherlands Economic Institute no. 33A, Haarlem, Erven F. Bohn N.V., pp. VIII, 78.

VERDOORN, P.J. (1947a) *Arbeidsduur en Welvaartspeil* (Hours of labour and economic welfare), Leiden, H.E. Stenfert Kroese, N.V., pp. VIII, 275.

VERDOORN, P.J. (1947b) *Loonshoogte en Werkgelegenheid* (Unemployment and the wage level), *De Economist*, vol. 95, 513–39.

VERDOORN, P.J. (1950) *Grondslagen en Techniek van de Marktanalyse* (Foundations and techniques of market research), Leiden, pp. XII, 667.

VERDOORN, P.J. (1952a) *Enige gegevens bettrefende de toekimstige behoefte aan medici* (Some aspects of the future demand for physicians) (with F.T. van der Maden), Report prepared for the Royal Netherlands Society of Physicians, Central Planning Bureau Reprints no. 21, pp. 48.

VERDOORN, P.J. (1952b) *De eigen markt der onderneming* (The market of a single business unit), Leiden, H.E. Stenfert Kroese, pp. 28.

VERDOORN, P.J. (1952c) *Welke zijn de achtergronden en vooruitzichten van de economische integratie in Europa en welke gevolgen zou deze integratie hebben, met name voor de welvaart in Nederland* (The Netherlands and the Economic Consequences of an Economic Integration of Western Europe), Central Planning Bureau Reprints no. 22, pp. 95.

Publications in English

The selection includes all titles in English listed in the Selected Bibliography of Professor Dr P.J. Verdoorn contained in Van Bochove et al. (1977), pp. 353–5, plus a few other titles (earmarked with an asterisk) found through personal research.

*VERDOORN, P.J. (1949) 'Fattori che regolano lo sviluppo della produttività del lavoro', *L'Industria*, 1, 3–10. English Translation by A.P. THIRLWALL, 'Factors governing the growth of labour productivity', in D. IRONMONGER, J.O.N. PERKINS, T. VAN HOA (eds), *National Income and Economic Progress*, London: Macmillan Press, 1988, pp. 199–207. Reprinted in L.L. PASINETTI (1993), *Italian Economic Papers*, vol. II, Bologna: Il Mulino, New York and Oxford: Oxford University Press, pp. 59–68.

*VERDOORN, P.J. (1950) 'On an Empirical Law Governing the Productivity of Labor', paper presented at the Varese Meeting of the Econometric Society, Sep., (an abstract of this paper is in *Econometrica*, vol. 19, 209–10, 1951).

VERDOORN, P.J. (1954) 'A Customs Union for Western Europe: Advantage and Feasibility', *World Politics*, vol. 6, 481–500.

VERDOORN, P.J. (1956a) 'Complementarity and Long-range Projections', *Econometrica*, vol. 24, 429–50.

VERDOORN, P.J. (1956b) 'Marketing from the Producer's Point of View', *Journal of Marketing*, vol. 20, no. 3, 221–35.

VERDOORN, P.J. and C.H. VAN EIJK (1958) 'Experimental short-term forecasting models', The Hague: Central Planning Bureau, pp. 103, paper presented to the 20th European Meeting of the Econometric Society, Bilbao, September.

VERDOORN, P.J. (1959a) 'The Role of Capital in Long-Term Projection Model', *Cahiers Èconomique de Bruxelles*, vol. 5, 49–57.

*VERDOORN, P.J. (1959b) 'Capital and Technical Development in Long-Term Projection Model', *Cahiers Economique de Bruxelles*, vol. 5, 59–69.

VERDOORN, P.J. (1960) 'The Intra-Block Trade of the Benelux', in E.A.G. ROBINSON (ed.), *Economic Consequences of the size of Nations*, London: Macmillan, pp. 291–329.

VERDOORN, P.J. and R. FERBER (1962) *Research Methods in Economics and Business*, New York: Macmillan, p. 573.

VERDOORN P.J. and J.J. POST (1964a) 'Capacity and Short-Term Multipliers', in HART P.E., G. MILLS and J.K. WHITAKER (eds), *Econometric Analysis for National Economic Planning*, Colston Paper no. 16, London: Butterworth, pp. 179–98.

VERDOORN, P.J. and J.J. POST (1964b) 'Short and Long Term Extrapolations with the Dutch Forecasting Model 1963–D', in WOLD H.O.A (ed.), *Modelbuilding in the Human Sciences*, Monaco: Union Européenne d'Editions, pp. 89–123.

VERDOORN, P.J. and F.G.M. MEYER ZU SCHLOCHTERN (1964) 'Trade Creation and Trade Diversion in the Common Market', in *Intégration européenne et réalité Économique*, Collège d'Europe: Cahiers de Bruges, Brugge: De Tempel, pp. 95–138.

VERDOORN, P.J. (1965) 'Government–Industry Planning Interrelationships', *California Management Review*, vol. 8, no. 2, 51–8.

VERDOORN, P.J. (1967) 'The Short-Term Model of the Central Planning Bureau and its Forecasting Performance (1953–63)', in *Macro Economic Models for Planning and Policy Making*, Geneva: United Nations, pp. 35–51.

VERDOORN, P.J. and J.J. POST (1969) 'Comparison of the Prewar and Postwar Business Cycles in the Netherlands', in BRONFENBRENNER M. (ed.), *Is the Business Cycle Obsolete?*, New York: Wiley, pp. 436–66.

*VERDOORN, P.J. and J.G.D. HOOGLAND (1971) *Commodity Imports by Four Main Categories for the Netherlands, 1952–68*, The Hague: Central Planning Bureau, Occasional Papers, no. 1.

*VERDOORN, P.J. and Y. VAN HAITOVSKY (1972) 'A Note on the Efficiency of the first Difference Least Square Estimators', Jerusalem: Hebrew Univesity of Jerusalem, Dept Of Economics, pp. 10.

VERDOORN P.J. and A.N.R. SCHWARTZ (1972) 'Two Alternative Estimates of the Effects of EEC and EFTA on the Pattern of Trade', *European Economic Review*, vol. 3, 291–335.

VERDOORN, P.J. and C.A. VAN BOCHOVE (1972) 'Measuring Integration Effects', *European Economic Review*, vol. 3, 337–49.

VERDOORN, P.J. (1973) 'Some Long-Run Dynamic Elements of Factor Price Inflation', in H.C. BOS, H. LINNEMANN, P. de WOLFF (eds), *Economic Structure and Development: Essays in Honour of J. Tinbergen*, Amsterdam: North Holland, pp. 111–37.

*VERDOORN, P.J. (1980) 'Verdoorn's Law in Retrospect: a Comment', *Economic Journal*, vol. 90, 382–5 June.

Notes

1. 'Fattori' is the only work by Verdoorn that was published in Italian. The reason why this was the case is still unclear. Through the kind involvement of Ms. Jacqueline Timmerhuis of the CPB Netherlands Bureau for Economic

Policy Analysis, Professor Van Den Beld, former CPB Director and Professor of Economics at the Erasmus University of Rotterdam, has been contacted. Although he had been working with Verdoorn for several years, he could not give an explanation of this. We wish to thank Ms Timmerhuis for her valuable help in finding some biographical and bibliographical information on Professor Verdoorn.

2. All references to Verdoorn in this chapter are to be found in Appendix II of the chapter.
3. In the second edition of *The Conditions of Economic Progress*, published in 1951, Colin Clark simply thanked Dr Verdoorn for providing him with the national income estimates for the Netherlands for 1946. See Clark (1951, p. 86).
4. See Colin Clark (1957, p. 357n1). The same note also makes reference to one of Verdoorn's works (1952c). This article, which was written in Dutch, is listed (with just the English translation of the title) in the bibliography of Verdoorn's works published in *Econometrica*, when he was elected Fellow of the Econometric Society (Colin Clark had been elected ten years earlier). See the selected bibliography of Professor Verdoorn's works in our Appendix II. On the same topic, Verdoorn also submitted a full report to the Annual Meeting of the Dutch Economic Association in 1952, of which however there is no written text. See van Eijk (1977, p. 3).
5. Perhaps it is also worth noting that Beckerman (1962) conjectured a very similar relation to that presented by Verdoorn, although he referred to the relation between the growth rates of output per worker and exports, rather than output. As is well known, this model prompted a new literature on export-led growth.
6. The English translation of 'Fattori' by Thirlwall was first published as an appendix to a work by Thirlwall, on the analysis of the relation between population growth and economic development. Strangely enough (or was it done on purpose?), this work by Thirlwall is part of a collection of essays dedicated to Colin Clark. Actually there are also reports – confirmed by Thirlwall (1980a) – of a previous translation by A.P. Thirlwall and G. Thirlwall. Another curious thing about this translation is that it was being circulated privately in English academic circles at the end of the 1970s and, although referred to as published in *Research in Population and Economics* in 1979 (see, for example, Harris and Lau, 1998, p. 212), in reality, it never appeared in that journal. This was because Verdoorn, for some unknown reason, refused to give permission for the translation to be published.
7. The publication, under the patronage of the 'Società italiana degli economisti', of the *Italian Economic Papers* series edited by Luigi Pasinetti, actually aimed at 'making available, to the vast international community of English-reading economists, contributions to economics that would otherwise remain within the bounds (and the privilege) of the happy few who know the language of Dante' (Pasinetti, 1992, p. 7). Hopefully, the 'Dutch Economic Association will soon follow suit with a similar initiative'.
8. For example, Colin Clark compared the British with the US experience and noted that Verdoorn's coefficient, generally speaking, took values other than 0.5. Also, it appeared that it was subject to changes over time. Therefore, while confirming the importance of the rule discovered by Verdoorn, Clark invited his colleagues not to rely too much on the specific values (and constant nature) of the parameters of this relation. See Colin Clark (1957, p. 359).
9. Announced in volume 18 of *Econometrica*, issues nos 1 and 2, the European Meeting of the Econometric Society was held in Varese on 6–8 September 1950.

Members of the Programme Committee of the Meeting were Professor Felice Vinci of the University of Milan (chairman and in charge of the preparation of the report), Professors R.G.D. Allen of the London School of Economics; Ragnar Frisch of Oslo University; René Roy, of the Office of Statistics of the University of Paris and Eraldo Fossati, of the University of Trieste, who was responsible for making the local arrangements for the meeting (see *Econometrica*, vol. 19, no. 2, p. 190).

10. On this point, for example, in Thirlwall's translation (1988, p. 199n1), it is stated that 'Verdoorn died in 1985 and the translation was not authorised by the author prior to his death' (this note was not included in the version published in the collection edited by Pasinetti). Actually, Verdoorn died three years earlier, in 1982. This is indirectly confirmed by the fact that, as early as in January 1983, Verdoorn was no longer included in the list of Fellows of the Econometric Society. See *Econometrica*, 1983, vol. 51, no. 3, p. 876. Also, as far as we know, news of his death has never been published in this journal, nor has his obituary, as was usually the case with other renowned Fellows, such as Leif Johansen (1930–82), Robert C. Geary (1896–1983), and John Lintner (d.1983) as well as Gerhard Tintner (1907–83). See *Econometrica*, 1983, vol. 51, no. 3, 5 and 6, and 1984, vol. 52, no. 3.
11. The scarce biographical data about Verdoorn, used to write this paragraph, have been obtained from the biographical note annexed to 'Fattori' (which is not included in the English translation by Thirlwall); the Preface to *liber amicorum*, edited by Van Bochove et al. (1977); and the essay by Van Eijk, published in the same volume. We have also obtained some information from Mrs Timmerhuis, of the CPB Netherlands Bureau for Economic Policy Analysis.
12. Apart from Verdoorn, the other Fellows of the Econometric Society elected in 1953 were William J. Baumol of Princeton University, Marcel Boiteux of the Service Commercial National in Paris, George B. Dantzig of the RAND Corporation in Santa Monica, Clifford Hildreth of the North Carolina State College and Don Patinkin of the Hebrew University of Jerusalem. See *Econometrica*, vol. 22, no. 1, pp. 133–5.
13. The CPB, of which Professor Tinbergen was the director, is a government institution established after the Second World War and concerned with planning economic development in the Netherlands. As reported by Mrs Timmerhuis, Verdoorn had always kept in contact with Professor Tinbergen, who, apart from holding him in great esteem, considered him to have a remarkable talent for scientific issues and an exceptional working stamina.
14. The outcome of the investigations carried out by Verdoorn (1947) on the relation between productivity, hours worked and production, which is reported in the appendix of that paper, was used by Verdoorn (as reported by his biographer) 'in different forms in several studies' (including the 'Fattori') (Van Eijk, 1977, p. 2).
15. It refers to the report by the CPB on *An Exploration of the Economic Perspectives of the Netherlands, 1950–70*, published in 1955 and available only in Dutch. Verdoorn also played an important role in the construction of a second and more complex econometric model for the short-term analysis of the Dutch economy. The guidelines and forecasts for the period 1953–63 supplied by this second model are contained in another paper by Verdoorn (1967). Moreover, with reference to econometric models, it is worth while recalling here that Verdoorn also took part in the Link project for the integration of national econometric models, which aimed to improve the estimates of world foreign trade (Van Eijk, 1977, p. 6).

16. This work (Verdoorn 1952c) was first noted and cited by Colin Clark (1957, p. 357n1).
17. The second of these two methods is an extension of the approach used by Verdoorn in a previous work (Verdoorn and Meyer zu Schlochtern, 1964).
18. Mention of this collection, processing and evaluation of data on domestic production is found in the first edition of *The Conditions of Economic Progress* by Colin Clark. In chapter III, he refers to Dr Verdoorn as well as to Professor Tinbergen. As reported by Clark, the former had given him the national income figures produced by the CPB for the Netherlands for 1946 (at 1938 constant prices). The latter, in a private communication, had given him the national income estimates in the Netherlands for 1947, as well as a comparison between these latter figures and those on employment for 1938. See Colin Clark (1951, p. 86).
19. Except otherwise specified, the page numbers of 'Fattori' refer to Thirlwall's translation reported in Thirlwall (1988, pp. 199–207).
20. The publisher of *L'Industria* made a note clarifying that the statistical information available to Verdoorn referred to August 1948.
21. Curiously enough, with regard to Italy, Verdoorn, based on the figures of the Piano Saraceno, also included the 'Public Utilities' sector (with an elasticity of 0.11). The average intersectoral value was 0.52 (including Mining).
22. Data on industrial production and employment reported in Table I of 'Fattori' (most likely collected by the CPB, since no reference is made to their source), concern the following: (a) four countries (Sweden, United Kingdom, United States and Germany) for the period before the First World War; and (b) 14 countries (Sweden, Japan, Finland, Hungary, Holland, Norway, Denmark, Poland, UK, United States, Canada, Czechoslovakia, Estonia and Italy) for the period between the two wars. See Verdoorn (1949, p. 200).
23. Table I of 'Fattori' also reports the results of a regression equation obtained, as specified in the report *On an Empirical Law Governing the Productivity of Labour*, from the relation $v/a = v^{\alpha}e^{\beta t}$ (where v indicates the level of production and a the level of employment). By taking logs and differentiating this latter expression with respect to time, one obtains the linear form of growth rates ($d\ log\ v/a = 0.573\ d\ log\ v + 0.00239$) which is reported in Table I of 'Fattori'. Among the curious things about Verdoorn, we can add that, on the basis of the data given in this table, we were unable to determine the same parameters obtained by Verdoorn. Vaciago, who most probably also realised it, complained that the statistical criteria used by Verdoorn to support his 'Law' were not rigorous enough. He therefore calculated the regression line again, and obtained a slope, or Verdoorn, coefficient of 0.605 and a constant of 0.480 (with a correlation coefficient of 0.687) (Vaciago, 1968, p. 328). The same results were later referred to also by Vaglio (1990, p. 166).
24. It should be pointed out here that the rule that Verdoorn thought to identify, as it was expressed, actually consisted of two separate propositions. First, the level of output per worker is linked to industrial production, depending on its elasticity. Secondly, this elasticity takes a specific constant value.
25. In order to justify the importance of this, Verdoorn wrote that 'While the hypothesis of constant elasticity is not in practice very suitable for making forecasts, it can nevertheless be used profitably as one criterion for making a judgement, on the basis of past experience, about the realisation of long term plans' (Verdoorn, 1949, p. 200).
26. 'On the Theory of Trend Movements' was written by Tinbergen while he was in Germany and was originally published in German (See *Weltwirtschaftliches*

Archiv, 1942, 55, pp. 511–49). This article, which is now held to be a milestone in the neoclassical theory on growth, remained practically unknown until its publication (this time in English) in the collection of *Selected Papers* by Jan Tinbergen, edited by L.H. Klaassen, L.M. Kayck and H.J. Witteveen, Amsterdam: North Holland, 1959, pp. 182–219.

27. With reference to the relation reported in note 22, for the ratio between output per worker and production growth rates to be constant, the regression constant must be equal to zero. Only in this case will the ratio correspond to the total elasticity. Most probably, Verdoorn was convinced that elasticity had to be (approximately) equal to 0.5, based on the outcome of his own calculation, which would indicate that the constant was not much different from zero and the elasticity very close to 0.5.
28. The note preceding the Table of Contents of the report, stating that Professor Felice Vinci of the University of Milan was given 'the responsibility for preparation of the Report', would indicate that he was also the author of the summaries included in the same Report. (see *Econometrica*, 19(2), April 1951, p. 190).
29. The work of the CPB's Division, co-ordinated by Verdoorn and which was in charge of research work on planning and development problems, culminated with the publication, in 1955, of the abovementioned report on the perspectives of the Dutch economy for the twenty-year period, 1950–70 (available only in Dutch).
30. According to Verdoorn, the world represented by the 'complementarity' of the factors of production was strange because such an assumption was to lead 'in many cases to pessimistic conclusions with respect to the possibilities of durable equilibrium' (Verdoorn, 1956a, p. 442). This seemed to be particularly true of open economies, although those who 'are thinking in terms of input–output analysis or linear programming and who define reality in terms of finite series of discrete technical processes and inflexible boundary conditions will, however, probably feel more at home with this view' (Verdoorn, 1956a, p. 442).
31. In particular, it refers to the functional form reported in note 22 above, in which, this time, Verdoorn omitted the autonomous part. However, by doing so, it is no longer possible for the level of output per worker to grow also for (unspecified) reasons, other than those that are dependent on the growth in the volume of production (see Verdoorn, 1956a, p. 433).
32. Verdoorn, however, pointed out that in the case in which 'the rate of increase of the working population is comparatively low, special allowance should perhaps be made for an autonomous increase in productivity' (Verdoorn, 1956a, p. 443). In this case, as can easily be verified from the formula reported in note 22, the elasticity of output per worker with respect to the level of production will not be a total, but a partial elasticity.
33. Fellner (1969) pointed out that the learning process could be interpreted in two ways – namely a process linked to doing more, which implies a positive and constant production growth rate, or one linked to doing it longer, which, conversely, is compatible with a constant production level. In the first case – the one considered by Verdoorn – the level of output per worker depends on the volume of production, whereas, in the second case, it depends exclusively on time. See also Nadiri (1970).
34. Actually, the only difference from the original formulation of levels was the presence of a constant term, which, as such, had no impact whatsoever when moving on to the relation in growth rates. The approach outlined by Verdoorn in *Complementarity and Long-Range Projections*, raised the interest not only of

Clark (1957) and Arrow (1962, p. 160), but was later followed by other authors as well. See also the works by Kennedy and Thirlwall (1972), McCombie (1982) and Soro (1983).

35. McCombie (1982) highlighted an apparent paradox in the estimates of Verdoorn's law using cross-sectional data. It arises from the fact that the law is confirmed only if it is estimated in a dynamic form (i.e. using growth rates), not in a static one (namely using the log-levels of variables). He also detected a specification mistake: when this law is interpreted in terms of a learning function, it is subject to estimation in its static form (McCombie, 1982, p. 290). On this point, see also Vaglio (1990, pp. 157–8).
36. This aspect of the problem was clearly highlighted in UNECE's report of 1977. This report first of all pointed out that Verdoorn's elasticity had to be read as production growth rates (always) being equal to the double of the growth rates of output per worker, while the regression coefficient indicates that a one percentage point increase in the production growth rate leads to one-half of a percentage point increase in the productivity growth rate. Therefore, the elasticity of Verdoorn had to be correctly identified as a total elasticity, 'differing from the regression coefficient to the extent that the intercept term is large' (UNECE, 1977, p. 85 and n11).
37. The importance of the autonomous component of productivity growth in the regression estimates of Verdoorn's Law has been confirmed by several studies conducted at the geographical as well as the sectoral level. For example, an increasing importance of the autonomous component of the law has been found by UNECE (1977) and Rayment (1981). Similar trend has also been found for the Italian regions (Soro, 1986).
38. One of these exceptions is undoubtedly the work by Katz (1968). This author, in a very interesting article on the 'perfect' substitutability between the factors of production, examined the link between the elasticity of Verdoorn, returns to scale and the elasticity of factor substitution. Another exception is Boulier (1984). Participating in the debate on the interpretation made by Rowthorn of Verdoorn's Law, this author showed that 'the elasticity of labour productivity with respect to output depends in a complicated way on characteristics of the production function, factor supply, and output demand and that differences in empirical values of this elasticity offer little insight into the nature of the underlying economic circumstances that give rise to these differences' (Boulier, 1984, pp. 264–5).
39. Note that the result obtained by Verdoorn depended on two particular assumptions. First, the elasticity of output per worker with respect to output referred to the *total* elasticity; and, secondly, that there was no technical progress.
40. Verdoorn knew that Tinbergen had developed a growth model – 'the first example of a model of this kind' – based on the assumption of a 'perfect' substitutability of factors (Verdoorn, 1980, p. 382n2). That model consisted of five equations: a Cobb–Douglas production function, two equations of labour market performance, an equation of capital supply and an equation of exogenous population growth. Curiously enough, in that model, the capital market performance, unlike the labour one, was exclusively represented by one equation concerning the 'supply of capital'. This fact, together with technology being represented by a Cobb–Douglas production function, was to pave the way to the dual interpretation of Verdoorn's Law highlighted by Rowthorn (1979). By solving that model, Verdoorn could reach a definition of its elasticity by just combining a few parameters which, duly selected, would make the elasticity

range around 0.5. Thirlwall, in his translation of 'Fattori', added a 'translator's note', providing the specific parameters so that that elasticity would actually be equal to 0.5. See Verdoorn (1949), in Thirlwall's translation (1988, p. 207).

41. When taking the view of the 'perfect' substitutability between the factors of production, one too often forgets that, in order to attain a homogeneous growth, the various sectors and demand components must grow by the same rate (something which is clearly contradicted by what happens in the real world). This is actually one of the reasons why Kaldor (1986) rejected this approach in favour of a theory on international growth rate differences.
42. More generally, as has been pointed out by Soro (1983, p. 586), in the case of homogeneous production functions (and thus not necessarily Cobb–Douglas type functions), when faced by an equally proportional growth of production factors, the Verdoorn coefficient will equal the complement to one of the reciprocal of the sum of coefficients of the production function.
43. As also pointed out by Heimler and Milana (1984, p. 136), this fact becomes particularly important 'when the elasticity is examined in periods of strong price variations and intensity of factors'. Furthermore, these authors quite correctly noticed that Verdoorn, in 'Fattori', by not imposing a specific value on the elasticity of the capital–labour ratio, had implicitly considered the possibility that factor intensities could be subject to changes in the long term (Heimler and Milana, 1984, p. 136).
44. This implication of Verdoorn's Law, namely that marginal labour productivity is twice as high as the average, is also the foundation of Kaldor's third law, which relates the growth of aggregate productivity to the rate of intersectoral transfer of labour. It is also the basis of the economic rationale for the Selective Employment Tax. See Soro (1997).
45. It is just worth mentioning here that, in Kaldor's opinion, increasing returns are not to be intended in a microeconomic sense of static returns to scale, but they must be seen from a macroeconomic point of view (Young-style). In other words, they do not depend on the growth of each single enterprise or industry, but on the growth 'of the manufacturing system as a whole' (Targetti, 1988, p. 238).
46. In addition to the already considered limitations and the numerous problems associated with the estimation of Verdoorn's Law in its various formalisations (all of them brutally excluded from our analysis), Heimler and Milana (1984) also pointed to the danger of considering the value added at constant prices as a measure of output. Those who, just like these two authors, have had the opportunity to deal with the construction of input–output tables, know the difficulties (and limitations) of measuring this aggregate. 'Using *real* added value as a concept for output', remarked Heimler and Milana, 'can be justified from a theoretical and empirical point of view only under very restrictive theoretical conditions concerning the separability of primary factors from the other inputs' (Heimler and Milana, 1984, p. 137).

4

Increasing Returns and the Verdoorn Law from a Kaldorian Perspective

John McCombie[1]

> There seem to be two traditions, which persist. On the one hand there are those who are so impressed by what has been done by the CRS (constant returns to scale) method that they have come to live with it; on the other, those for whom scale economies are so important that they cannot bring themselves to leave them aside. I do not see that between these views there can be any easy reconciliation.
>
> (John R. Hicks 1989, p. 12)

Introduction

It is somewhat ironical that without Kaldor's celebrated inaugural lecture of 1966 the widespread use of the term 'Verdoorn's Law' (Verdoorn, 1949) to describe the relationship between productivity and output growth may never have come to pass. Moreover, Verdoorn himself made no further major contribution after his seminal 1949 paper to the extensive literature that has developed concerning the law. Indeed, the main impetus for the subsequent revival of interest in the law ironically may be traced back to Rowthorn's (1975a) critique of Kaldor's specification of the law. Verdoorn's (1980) only other notable article was to reinterpret the law within a neoclassical framework and simultaneously to distance himself from it.[2,3]

The purpose of this chapter is to assess Kaldor's views on economic growth, especially since 1966, with especial reference to his emphasis on increasing returns to scale and the Verdoorn Law. We shall also survey some of the theoretical and empirical issues that have arisen with respect to the law.

Kaldor left a legacy of two major insights into the growth process. The first, which has not been accepted by the orthodoxy, was that, in the long run, growth is not determined solely by the supply side – notably the rate of exogenous technical change and the growth of the labour force. The key to understanding growth is the determinants of the exogenous component of the growth of demand. Initially, it was demand that emanated from the agriculture sector that was important, later to be replaced by export growth.

This latter was developed by Thirlwall (1979) in the context of the balance-of-payments constrained growth model, with which Kaldor was fully in accord. The now substantial literature on 'Thirlwall's Law' has been discussed recently elsewhere (McCombie and Thirlwall, 1994; McCombie and Roberts, 2002) and will not be considered in any depth here.

The second insight was the importance of increasing returns, broadly defined, in understanding the economic growth process. In many ways, the recent developments of endogenous growth theory and path-dependent models of growth show just how far ahead of his time Kaldor was. For example, Kaldor noted not only that output growth is invariably associated with productivity growth, but also that there is no correspondingly secular increase in the capital–output ratio. The approach of the Solow–Swan model was to bring in Harrod-neutral technical change, deus ex machina, to account for this. But as Kaldor (1979, p. 285) noted: 'The observed phenomena are, of course, capable of a much simpler explanation: the existence of increasing returns to scale, which makes it possible to use more and more capital with an increase in the scale of production, *without encountering diminishing returns*' (emphasis added).[4]

However, it is a matter of conjecture to what extent Kaldor would have approved of all the developments within endogenous growth theory, especially its neglect of both the importance of factors determining the growth of demand and also the role that the different sectors of the economy play. Kaldor's pioneering work has still received little credit from the mainstream approach. Part of this may be due to the fact that since his inaugural lecture (Kaldor, 1966) he had painted with very much a broad brush and had abandoned the production of narrow formal models, finding them too limiting. When he was elevated to a personal Chair at Cambridge, Kaldor was already 56. Most of the expositions of his views on economic growth subsequent to 1966 were in the form of public addresses before distinguished audiences. This meant that his presentations had to be in a suitable verbal form for a lecture.[5] However, I shall leave further speculations as to the reason for the neglect of recognition of Kaldor's work to the historians of economic thought.

Kaldor, certainly in his later works, argued that economic theory had to be grounded in empirical relevance, which accounts for the importance of the Verdoorn Law to his argument.[6] It provided empirical evidence, even if only regarded as a stylised fact, of the importance of increasing returns to scale and formed the basis of the cumulative causation model of economic growth on which Kaldor placed a great deal of emphasis. (See Toner (1999) for a detailed discussion of the historical development of the cumulative causation model.)

Economic theory and increasing returns in a historical context

Two centuries ago, there was very little difference between the absolute living standards in various parts of the world. Those areas with greater fertility as a result generally supported a greater population density thereby tending to equalise differences in prosperity, although not completely eliminating them. So why is it, Kaldor (1977) asked, that the most advanced countries now have per capita incomes that are more than thirty times that of the poorest? Or, to put the question another way, why have some countries experienced sustained per capita income growth over a long period while others have barely developed at all?

This is, of course, almost an impossible question to answer comprehensively, but, nevertheless, an important insight can be found in the very first paragraph of Book One of Adam Smith's *The Wealth of Nations* (1776). 'The greatest improvement in the productive powers of labour, and the greater part of the skill, dexterity, and judgement with which it is anywhere directed, or applied, seem to have been the effects of the division of labour.' Smith illustrated this by his famous example of a pin factory. He considered that a workman with no previous experience of making pins could hardly 'make one pin a day, and scarcely twenty'. Even a blacksmith who had made nails in the past could probably make upward of only a thousand nails a day. But with the internal division of labour, and with ten men performing two or three separate operations, Smith noted each could produce about 4,800 pins. Moreover, an increase in the division of labour brought further benefits as, he argued, it induces technical change: 'It is unnecessary to give an example. I shall only observe, therefore, that the invention of all those machines by which labour is so much facilitated and abridged seems to have been originally owing to the division of labour.' Thus, the origins of endogenous growth can be traced back over two hundred years!

Kaldor (1977) considered that the greatest gains in productivity in the industrial revolution resulted from the development of the factory system. Prior to this, the gains from the division of labour were limited by the putting-out system. This was where artisans worked with their own capital (the spinning wheel or the loom) in their own cottages. It was only when the factory system developed that both the scope for a significant division of labour and the supervision of labour (through the use of piece rates and other methods) was possible. Another important factor in the industrialisation process was the agricultural revolution, which released labour on a scale that made the factory system possible.

In his famous paper on increasing returns, Allyn Young (1928, p. 529) considered that Smith's dictum that 'the division of labour depends upon the extent of the market to be one of the most illuminating and fruitful generalisations to be found anywhere in the whole literature of economics'. (Young was Kaldor's mentor at the LSE and had a profound effect on Kaldor's views of the growth process, as we shall see. Kaldor's (1972) famous paper on the irrelevance of equilibrium economics was very heavily influenced by Young.)[7] This dictum is more than a mere tautology because it forms the heart of the cumulative causation model. As production grows (the extent of the market increases), so there is greater scope for specialisation (the division of labour) and increased productivity, which further increases the extent of the market. In the industrial revolution, this widening of the extent of the market was initially due primarily to the spatial extension of the market. Prior to the industrial revolution, though, the improvement of communication between towns reduced the power of the guilds with their restrictive practices of apprenticeships (Olson, 1982). This also increased the scope for specialisation.

One of the major implications of the division of labour is that the degree of roundaboutness of production (the capital–labour ratio) is not determined primarily by the ratio of wages to the rental price of capital (as in the neoclassical schema), but by the scale of production. 'It would be wasteful to make a hammer to drive a single nail; it would be better to use whatever awkward implement lies conveniently at hand' (Young, 1928, p. 530). This is not to say that there is *no* substitution of labour for capital as factor prices vary, but rather that techniques of production are predominantly determined by the scale of production. Under constant returns to scale, however, and the usual neoclassical assumptions, the capital–labour ratio of the firm is uniquely determined by the wage–rental price of capital ratio.

However, Adam Smith's insight became neglected in the subsequent development of economics. As Smith himself accepted, the scope for the division of labour was very much limited in the case of agriculture. Against a background of rising corn prices resulting from the war with France, Ricardo and Malthus developed the principle of diminishing marginal productivity in agriculture, which led to the prediction of the dismal stationary state. As Kaldor (1955–56) has succinctly shown, this principle was, after the marginal revolution, applied to capital within the confines of the aggregate production function. The latter can be traced to the writings of Wicksell, who has claims to be the originator of the 'Cobb–Douglas production function'. By the middle of the nineteenth century, the elements that were to become central to the Solovian neoclassical growth model could already be discerned: diminishing returns to factors of production, constant returns to scale, and the necessity of an improvement in the knowledge of production to offset the progressive decline in the gains from capital accumulation.[8] The principle of perfect competition and convexity became central to the proofs of the uniqueness and existence of Walrasian general equilibrium – for a long time the lack of mathematical tools that could deal with non-convexity determined the path of economic theory.

As Stigler (1951) points out, Adam Smith, in fact, created a dilemma – as increasing returns lowered costs as production expanded, the eventual outcome should be monopoly, yet some competitive industries existed. But to assume perfectly competitive markets meant that Smith's theorem was empirically insignificant, which was highly implausible. As value theory moved to bring microeconomic production and consumer theory to the centre of the stage, and with the former, the theory of the firm, Alfred Marshall (1890) tried to resolve the dilemma in three ways.

First, he introduced the concept of external economies of scale. Thus, a firm increasing its output would not find its costs falling: this would only occur as the size of the industry, as a whole, increased. This meant that the concept of perfect competition could be maintained. This was never wholly convincing because it was difficult at the time to find convincing examples of external economies of scale, apart from the benefits of a common pool of skilled labour or a trade journal. Secondly, Marshall postulated the lack of sufficient entrepreneurial ability as the firm grew which offset the gains from increasing returns to scale, but this, together with his analogy of trees in the forest, was never persuasive.

His third suggestion, which was to postulate that firms faced a downward-sloping demand curve, was difficult to reconcile with the notion of perfect competition. Hence, it was not taken seriously until it was rediscovered by Sraffa (1926) and developed by Joan Robinson and Chamberlin in the 1930s as the theories of imperfect and monopolistic competition. But even then, it did not become central to orthodox theory until it was adopted by the new growth theory and the new trade theory in the 1980s.

Stigler's (1951) approach was to follow a suggestion implicit in Allyn Young (1928). Young had argued that increasing returns were essentially a macroeconomic phenomenon: increasing returns arise because of increasing specialisation between firms, the emergence of new subsidiary industries and new processes. (Here he diverged somewhat from Adam Smith who had emphasised the division of labour within the individual firm.) Thus, increasing returns cannot be 'discerned adequately by observing the effects of variations in the size of the individual firm or of a particular industry' (Young, 1928, p. 539).

Stigler considered that a particular firm has a number of production processes, some of which are subject to decreasing, and others to increasing, costs. Let us call one of the processes subject to decreasing costs, *Y*. As the industry grows, it becomes profitable for a firm to hive off *Y* as a specialist firm, in order to take advantage of the greater benefits from economies of scale that this would bring. In other words, while the firm would have benefited from the cost of the product produced by *Y* falling as its own output expands, it benefits to an even greater extent as the specialist firm's output will increase even more as it produces for the industry as a whole. This specialisation can only occur when the size of the industry is such that it can support the separate specialist firm. The latter is initially a monopoly and faces a less-than-perfectly-elastic demand curve. But, anticipating the theory of contestable markets, Stigler argues that it cannot charge more than the cost of production that would have been incurred by the original firms had they continued with *Y* themselves. As the industry continues to grow, more specialised firms enter, increasing the competition. Over time, these firms will also hive off those processes they have which are subject to increasing returns. A similar practice occurs for increasing cost processes, with one exception. 'When the industry grows, the original firms need not wholly abandon the increasing-cost processes. Part of the required amount of the process (say, engine castings for automobiles) may be made within the firm without high average (or marginal) costs, and the remainder purchased from subsidiary industries' (Stigler, 1951). Thus, Young and Stigler tend to follow the Marshallian approach in trying to maintain perfect competition and increasing returns through externalities.

The renaissance in growth theory due to the work of Solow (1956, 1957) and Swan (1956) was firmly grounded in the assumption of constant returns to scale and the concept of perfectly competitive markets and the marginal productivity theory of factor pricing. Indeed, almost the whole of the applied work of 'growth accounting' that really started with Denison (1962) attempting to account for the sources of economic growth is grounded in these three assumptions. This allows the output elasticity of a particular factor input (and hence its weight in calculating its contribution to the growth of output) to be accurately measured by its factor share. However, much of the late 1970s and early 1980s, further development of neoclassical growth theory seemed to make little progress.

This changed with the publication of Romer's (1986) celebrated paper that was one of the first, if not the very first, to develop a neoclassical model of endogenous growth. According to Romer, growth was endogenised in the sense that changes in government policy or in the decisions of entrepreneurs, such as to increase the investment ratio, could raise the steady-state growth rate. (In the Solow–Swan model such an increase would only have a 'level' effect and growth would only increase temporarily.) The key assumption was that the produced factor of production was not subject to diminishing returns. The problem was that this produced a 'knife-edge' problem. The output elasticity of capital, broadly defined, had to be exactly equal to unity and there was nothing in these models that ensured that this would be the case. If the degree of returns to capital was large but less than unity, then the Solovian result remained, although the time to return to steady-state growth from, say, an exogenous shock might be long. However, if the output elasticity of capital was just above unity, say 1.05, the model predicts infinite output after a finite period of time, which could be as little as two centuries (Solow, 1994). The second-generation models have continued to model the determination of technical progress within the usual neoclassical framework, but with the difference that without exogenous population growth, per capita income growth eventually comes to a halt. For this reason these models are often called semi-endogenous.

However, as Mankiw et al. (1992) have pointed out, postwar international growth differences can equally be explained by the Solow–Swan model augmented by human capital and still retain the assumption of constant returns to scale. Clearly, even now, there are still fundamental disagreements about the empirical importance of increasing returns to scale.

Allyn Young's concept of increasing returns and the Verdoorn Law

Although Kaldor (1966) only made a very general connection between Young's concept of increasing returns being external to the firm and the Verdoorn Law, it is possible to show this formally. The Verdoorn Law is the relationship between the growth of manufacturing productivity and output given by the equation $p = \varphi + \lambda q$, where p and q are the growth rates of productivity and output, and φ is the rate of exogenous technical progress. An estimate of the Verdoorn coefficient (λ) that is statistically greater than zero indicates, according to Kaldor (1966), the presence of increasing returns to scale. (This interpretation needs an assumption to be made about the rate of growth of the capital stock, k: for example, that it conforms to one of Kaldor's stylised facts and is equal to q. This is discussed below.) In practice, the Verdoorn coefficient in a wide variety of studies usually takes a value of around one-half.

Consider an economy consisting of a large number of firms each having a Cobb–Douglas production function:[9]

$$Q_i = A_0 e^{\varphi t} K_i^{\alpha} L_i^{(1-\alpha)} Q^{\xi} \tag{4.1}$$

where Q, K and L denote the levels of output, capital and labour and A_0 is a constant. φ is the rate of exogenous technical progress that is common to all firms and α and $(1 - \alpha)$ are the output elasticities of capital and labour, respectively. We deliberately assume that each individual firm exhibits constant returns to scale. Apart from the conventional inputs, the output of each firm is also a function of the volume of *total* industrial output. However, the firm treats this as independent of its own production decisions. As will be shown, this captures Young's notion of the degree of returns to scale being a function of the extent of the market, but preserves perfect competition. ξ is the elasticity of industry i's output with respect to total output. Taking logarithms and differentiating equation (4.1) with respect to time, we obtain an equation for the growth of each firm's output:

$$q_i = \varphi + \alpha k_i + (1 - \alpha)\ell_i + \xi q \tag{4.2}$$

Multiplying equation (4.2) by $\theta_i = Q_i/Q$, where $\Sigma\theta_i = 1$, and summing over the firms gives:

$$q = \varphi + \Sigma\theta_i \alpha k_i + \Sigma\theta_i(1 - \alpha)\ell_i + \xi q \tag{4.3}$$

If we assume that the capital–output ratio is identical between firms so that $K_i/Q_i = K/Q$, (recalling that a constant capital–output ratio is one of Kaldor's 'stylised facts', although, strictly speaking, for industry or the whole economy) and that there are no differences between firms in productivity, then equation (4.3) may be written as:

$$\begin{aligned} q &= \varphi + \alpha k + (1 - \alpha)\ell + \xi q \\ &= v\varphi + v\alpha k + v(1 - \alpha)\ell \end{aligned} \tag{4.4}$$

where $v = 1/(1 - \xi)$ is the degree of 'macro' increasing returns to scale and $v > 1$, provided $\xi < 1$.

The Verdoorn Law is given by:

$$p = \frac{\varphi}{(1-\alpha)} + \frac{(1-\alpha)v - 1}{(1-\alpha)v} q + \frac{\alpha}{(1-\alpha)} k \tag{4.5}$$

or, given the assumption that $q = k$, by:

$$p = \frac{\varphi}{(1-\alpha)} + \frac{v - 1}{(1-\alpha)v} q \tag{4.6}$$

As the typical value for the Verdoorn coefficient (the coefficient of q in equation (4.6)) is 0.5 and the share of capital in manufacturing is roughly a half, this implies that $v = 1.33$ and a value of ξ of 0.25.

Factors are assumed to be paid their marginal products and so $\partial Q_i/\partial K_i = R_i = \alpha Q_i/K_i$ and $\partial Q_i/\partial L_i = W_i = (1 - \alpha)Q_i/L_i$, where W and R are the wage rate and the rate of profit. The accounting identity $Q_i = R_i K_i + W_i L_i$ must hold for each firm and it can be seen that the factor payments exhaust the total output. Furthermore, α and $(1 - \alpha)$ equal capital's (a) and labour's shares $(1 - a)$ in total output. Consequently, the neoclassical theory of factor pricing holds in spite of the presence of substantial increasing returns because of the Marshallian assumption that these are external to the firm. A corollary is that the private returns to the factors of production are less than the social returns.

Taking the logarithm of the accounting identity of the individual firm and differentiating this with respect to time, we obtain:

$$q_i = ar_i + (1 - a)w_i + ak_i + (1 - a)\ell_i \tag{4.7}$$

where r and w are the growth rates of the profit and real wage rates.

Comparing this with equation (4.2), it can be seen that the weighted growth of wages and the rate of profit (what may be termed the growth of total factor productivity, or the Solow residual, from the viewpoint of the firm) is given by the equation $ar_i + (1 - a)w_i = \xi q + Q$.

Given the fact that with constant shares and a constant capital–output ratio, there is no growth in the rate of profit, it follows that that the growth of wages is given by $w_i = (\xi/(1 - a))q$ when there is no exogenous technical progress.

Kaldor would not have approved of the use of the marginal productivity theory. Nevertheless, the Verdoorn relationship does not depend upon it, as equation (4.6) makes no use of the theory. An alternative theory of distribution is to assume that prices are determined by a mark-up on unit labour costs, and that the size of the mark-up is determined by the relative bargaining power of labour and capital, or some other mechanism such as the degree of monopoly. Hence, if $(1 + \chi)$ is the mark-up, labour's share is equal to $1/(1 + \chi)$ and if the mark-up is constant, so will be the share. The wage rate is equal to $\frac{1}{(1+\chi)}\frac{Q_i}{L_i}$.

At this level of abstraction, the data cannot discriminate between the two competing theories, although the implications of each are radically different.

Work by Romer (1987) has provided another way to formalise the Allyn Young approach (see also Romer, 1989, 1990). He assumes that the production function of an industry consists of labour and separate intermediate inputs (s), the number of which could potentially be infinite. These intermediate goods could be regarded as capital goods, but it is more plausible to regard them as any type of intermediate good (including capital). Output is therefore gross output, although we shall continue to denote it by Q.

The production function of the industry is given by:

$$Q = A_0 L^{(1-\alpha)} \Sigma s_i^{\alpha} \tag{4.8}$$

which exhibits constant returns to scale and the industry is competitive. For mathematical ease Romer takes a continuous version of Σs_i^{α}, replacing this term by $\int s_i^{\alpha}$, defined over the interval [0, M].

Let $Z = \int s_i^{\alpha}$, where Z is the cost of resources devoted to the production of the s's. It can be seen for a fixed Z, a greater variety of s increases output. Thus, the greater the degree of specialisation of the firms making s, i.e. the greater the division of labour, the greater will be the level of productivity. Consequently, at any given moment there must be a factor that limits the number of s_i. This is the presence of fixed costs (Romer suggests arising from R&D expenditure) in the production of the s_i's, which means that firms producing these goods are not price takers and their demand curves will be downward-sloping. But as output, or the extent of the market, increases so will the number of different types of s. (The similarity with the argument of Stigler (1951), discussed above, will be readily apparent.) However, as in models of imperfect competition, the entrance of new firms will ensure that there are no abnormal profits being made. Under the assumptions of the model, all the s_i's are of the same size. Consequently, $\int s_i^a = M(Z/M)^\alpha = M^{(1-\alpha)}Z^\alpha$. What happens if we double the amount of resources devoted to the intermediate good? This will result in a doubling of the number of different types of intermediate goods and so, with a suitable choice of measurement units for Z, the production function is given by

$$Q = A_0 L^{(1-\alpha)} Z \tag{4.9}$$

Thus, there are no diminishing returns to the use of the intermediate products. (The introduction of a new intermediate good does not reduce the marginal productivity of the existing intermediate goods. There are no diminishing returns to Z so long as there are inexhaustible opportunities for introducing new types of intermediate goods.)

This model produces steady-state growth, even though there is no exogenous technical progress because of the absence of diminishing returns to scale to the produced means of production. However, if the possibility for progressive specialisation of the intermediate inputs for a particular industry declines, as in intuitively would seem to be the case, diminishing returns to Z would eventually set in.

The question of the Verdoorn Law and steady-state growth is examined by Pugno in chapter 10 of this volume and so only a passing mention will be made here. The empirical evidence makes it unlikely that capital (broadly defined) is subject to constant returns. A Verdoorn coefficient of one-half implies from equation (4.6) that the output elasticity of capital < 1 (see, for example, McCombie and de Ridder, 1984). Neoclassical growth theory (of both the Solow and endogenous growth models) have been almost exclusively concerned with steady-state growth. However, as Valdés (1999, pp. 172–3) notes, 'some economists, however, begin to question whether this framework, productive as it has been, is flexible enough to let us progress much further in the analysis of economic growth'.

Kaldor (1972), on the other hand, does not consider general equilibrium analysis to be useful. In accounting for the postwar growth of the advanced countries, he argues that the growth of the manufacturing labour force was not exogenous. There was disguised unemployment in the agricultural or service sector or sufficient immigration to ensure that there was an elastic supply of labour to manufacturing. (See Cornwall (1977) for a review of the evidence that supports this contention.) This is also likely to be true for many less developed countries. Industrial output growth is not determined by factors that determine the growth of the factor inputs, but rather it is the growth of the demand for output that determines the growth of the factor inputs and the rate of induced technical change. Manufacturing growth determines both the growth of capital accumulation and the flow of labour into the sector. As Dixon and Thirlwall (1975) have shown, it is possible to construct models within this framework and where the Verdoorn Law plays a pivotal role that exhibits steady-state growth, but the underlying model is radically different from the neoclassical approach, focussing on demand factors such as the price and income elasticities of demand. This is discussed further below.

The Verdoorn Law and 'learning by doing'

There are other ways of providing a foundation for the Verdoorn Law by partly or wholly endogenising technical change. For example, the Verdoorn Law may also be derived at the microeconomic level from the firm's learning function. (This was explicitly cited by Kaldor, 1966.) As Arrow (1962, p. 156) pointed out, 'the number of labour hours expended in the production of an airframe (airbody without engines) is a decreasing function of the total number of airframes of the same type previously produced'. On the basis of this Arrow went on to construct his well-known model where the acquisition of knowledge was a function of cumulative gross investment. However, many of the empirical studies found that, as in Arrow's quote above, the fall in costs was a function of cumulated output, even though there was no investment.[10] Hence, a learning function may be postulated as an index of technology A(t) as a function of cumulative output $\int Qdt$. Under certain assumptions this gives a learning elasticity of $\frac{d \ln A_i}{d \ln Q_i} = \psi_i$. If the underlying production function of the firm is of the form $Q_i = B_0 e^{\varphi t} K_i^{\alpha} (A_i L_i)^{(1-\alpha)}$ (dropping the *i* subscript for notational convenience and assuming the learning elasticity is the same for all firms), then it may simply be shown that the degree of returns to scale is $v = 1/(1 - \psi(1 - \alpha))$. As the denominator is less than unity, this implies $v > 1$ or increasing returns to scale.

The Verdoorn Law is given by:

$$p = \varphi + \frac{\psi(1-\alpha)-\alpha}{(1-\alpha)} q + \frac{\alpha}{(1-\alpha)} k \qquad (4.10)$$

or if we assume, once again, the stylised fact that $q = k$

$$p = \varphi + \psi q \qquad (4.11)$$

With suitable aggregation, a functional form similar to equations (4.10) and (4.11) will hold at the industry level. Two comments are in order here.

First, it can be seen that in equation (4.11) the simple Verdoorn coefficient is positive, whereas if there were no 'learning by doing' it would be zero, and productivity growth would be merely equal to the exogenous rate of technical progress. Secondly, for plausible values (e.g., $\alpha = 0.5$ and $\varphi = 0.5$) this simple model cannot generate endogenous growth. A similar model may be derived if the learning function is a function of cumulative investment or the capital–labour ratio (see Romer, 1986 and Pugno, chapter 10 of this volume). However, this will not be pursued here. The point to be made is simply that the Verdoorn Law may result from a combination of 'learning by doing' and increasing returns at the firm level, together with an increasing degree of specialisation at the inter-firm or inter-industry level.

Increasing returns and path dependency

Young attempted to rescue the concept of perfect competition by postulating that increasing returns were external to the firm. Therefore, the individual firm could not benefit from increasing returns to scale by increasing the volume of its own output, because we have assumed that its output was only a small proportion of the total. Kaldor, on the other hand, saw the existence of increasing returns as undermining the whole notion of Walrasian general equilibrium.

> The very notion of 'general equilibrium' carries the implication that it is legitimate to assume that the operation of economic forces is constrained by a set of exogenous variables which are 'given' from the outside and stable over time. It assumes that economic forces operate in a system that is 'imposed' on the system in the sense other than being just a heritage of the past – one could almost say an environment which, in its most significant characteristics, is independent of history. (Kaldor, 1972, p. 244).

But with increasing returns, 'the forces making for continuous change are *endogenous* – "they are engendered from within the economic system"[11] – and the actual state of the economy during any one "period" cannot be predicted except as a result of the sequence of events in previous periods which led up to it'. Here, Kaldor is arguing that historical time, as opposed to logical time, is crucial for understanding the growth path of the economy. The position of the economy at time t depends upon where it was in $t - 1$, $t - 2$, and so on. Consequently, economic growth is path-dependent. We may adopt the analysis that Young (1928) put forward in the appendix to his paper to demonstrate this argument more clearly. It is necessary to modify it, however, because it is difficult not to agree with Kaldor (1972) that the original discussion by Young is somewhat 'obscure'.

Figure 4.1 follows Young, but with a number of differences, and uses the traditional transformation curve showing the possible combinations of goods *X* and *Y* for a given utilisation of resources. One important difference is that the utilisation rate is such that total resources are not fully employed. In other words, the transformation curve is inside the production possibility curve. (For a justification of this, see Kaldor (1977a), including his Figure 1.) Alternatively, we can regard the figure as representing the production possibility curve for manufacturing which is technically efficient, while there is disguised unemployment in the remainder of the economy. *I* denotes the social welfare function with $I_3 > I_2 > I_1$. Following Young (1928), if the transformation curve took the convex form TT´ then the unique Pareto preferred allocation would be at *b*, as in the orthodox analysis. But let us assume, rather, that the transformation curve takes the form TT˝. The figure represents only one part of the production possibility curve and is now subject to local decreasing and increasing returns to scale. Let us further assume that the economy is initially at point *a*. It can be seen that this is not an optimum, as a rearrangement of the quantities of *X* and *Y* produced will increase welfare.

Let us assume that the economy can move along the transformation curve per period in either direction. We assume that there is a cost associated with move of a unit distance that is the same whichever direction is chosen. But this cost is less than the gains in output achieved from the move away from *a*. However, there are increasing average costs incurred as

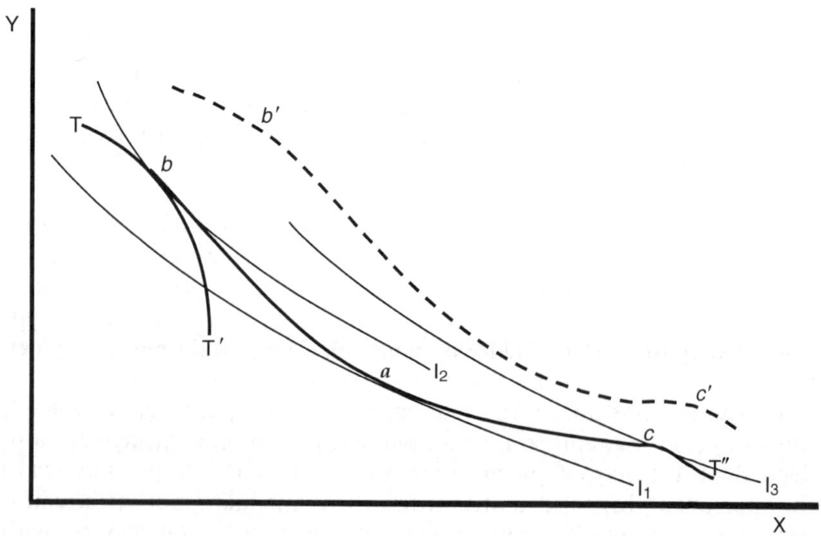

Figure 4.1

the number of units moved in any one period of time increases. To make the exposition simple, let us assume that to move two units in one period would cost more than the gain in output, but this would be not be true if the same move occurred over two periods. There is, by assumption, no difference in the distance from *a* to *b* and *c*.

The question now arises – which way will the economy move? Towards *b* or *c*? Either path would increase welfare, but *c* would provide the higher level. This is where recent developments in the theory of path dependency come in (Arthur, 1989, 1994). Let us assume that there is only knowledge of the local area around *a*. In other words, it is only known that moving either way from *a* will increase utility, but not that an eventual movement to *c* would be preferable to *b*. Let us further assume that the initial movement away from *a* is due to chance. But as movement in one direction occurs, so utility increases and we assume that the possibility of a further increase in utility by moving in that direction becomes apparent. There is a learning process. A more sophisticated analysis assumes that after each movement, the direction taken at the next stage is determined by a stochastic process. Consequently, the probability of the movement in a particular direction is non-linear. As the economy moves in one direction, the probability of a further move in the same direction increases. Thus, let us assume that the movement is initially towards *b*, then there is a high probability, but not necessarily a certainty, that the economy will eventually move to *b*.

We are assuming here that there is a non-zero probability of a move back towards *a* even though it involves an immediate loss of utility. This is because there is an expectation that a further movement towards *c* might eventually lead to a higher level of utility. The further we move towards *b*, the smaller this probability becomes because of the progressively greater loss in utility from moving back to *a*. In other words, we have lock-in. Alternatively, we could assume that because of technical change, there is a probability that a movement back would increase utility more than movement in the original direction, but this probability also decreases the further towards *b* the economy has moved.

The point *b* is a locally stable equilibrium, because once there the cost of moving from *b* to *c*, even if it became known that point *c* gave greater utility, may be prohibitive. The economy is locked into point *b*.

The process that has been followed here is similar to the 'Polya urn scheme' where an urn with coloured balls is repeatedly sampled, with a replacement of the same coloured ball that has just be drawn, together with the addition of another ball of the same colour. The probability of a ball of a particular colour being drawn is thus an increasing function of the number of balls of that colour that are already in the urn. Under these circumstances, if the process is carried on indefinitely there is a probability of unity that the all the balls converge to one colour.

Over time there is increase in demand for *X* and *Y* with a resulting increase in their production. This has the result of shifting the transformation curve upwards to the right. Let us assume that in both cases there are increasing returns but that they are greater as the trransformation curve shifts outward from *b* than at *c*. Thus, over time the transformation curve moves out to the right but not symmetrically. If the path of the economy is from *b* (or rather *a*) to *b´*, it would lead to a higher level of welfare than if the path was from *c* (or *a*) to *c´*. In other words, the social indifference curve at *b´* is higher than that at *c´* (these curves are not shown in Figure 4.1). Again, we assume that only the outcome of the movement along a particular path is known to the actors in the economy. What then becomes of the concept of the Pareto optimum? Clearly, in a static context, from our perspective, a movement from *a* to *c* would be Pareto preferred than from *a* to *b*. But in a dynamic context the converse could be true. This provides an admittedly simple illustration of Kaldor's (1972, p. 1245) argument that:

> When every change in the use of resources – every reorganisation of productivity activities – creates the opportunity for a further change *which would not have existed otherwise*, the notion of an 'optimum allocation of resources' – when every particular resource makes as great or greater contribution to output in its actual use as in any alternative use – becomes a meaningless and contradictory notion. The pattern of the use of resources at any one time can be no more than a link in the chain of an unending sequence and the very distinction, vital to equilibrium economics, between resource-creation and resource-allocation loses its validity.

Young's own diagram in his appendix is similar to ours in that the movement of the economy (but in one direction only) along the transformation curve from its initial position, denoted by P in his figure, to P_1 takes the economy on to a higher indifference curve. In order to explain why the economy will not automatically move to P_1, 'simply by altering the proportions of the two commodities produced annually', Young (1928, p. 541) also assumes that there are transformation costs involved. However, as was noted above, this argument is somewhat difficult to follow.[12]

The question then arises as to how the presence of increasing returns per se generates a process of cumulative causation. As Kaldor (1972) pointed out, Young realised that Say's Law and Adam Smith's dictum are not sufficient to ensure that an increase in output necessarily propagates itself in a cumulative fashion. Something else is required to ensure that an increase in supply provides an increase, rather than a decrease, in demand, for other goods and services. Young, lacking the insights of Keynesian economics, sought to explain this, somewhat inadequately according to Kaldor, in terms of Marshallian 'offer curves'. According to Young (1928,

p. 534), when a good is produced under conditions of elastic demand 'in the special sense that a small increase in its supply will be attended by an increase in the amounts of other commodities which can be had in exchange for it', an expansion in production will be self-propagating.[13] In other words, the increase in supply of, say, steel gives rise to a fall in its price through increasing returns to scale, but may also lead to an increase in its factor's rewards. The fall in the price of steel reduces the cost of, for example, the automobile industry which uses steel as an input. This, in turn, may lead to a fall in the price of cars, or a rise in the industry's profits, or both. The fall in price of cars leads to an increase in their demand and hence to an increase in demand for steel. The higher factor incomes also lead to the increase in demand for this and other commodities. As Young (1928, p. 534) put it, 'under such conditions an increase in the supply of one commodity *is* an increase in the demand for other commodities, and it must be supposed that every increase in demand will evoke an increase in supply'(emphasis in the original).

Kaldor, however, pointed out that it was by no means certain in such situations that an increase in the supply of one commodity would necessarily lead to an increase in demand, and hence supply, of the total value of all other commodities. It would be perfectly possible for the change in relative prices to lead to a fall in the demand for some commodities as consumers substituted away from them. According to Kaldor, what leads to a guarantee of increased total expenditure is the willingness of traders in the commercial sector, and of the producers themselves, to accumulate stocks and inventories when there is a temporary excess supply and vice versa. This ensures that temporary excess in supply does not lead to a fall in demand, thereby breaking the process of the cumulative increase in output. As Kaldor (1972, p. 1249) commented:

> It is a hen-and-egg question whether historically it was the growth of commerce which continually enlarged 'the size of the market' and thereby enabled increasing returns to be realised, or whether it was the improvement of techniques of production and the improvement of communication which led to the growth of commerce. In the process of the development of capitalism the two operated side by side. And it involved a tendency for a continual rise in the *value* (and not just the volume) of stock carried by traders in the markets, which meant in turn that the growth of production resulting from any favourable change on the supply side led to a growth in incomes which in turn generated an increase in effective demand for commodities.

However, notwithstanding Hahn's (1989) formalisation of the argument within the framework of an optimising model, this aspect of Kaldor's view of the growth process has received scant attention in the literature.

Hahn on Kaldor and returns to scale

Kaldor's (1972) paper was an attack on the relevance of Walrasian general equilibrium theory, and he argued that once one allows for increasing returns to scale (removes 'the scaffolding'), the whole concept becomes untenable. In his inaugural lecture Hahn (1973) provided a robust defence of general equilibrium theory, taking explicit account of some of Kaldor's (1972) criticisms.[14] While Kaldor did make one or two slips in his criticisms of general equilibrium theory,[15] there remain two substantial issues between Kaldor and Hahn. The first one is methodological and the second one concerns the implications of increasing returns to scale.

I do not wish to spend much time on the first issue – I leave it to others to determine the appropriate perspective from which to view Kaldor's methodological stance (see, for example, Boylan and O'Gorman, 1999). However, while he conceded that general equilibrium theory is not intended to describe reality, he argued that it is regarded as a necessary starting point for any explanation of how a decentralised system works. 'This belief sustained the theory despite the increasing (*not* diminishing) arbitrariness of its basic assumptions – which were forced upon its practitioners by ever more precise cognition of the needs of logical consistency' (Kaldor, 1972, p. 1238, emphasis in the original). In Hahn's words, 'Professor Kaldor believes that the received theory is vacuous by virtue of being unfalsifiable' (Hahn, 1973, p. 22). For Hahn the usefulness of a rigorous general equilibrium theory is its essentially negative role. For example, if someone argues that there is no need to worry about exhaustible resources, as increasing scarcity will be captured by the price mechanism, all one needs to do is to look at the stringent conditions for this to be true as set out by the general equilibrium theorists to realise how implausible this assertion is.

As far as the second issue is concerned, Hahn (1973, pp. 12–13, emphasis added) argues that 'an Arrow–Debreu equilibrium may exist when there are increasing returns. Not only is this so when these increasing returns are not internal to firms, but even if they are, *provided they are not too large*'. Since this would seem to be a major criticism of Kaldor, it is worth briefly considering under what conditions increasing returns *do not* pose difficulties for general equilibrium theory. In doing this I shall follow the seminal paper of Farrell (1967) which was cited by Hahn (1973).

Let us assume that there are a large number of firms that are subject to increasing returns to scale. Figure 4.2 considers a firm which can produce two goods, *X* and *Y*, subject to increasing returns to scale. Thus, the firm's transformation curve is given by the solid curved line *tt'*.

If the price ratio of *X* to *Y* is less than this (i.e. $\Omega_1 < \Omega_0$ where Ω_0 is the slope of the straight line between *t* and *t'*), then only *Y* will be produced by the firm and if the price ratio $\Omega_1 > \Omega_0$, then only *X* will be produced. If all firms have identical production functions, the economy transformation curve will be a

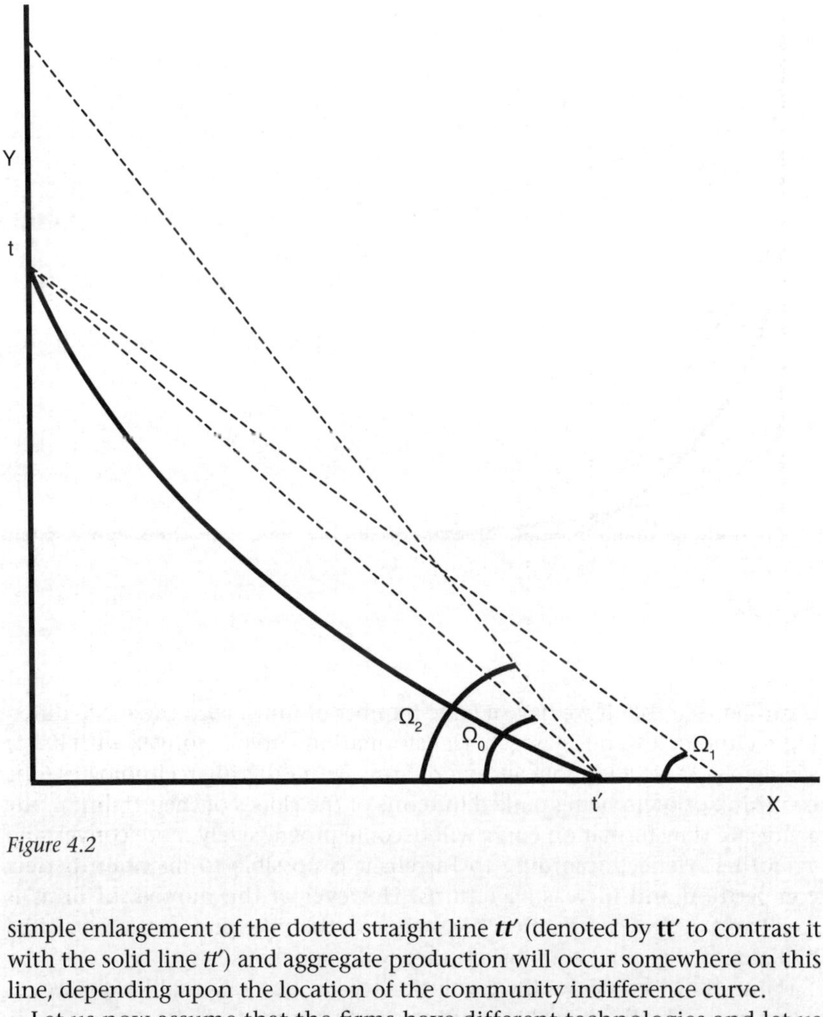

Figure 4.2

simple enlargement of the dotted straight line ***tt′*** (denoted by **tt′** to contrast it with the solid line *tt′*) and aggregate production will occur somewhere on this line, depending upon the location of the community indifference curve.

Let us now assume that the firms have different technologies and let us rank them in terms of their slopes of **tt′**. The aggregate production curve will be convex. We may see this most easily by considering just two firms. In Figure 4.3, the transformation curve of firm 1 is given by t_1t_1' and firm 2 by t_2t_2' where the slope $\mathbf{t_1t_1'}$ (Ω_3) > the slope $\mathbf{t_2t_2'}$ (Ω_4). The following scenarios are possible where Ω is the price ratio:

- If $\Omega > \Omega_3 > \Omega_4$ both firms will produce *X* and the economy will be at T**
- If $\Omega_3 > \Omega > \Omega_4$ firm 1 will produce *Y* and firm 2, *X*, and the economy will be at T*
- If $\Omega_3 > \Omega_4 > \Omega$ both firms will produce *Y* and the economy will be at T.

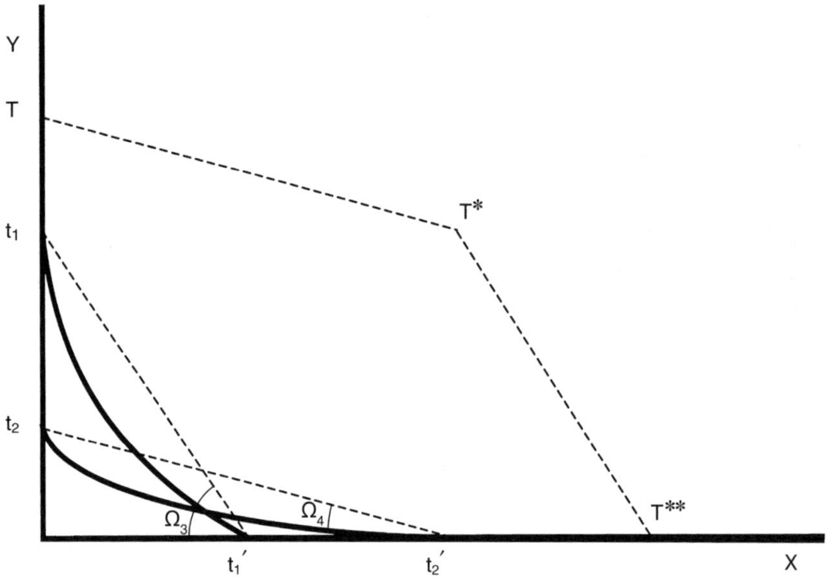

Figure 4.3

It can be seen that if we have a large number of firms, with these two differing technologies, the aggregate transformation curve is convex with linear segments. As we add more and more firms with differing technologies (one can think of them being ranked in terms of the slopes of their **tt′** lines), the aggregate transformation curve will become progressively more convex and smoother. Hence, according to Farrell, it is possible to maintain perfect competition and increasing returns. However, if the number of firms is small and perfect competition breaks down, then the problems emphasised by Kaldor for general equilibrium theory do materialise.

Hahn, however, denies the revolutionary implications that Kaldor sees as being caused by the prevalence of increasing returns to scale:

> Now we say that a given path taken by the economy is production inefficient if there is an alternative one which gives us more of some good at some time and not less of any good at any time. There is nothing in the economy here discussed which makes such an ordering impossible. If we take finite time horizons, as long as we like, and suppose the set of alternatives closed, then an efficient path also exists. It is simply a muddle to go from the difficulties increasing returns impose for perfect competition to the view that allocation does not matter. Indeed, the truth is orthogonal to the view. For the more impor-

tant increasing returns are, especially the dynamic variety, the greater the potential losses from misallocation. (Hahn, 1973, p. 31)

This is not being totally fair to Kaldor, who did not say that allocation did not matter, but rather suggested that the whole notion of a unique optimal allocation of resources loses all meaning, except in the short run. As we have seen when we consider the notion of path dependency, the economy may be moving at any particular point in time along a path that increases efficiency possibly more than any other path, but may end up locked-in to a technology that, from a longer-run perspective, does not maximise welfare. Moreover, if the path of the economy opens up new opportunities which only become apparent when the economy moves along that path because of increasing returns to scale, there may be other unknown paths that would have been preferable if they had been apparent.

Cumulative causation and path dependency

As we have noted, Kaldor's developments of the cumulative causation model were sketched on a broad canvas and were largely verbal (see, for example, Kaldor, 1970). However, in 1975, Dixon and Thirlwall first developed what may be justifiably now regarded as the 'standard' cumulative causation model and which has provided the basis for subsequent theoretical developments. Since this model is well known, it will only be briefly considered here. However, as Setterfield (1997a) has pointed out, in its original form it does not capture Kaldor's emphasis on path dependency.

The model consists of four equations:

$$x = \varepsilon z + \eta(pr_d - pr_f) \qquad \text{Export demand equation} \qquad (4.12)$$

$$q = \gamma x \qquad \text{Harrod dynamic foreign trade multiplier} \qquad (4.13)$$

$$pr_d = w_n - p + \tau \qquad \text{Pricing equation} \qquad (4.14)$$

$$p = \varphi + \lambda q \qquad \text{Verdoorn's Law} \qquad (4.15)$$

where x, q and z are the growth rates of exports, domestic output, and the output of the rest of the world. The variables w_n, pr_d, pr_f, p, φ are the growth rates of nominal wages, domestic prices, foreign prices (both expressed in a common currency), productivity growth and exogenous technical change. The parameters ε and λ are the income elasticity of demand for exports and the Verdoorn coefficient. η (< 0) is the price elasticity of demand for exports. Prices are determined by a mark-up on unit labour costs and so the rate of growth of domestic prices is determined by the growth of nominal wages, productivity, and the rate of change of the mark-up (τ).

The equilibrium solution to this model is (if the mark-up does not change over time):

$$q = \frac{\gamma\left[\eta\left(w_n - \varphi - pr_f\right) + \varepsilon z\right]}{(1 + \gamma\eta\lambda)} \tag{4.16}$$

This is essentially a partial equilibrium model, as the growth of the region under consideration does not affect the growth of the rest of the world. Dixon and Thirlwall introduce dynamics into the model by assuming that x is a function of the growth of relative prices and income in the rest of the world lagged by one period.[16] The growth rate is stable (that is, it will converge to an equilibrium rate) if $-\gamma\eta\lambda < 1$. Dixon and Thirlwall (1975) argue that if $\gamma \approx 1$, this condition is likely to be met as $\lambda = 0.5$ and $|\eta|$ is likely to be less than 2.[17]

The model does not, however, demonstrate path dependency, because, regardless of the initial growth rate, the region will converge to the same equilibrium growth rate. This is most readily seen from a diagrammatic representation of the model. (See, for example, Dixon and Thirlwall (1975) or McCombie and Thirlwall (1994, Figure 8.1, p. 462).) If the initial condition is such that the initial growth rate is below the equilibrium growth rate, then growth will accelerate until it converges to the latter. Conversely, if the initial growth rate is above the equilibrium growth rate the converse will occur. This has parallels with the convergence and steady-state results of the Solow model, although, of course, the underlying assumptions and implications are very different.

In the steady state, differences in growth rates will be due differences in the values of the parameters γ, $|\eta|$, and ε. The higher these are, the higher will be the equilibrium growth rate. Moreover, the Verdoorn coefficient only serves to amplify the existing regional growth rate disparities – it is only a cause of differences in growth rates if its value differs between regions or nations. Observed growth rate differences could be due to countries being in the transition state and not at their steady state growth rates.

While the model is a useful formalisation of the cumulative causation, it is only a beginning. One of the facts stressed by Kaldor, as we have noted, was that in the context of growth over the last two centuries, some countries have taken off into sustained growth – to use Rostow's term – while others have virtually stagnated. This could be modelled as the latter having low values of γ, $|\eta|$, and ε. However, another, and perhaps more satisfactory, approach is to include some form of low-level equilibrium trap in the model (Nelson, 1956). In, for example, the Nelson model, when per capita income is low, there are negative feedback effects caused by the positive relationship between population growth and savings. This causes any increase in a less developed country's growth rate to return eventually to its former low growth rate, unless it achieves a sufficiently fast growth rate that exceeds a crucial threshold level. Thus, this explains why a poor country may never reap the positive benefits from cumulative causation as it is caught in a vicious circle of growth.

The standard model has been extended in a variety of other ways. Pugno (1996b) and Roberts (chapter 7 of this volume) have introduced a supply side and León-Ledesma (2002) has developed a model that contains elements of both convergence and divergence (see also chapter 8, this volume). The export equation contains a technology variable that is a function of cumulative output, education and a technological catch-up variable. The productivity growth equation also depends upon the level of technology and the technological gap. The parameters of the model determine whether there is convergence or divergence.

Alternatively, one could follow Setterfield (1997a) and argue that the transition dynamics, from the initial to the equilibrium growth rate, are more interesting and that path dependency will occur if the parameters of the model change over this period.[18] In particular, Setterfield argues that path dependency will occur if both the size of the Verdoorn coefficient and the income elasticity of demand for exports are functions of the rate of growth of output. In other words,

$$\lambda_t = f(q_0, q_1, q_2 \ldots q_t); \quad f'_i \neq 0 \text{ for some } i = 0 \ldots\ldots t \tag{4.17}$$

$$\varepsilon_t = g(q_0, q_1, q_2 \ldots q_t); \quad g'_i \neq 0 \text{ for some } i = 0 \ldots\ldots t \tag{4.18}$$

A priori, the exact relationship between the rates of growth and the values of λ_t and ε_t could be either positive or negative. It is possible that a faster growth of output could lead to a more efficient inducement of technical change, which would increase the size of the Verdoorn coefficient. On the other hand, Setterfield suggests that technological lock-in may eventually occur for those regions with the faster growth rates, which would reduce the size of the coefficient. Specifications of the Verdoorn Law for estimation purposes have assumed that the value of the Verdoorn coefficient is the same for all regions/nations, but given the size of the standard error, it would be possible for the value of the coefficient to vary to some extent between regions.

In the case of the income elasticity of demand for exports, to the extent that this represents the degree of non-price competitiveness and the structure of production, the value could also be a function of past growth rates. A faster growth of output, by inducing greater capital accumulation, could through various channels improve certain aspects of non-price competitiveness. A fast growth could also lead to a country moving into high-technology industries for which ε is high. There is evidence that both the

Verdoorn Law differs between regions (Soro, 1986; Bernat, 1996), and that ε differs substantially between countries (McCombie and Thirlwall, 1994). The latter is also likely to differ considerably between regions.

The cumulative causation model may be extended to incorporate an explicit balance-of-payments constraint. With balanced trade and no changes in relative prices, we may derive Thirlwall's Law, $q = \varepsilon z/\pi$, where π is the income elasticity of demand for imports. As Posner and Steer (1979) have noted, exchange rate adjustments help firms to keep their costs and prices in line with competitors, while they compete in terms of gaining market share by improving non-price competitiveness. Alternatively, if the sum of the absolute values of the price elasticities equals unity, changes in relative prices will have no effect on the current account and hence on the balance-of-payments equilibrium growth rate and Thirlwall's Law results.

It can now be seen that the Verdoorn coefficient does not play an explicit role in the determination of the equilibrium growth rate. Productivity growth is still determined by the growth of output through the Verdoorn Law, but the benefits of faster growth of productivity are not passed on in the form of a relatively slower growth of relative prices, but in the form of a higher growth of real wages. Consequently, path dependency of the output growth rate comes through ε/π being a function of past growth rates, along the lines outlined above. It is, however, important to emphasise that these changes are likely to occur only slowly. In the medium term, they are likely to show little variation and in particular do not change in the short run to equilibrate the balance of payments at the full employment of resources (see McCombie and Roberts, 2002).

It is possible, however, that a long period of slow growth could induce institutional and other changes that actually increased the value of ε. There comes a point where there are institutional changes or radical policy decisions to arrest and reverse the secular decline. There is some evidence that ε may have increased for UK in the early 1980s (Landesmann and Snell, 1989). Or a sustained period of fast growth could, through locking the economy into industries that have a progressively lower ε, lead to a low aggregate value of ε. (This is modelled in McCombie and Roberts, 2002.) There is nothing immutable about the vicious and virtuous circles of growth in which regions or countries find themselves, even though there are strong economic forces that seek to perpetuate them.

Kaldor's laws of economic growth

Kaldor argued that any theoretical analysis should be capable of explaining the 'stylised facts' of economic growth. In his inaugural lecture, Kaldor (1966) propounded two empirical regularities (or laws) of economic growth which he considered crucial to the understanding of why growth rates differ. This was supplemented later by a third law which arose from an exchange of views with Wolfe (1968) (see Kaldor, 1968) and Rowthorn (1975a and 1975b) (see Kaldor, 1975a). The laws have generated a good deal of attention over the last thirty years or so, and their rationale has been extensively discussed in the literature (see, for example, McCombie, 1983; Thirlwall, 1983a; McCombie and Thirlwall, 1994, chapter 2). Consequently, it is not proposed to present a detailed discussion of the issues here. Nevertheless, given the fact that Kaldor's 'second law', the Verdoorn Law, is deceptively simple and many of the issues seem either to have been overlooked or rediscovered sometime later, it will be considered in the next section in greater detail.

Kaldor's three laws are as follows:

(i) *Kaldor's First Law*. A faster growth of manufacturing will cause a faster growth of GDP. In this sense, manufacturing is seen as 'the engine of growth'. In order to remove the element of spurious correlation due to manufacturing being a substantial component of GDP, this law has been reformulated in terms of non-manufacturing and manufacturing output. The former is sometimes disaggregated to consider individual sectors (such as agriculture, mining, services and so on) separately. The law is specified as $q_i = c + b_1 q_{MAN}$, where q is the growth of output, the subscript i denotes GDP, non-manufacturing, or any other individual non-manufacturing sector and *MAN* is manufacturing.

(ii) *Kaldor's Second Law (the Verdoorn Law)*. As we have noted above, faster growth of industrial or manufacturing output will, through the effect of increasing returns to scale, lead to a faster growth of productivity. The simplest specification of the law is specified as $p = \varphi + \lambda q$, where p is the growth of productivity. A Verdoorn coefficient (λ) that is significantly greater than zero is seen as providing evidence of increasing returns to scale. However, under most circumstances it is necessary to either explicitly include the rate of growth of the capital stock in the Verdoorn equation or make some assumption about its relation to q. See the next section.

(iii) *Kaldor's Third Law*. The growth of GDP per worker is positively related to the growth of manufacturing output and negatively related to the growth of non-manufacturing employment, i.e., $p_{GDP} = c + b_2 q_{MAN} - b_3 \ell_{NM}$, where the subscripts *MAN* and *NM* are manufacturing and non-manufacturing. The rationale for this regression is that a faster growth of manufacturing will increase manufacturing productivity (and hence GDP per worker) through the Verdoorn Law. However, with surplus labour in the agricultural and service sectors, a faster growth of manufacturing will also increase productivity growth in this sector by increasing the sectoral transfer of labour from the rest of the economy into manufacturing. As labour is drawn from agriculture where the marginal productivity is low to manufacturing where it is higher, productivity will increase for purely arithmetical reasons. Hence, a faster rate of decline of non-manufacturing employment will increase the growth of non-manufacturing productivity. However, McCombie (1981) has shown that the estimates of this law do not tell us anything new; it is just a misspecified identity, with the degree of bias resulting from the relationships given by the first two laws.

The Verdoorn Law: some theoretical issues

The most famous of Kaldor's Laws is, of course, the Verdoorn Law, an empirical regularity for industry (or manufacturing) that forms a central plank in the cumulative causation model of economic growth. The relationship is estimated as (although it may be embodied in a more complex set of simultaneous equations):

$$p = c + b_4 q + b_5 k \tag{4.19}$$

If, and it is a big if, the underlying relationship is a Cobb–Douglas production function, where α and β are the output elasticities of capital and labour, the Verdoorn equation can be written as

$$p = \varphi + ((\beta - 1)/\beta)q + (\alpha/\beta)k \tag{4.20}$$

As Kaldor (1970, p. 339) argues, however, the rate of growth of capital is itself a function of the growth of output. 'It is as sensible – or perhaps more sensible – to say that capital accumulation results from economic development as that it is a cause of development. Anyhow the two proceed side by side.' Hence, the growth of capital is endogenous to the model and is a function of the growth of output:

$$k = c + b_6 q \tag{4.21}$$

Given the stylised fact of a constant capital–output ratio, we should expect the estimate of b_6 to be around unity (see McCombie and Thirlwall, 1994, p. 176, n.5).[19] Substituting $k = q$ into equation (4.20) gives the traditional specification of the Verdoorn Law as $p = \varphi + \lambda q$, where $\lambda = (\alpha + \beta - 1)/\beta$ is the Verdoorn coefficient and is often found to take a value of around one-half. Kaldor argued that this provided evidence of substantial returns to scale. If α and β are equal, which is plausible for industry, then a Verdoorn coefficient of one-half implies returns to scale of 1.33.

The parameter φ is the growth of exogenous technical change, but in practice a substantial part of this may be induced by the growth of output. Consequently, $\varphi = \varphi' + \zeta q$ and λ now equals $(\alpha + \beta + \zeta - 1)/\beta$ and hence it can be seen that the law 'is a dynamic rather than a static relationship... primarily because technological progress enters into it, and it is not just a reflection of the economies of large-scale production' (Kaldor, 1966, p. 10). The Verdoorn Law is, as was shown above, one of the earliest (and largely unrecognised) endogenous growth models. (However, most estimates of the Verdoorn Law, while they show substantial increasing returns to scale, find the output elasticity of capital substantially below unity. Thus, the model is not endogenous in the sense of the *AK* model.)

Other specifications of the law include the growth of the capital stock or, as a proxy, the gross investment–output ratio in the law and estimate it as equation (4.19). The Verdoorn Law is not normally found to hold for any of the other sectors (although see León-Ledesma, 2000), which Kaldor argues are subject to either constant or diminishing returns to scale. (Kaldor was well aware that some services might be subject to economies of scale – the rise of the large out-of-town hypermarkets bears evidence of this in the retail and wholesale industries. However, in many of the service sectors output growth is measured as merely the growth of the inputs, with often an arbitrary allowance for productivity growth.)

As we have noted above, following Allyn Young (1928), Kaldor (1966) argued that increasing returns were essentially a 'macro-phenomenon'. Because such a large part of economies of scale results from increased specialisation, the emergence of new processes and new subsidiary industries, they cannot be observed at the firm or industry level. In fact, the evidence is not conclusive on this point. McCombie (1985a) estimated the Verdoorn Law using US state data at the 2-digit industry level SIC and found well-defined Verdoorn coefficients. The inclusion of the growth of total manufacturing in the individual industry regression to capture any externality effects due to increasing returns proved statistically insignificant. This does not mean, however, that they are not important at the *firm*, as opposed to the industry, level.

It is probably best to view the Verdoorn Law as a production relationship, akin to Kaldor's technical progress function. The technical progress function was an attempt by Kaldor to remove what he saw as the artificial distinction between shifts *of* the production function and shifts *along* the production function. The technical progress function was originally specified as a non-linear relationship between the growth of labour productivity and the growth of the capital–labour ratio (later within a vintage model). It differs from the Verdoorn Law notably in that it assumes constant returns to scale. The technical progress function never really caught on, once it had been pointed out that, having linearised it around the steady state, it could be integrated to give a conventional Cobb–Douglas production function (Black, 1962). We shall return to this point below.

Verdoorn's interpretation of Verdoorn's 'rule'[20]

In chapter 3, Soro described how Verdoorn's interpretation of his 'rule' differed from that of Kaldor and that one theoretical justification for the rule and its stability was to be found in the Appendix to his original paper (Verdoorn, 1949). Verdoorn's rule was simply that the total elasticity of productivity with respect to output growth is defined as $V \equiv p/q$ and took a value of around 0.5 for a wide variety of data sets.

Indeed, as Soro points out it is almost as if the text of Verdoorn's paper was an appendix to the Appendix. In a short note, however, Rowthorn (1979) pointed out that there was a contradiction between the Appendix and the rest of the paper, to the extent that in the latter the explanation of the rule was couched in terms of economies of scale (that is, referring solely to production technology) while in the Appendix, the theoretical definition of the rule contained a hybrid of production and labour market parameters. However, by 1980, as Soro reminds us, Verdoorn had disavowed his rule. Moreover, he abandoned the model of the Appendix and his argument was now couched in terms of the Solow–Swan model (Verdoorn, 1980, p. 386). Although this abstracted from the labour market, he argued that the rule under this formulation would only be stable in conditions of steady-state growth. (The issues of steady-state growth and Verdoorn's elasticity are examined by Pugno in chapter 10.)

Thirlwall (1980, p. 386), however, in commenting on Rowthorn (1979) considered that he found 'it difficult to agree with Rowthorn's interpretation of the law; in particular, his implied suggestion that the two distinct relationships between productivity growth and output growth, which can be derived from Verdoorn's systems of equations, can themselves be interpreted as "Verdoorn" coefficients'. The purpose of this section is to assess Verdoorn's arguments from the Kaldorian viewpoint.

Kaldor considered that the steady-state properties of growth models, and the associated discussions of stability that invariably accompanied them were of little, or no relevance, for the understanding of the growth and development of actual economies. Indeed, as we have seen, many of his writings post-1966 were about the irrelevance of this approach. Consequently, the question arises: 'does Verdoorn's recantation undermine the Kaldorian interpretation of the Verdoorn Law?' The answer, as we shall see, is that it has no adverse implications for the Kaldorian interpretation of the law.

The debate over Verdoorn's rule has been complicated by the fact that it conflates three issues. First, there is Verdoorn's definition of the rule as $V \equiv p/q$ rather than using the Verdoorn coefficient, λ. Secondly, there is the question as to whether the rule refers solely to the production technology or is a hybrid production/factor supply relation and consequently whether it can be unambiguously interpreted as a measure of returns to scale. (That it cannot be was Rowthorn's (1979) point.) Thirdly, there is the problem as to whether V is stable (or under what conditions it is stable). The degree of confusion can be seen from the fact that Turner (1983) in his, admittedly brief, survey of the debate, makes no mention of Rowthorn's original critique but confines himself to discussing the rule only in terms of the production function.

We begin with a consideration of Verdoorn's (1949) model as set out in his appendix. This is, as Soro (chapter 3, this volume) has noted, similar to Tinbergen's early growth model, and consists of five equations (see chapter 2, this volume).

$$Q = AK^{\alpha}L^{\beta} \qquad (\alpha + \beta > 1) \tag{4.22}$$

$$W = \beta\frac{Q}{L} \tag{4.23}$$

$$W = \beta\left(\frac{L}{N}\right)^{\rho} e^{\mu t} \tag{4.24}$$

$$k = \phi\frac{Q}{K} \tag{4.25}$$

$$N = e^{nt} \tag{4.26}$$

where, with the same notation as before, N is the total active population, W is the wage rate, ρ is the elasticity of the wage rate with respect to the labour supply (strictly speaking, the participation rate), μ and n are the exogenous growth rates of W and N, respectively and ϕ is a constant.

Equation (4.22) is a *static* Cobb–Douglas production function with no exogenous technical progress and equation (4.23) describes the labour demand function that is derived from the marginal productivity conditions. (It is difficult to reconcile this with the assumption that $\alpha + \beta > 1$.) Equations (4.24) and (4.25) are the labour and capital supply functions while equation (4.26) represents the autonomous growth of the labour force.[21] (It should be noted that $k = \phi Q/K$ implies $I = \phi Q$, and that that each country invests the same proportion of income or, in other words, has the same investment-output ratio. This is an unconventional capital supply function, to say the least.)

Confining our attention initially to the production function, equation (4.22) may be written in growth rates simply as $q/\ell = \beta + \alpha(k/\ell)$, from which the Verdoorn elasticity V, as defined by Verdoorn, may be derived as:

$$V = \frac{p}{q} = 1 - \frac{1}{\left(\beta + \alpha\frac{k}{\ell}\right)} \tag{4.27}$$

This is Verdoorn's equation (I) and Thirlwall's (1980) equation (6). There are two points to note with respect to V. First, it will only be stable to the extent that the ratio of the growth of capital to that of labour is constant. Secondly, it is not possible to infer anything about the degree of returns to scale ($v = \alpha + \beta$) solely from the value of V except in the unlikely case that k equals ℓ. A knowledge of the growth rates of k and ℓ is necessary. If, following Verdoorn, we assume that capital and output grow at the same rate and $Q/k = 1$, then equation (4.27) becomes $V \equiv p/q \equiv (\alpha + \beta - 1)/\alpha$, which is the same as the 'Verdoorn coefficient', λ, under the same assumption.[22,23] As we have noted, provided we are prepared to make some assumption of the relative magnitudes of α and β (such as for manufacturing that they are roughly equal), an estimate of returns to scale can be obtained.

The specification of the Verdoorn Law as a production relationship is:

$$p = \frac{\beta - 1}{\beta} q + \frac{\alpha}{\beta} \phi \tag{4.28}$$

However, Verdoorn (1949) attempted to determine the stability of V by deriving it from the simultaneous equation model, rather than just the production function given by equation (4.28). In order to do this, Verdoorn first derived the rate of growth of the labour supply. From equation (4.24), the constant growth of wages is given by:

$$w = \rho\ell + \delta \tag{4.29}$$

where $\delta = (\mu - n\rho)$. However, from equation (4.23), the growth of wages also equals the growth of productivity:

$$w = p \tag{4.30}$$

Combining equations (4.29) and (4.30) and using the identity $p = q - \ell$ gives:

$$p = \frac{\delta}{1 + \rho} + \frac{\rho}{1 + \rho} q \tag{4.31}$$

Thus implicit in Verdoorn's model are two relationships between productivity and output growth, given by equations (4.28), the production relationship, and (4.31) the labour supply function. As by definition, $p \equiv q - \ell$, an expression for Verdoorn's rule may be obtained (this is Verdoorn's equation IV):

$$V = \frac{\rho\left(1 - \frac{(1-\beta)n}{\alpha\phi}\right) + \frac{(1-\beta)\mu}{\alpha\phi}}{\rho\left(1 + \frac{\beta n}{\alpha\phi}\right) + 1 - \frac{\beta\mu}{\alpha\phi}} \qquad (4.32)$$

Verdoorn (1949) concludes that the stability of the elasticity 'can easily be seen taking different combinations of n and μ (taken as given α, β, and ϕ). It appears therefore, that quite considerable modifications would be necessary for V to lie outside certain limits, for example ± 0.15 around an initial value of 0.45. Analogous conclusions would be reached if variations in α, β and ϕ were taken for fixed values of n and μ.' (The notation has been changed to make it consistent with the text.)

However, it is not the stability of V that really matters, but, rather, whether it can be unambiguously interpreted as a measure of returns to scale. It is clear that it cannot. As the elasticity is a function of both *production* and *labour and capital market* parameters, it is not possible to identify the sum of α and β from the numerical value of V. Hence, the elasticity or rule, per se, can give no indication whatsoever of the degree of returns to scale. It is possible for a Verdoorn elasticity of one-half to be compatible with the sum of α and β to be greater than, less than, or equal to unity depending upon the values of the other parameters. The problem, as Rowthorn (1979, p. 386) noted, is that there is, in effect, an identification problem, with there being two separate relationships between p and q, one (equation (4.28)) representing a production relationship and the other one derived essentially from the labour and capital supply and labour demand functions (equation (4.31)).

What are the implications of this for the statistical estimation of the law and Kaldor's interpretation of the relationship? The first thing to note, is that the 'interpretation problem' arises because Verdoorn treats as constants or parameters what are in fact variables – for example, the investment–output ratio, ϕ, which empirically varies considerably across countries. The other growth rates, n and μ, are also likely to vary both over time and between countries. Once this is appreciated there is in fact no identification problem in the statistical sense. We have a two-equation model, given by equations (4.28) and (4.31).

However, the model is identified by the exogenous variables n, μ and k (which with cross-country data are not constant) and hence the simultaneous equation model can be estimated by a suitable estimating procedure.[24] McCombie (1986) estimated such a model, using cross-country data for the advanced countries over the early postwar periods, along these lines and found that the parameters of the Verdoorn Law and labour supply function were statistically insignificant when using three stage least squares. The Verdoorn relationship was, however, confirmed for the period until the late 1960s using OLS and then, like other studies, it was found to have broken down for this data set. This did not occur, however, when the growth of total factor productivity was regressed on that of output.

Related to this is the fact that Kaldor argued that the growth of the manufacturing sector was demand- and not supply-constrained and that, at the going manufacturing wage, the labour supply to manufacturing was perfectly elastic. Under these circumstances, the estimation of the Verdoorn Law as a single equation model would correctly measure the degree of returns to scale.

Verdoorn's (1980) reformulation is, as we have noted, to abandon the labour supply relationship and to discuss the Verdoorn coefficient in terms of the Solow–Swan model, but with increasing returns to scale. He considers both the steady state and the transition path to the steady state (which require $\alpha < 1$). The production function is again the static Cobb–Douglas, but this time with exogenous technical progress. This version of the model is thus supply-driven, with growth being determined, as in the 'old' growth models, by the growth of the labour force and exogenous technical progress.

Confining our attention to the steady state, Verdoorn (1980) derives the standard neoclassical result that $q = (\beta\ell + \varphi)/(1 - \alpha)$. It has long been known that if increasing returns to scale is compatible with steady-state growth, provided the output elasticity of capital does not exceed unity. However, Conlisk (1968) has shown that this requires a Cobb–Douglas production function, except for some improbable exceptions. The Verdoorn coefficient is now given by $V = ((\alpha + \beta - 1)\ell + \varphi)/(\beta\ell + \varphi)$ and Verdoorn points out that when cross-country comparisons are made V will be unstable to the extent that ℓ varies between countries and as $\ell \to 0$, so $V \to 1$.

However, this occurs because Verdoorn considers again the total rather than partial elasticity of productivity with respect to output. The steady-state condition can be written alternatively as $p = \varphi/\beta + [(\alpha + \beta - 1)/\beta]q$. The Verdoorn coefficient is λ and this equals $[(\alpha + \beta - 1)/\beta]$ which is stable, whereas $p/q \equiv V \equiv \varphi/\beta q + (\varphi + \beta - 1)/\beta$, which is a function of q, will not be constant. Verdoorn (1980) was clearly concerned with the steady-state properties of the model. Kaldor was more concerned with formulating empirical regularities or 'laws of growth'. What matters are not the steady-state properties of the model, but whether empirical estimates of the Verdoorn Law, augmented by the growth of the capital stock, provide evidence of increasing returns. We turn to a consideration of this next.

The Verdoorn Law: some empirical issues

As we have noted above, the Verdoorn Law has not been without its problems or critics and we now turn to a brief consideration of the more important issues to do with its estimation.

Simultaneous equation bias

The possibility and implications of simultaneous equation bias in the estimation of the Verdoorn Law has been appreciated for a long time, and first rose to prominence during the celebrated debate between Rowthorn and Kaldor (Rowthorn, 1975a, 1975b; Kaldor, 1975a). Rowthorn noted that in Kaldor's inaugural lecture, Kaldor ascribed the low rate of manufacturing productivity growth in the UK to the exhaustion of surplus labour in the other sectors of the economy. Thus, the UK suffered from what Kaldor termed 'premature maturity' and manufacturing growth was constrained by labour shortages. It was, hence, not able to reap the benefits of increasing returns to scale to such an extent as other countries which still had substantial degrees of underemployment. But, if this is the case, then the regressor, Rowthorn argued, should be employment, ℓ, and not output growth, q. But when the inverse regression is estimated, and Japan dropped as an outlier, there is no significant relationship between p and ℓ. Under Kaldor's assumptions, this implies constant and not increasing returns to scale.

The econometric reason for this is straightforward. Consider the Verdoorn Law as $p = a + bq$. Since $p \equiv q - \ell$, the law may be written equivalently as $\ell = -a + (1 - b)q$. (This has the advantage that it removes the spurious correlation inherent in q being included in the regressand through the identity, $p \equiv q - \ell$.) The alternative Rowthorn specification may also be written as $q = c + d\ell$. If the statistical fit were exact, i.e., if $R^2 = 1$, then both statistical estimations would give the same result, that is to say, $(1 - \hat{b}) = 1/\hat{d}$, where $\hat{b}$ and $\hat{d}$ are the estimate values of b and d. This is because the relationship between the two estimates is given by $(1 - \hat{b})\,\hat{d} = R^2$. Thus, if R^2 is less than unity, then $(1 - \hat{b}) < 1/\hat{d}$. The Verdoorn Law will, in these circumstances, always give a higher estimate of returns to scale. For example, a Verdoorn coefficient of 0.5 and an R^2 of 0.5 imply that $\hat{d}$ is 1.0, and constant returns to scale prevail, rather than 2.0 and increasing returns to scale. In the late 1970s, Rowthorn reworked a large number of cross-industry studies of the Verdoorn Law to see what the inverse regression would have produced. In nearly all cases $\hat{d}$ was not significantly different from unity even though the Verdoorn coefficient was nearly always significant.[25] The former result refutes the hypothesis of increasing returns to scale provided that it is correct to choose ℓ as the regressor. Kaldor's (1975a) riposte was that it was only in the case of the UK that he postulated that the growth of the labour supply constrained the rate of growth of manufacturing and, even here, on the basis of subsequent evidence, he conceded he was wrong.

Output growth is demand and not supply constrained and q not ℓ should be the regressor. Dropping Japan does not now greatly affect the value of the Verdoorn coefficient. This is not the end of the story, however, because the notion of cumulative causation implies both q and ℓ are endogenous. A faster growth of output increases productivity growth but this, in turn, through improving a country's (region's) price competitiveness, stimulates an increase in the growth of output. In these circumstances, the Verdoorn coefficient in both Kaldor's and Rowthorn's specifications will be subject to simultaneous equation bias and all one can say is that $1/\hat{d} < \hat{\lambda} < (1 - \hat{b})$. $1/\hat{d}$ and $(1 - \hat{b})$ are not the extreme values, as both will have an associated standard error. The problem of simultaneous equation bias is largely a result of the poor goodness-of-fit since as this improves so Wold and Faxer's (1957) 'proximity theorem' shows the bias will be progressively reduced. An obvious way around the problem is to use an instrumental variable approach. McCombie (1981) attempted this using, inter alia, Durban's ranking method, which uses the ranks of the regressor as an instrument. However, the method of normalisation still proved crucial and this procedure did not resolve the controversy. The reason is that we have a different instrument depending on whether q or ℓ is taken as the regressor. Generally, unless the equation is exactly identified, the method of normalisation will be important even if the instruments are the same.

Parikh (1978) specified and estimated a simultaneous equation model, but there are a number of serious problems associated with his procedure; most notably that export growth and I/Q were specified as exogenous and hence not a function of a potential supply constraint. Therefore, although he suggests that the results confirm Kaldor's arguments, the results should be treated with a great deal of caution.

Attempts have been made to test whether output growth Granger-causes productivity growth, productivity growth causes output growth, there is a two-way relationship, or no relationship at all (see, for example, Fase and van den Heuvel, 1988). This test requires the use of time–series data, which suffers from a number of problems discussed below. Furthermore, Granger causality is not causality in the conventionally understood sense of the term and does not provide an unambiguous way of resolving the issue.

The impact of the diffusion of technical change and the heterogeneity of the sample

An outlier should not be omitted from a regression without good cause and Rowthorn argued that much of Japan's phenomenal growth rate during the postwar period was due to its catching-up with the technologically more advanced countries. If this is generally an important factor then it could lead to the generation of a spuriously significant Verdoorn Law. In

McCombie and Thirlwall (1994) it was argued that while this may have been important in the case of Japan, it was extremely unlikely that the European countries did not have access to the same blueprint of technology as the United States (Van der Wee, 1987). Moreover, this factor has been tested for by including the initial level of productivity relative to that of the United States as an additional regressor. The more backward a country, the more it will be able to benefit from the diffusion of technology. Hence, if this were important, the coefficient on the level of productivity should be negative. There is, however, a problem here in that the levels of productivity should vary between countries because of the existence of increasing returns to scale – even though both have access to the same technology.

Kaldor's original sample of the advanced countries also varied considerably in their socio-economic complexions. It could be argued, with some justification, that this could lead to substantial biases in the regression estimates. There may be many other factors affecting productivity that differ between countries and such productivity shocks may well mask the underlying Verdoorn relationship. Regional data has the advantage of not being subject significantly to either of these problems, namely differences in technology and socio-economic characteristics.

Time-series estimates: Okun's or Verdoorn's Law?

The Verdoorn law is a long-term relationship in the sense that a faster *trend* rate of growth of output, both through induced technical progress, and static and dynamic increasing returns to scale, leads to a higher *trend* rate of growth of productivity (and a faster induced rate of capital accumulation). However, a number of studies have used time-series data. The problem is that, over the cycle, variation occurs in the intensity of use of both labour (labour hoarding occurs during the downswing of the cycle) and the capital stock. This will lead to a positive relationship between the growth of productivity and output, but one that is due merely to these short-term cyclical factors and has nothing to do with the presence of increasing returns to scale. This short-term relationship is known as Okun's law.

The capital stock often proves to be statistically insignificant in time-series estimates of production functions and the Verdoorn Law because of the failure to adjust for variations in capacity utilisation (Lucas, 1970). It is true that there have been attempts to correct for changes in capacity utilisation, but the estimates of the Verdoorn coefficient prove very sensitive to the exact method of adjustment adopted. Attempts to construct such capacity utilisation indices by using the existing data (for example, by using the deviations from the trend increase in output or the output–capital ratio or by using the unemployment rate) are also not altogether satisfactory. Moreover, the degree of factor utilisation may vary between different cycles. A severe recession may lead to a proportionally higher shake-out of labour and greater scrapping of capital than a milder recession. The degree of shake-out for a recession of a given severity may vary over time as institutional factors change such as the labour laws, leading especially to the deregulation of the labour market. This will pose problems for attempts to model changes in factor use by partial adjustment models. To the extent that a severe recession drives firms with the lowest levels of productivity out of business, this will raise the overall level of productivity for purely arithmetical reason, which have nothing to do with increasing returns to scale.

Moreover, the rate of exogenous technical progress is not likely to be constant, but will show a random fluctuation, which may be large relative to the trend rate of growth (see Solow (1957) for an admittedly neoclassical demonstration of this). Thus, the Verdoorn Law may be misspecified as the exogenous growth of productivity growth is assumed to be constant.[26] Finally, the relative lack of variation in the data is likely to lead to imprecise estimates of the coefficients of the Verdoorn Law – especially when compared with cross-regional data. Indeed, if we were to use the trend rates of growth of the variables, these would be virtually constant.

It is not surprising that such estimates of the 'Verdoorn' law (if, indeed, it is the Verdoorn Law) are either not well determined or show structural instability. It is for this reason that the most appropriate method is to follow Kaldor and to use average growth rates for cross-sectional data calculated over several years, with peaks of the growth cycle for initial and terminal years. This minimises the effect of variations in capacity utilisation in biasing the results.

The stability of the results

There is a certain irony in the fact that the simple Verdoorn Law for the advanced countries seemed to break down from the mid- or late-1960s, just at the time when Kaldor was stressing its importance. However, it is important to note that the law broke down in the sense that there was no well-defined relationship between p and q. It did not suggest the presence of constant returns to scale – the statistical fit was just so poor that no inferences could be drawn. This is an important point to note. A breakdown in the law does not necessarily imply that the estimates suggest constant returns to scale. It could be that the standard errors are so large that it is not possible to say anything about the degree of returns to scale. What is crucial is not whether the estimate of the growth of exogenous productivity is higher in one period than another, and the estimated Verdoorn coefficient is lower, but whether these differences are statistically significant. (For an interesting discussion of the reasons for this in terms of a simultaneous equation approach, see Boyer and Petit (1991).)

The importance of this is confirmed by the findings of Michl (1985). While Michl (1985, p. 482) found that using international data for the advanced countries, there 'is an unmistakable trend toward a looser statistical fit' in the growth cycles for 1970–74 and 1974–79 compared with those from 1950–70. Nevertheless, the Verdoorn coefficient still takes a value of over 0.5, which is statistically significant. The exogenous component of the growth of productivity does increase over the cycles. But when an allowance is made for the growth of capital intensity, there is no statistically significant growth of autonomous technical progress and no evidence of statistically significant shifts in either the slope or the intercept in the last growth cycle.

It is also not coincidental, for reasons outlined in the above section, that most cases where the law breaks down are when time-series data are used. Cross-country, cross-regional or cross-industry estimates do not generally suffer from this problem. Pugno (1995), for example, using an augmented Verdoorn Law and cross-country data for advanced and less developed countries, finds a statistically significant Verdoorn coefficient which does not suffer from this instability problem. Regional estimates of the Verdoorn Law are also temporally stable. (Compare, for example, McCombie and de Ridder (1984) and Bernat (1996).) This is discussed further below.

The Verdoorn Law, the technical progress function, and the static production function

As we have seen, Kaldor, following Adam Smith, Alfred Marshall, and Allyn Young, stressed the importance of both static and dynamic increasing returns to scale. Static increasing returns to scale lead to increased productivity as the scale of production increases, for reasons such as the three dimensional nature of space (Kaldor, 1972, Appendix). The dynamic factors increase the rate of growth of productivity through, for example, 'learning by doing' and induced technical change. The former returns to scale are, in principle, reversible, while the latter are not, as emphasised by Marshall in his famous Appendix H to the *Principles*. As Kaldor (1966, p. 9) put it: 'Learning is the product of experience – which means as Arrow has shown, that productivity tends to grow the faster, the faster output expands; it also means that the *level* of productivity is a function of cumulative output (from the beginning) rather than just the rate of production per unit of time'. Kaldor argued that the Verdoorn Law captures, in particular, the latter. 'It is a dynamic rather than a static relationship – between the rates of change of productivity and of output, rather than between the *level* of productivity and the *scale* of output – primarily because technical progress enters into it, and is not just a reflection of the economies of large-scale production' (Kaldor, 1966, p. 10).

In this respect, the basis of the Verdoorn Law would seem to be a linear Kaldorian technical progress function with an allowance for increasing returns. But matters are not so straightforward. The technical progress function has been through a number of versions; but they all share one rationale in common. This is that the rate of technical progress cannot be treated solely as a function of time, but is also a result of the rate of capital accumulation. It makes no sense to try to distinguish *shifts of* a production function from *movements along* the function. New knowledge is a function of learning which, in turn, is a function of the rate of increase of output (or, under certain assumptions, the level of cumulative output) or, alternatively, capital growth and the rate of investment. The first version of the technical progress function was $p = f(k - \ell)$, where $f' > 0$ and $f'' < 0$. In other words, the rate of productivity growth increases with the rate of growth of capital per worker but at a diminishing rate. Productivity is assumed to increase even when $k - \ell$ is zero. This is the exogenous increase in new knowledge, but the rate at which these ideas are exploited or developed is a function of the rate of growth of capital (holding employment constant). Thus technical progress consists of two elements: the exogenous growth of knowledge together with the rate of its adaptation, the latter being a function of the rate of growth of capital. 'There is therefore no *unique* rate of technical progress – no *unique* rate at which a constant rate of growth can be maintained. There is a whole series of such rates, depending on the rate of accumulation of capital being relatively small or large' (Kaldor, 1961, p. 209). The technical progress function is not therefore integratable to give a relationship between the levels of the variables.

However, in his modelling, Kaldor uses a linear version of the technical progress 'for convenience', although it could equally be regarded as a linear approximation around the steady state point (where $p = k - \ell$). Unfortunately, as a number of people (including Meade, Hahn and Black) quickly pointed out, this could be derived from a Cobb–Douglas production function with constant returns to scale. In other words, differentiating $Q = A_0 e^{\varphi t} K^{\alpha} L^{(1-\alpha)}$ with respect to time and rearranging gives $p = \varphi + \alpha(k - \ell)$, the linear technical progress function. Likewise, as we have seen above, introducing increasing returns to scale, the Cobb–Douglas production function can be differentiated to give $p = \varphi + (\beta - 1)/\beta q + (\alpha/\beta)k$, where β is the output elasticity with respect to employment. Assuming $k = q$, this may be expressed as $p = \varphi + [(\alpha + \beta - 1)/\beta]q$, which is none other than the Verdoorn Law. Even if we assume, following Arrow (1962), that $\varphi = \varphi_0 + \xi k$, (i.e., part of technical progress is induced by the growth of capital), the Verdoorn Law, $p = \varphi_0 + [(\alpha + \beta + \xi - 1)/\beta]q$ may also be derived from a *static* production function (or, in other words, it is capable of being specified in levels of the variables).[27]

This, needless to say, considerably reduced the novelty of Kaldor's approach. Kaldor's response was to argue that the Cobb–Douglas production function assumes malleable capital whereas the rate of the embodiment of technical progress is dependent upon the rate of capital accumulation. If one of the reasons is because new technology needs to be embodied then it may not be possible to integrate the technical progress function to give a static production function. This is because output will be a function of 'the distribution of capital according to age as well as (in a multi-commodity world) the distribution of capital and labour between industries and firms' (Kaldor, 1961, p. 215). It is for this reason that subsequent versions of the technical progress function adopted a vintage approach and in Kaldor and Mirrlees (1962), productivity growth on the latest vintage is related to the rate of increase of gross investment. However, in the steady state, the age distribution of the capital stock will not vary (a point made by Kaldor himself in a rejoinder to a criticism by Wolfe (1968)) and, moreover, the Verdoorn Law does not encompass the vintage effect.

The static Verdoorn Law

Consequently, notwithstanding Kaldor's insistence on the importance of the rate of growth in the Verdoorn Law, estimating the law using cross-sectional data in growth rates or logarithms of the levels could give the same estimates of the Verdoorn parameters. However, in nearly all cases this does not prove to be the case. The estimation of the static Verdoorn law, specified as either (where P is the level of productivity)

$$lnP = c + b_7 lnQ + b_8 lnK \tag{4.33}$$

or in terms of total factor productivity (TFP)

$$lnTFP = c + b_9 lnQ \tag{4.34}$$

gives an estimate of returns to scale that is generally not significantly different from unity.[28] Moreover, Rowthorn's specification also does not refute the hypothesis of constant returns to scale.[29]

Table 4.1 reports the results of estimating the static Verdoorn Law specified as $lnL = lnA + (1/\beta)lnQ - (\alpha/\beta)lnK$, as an illustration using US state data for manufacturing for 1987. lnL was chosen as the regressand to remove the spurious correlation engendered by the use of lnP. The estimate of the capital stock was the sum of the gross book value of depreciable assets and rental payments capitalised using a gross rate of profit of 13 per cent. An IV estimating method with the ranks of the variables as the instruments was used because of the possible problem of simultaneity. However, the OLS estimates are virtually identical to the IV estimates.

If there were constant returns to scale and $\alpha = \beta$, so that both α and β equal $\frac{1}{2}$, then we should expect the estimated coefficient of lnQ to be about 2. However, as may be seen from equation (i), it is nearly unity. The problem is that, as the auxiliary equation (ii) shows, there is strong multicollinearity between lnQ and lnK. (This confirms Kaldor's stylised fact of a constant capital–output ratio.) While it is not possible to estimate the

Table 4.1 The static Verdoorn Law: US manufacturing industry, state data, 1987, IV estimates

(i)	$\ln L = -3.863 + 1.075\ln Q - 0.091\ln K$ (–17.39) (11.42) (–0.92)	SER = 0.151	$\overline{GR}^2 = 0.942$
(ii)	$\ln K = 1.686 + 0.934\ln Q$ (6.53) (34.05)	SER = 0.263	$\overline{GR}^2 = 0.936$

Notes: Figures in brackets under the estimates of the coefficients are the *t*-values.
$\overline{GR}^2$ is the generalised R-bar-squared statistic.
Number of observations = 51

Source: US Census of Manufactures, 1987.

individual coefficients precisely, fortunately, this is not true of their sum. Thus, with constant returns to scale, we should expect the sum of the coefficients not to be significantly different from unity (i.e. $1/\beta - \alpha/\beta = (1 - \alpha)/\beta = 1$). The sum of the coefficients is 0.974, which does not significantly differ from unity at the 0.01 confidence level. The use of OLS does not make a great deal of difference to the results.

These results confirm those obtained by the author (McCombie, 1982a; McCombie and de Ridder, 1984) for earlier years and contrasts with the statistically significant dynamic Verdoorn coefficient found by McCombie and de Ridder (1984) and Bernat (1996) for US data. See also Fingleton and McCombie (1998), where similar results occur using European regional data but where the Verdoorn Law shows substantial increasing returns to scale when growth rates are used.

Thus, we have a paradox, in that it might be supposed that both the static and dynamic specifications should give the same result. One possibility is that while the static law may be derived from a Cobb–Douglas, it does not necessarily follow that the converse is true – that is, that the Verdoorn Law is integratable into a Cobb–Douglas. This is because the constant of integration is undetermined and is fixed by initial conditions and these may differ between countries. So that if we estimate a common static production function, we may get biased estimates. Other specifications of static production functions that may also be compatible with the Verdoorn Law are considered in McCombie (1982a).[30]

It is clearly unsatisfactory from a theoretical point of view that the Verdoorn Law can, under certain assumptions, be integrated into a static Cobb–Douglas production, because this implies that if there are increasing returns to scale the level of productivity is positively correlated with the *size* of output–a conclusion that is contradicted by the empirical evidence. Switzerland, with a manufacturing sector only a fraction of the size of that of the United States, does not have a level of productivity that is significantly smaller. (The dynamic Verdoorn Law is not scale-dependent in this way.) This raises the whole question of what is the appropriate unit of observation. Is it the total output of an industry of a particular country, which runs into the above problem? Is it the output of a region within a particular country and, if so, by what economic criteria should the region be defined? Is the city (or the so-called functional economic area) the appropriate unit of observation? One other possibility is that, *pace* Allyn Young, the correct method is to divide the values of the output and the input by the number of firms. Thus, the production relationships are estimated using *per firm* data and the underlying static production function is given by

$$P/F = A_0 e^{\varphi t}(Q/F)^{(\beta - 1)/\beta}(K/F)^{\alpha/\beta} \tag{4.35}$$

where F is the number of firms and the dynamic Verdoorn Law is given by equation (4.35) expressed in growth rate form.

These specifications have only been estimated, so far as I am aware, by McCombie and de Ridder (1984), and they found that it did not resolve the paradox. The dynamic Verdoorn Law using per establishment data still gave an estimate of substantial increasing returns to scale and the static Verdoorn Law, constant returns to scale. (Using the same US state data set as above, the estimates using per firm data in the static specification were almost identical to those reported in Table 4.1.)

The dynamic Verdoorn Law

An alternative approach is to adopt Maurice Scott's (1989) 'new view' of economic growth, which in many ways is similar to that of Kaldor – namely, that it makes no sense to talk about a production function which shifts over time. According to Scott, all that one can reasonably do is explain the *changes* in output. However, his reasoning differs fundamentally from Kaldor's and is more controversial. (What is perhaps surprising is that Scott's approach has generally been ignored by the growth theorists, with the exception of Denison (1991) and Oulton (1995), both of whom find it unconvincing and van de Klundert and van Schaik (1996), who are more sympathetic.)

Scott's argument is quite subtle and there is not space here to go into it in detail. The reader is referred to Scott (1989, 1991) and McCombie and Thirlwall (1994). Briefly, it concerns the correct way to measure capital. Scott argues that omissions in the national accounts in the level of investment offset the amount of depreciation due to 'wear and tear'. Thus, in the conventional approach scrapping should only reflect depreciation due to relative price changes. But Scott (1991, p. 6) argues that

> relative price changes are symmetrical in as much as they result in appreciation that equals and offsets depreciation. Depreciation does not,

therefore, subtract from the growth of output. It is, instead, a transfer of income from capitalists to workers, whose human capital appreciates. It is therefore gross investment, not gross investment minus depreciation, which is the right way to measure changes in capital input, and which is most closely analogous to the way in which the change in the labour input is measured. If this right way is chosen, there is no reason to expect any unexplained residual, due to technical progress, greater knowledge, increased total factor productivity or what have you.

Scott (1989, chapter 6) further argues that the correct procedure is to relate the growth of output to that of quality-adjusted labour and the gross investment–output (I/Q) ratio and there is no role for technical progress. Furthermore, Scott argues that it makes little sense to postulate an underlying *static* production function, and the conventional estimates of the level of capital stock (either gross or net) and its rate of growth are not appropriate measures of the capital input or its growth rate (see Scott, 1989, p. 97). Hence, it is erroneous to estimate a production function in levels form.

Thus Scott estimates his model using the relationship using pooled cross-country data for the whole economy from the mid-nineteenth century for some countries to the mid-1980s. The estimating equation is $q = c + b_{10}\ell + b_{11}I/Q$. He finds that the estimate of the intercept is not significantly different from zero, i.e. there is no *exogenous* technical progress. There is a certain irony here. The variable I/Q had been included in the Verdoorn Law by Kaldor (1967) to capture the contribution of the growth of the capital stock. But it was very much *faute de mieux* as estimates of net investment or the capital stock were not available. But Scott now argues that this was the *correct* measure in the first place![31] Scott himself sees little room for increasing returns in economic growth, and in this respect differs from Kaldor, but this is an empirical matter.

Scott (1989, chapter 12) replicates Kaldor's regression of the Verdoorn Law using his (Scott's) data for the postwar period. Regressing the growth of quality-adjusted employment on output, he confirms Kaldor's result that the regression coefficient is significantly less than unity. But he discounts this result by arguing that it is misspecified because the growth of capital (or the investment–output ratio) and a catch–up variable is missing. Scott uses the ratio of productivity in the country concerned to that of the United States. (However, there is a problem that to the extent that there are increasing returns to scale, productivity levels will vary because of this, even though both countries have the same level of technology and there is no scope for catch up.) This criticism overlooks the fact that Kaldor (1967) did explicitly include the I/Q and it made little difference to the interpretation of the results. Kaldor (1975a) discounted the importance of the diffusion of technology, at least between the advanced countries. Including the

I/Q and catch-up variable did not significantly alter the results (see McCombie and Thirlwall, 1994).

Extending the analysis, Scott's (1989) full data set was used for ten of the now advanced countries using growth rates calculated over subperiods from 1856 (in the case of the UK) or later to 1984 (in the case of Japan) or earlier. The estimation method was an IV procedure with the ranks of the regressors as instruments. Following Scott, a postwar dummy for the investment–output ratio was introduced. In the first regression, the growth of employment was the numbers of full-time workers employed. A catch-up variable (*lncu*) was also included and this was the ratio of productivity in the country concerned to productivity in the technological leader, the United States. (This is notwithstanding the problems, noted above, with the interpretation of this variable.) However, dropping it from the regression does not significantly alter the estimate of the Verdoorn coefficient. The latter is one minus the coefficient of the growth of output in the estimated equation reported in Table 4.2. From the table it can be seen that serial correlation is not a problem.

What is surprising is the lack of statistical significance of the investment–output ratio for the pre-Second World War period. The implicit Verdoorn coefficient (0.671 with a *t*-value of 7.98) and the catch-up variable are statistically significant and the growth of exogenous technical progress is negligible.

To conclude, if we accept Scott's argument, it is incorrect to estimate the Verdoorn Law in its static form and the law is a relationship only between growth rates of productivity and output (and the gross investment–output ratio but not the growth of the net or gross capital stock). Thus, because of the inappropriate measure of the capital input, the static Verdoorn Law will give misleading estimates of the degree of returns to scale. Hence, the results of estimating the modified Verdoorn Law using Scott's data give support for Kaldor's contention of the importance of increasing returns to scale (broadly defined).[32]

Table 4.2 The dynamic Verdoorn Law: advanced countries, mid-nineteenth century to mid-1980s, IV estimates

$$\ell = \underset{(1.68)}{0.007} + \underset{(3.91)}{0.329q} - \underset{(-0.73)}{0.021I/Q} - \underset{(-1.99)}{0.033d^{*}I/Q} + \underset{(2.39)}{0.008lncu}$$

$SER = 0.005$; $\overline{GR}^2 = 0.245$
SC $\chi_1 = 0.730$ [0.39]

Notes:
See Table 4.1.
SC is the Lagrange multiplier test of serial correlation. The figure in square brackets is the probability value.
d*I/Q is a postwar dummy variable for I/Q. d = 1 for the postwar period and 0, prewar.
Number of observations = 29
Countries: UK, US, Belgium, Denmark, France, Germany, Netherlands, Norway, Italy.
Source: Scott (1989, table SA I).

Recent estimates of the Verdoorn Law

In the three decades since the publication of the inaugural lecture there have been numerous studies estimating the Verdoorn Law using a variety of different data sets. The picture that emerges is, notwithstanding the instability of the law at the level of the advanced countries and with some time-series data sets, that the Verdoorn Law estimates are particularly robust with values of the Verdoorn coefficient in the range of 0.3 to 0.6 and statistically significant. In this section, we consider some of the more recent studies and, although no claim is made of comprehensiveness, these studies provide strong confirmation of the Verdoorn Law. (See the Appendix to the Introduction to this volume for a full listing.)

However, it is useful to commence with a rather old study, McCombie and de Ridder (1984), since their approach had certain advantages over previous studies. They used state data for the US to estimate the Verdoorn Law. The data were growth rates for the US states calculated over the ten-year period from 1963 to 1973. The length of time removes the problem posed by Okun's Law (and both 1963 and 1973 were peak years). They explicitly calculated and included measures of the growth of the capital stock. There are a number of advantages of using regional data to estimate the law. First, the US states do not differ greatly from each other in the socio-economic characteristics (especially when compared to the differences between the advanced countries) and in the effect of macroeconomic policies. Secondly, it is reasonable to assume that they have access to the same blueprint of techniques and so the spatial diffusion of innovations is unlikely to bias the Verdoorn coefficient. Finally, the estimate is likely to be conservative and biased in favour of rejecting the hypothesis, since the estimate of the Verdoorn Law will not capture the effects of the growth of national manufacturing output on regional productivity growth.

The results provided strong support for the Kaldorian thesis. The preferred specification of the Verdoorn Law, augmented by the growth of the capital stock, gave a value of degree of returns to scale of 1.45, which was statistically significant at the 99 per cent confidence level. It is interesting to note that Rowthorn's specification also gave a statistically significant estimate of 1.33.

Bernat (1996) updated this study for the period 1977–90, although he did not include the growth of the capital stock. He was able to take advantage of recent developments in spatial econometrics to take account of the effect of spatial autocorrelation. Basically, under what is known as the *spatial lag model*, spatial dependence acts as if there were an additional explanatory variable. In other words, the growth of a state will be affected by the productivity growth of the surrounding states. There is an alternative model known as the *spatial error model* where the error term exhibits spatial dependence. This is likely to occur because the unit of measurement, the state, is defined on administrative or political rather than economic criteria. Thus, it would not be surprising if a region's residuals were highly correlated with that of its neighbour. As Bernat points out, the implications of the two models are subtly different. Ignoring spatial dependence in the spatial lag model induces a bias on the Verdoorn coefficient, whereas if the true model were the spatial error model the estimate would be unbiased but inefficient. In the former case, a high growth rate in one state would exert a positive effect on a neighbouring state, even if the growth of the latter were not high. In the spatial error model, the spatial effect would only occur if the neighbouring state had a growth rate either substantially above or below that predicted by the regression equation. Bernat finds the spatial error model to be preferred and this gives a statistically significant Verdoorn coefficient of 0.314 (compared with an OLS estimate of 0.271). 'The results also indicate that a 10 per cent deviation in neighbouring states' growth would have more than twice the impact on a state's manufacturing productivity growth rather than an equal increase in the state's own manufacturing output.'[33] (This actually seems to be a rather implausible result.) While Bernat considered that the results clearly support the Verdoorn Law, he noted that the law did not apply uniformly across the region.

Fingleton and McCombie (1998) estimated the Verdoorn Law for manufacturing for 178 regions of the European Union. Apart from the advantages of using regional data noted above, this gave a large number of degrees of freedom. The OLS results gave a highly significant Verdoorn coefficient of 0.575, but the Moran's I statistic suggested the presence of significant spatial autocorrelation. Consequently, a spatially lagged variable of productivity growth was included in the regression. The maximum likelihood estimates gave a virtually unchanged Verdoorn coefficient of 0.569 (*t*-ratio of 7.36) and the coefficient of the spatially lagged productivity suggests that an increase of productivity growth by one percentage point increased neighbouring regions' productivity growth by 0.2 of a percentage point.

When the initial level of productivity was included as a proxy for differences in the level of technology (and hence the effect of diffusion from the more to the less technically advanced regions), it proved statistically significant. However, the use of the level of productivity may be misleading because regional differences in this are not solely due to disparities in technology, but also to the effect of increasing returns to scale. Once an allowance has been made for this, the variable is still significant, and the value of the Verdoorn coefficient is virtually unaffected. These results therefore provide strong support for Kaldor's inferences concerning the Verdoorn Law.

Since the Verdoorn Law is essentially a technological relationship, it should not be dependent upon the type of economic organisation of a country. Thus, the study of Hansen and Zhang (1996) for China is of particular interest. They estimated the law using pooled time-series data (from 1985–91) for 29 Chinese regions. They found a statistically significant

Verdoorn coefficient of 0.71 (*t*-statistic 19.10). This is rather higher than is conventionally found and it may be partly due to the effect of a rapid growth of capital (that is, the capital–output ratio may be falling over time) or to the Okun effect which will bias the Verdoorn coefficient upwards. (No attempt was made to adjust for changes in capacity utilisation.) Nevertheless, it is difficult not to agree with the authors when they state that 'the relation [Verdoorn law] highlights industrial growth as a key factor in productivity growth' (Hansen and Zhang, 1996, p. 685).

León-Ledesma (2000) has estimated the Verdoorn Law for the 17 Spanish regions using pooled data for 1962–73, 1973–83 and 1983–91. Using OLS, the capital augmented Verdoorn Law gave a good statistical fit with a Verdoorn coefficient of 0.448 in the multiple regression and a statistically significant value of increasing returns to scale of 2.24.[34] As in McCombie and de Ridder (1984), Rowthorn's specification gave a smaller value of returns to scale at 1.37, but this was still highly statistically significant.

Further confirmation was found for the Verdoorn Law for Greece using time-series data for the period 1967 to 1988 (Drakopoulos and Theodossiou, 1991). The Verdoorn coefficient was highly significant and took a value of 0.804 which is again higher than that usually found. The intercept (capturing exogenous productivity) was negative, but statistically insignificant. But one of the problems with time-series data, as we noted above, is that the Verdoorn coefficient may be biased upwards because of Okun effects. The authors were aware of this, and introduced a capacity utilisation index as a regressor. The index was calculated as $CU_t = Q_t/Q_t^*$ where Q_t is the actual and Q_t^* is the full-capacity level of output. The inclusion of this, surprisingly, made no significant difference to the estimated value of Verdoorn coefficient.[35]Finally, mention should be made of Harris and Lau (1998), who used time-series data and the more fashionable cointegation technique. They estimated the Verdoorn Law for 13 2-digit SIC industries separately for the 10 standard UK regions and then weighted the estimates by net output to get an aggregate figure for manufacturing. They also found strong support for the Verdoorn Law, although the problem of sensitivity of the results to the precise proxies for changes in capacity utilisation remain. (Harris and Lau calculated the peak-to-peak output–capital ratio and then divided this by the actual output–capital ratio to calculate a measure of capacity utilisation.) Generally, most of the industries exhibited increasing returns to scale (some values of which were quite substantial, with a statistically significant value of returns to scale of over 3). The aggregate degree of increasing returns to scale ranged from 2.12 in the North to 1.47 in the East Midlands. They conclude that the 'results indicate that there is substantial evidence that increasing returns are the norm for the majority of manufacturing industries in Britain'.

Roberts (2001) found a statistically significant Verdoorn Law for the UK counties. It made little difference to the results whether OLS or an IV approach was used. The specification of the Verdoorn Law included both the investment–output ratio and a human capital variable.

Finally, Pugno (1995) tested the various neoclassical and Kaldorian growth models using a common data set for advanced and less developed countries over the period 1960–88. The importance of his approach was this comparative analysis and testing. He found a significant Verdoorn coefficient regardless of whether the conventional Verdoorn Law was estimated or it was specified as part of a reduced form equation with variables included for the initial level of human capital, a catch-up effect, innovative effort, and initial manufacturing share. The model also incorporated a Kaldorian export-led growth relationship.

Conclusions

In this essay we have considered the role of increasing returns in economic growth and briefly placed it in its historical context. It was shown how Kaldor built upon the earlier work of Adam Smith and, in particularly, Allyn Young. We explicitly derived the Verdoorn Law from the verbal model of Allyn Young in which he emphasised the fact that that increasing returns were essentially external to the firm. By this means, like Alfred Marshall before him, he attempted to reconcile increasing returns with perfect competition. There is a certain irony in the fact that Kaldor had precisely the opposite intention in mind. We then considered the criticisms of Kaldor by Hahn. While it is possible to have convexity in the aggregate transformation curve, this can only occur provided that the degree of returns to scale are small in relation to the size of the economy (or the number of firms is large). Presumably Kaldor had in mind the prevalence of substantial economies of scale. Verdoorn's own interpretation of the law was considered and it was shown that this was considerably different from the Kaldorian. Some recent studies of the Verdoorn Law were considered next. While all statistical estimation is open to some objection, and it was shown that there are a number of problems that beset the estimation of the Verdoorn Law, the vast majority of the evidence confirms Verdoorn's original results – industry is subject to substantial increasing returns. Clapham's (1922) 'empty boxes' seem now at least partially full.

Notes

1. I am grateful for the helpful comments of Maurizio Pugno, Bruno Soro and Tony Thirlwall.
2. Verdoorn actually refused permission for an English translation of his paper (the original was in Italian) and it was not until after his death that this occurred (see footnote 1, chapter 3 of this volume). Kaldor was, however, not the first to cite

this relationship. See chapter 3 for a discussion of the origins of the law. However, there is no doubt that it was Kaldor who really brought the relationship to prominence.

3. Verdoorn's Law is generally taken to refer to the relationship between the growth of productivity and output for total manufacturing or for a particular manufacturing industry. But a similar relationship has also been found using cross-industry data, as indeed may be found in Verdoorn (1949). (One of the earliest studies was Fabricant (1942), which actually predates Verdoorn's article.) Moreover, it is further found in these studies that productivity growth is negatively correlated with the growth of wage costs per unit of output and with the rate of growth of prices. These are sometimes called Fabricant's laws. (See Salter (1966) and Kennedy (1971) for detailed discussions.)
4. Strictly speaking, this requires the output elasticity of capital (broadly defined) to be equal to, or greater than, unity. In other words, increasing returns to scale is a necessary but not sufficient condition as it is possible to have both increasing returns and diminishing returns to capital.
5. To name just a few: *The Causes of the Slow Rate of Economic Growth of the United Kingdom* (1966) was Kaldor's inaugural lecture. The 'Case for Regional Policies' (1970) was the Fifth Annual Scottish Economic Society lecture. 'Conflicts in National Economic Objectives' first saw the light of day as the 1970 Presidential Address to Section F of the British Association and was published in the following year. The 'Irrelevance of Equilibrium Economics' (1972) was the Goodricke Lecture delivered at the University of York. 'What is Wrong with Economic Theory' had its origins as a Political Economy lecture given at Harvard University in 1974 and was published in 1975. 'Inflation and Recession in the World Economy' was the 1976 Presidential Address to the Royal Economic Society.
6. Just as a distinction has been drawn between J.R. Hicks and John Hicks in terms of Hicks's contribution to economics, it is tempting to make a similar distinction between Mr Kaldor and Professor Kaldor, as 1966 marks a watershed in the development of Kaldor's ideas on growth.
7. Kaldor took detailed notes of Young's lectures at the LSE (see Sandilands, 1990 and Blitch, 1990).
8. It should be pointed out, however, that Ricardo, Senior, and J.S. Mill accepted the presence of increasing returns to scale in manufacturing.
9. There is a question as to whether or not the underlying technology of the Verdoorn Law is the *static* Cobb–Douglas production function. If it is considered that it is not, then the analysis could start with equation (4.2) below. This is discussed below.
10. Arrow chose cumulative investment to stress the fact that the learning function, in practice, requires the introduction of new techniques of production. With only one specific type of technology the gains from learning by doing in the long run may eventually become exhausted (the learning elasticity will eventually fall to zero).
11. Young (1928, p. 530).
12. For example, Young (1928, p. 541) argues that:

    > To diminish the amount of the one commodity which must be sacrificed for a given increment of the other, some of the labour hitherto devoted to its production must be used indirectly, so the increase in the annual output of the one lags behind the other.

> This new element of cost might be taken into account by utilising a third dimension, but it is simpler to regard it as operating upon ΔX, the increment in X accompanying movement from P to P_1, so as to move the indifference curve upon which P_1 lies to the left. It would be an error, however, to think that the combination of X with Y and $X + (\Delta X)$ with $Y - \Delta Y$ (where (ΔX) is the contracted form of ΔX) are themselves indifferent, so that P_1 is, in effect, brought over to the original indifference curve, I, and no advantage reaped. The path P to P_1 is the *preferred* route, not merely a segment of an indifference curve. The cost of moving along this route is a function of the *rate* in time of the movement. (Emphasis in the original)

Unlike in our diagram, Young draws the indifference curves such that a move from P to P_1 (*b* to *c* in Figure 4.1) as always leads to an increase in utility.

A more sympathetic view of Young's approach, however, is taken by Reid (1989, pp. 146–51) who regards the note to Young's article as 'being of central importance'. According to Reid, Young considers a path of the economy along the traditional production possibility curve diagram that exhibits local increasing returns to scale and is drawn in the commodity space of two goods, X and Y. But the movement is not seen as costless by Young, as evidenced by the above quotation from him. The costs depend not only upon the distance of the path but also on the speed of movement. As Reid points out, Young tries to incorporate this effect (which is difficult to accomplish in terms of the traditional geometry of the production possibility frontier diagram) by making the position of the community indifference curves contingent on the path that the economy follows. Thus, there is a family of indifference curves before the move and these shift downwards to the south-west as a consequence of the move. According to Young, the indifference curves become 'contracted' by costs. 'Thus given any point in the commodity space, a *lower* lever of utility is attained at that point after a modification of the production possibility curve because of the cost incurred in achieving it' (Reid, 1989, p. 150, emphasis added).

However, from a consideration of Reid's interpretation of Young, it would seem that any point in the XY space after the move should confer a *greater*, not *lesser*, amount of utility than it did before. A shift down of the indifference curves means that a higher indifference curve now passes through a particular point with a given combination of X and Y, e.g. the initial or terminal points. Nevertheless, there are problems regardless of whether the shift actually increases or decreases utility at a particular point. The analysis suggests that as a consequence of the shift of the indifference curves, the same combination of goods X and Y at a point in the commodity space now gives a different level of utility. As the arguments of the utility function are simply the goods X and Y (at least no other argument is specified), the rationale for this is not clear. Utility is a function of the goods consumed and any changes in the costs of production should be reflected on the production side, presumably by a shift inwards of the production possibility curve. The relationship between the costs incurred by the change in the production and the levels of utility is not clearly spelt out and can only be described as 'obscure'. Nevertheless, perhaps more sense can be made of Young's argument by assuming that the production possibility curve shifts downwards as a result of the path of the economy (and the indifference curves are fixed) and the degree to which it shifts is a function of the speed of movement. In other words, the slower the speed, the lower the costs of adjustment and the less the production possibility curve shifts. Thus, the final level of utility achieved after the move depends on the speed of movement, but there is nothing to say that that it will be back at the old level of utility, so the end result is that the level of utility is increased.

13. This process is very similar to what Scitovsky (1954) later termed 'pecuniary external economies'. These are external economies that occur through the price mechanism, in contradistinction to technological external economies, which do not. Pecuniary external economies occur when 'the profits of the firm depend not only on its output and factor inputs, but also on the output and factor inputs of other firms' (Scitovsky, 1954, p. 146). His argument echoes Young. 'Investment in an industry leads to an expansion of its capacity and thus may lower the prices of its products and raises the prices of the factors used by it. The lowering of the product price benefits the users of these products; the raising of factor prices benefits the suppliers of the factors. When the benefits accrue to firms in the form of profits, they are pecuniary external economies.' He further continues that this seems to be in direct conflict with general equilibrium theory. Scitovsky gives two related reasons why this is the case. first, there are increasing returns due to fixed costs. Secondly, 'investment, however, need not bring the system closer to equilibrium; and when it does not the results of equilibrium theory may not apply'. A conclusion of all this is that investment may be below the social optimum. An individual firm when deciding upon its level of investment does not take into account the positive effect that this has on the profits of other firms.
14. Both Kaldor and Joan Robinson were present at the lecture, sitting in the front row. As with a maiden speech in the House of Commons, unfortunately no questions were permitted.
15. General equilibrium theory does not postulate linear-homogeneous and continuously differentiable functions, nor does it necessarily assume perfect foresight. But, as Hicks (1989, p. 112) points out, Walras 'does not have a production function, even a Ricardian production function; he just has a matrix of coefficients, which are stated to be independent of outputs so that they obey the rule of CRS [constant returns to scale]. ... There is not much difference between [the] later form of Walras's model and the all-round marginal productivity doctrine; it is all CRS.'
16. Setterfield (1997a) uses the standard model but assumes instead that productivity is a lagged function of output growth. This does not make any difference to the stability of the model.
17. The stability of the two-region model where the growth of one region can affect the growth of another is more complex and depends upon the various parameters of the model (see Guccione and Gillen (1977) and Dixon and Thirlwall (1978)). Some of the possibilities have been examined by Roberts (2002a) who finds that the values assumed by Dixon and Thirlwall do once again produce stability. One interesting finding is that in many cases instability leads to *both* regions exhibiting explosive growth. This stands in marked contrast to the neoclassical model (where there are infinite price elasticities) and where, with increasing returns to scale, the rapid growth of one region is always at the expense of another region (Faini, 1984, and Bertola, 1993). This is also the scenario emphasised by Kaldor. However, to take just one example, namely, when the sum of the price elasticities is greater than 4 in absolute value. If the value of $|\eta|$ is greater for the initially more slowly growing region, then both regions' growth rates collapse to $-\infty$. Conversely, if the initially more slowly growing region had the lower price elasticity, then both regions would grow without

bound. Intuitively, the reason for this complementarity is that the regions' growth rates are linked to each other through the export function and the income elasticity of demand. While this is not sufficient to cause complementarity of growth for all parameter values, it does so for a large number of cases.

18. However, Roberts (2002a) has shown that the convergence rate to equilibrium is very rapid.
19. An approximately constant capital–output ratio (implying that capital and output grow at roughly the same rate) is one of Kaldor's stylised facts or empirical regularities. Given that factor shares are constant (because of, say, a constant mark-up) and there is no discernible trend to the rate of profit, there will be no change in the capital-output ratio. This result is also necessary for steady-state growth. It should be noted, however, that the discussion in the text actually requires a weaker condition than this. It merely requires that the estimate of the coefficient b_3 is approximately unity. This is compatible with k being either greater than or less than q, depending upon the sign of the intercept in equation (4.21).
20. This argument is based on McCombie (1986).
21. It is not clear why the coefficient β is included in equation (4.24), but as we are dealing with growth rates, it plays no part in the dynamic labour supply function.
22. This is best regarded as a stylised fact of economic growth, although it is also a condition of steady-state growth. It implies that $q = k = \ell$.
23. If there is exogenous productivity growth, denoted by φ, then $V \equiv 1 - \dfrac{1}{\left(\dfrac{\varphi}{\ell} + \beta + \alpha\dfrac{k}{\ell}\right)}$

    Even if $k = \ell$, it will not reflect only increasing returns to scale as it includes exogenous technical change. It will also be unstable to the extent that φ varies.
24. In fact, μ is not observable. However, an alternative equation for the determination of the growth of real wages in the spirit of this model is to replace equations (4.23) and (4.24) in growth rate form by $w = (q - \ell) + \rho(\ell - n)$. This implies that when employment is growing as fast as the labour force, wages are determined by the growth of productivity. However, when a labour shortage occurs as evidenced by a rate of growth of employment that is faster than that of the labour force, this leads to an increase in the real wage above that warranted by the growth of productivity (see Verdoorn (1949) and chapter 2, Appendix, section 3-I.)
25. Personal communication.
26. This may also be true of regional data but the inter-regional variations in the growth of exogenous productivity are likely to be small compared with variations in the other growth rates.
27. It is possible to specify the Verdoorn Law as a non-linear function but most econometric specifications use the linear function. One notable exception is Bairam (1995) who uses a Box–Cox model to estimate the technical progress function. His results for 23 OECD countries over the period 1988–92 'conclusively refute the hypothesis that suggests that the technical progress function is linear and confirm Kaldor's original hypothesis that suggest that it is "convex upwards"' (Bairam, 1995, p. 304). Limitations of this approach are the short time span over which the growth rates are calculated (four years) and the fact that the growth of the capital stock is proxied by the gross investment–output ratio. Thus, the results must be considered suggestive, rather

than conclusive, and it would be interesting to see if this finding is repeated using other data sets.

28. *lnTFP* is the logarithm of the level of total factor productivity and defined as $lnQ - alnK - (1 - a)lnL$, where a and $(1 - a)$ are capital's and labour's share in value added. The advantage of this specification is that it avoids the problem inherent in equation (4.29) which results from the fact that *lnK* is endogenous. The disadvantage, from a Kaldorian perspective, is that it is derived using the marginal productivity theory of factor pricing.
29. An exception is the results of León–Ledesma (2000), who finds the static specification gives strong returns to scale, but Rowthorn's specification still gives constant returns to scale.
30. Kaldor's (1961) discussion of this criticism was as follows: 'However, as was pointed out to me by H. Uzawa of Stanford University, in integrating the technical progress function , the constant of integration $B = B(Y_0,K_0)$ is a function dependent upon the initial amount of capital K_0 and of output Y_0, whereas a production function of the type $Y_t = f(K_t t)$ requires that the function should be independent of the initial conditions.' But, as Wulwick (1993, p. 330) noted, this is puzzling as the 'Cobb–Douglas production function includes a term for time and so depends upon initial conditions.'
31. Likewise Bairam's (1995) use of I/Q could be justified on these grounds as the correct variable for the growth of the capital input.
32. Ghosh and Banerjee (1993) develop a model where the technical progress function is not integratable into a Cobb–Douglas production function when savings and investment plans are not realised. It is not possible to test this specification as it contains an unobservable variable – namely, planned savings.
33. The results of McCombie and de Ridder (1984) may therefore be inefficient. However, this is likely to be minimised by the fact that they used regional dummies that will counteract the effect of spatial autocorrelation. They also estimated the law using only the largest twenty states (the smallest states are very small compared with the largest and may therefore be affected by exogenous productivity shocks to a much greater extent). The use of the largest twenty states considerably reduce the degree of spatial contiguity.
34. The use of one-way fixed and random effects models gave virtually identical results. Because of the endogeneity of the growth of the capital stock (it is a function of the growth of output), including it as a regressor could lead to simultaneous equation bias. One method of avoiding this suggested by McCombie and de Ridder (1984) is to regress $tfi = c + b_{12}\, q$ where tfi is the growth of total factor inputs, defined as $a\ell + (1 - a)k$ where a and $(1 - a)$ are the shares of labour and capital in total income (although it could be objected that there are no firm foundations for this weighting procedure). The degree of returns to scale is given by $1/b$. León-Ledesma found that this specification (together with the equivalent Rowthorn specification) gave virtually the same estimates of returns to scale as the more traditional specifications.
35. It would have been interesting to see whether the *rate of change* of CU had any effect on the estimate; given that the model is specified in terms of growth rates, this would seem to be preferable.

5

A Reappraisal of Verdoorn's Law for the Italian Economy, 1951–1997

Carluccio Bianchi

Introduction

Verdoorn's Law postulates the existence of a significant positive relationship between the growth rate of labour productivity and that of output, at least in manufacturing. The relationship is generally interpreted to be of a technological nature, reflecting the existence of both static and (mainly) dynamic economies of scale and thus the presence of increasing returns to scale.

Kaldor (1966) tested the validity of the law for a cross-section of industrial countries for the period 1953–64, finding a value for the so-called Verdoorn coefficient – that is, the marginal elasticity of labour productivity with respect to output – of about 0.5.[1] Since the marginal elasticity of employment, which by definition is one minus the value of the Verdoorn coefficient, had the same approximate value, Kaldor argued that a one percentage point increment in the growth of output required an increase in employment growth by only half a percentage point, as a consequence of the estimated rise in productivity growth of half a percentage point. Thus, apparently convincingly, he claimed that the empirical finding of a marginal elasticity of employment of less than one would be proof of the existence of increasing returns to scale – a feature he deemed to be typical of the industrial sector. Indeed, when checking for the validity of the law in various sectors of the economy, Kaldor found it was unambiguously confirmed only in the case of industry (comprising the manufacturing, public utilities, and construction sectors), while elsewhere the evidence was either controversial or weak.

After Kaldor's seminal work, Verdoorn's Law was tested in a variety of studies and ways, concentrating on the manufacturing sector. Cross-country studies were progressively abandoned in favour of cross-regional or time-series analyses, since it was recognised that the former could give rise to spurious correlations, if the various countries involved had different technological features or were at different stages of economic development.[2] Cross-regional studies yield promising (and probably unbiased) results only when, by the same token, the technological characteristics of the various territorial areas of a country are fairly similar. This does not seem to be the case for the Italian economy, which has a dualistic nature, with large technological differences between regions.[3] With reference to the Italian economy, then, in order to test the validity of Verdoorn's Law, it seems preferable to use a time-series approach. This kind of procedure, moreover, appears to be the natural framework within which to examine the possible existence of temporal structural breaks in the relationship – a phenomenon that the literature on the subject indicates occurred worldwide after 1973.[4] The use of time-series data enables the study of the value of the relevant coefficients in selected subperiods, with the further advantage of avoiding a necessary, albeit arbitrary, choice of specific time horizons inherent in the alternative techniques, in an attempt to eschew the influence of cyclical fluctuations.[5] With regard to these, a possible critique raised about the use of a time-series approach in estimating Verdoorn coefficients relates to its alleged incapacity to disentangle short-run and long-run effects and thus to distinguish between Okun's Law and Verdoorn's Law. This objection, however, can be overcome in a number of ways, such as through the use of annual (instead of quarterly) data,[6] by a suitable choice of employment variables (standard labour units instead of persons employed[7]), and by the use of appropriate techniques (such as a partial adjustment model) capable of distinguishing between the short- and long-run values of the desired coefficients.

This chapter tests the validity of Verdoorn's Law for the Italian economy, both in general and for some specific sectors, using annual data for the period 1951–97.[8] A preliminary analysis of the traditional approach is followed by two possible extensions of the basic framework. The first of these introduces a partial adjustment mechanism ensuring that in the long run the actual employment level is equal to the desired one, and thus eliminating the short-run bias in the estimates of the Verdoorn coefficient. The second one removes some simplifying assumptions concerning Kaldor's original interpretation of the law by examining a formulation in which the effects of capital growth on output dynamics are explicitly considered. As will be shown, while the traditional estimates suggest that there are increasing returns to scale in Italy, both for the whole economy and for each of the individual sectors, the partial adjustment model and, in particular, the explicit consideration of the role of capital growth seem to indicate, by contrast, that increasing returns to scale may be found only in the case of industry and for the entire sample period.

Finally, an international comparison with the corresponding experience of the European Union and the United States, though limited to the period 1960–97 and to either manufacturing or the whole economy, is undertaken.[9] These comparisons show the existence of wide differences between these areas. Indeed, while the estimates for the European Union suggest a generalised presence of increasing returns to scale, the United States data never allow the rejection of the hypothesis of constant returns.

The chapter proceeds as follows. The next section presents the traditional estimates of Verdoorn's Law for the Italian economy for the period 1951–97. This is followed by a section that examines the possible extensions of the traditional formulation by introducing both a partial adjustment mechanism and explicit capital growth. The subsequent section considers an international comparison between Italy, Europe and the US. Finally, some brief conclusions drawn from the previous analyses are presented.

The traditional formulation

The traditional specification of Verdoorn's Law implies estimating the following equation:

$$g_p = a + bg_y \tag{5.1}$$

where g_p is the rate of growth of labour productivity and g_y is the corresponding rate of growth of output (value added). The parameter a is generally supposed to be related to the rate of autonomous (and thus exogenous) technical progress, while the coefficient b defines the nature and size of returns to scale in the way specified below.

Since, by definition, $g_p = g_y - g_n$, where g_n is the rate of growth of employment, equation (5.1) is equivalent to:

$$g_n = -a + (1 - b)g_y \tag{5.2}$$

This formulation is preferred by Kaldor since labour productivity is actually no more than a definition (just like the velocity of money) and is equal to Y/N, where the relevant variables are output Y (assumed to be exogenous, as determined by aggregate demand) and employment N (assumed to be the relevant decision variable of the firms). Kaldor's interpretation seems sensible not only from an economic standpoint, but also from a statistical one, as regressing g_p on g_y yields spurious correlations because g_p is a component of g_y. Furthermore, equation (5.2) enables the estimation of long-run Verdoorn coefficients, when it is extended to consider a partial adjustment model of changes in employment to changes in output, in the manner discussed below.

Equations (5.1) and (5.2) can be related to a production function of the classical Cobb–Douglas form,[10] where labour (N) and capital (K) are assumed to be the only inputs, so that:

$$Y = Ae^{gt}K^{\alpha}N^{\beta} \tag{5.3}$$

where g is the exogenous rate of growth of total factor productivity (A) and α and β define the nature and size of returns to scale. From equation (5.3), taking logs of both sides and using low-case letters for the derived variables, we get:

$$y = logA + gt + \alpha k + \beta n \tag{5.4}$$

so that differentiating with respect to time yields:

$$g_y = g + \alpha g_k + \beta g_n \tag{5.5}$$

From equation (5.5) an implicit employment function can be derived, which is given by:

$$\begin{aligned} g_n &= -(1/\beta)g + (1/\beta)g_y - (\alpha/\beta)g_k \\ &= -c + dg_y - eg_k \end{aligned} \tag{5.6}$$

This is the general form of Verdoorn's Law that ought to be estimated (or alternatively equation (5.5), often labelled Rowthorn's reformulation[11]). However, the traditional estimates of the law, as given by equation (5.1) or (5.2), can still be used to yield unbiased measures of the size of returns if a few simplifying assumptions are made. Indeed, there are at least three different ways to reconcile equation (5.6) with equation (5.2). The first one is based on Kaldor's observations about the stylised facts of industrial countries and is related to the idea that, in the long run, the ratio between output and capital is constant. Thus if $K/Y = v$ and then $g_k = g_y$, by substituting the latter into equation (5.6) we get:

$$\begin{aligned} g_n &= -c + (d - e)g_y \\ &= -(1/\beta)g + [(1 - \alpha)/\beta]g_y \end{aligned} \tag{5.7}$$

Equation (5.7) is thus immediately transformed into equation (5.2), with the obvious implication that if the estimated marginal elasticity of employment is less than one then $\alpha + \beta > 1$ and returns to scale are increasing, while if the same coefficient is equal to (or less than) one then returns are constant (or decreasing).[12] Thus Kaldor (1975, p. 893) appears to be correct in stating: 'a sufficient condition for the presence of static or dynamic economies of scale is the existence of a statistically significant relationship between g_n and g_y with a regression ... coefficient which is significantly less than 1'. This quotation also makes it clear that Kaldor attributes the evidence of increasing returns to the existence of static and dynamic economies of scale. In this sense, the phenomenon is considered to be an intrinsic feature of manufacturing, while other sectors of the economy should typically exhibit decreasing returns (Kaldor, 1966).

The second way to get equation (5.2) from equation (5.6) is to assume that the dynamics of the capital stock is exogenous so that capital grows through time at a constant rate γ: at any moment, then, $K = K_0 e^{\gamma t}$. Under this assumption, we may write the production function (5.3) as:

$$Y = Be^{\rho t}N^{\beta} \tag{5.8}$$

where $B = AK^{\alpha}{}_0$ and $\rho = g + \alpha\gamma$. Again, taking logs and differentiating with respect to time yields an equation to be estimated that is similar to equation (5.2).[13] In this case, once again, since $1 - b = 1/\beta$, if the marginal elasticity of employment is less than one then, as Kaldor claims, this is a sufficient condition[14] for the existence of increasing returns to scale.

A third way to reconcile equation (5.6) with equation (5.2) is based on Verdoorn's observation that the coefficient associated with his name depends upon the relative growth rates of capital and employment.[15] If the ratio between these growth rates is constant, as it happens in steady-state growth and, as Thirlwall (1980) suggests, is another stylised fact of industrial economies, then

$$g_k = fg_n \tag{5.9}$$

so that, substituting into equation (5.5) and rearranging yields:

$$g_n = g/(\alpha f + \beta) + [1/(\alpha f + \beta)]g_y \tag{5.10}$$

In this case, however, since normally, $f > 1$, the fact that the estimated marginal elasticity of employment is less than one does not guarantee that returns are increasing.[16]

Keeping these considerations in mind, the rest of this section is dedicated to estimating traditional Verdoorn equations for different sectors of the Italian economy using annual data for the 1951–97 period.[17] The results of the computations derived from estimating equation (5.2), using the OLS technique, are reported in Table 5.1.

The scatter plots of the data relating productivity growth to output growth for the same period, are shown in Figure 5.1.

The diagrams are exactly comparable in scale, so that the slope of the regression line drawn reflects the value of the traditional Verdoorn coefficients. Figure 5.2 shows the logarithms of employment and output for the various sectors. It provides useful supplementary information on the underlying dynamics of output and employment that generate the path of productivity that is the object of this study. In particular, it is interesting to note that standard labour units in agriculture decrease during the whole period.[18] Industrial employment shows an upward trend until 1980, subsequently followed by a marked decline, thus justifying the idea of the

Table 5.1 Estimates of the marginal elasticity of employment in the traditional Verdoorn equation: Italy

Period	*Agriculture*	*Industry*	*Non-tradables*	*Non-agriculture*	*Whole economy*
1951–97	0.11++	0.35*	0.24++	0.29*	0.17*
1960–97	0.12++	0.33*	0.33++	0.32*	0.20*
1951–73	0.02++	0.25*	0.49++	0.44*	0.24*
1973–97	0.18**	0.34*	0.53++	0.39*	0.37*
1980–97	0.36*	0.54*	0.73++	0.49*	0.52*

Notes:
* Significant at the 5% level: null hypothesis constant returns.
** Significant at the 10% level: null hypothesis constant returns.
++ The model is not significant.

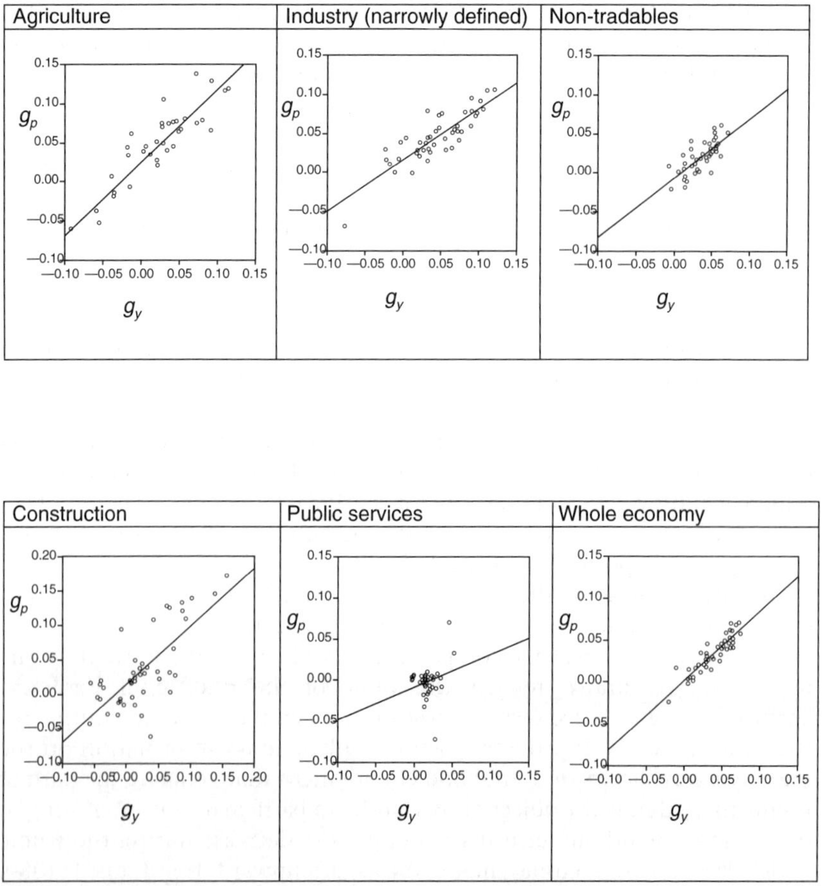

Figure 5.1 Verdoorn's Law for the Italian economy, 1951–1997

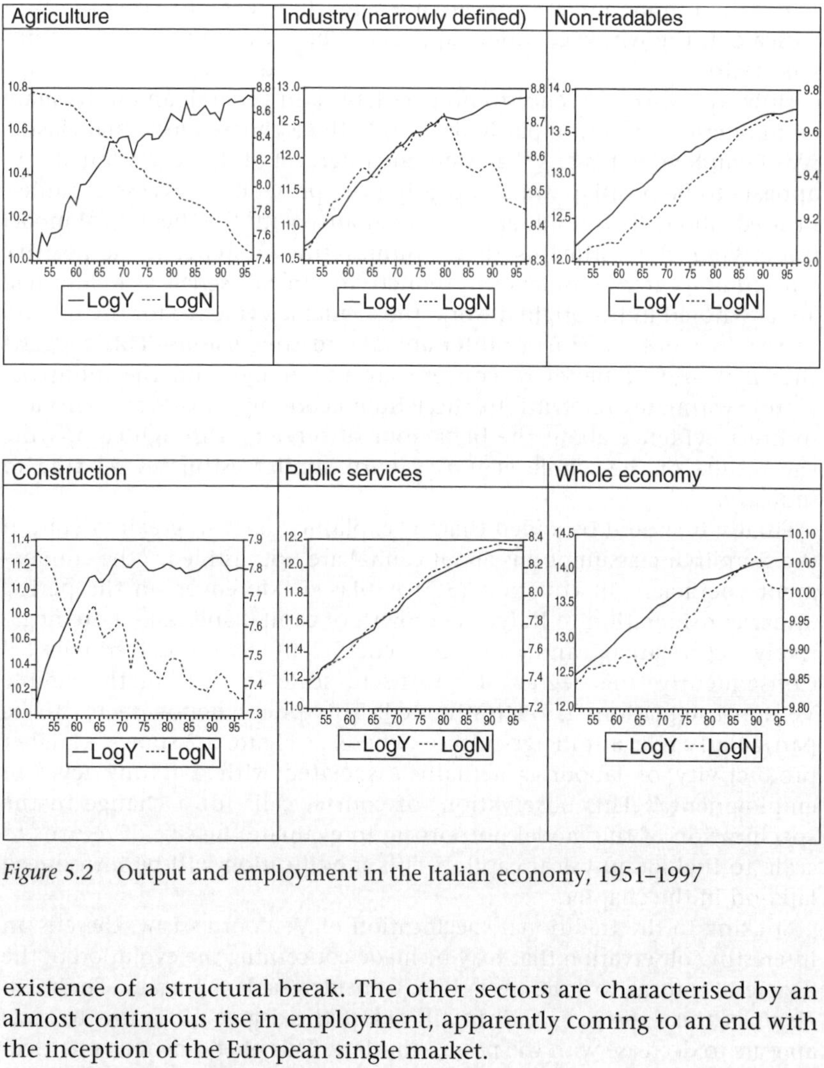

Figure 5.2 Output and employment in the Italian economy, 1951–1997

existence of a structural break. The other sectors are characterised by an almost continuous rise in employment, apparently coming to an end with the inception of the European single market.

As Figure 5.1 shows, contrary to some possible a priori beliefs, all sectors exhibit increasing returns. This is confirmed more formally by the standard tests on the estimated Verdoorn coefficient (or rather the marginal elasticity of employment), reported in Table 5.1. In particular, it is interesting to notice that the sector showing the greatest level of returns to scale, as a consequence of the peculiar features of its employment dynamics noted above, is agriculture, followed by non-tradables and finally by industry (narrowly defined – that is, excluding construction).[19] Only in public services are the increasing returns to scale slightly lower than in manufacturing. On average, therefore, the size of returns to scale in the whole economy appears to be greater than in the industrial sector.

However, with reference to non-tradables, in general, and to its main component, services, in particular, while the estimated marginal elasticity of employment is less than one, the intercept of the regression always appears to be positive, thus indicating the presence of excess or underutilised labour. This result appears at variance with the theoretical model underlying the estimates that assumes the existence of a positive autonomous growth of labour productivity. In this sense, as Kaldor had already noted in his original work, the available evidence for the tertiary sector does not allow us to infer any sound conclusions. This suggests that it would be better to concentrate the analysis on the industrial sector. Estimates referring to the whole economy, however, can yield indirect evidence about the behaviour of services, through comparing the results of the whole economy with similar estimates relating to industry.

Finally it should be added that, as explained later in greater detail, if the simplifying assumptions about capital are not justified,[20] the employment coefficient in equation (5.2) is biased. Moreover, in the period under consideration in Italy, the growth of capital and labour are negatively correlated, and so the coefficient is underestimated.[21] Consequently, the degree of returns to scale implicit in the simple Verdoorn equations is overestimated. This phenomenon seems to be particularly relevant in agriculture, where, as Figure 5.2 shows, a higher productivity of labour is actually associated with a falling level of employment.[22] This observation, of course, calls for a change in the specification of the model purporting to evaluate the size of returns to scale to include physical capital. This modification will be introduced later on in the chapter.

Sticking to the traditional specification of Verdoorn's Law, there is an interesting observation that may be made concerning the evolution of the degree of returns to scale over time. Consider Table 5.1 again. The main result of this exercise is that in all sectors the degree of returns to scale appears to decrease with the passage of time. This phenomenon is particularly relevant in the case of the non-tradable sectors, where the estimate of $(1 - b)$ in the most recent 1980–97 period is 0.73, but the associated statistical test cannot exclude the possibility that its true value is 1 or a little more (thus implying constant or even slightly decreasing returns to scale). This result is partly attributable to the performance of the public services, a sector where returns to scale appear to be very high in the 1951–73 period ($b > 1$!), but their value decreases both in the 1973–97 period and in the most recent 1980–97 subperiod.[23]

Extensions of the traditional formulation

The simple model previously described assumes that employment – the relevant decision variable by firms – is adjusted instantaneously. It is actually more plausible to assume that input adjustment is slow, owing to the existence of hiring and firing costs, uncertainty about demand, and contractual constraints. In order to see the consequences of a sluggish employment adjustment, we proceed as follows. Let us start from the production function given by equation (5.3) and let us assume, in a Kaldorian fashion, that the capital–output ratio is constant.[24] Then, since $K = vY$, we may rewrite equation (5.3) as:

$$Y = Ae^{gt}(vY)^{\alpha}N^{\beta} \tag{5.11}$$

and hence, letting $D = Av^{\alpha}$ and rearranging, we get:

$$Y = D^{1/(1-\alpha)}e^{gt/(1-\alpha)}N^{\beta/(1-\alpha)} \tag{5.12}$$

The derived employment function will then be:

$$N = D^{-1/\beta}e^{-gt/\beta}Y^{(1-\alpha)/\beta} \tag{5.13}$$

Taking logs, and using lower-case letters for the derived variables, we finally have:

$$n = [-logD - gt + (1-\alpha)y]/\beta \tag{5.14}$$

We may then use equation (5.14) to define the desired equilibrium values of the log of employment at any time t (denoted by n_t^*), while in the short run the actual values (n_t) adjust only slowly to the desired ones, according to the rule:

$$n_t = n_{t-1} + \lambda(n_t^* - n_{t-1}) = \lambda n_t^* + (1-\lambda)n_{t-1} \tag{5.15}$$

Substituting the value of n_t^*, derived from equation (5.14), into equation (5.15), one finally gets:

$$n_t = (-\lambda/\beta)logD - (\lambda/\beta)gt + (\lambda/\beta)(1-\alpha)y_t + (1-\lambda)n_{t-1} \tag{5.16}$$

so that, differentiating with respect to time, one can estimate:

$$g_n = (-\lambda/\beta)g + (\lambda/\beta)(1-\alpha)g_y + (1-\lambda)g_{n,-1} = -h + ig_y + jg_{n,-1} \tag{5.17}$$

where $g_{n,-1}$ stands for the lagged growth rate of employment. Using this partial adjustment model, coefficient i[25] in equation (5.17) can be interpreted as the short-run response of employment to output (the short-run marginal elasticity of employment), while the coefficients ratio $i/(1 - j)$[26] represents the equivalent long-run elasticity. The inverse of these coefficients can thus be regarded as representative of the equivalent short-run and long-run degree of returns to scale.

The empirical estimates of these coefficients for the Italian economy are reported in Table 5.2. It may be seen that the short-run coefficients substantially confirm the results previously obtained in the absence of a partial adjustment mechanism, and thus imply the existence of increasing returns in all sectors and periods (with the exception of public services in the most recent period). Allowing for a slow adjustment of labour inputs, however, changes the picture in the long run. First, all employment coefficients are higher, implying lower returns to scale. Secondly, in the most recent period (post-1973), all sectors, with the exception of agriculture (which has its own unique structural features), show employment coefficients very near to 1. Consequently, the hypothesis of constant returns cannot be excluded. Finally, with regard to non-tradables (and thus services) in the most recent period, there is a presumption of decreasing returns.

The previous estimates, as noted above, concern employment data defined as standard labour units. This is not, however, the most widely used measure of employment, since, for instance, unemployment figures are based on data about the number of persons. Thus, for future purposes as well,[27] it is useful to estimate employment coefficients, similar to the ones used until now, but using the alternative definition of employment in terms of persons employed. The results of this are reported in Table 5.3, with regard to the industrial sector and to the whole economy for the 1960–97 period.[28] As might be

Table 5.2 Estimates of the short-run and long-run marginal elasticity of employment in a partial adjustment model: Italy

Period	*Agriculture*		*Industry*		*Non-tradables*		*Non-agriculture*		*Whole economy*	
1951–97	0.11^{++}	0.12^{++}	0.31*	0.55*	0.25^{++}	0.44^{++}	0.28*	0.44*	0.18*	0.28*
1960–97	0.11^{++}	0.11^{++}	0.30*	0.55*	0.33^{++}	0.55^{++}	0.32*	0.50*	0.21*	0.34*
1951–73	0.02^{++}	0.03^{++}	0.31*	0.46**	0.52^{++}	0.64^{++}	0.48*	0.62^{+}	0.25*	0.27^{+}
1973–97	0.18*	0.19*	0.37*	0.78	0.44^{++}	0.96^{++}	0.39*	0.74	0.38*	0.75
1980–97	0.38*	0.47^{+}	0.53*	0.93	0.52^{++}	1.73^{++}	0.46*	1.07	0.47*	0.94

Notes:

* Significant at the 5% level: null hypothesis constant returns.

** Significant at the 10% level: null hypothesis constant returns.

$^{+}$ The hypothesis of the presence of a partial adjustment mechanism is rejected.

$^{++}$ The model is not significant.

expected a priori, the employment coefficients using the standard labour units are higher, since, when output increases, firms adjust both the number of people employed and the average working time to the new level of demand. The econometric evidence seems to suggest that an increase in output is accompanied by an equal relative change in employment and worked hours for the entire 1960–97 period. In the most recent period, however, if one takes into account the special circumstances of 1993, characterised by a very unfavourable cyclical situation, and thus introduces a specific dummy variable in the appropriate regressions, the employment coefficient estimated using standard units appears to be much higher, so that the level of returns to scale is much lower.

As noted above, however, the traditional formulation of Verdoorn's Law implies making some simplified assumptions about either the growth of capital or of the capital–output ratio. These hypotheses are obviously restrictive[29,30] and may also be considered to be responsible for the poor explanatory power of the simple model implied by equation (5.2). As we have seen, a more comprehensive approach requires the estimation of an equation such as (5.6),[31] which explicitly considers the effects of both labour and capital inputs on production. In this case a direct estimate of the production function, that is, Rowthorn's specification of Verdoorn's Law – equation (5.5), is preferable to the alternative estimation of a generalised employment function in order

Table 5.3 Estimates of the marginal elasticity of employment: standard labour units versus persons employed: Italy

	Industry				*Whole economy*			
Period	*S. l. u.*		*Persons*		*S. l. u.*		*Persons*	
1960–97	0.33*		0.18*		0.20*		0.10++	
1960–97 + DU93			0.21*		0.14*		0.00++	
1960–97 PA	0.30*	0.55*	0.16*	0.28*	0.21*	0.34*	0.15*	0.27*
1960–97 PA + DU93			0.19*	0.34*	0.16*	0.23*	0.05++	0.08++
1960–80	0.15*		0.12**		0.12++		0.01++	
1960–80 PA	0.20*	0.29+	0.15*	0.23**	0.17**	0.23**	0.10++	0.17++
1980–97	0.54*		0.07++		0.52*		0.60*	
1980–97 + DU93			0.19**		0.28**		0.13++	
1980–97 PA	0.53*	0.93	0.07++	0.11++	0.47*	0.94	0.63*	1.19
1980–97 PA + DU93			0.20**	0.32**	0.30*	0.52*	0.2++	0.32++

Notes:
PA = Model with partial adjustment: first figure is the short-run coefficient and the second is the long-run coefficient.
DU93 = Dummy variable for 1993 (1993 = 1; otherwise = 0).
* Significant at the 5% level: null hypothesis constant returns.
** Significant at the 10% level: null hypothesis constant returns.
\+ The hypothesis of the presence of a partial adjustment mechanism is rejected.
++ The model is not significant.

to exclude the presence of multicollinearity among the regressors (output and capital). Furthermore previous analyses of a generalised employment function lead to capital coefficients with the wrong sign, a result that cannot be justified on purely economic grounds.[32]

When capital is introduced, the nature of returns to scale can be inferred directly by computing the sum of coefficients α and β in equation (5.5). The estimates of this equation for the manufacturing sectors and for the whole economy of Italy are reported in Table 5.4. The OLS technique has been used because the weak exogeneity hypothesis has not been rejected by the appropriate check.[33] The Wald tests for the constant returns hypothesis[34] confirm the existence of increasing returns to scale in industry in the whole estimation period, using either standard labour units or numbers of persons employed (the coefficients add up to 1.7 approximately). Nothing definite can be established for the subperiods chosen, however, in the sense that despite the evidence that the coefficients sum to greater than 1 in the 1951–73 period, and around one later on, the case of constant returns to scale cannot be rejected in either case. With reference to the whole economy, it is never possible to determine the size of returns to scale in an unambiguous way, either for the entire 1951–97 period or for the chosen subperiods, since the sum of the estimated coefficients is never very different from 1 (and capital also appears to have the wrong sign in the most recent 1980–97 period). In the more general model defined by equation (5.5), if the possibility of a slow adjustment of output is introduced, the overall picture previously described does not change. In fact, a partial adjustment model is statistically significant for industry, but not for the system as a whole. In the industrial sector, however, the

Table 5.4 Estimates of returns to scale in the general model with capital growth: Italy

Period	*Industry*		*Whole economy*	
1951–97	1.67*		1.44	
1951–97 PA	2.32*	1.71*	1.38^{+}	1.44^{+}
1951–73	1.19		0.75	
1951–73 PA	0.69^{+}	0.76^{+}	0.54^{+}	0.68^{+}
1973–97	1.02		1.27	
1973–97 PA	1.75	1.15	1.56^{+}	1.21^{+}

Notes: The table reports the sum of the coefficients α and β and the result of the tests on the nature of returns to scale.

PA = Model with partial adjustment: first figure is the short-run coefficient and the second is the long-run coefficient.

* Increasing returns to scale. (An appropriate Wald test rejects the hypothesis of constant return to scale, so that $\alpha + \beta > 1$.)

$^{+}$ The hypothesis of the presence of a partial adjustment mechanism is rejected.

hypothesis of increasing returns to scale for the whole sample period is confirmed by the appropriate Wald tests.

An international comparison

The level of returns to scale estimated for the Italian economy can be usefully compared both to those of the European Union and to those of the United States. Figure 5.3 illustrates the scatter plots of the data, while Tables 5.5 and 5.6 report the relevant estimates of the employment coefficients.[35] According to the traditional formulation of Verdoorn's Law, returns to scale are larger for Italy, both in industry and for the economy as a whole. It is also interesting to notice that, with reference to the United States, the Verdoorn coefficient appears to be around 0.50 – a value in line with earlier estimates available in the literature. European manufacturing is very similar to the United States, while for the whole economy the degree of returns to scale are almost as high as those of Italy. All three economies show a tendency for the employment coefficients to increase over time. The worst performance is for that of Europe with respect to the whole economy. Using a model with a partial adjustment of labour does not change the overall picture, but, as expected a priori, all employment coefficients, in the long-run steady state, are higher. Indeed, one cannot exclude the possibility of constant returns to scale for the United States in both industry and the whole economy, for the entire observation period. This is also true for Europe in the most recent period.

Some quite different results are obtained by studying the more general equation, which includes capital growth as a regressor. With regards to the European Union, the tests performed seem to indicate the existence of increasing returns to scale across the whole economy for the entire period 1960–97, but mainly in the first subperiod, while nothing definite can be said about the second subperiod. With reference to the manufacturing sector, the basic model can never exclude the existence of constant returns, despite the estimate of returns to scale of 1.5 in the entire period (very close to the Italian figure). The size of the returns to scale, moreover, appears to be rapidly diminishing over time. However, a partial adjustment mechanism proves to be important in determining the magnitude of the degree of returns to scale in manufacturing. This specification implies the existence of increasing returns in this sector as well, with reference to the whole sample period and most of all to the earlier years considered in the estimates.

Finally, with regards to the United States, both for the industrial sector and for the economy as a whole, the tests performed can never reject the hypothesis of constant returns to scale, either for the entire observation period or for all the subperiods. In the case of manufacturing, there is

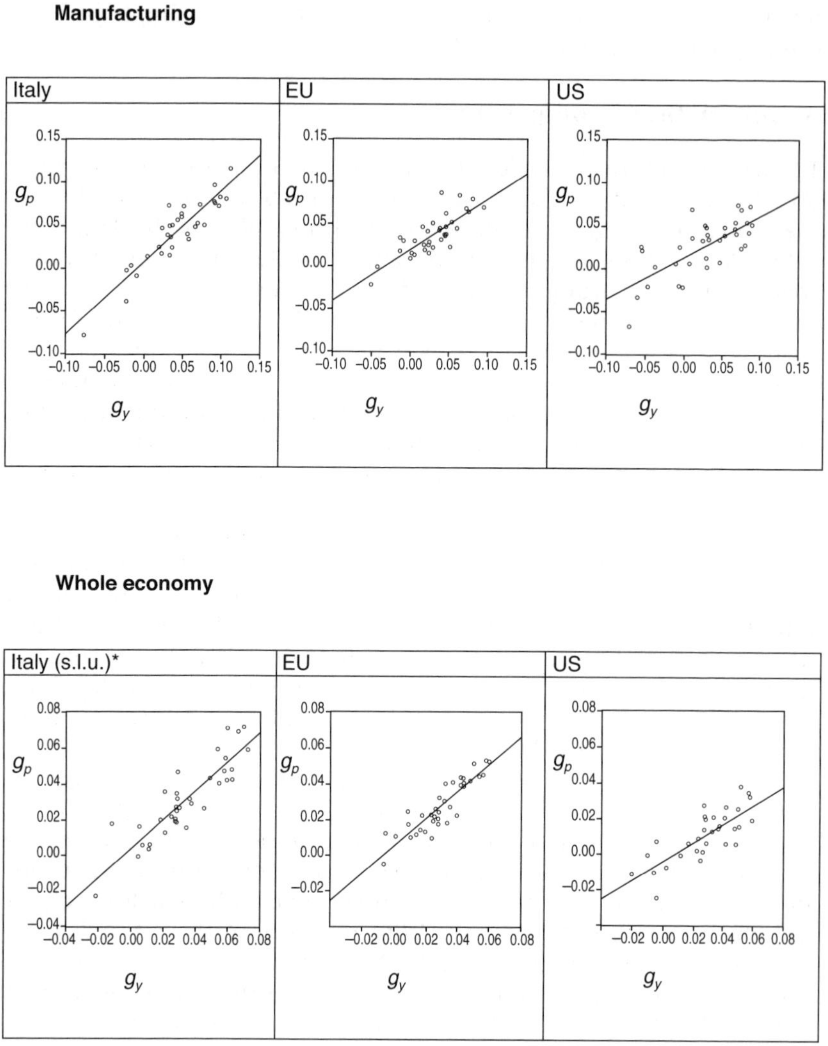

Figure 5.3 Verdoorn's Law – an international comparison, 1960–1997
Note: * In the case of Italy, with regard to the whole economy, the use of standard labour units (s.l.u.) is justified by the unsatisfactory statistical properties of the civilian employment series.

rather a presumption in favour of decreasing returns to scale, but all estimated regressions are rather unsatisfactory. The use of the partial adjustment model does not produce an improvement in our understanding of the possible degree of returns to scale in the United States economy.

Table 5.5 Estimates of the marginal elasticity of employment – an international comparison

Period	Industry						Whole economy					
	Italy		*Europe*		*USA*		*Italy*		*Europe*		*USA*	
1960–97	0.18*		0.41*		0.52*		0.20*		0.25*		0.48*	
1960–97 PA	0.16*	0.28*	0.32*	0.58*	0.57*	0.88	0.21*	0.34*	0.21*	0.51*	0.50*	0.76
1960–80	0.12**		0.29*		0.48*		0.12++		0.12*		0.40*	
1960–80 PA	0.15*	0.23*	0.31*	0.53*	0.56*	0.75	0.17**	0.23**	0.17*	0.41*	0.47*	0.78
1980–97	0.19**		0.49*		0.54*		0.52*		0.74		0.56*	
1980–97 PA	0.20**	0.32**	0.36*	0.72	0.57*	0.86	0.47*	0.94	0.60*	1.07	0.57*	0.76

Notes:
Industry: Industry narrowly defined for Italy; manufacturing for Europe and USA.
1980–97 Industry in Italy: estimates including a dummy for 1993.
Numbers of persons employed except for the whole economy of Italy which is standard labour units.
PA = Model with partial adjustment: first figure is the short-run coefficient and the second is the long-run coefficient.
* Significant at the 5% level: null hypothesis constant returns to scale.
** Significant at the 10% level: null hypothesis constant returns to scale.
\+ The hypothesis of the presence of a partial adjustment mechanism is rejected.

Table 5.6 Estimates of the degree of returns to scale in the general model with capital growth – an international comparison

Period	*Industry*						*Whole economy*					
	Italy		*EU*		*USA*		*Italy*		*EU*		*USA*	
1960–97	1.65*		1.51		0.33		1.42		1.63*		1.10	
1960–97 PA	2.35*	1.72*	2.68*	1.76*	0.87	0.68	1.62^{+}	1.41^{+}	1.22^{+}	1.55^{+}	1.33^{+}	1.19^{+}
1960–80	1.97		2.31		0.17		1.70		2.56*		0.80	
1960–80 PA	3.37*	2.25	4.58*	2.48*	0.58^{+}	0.42^{+}	2.19^{+}	1.70^{+}	3.41^{+}	2.47^{+}	1.02^{+}	1.01^{+}
1980–97	0.60		0.69		0.52		0.58		0.78		1.08	
1980–97 PA	0.94^{+}	0.80^{+}	1.34^{+}	0.93^{+}	0.79^{+}	0.69^{+}	0.31^{+}	0.39^{+}	1.27	0.88	1.32^{+}	1.10^{+}

Notes:
The table reports the sum of the coefficients α and β and the result of the tests on the nature of returns to scale.
PA = Model with partial adjustment. The first figure is the short-run coefficient and the second figure is the long-run coefficient.
* Increasing returns to scale. (An appropriate Wald test rejects the hypothesis of constant return to scale, so that $\alpha + \beta > 1$);
$^{+}$ The hypothesis of the presence of a partial adjustment mechanism is rejected.

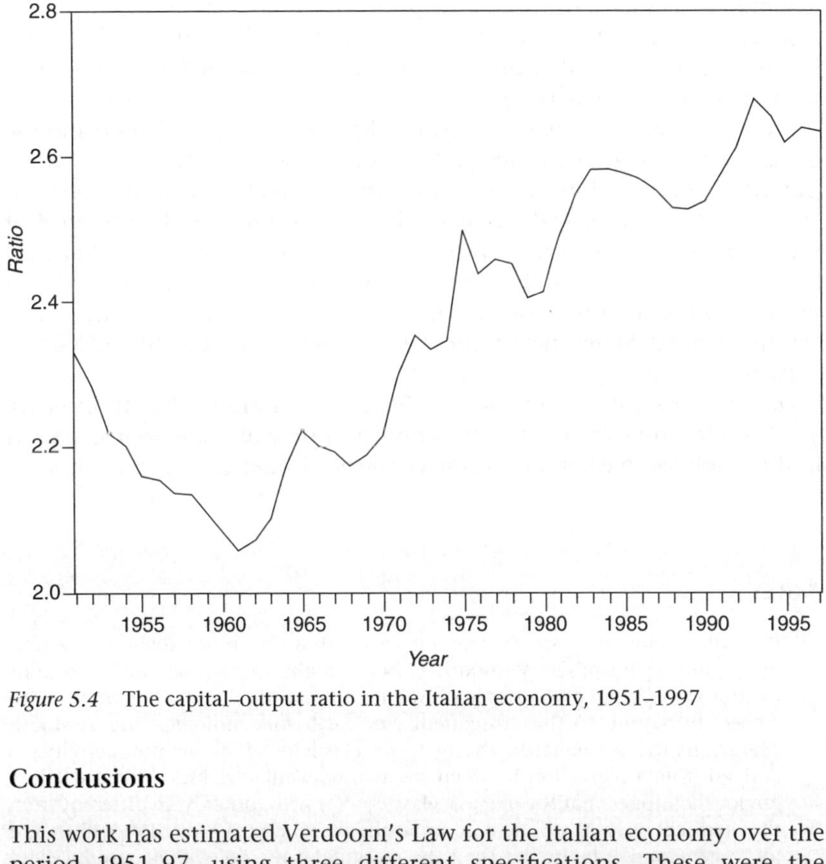

Figure 5.4 The capital–output ratio in the Italian economy, 1951–1997

Conclusions

This work has estimated Verdoorn's Law for the Italian economy over the period 1951–97, using three different specifications. These were the traditional Verdoorn equation, a partial adjustment model and a specification that included the growth of capital in the regressors.

Estimates of the traditional Verdoorn's Law suggest that there are increasing returns to scale both for the whole economy and for all of its sectors. The analysis conducted for selected subperiods indicates, moreover, that this general result appears to be robust, even though the size of returns to scale turns out to be decreasing over time.

The use of a partial adjustment model, however, confirms the presence of increasing returns to scale in the whole sample period and mainly in the earlier years preceding the first oil shock (1973–74), while estimates for the most recent period seem to indicate that returns to scale are increasing only in the short run: in the long run, constant returns to scale cannot be excluded, and there is even a suggestion of decreasing returns to scale in services. Estimates of the more appropriate specification that explicitly includes capital growth, however, confirm that the industrial sector exhibits increasing returns to scale over the whole sample period. This is true, even though the same result is not found in the various subperiods. Finally, nothing definite can be said with regards to the whole economy, with reference to any period.

An international comparison between Italy, the European Union and the United States shows disparities in the results obtained for the various areas. Indeed, the estimation of the more general equation considering both labour and capital growth leads to the conclusion that the presence of increasing returns to scale is justified for the European Union, both for industry and for the whole economy, in the overall sample period and most of all in the earlier years before 1980. On the other hand, the results for the United States never allow the rejection of the hypothesis of constant returns.

To summarise, Verdoorn's Law only seems to hold for Italian industry and both for industry and for the whole economy of the European Union in the whole sample period considered in the estimates.

Notes

1. It is interesting to note that in his original study, motivated by practical programming purposes, Verdoorn (1949) sought to analyse the conditions behind the existence of a stable *constant* elasticity of labour productivity with respect to output. In the subsequent empirical work, however, the Verdoorn coefficient was set equal to the *marginal* elasticity of labour productivity, as derived from a regression between the two relevant variables. This procedure obviously implies that the average elasticity (a) will normally be different from the marginal one, (b) will depend upon the actual rate of growth of output and (c) in general will be higher than the marginal one, since labour productivity growth usually has an autonomous (or exogenous) positive component. This means that the actual Verdoorn coefficient, and thus the degree of returns to scale, will generally be higher than those reported, even though they are not independent of output growth. Kaldor (1966, appendix b) seemed to be at least partially aware of this problem. In his original article, when commenting on the regressions for various sectors of the economy, he tended to attribute a minor significance to the evidence of a positive (marginal) Verdoorn coefficient in those sectors (as agriculture and construction) where the regressions indicated the existence of a high value of the intercept.
2. Bairam (1987a) provides an intuitive and convincing explanation of the reasons that might lead to spurious correlations when using cross-country data. The famous debate between Rowthorn (1975a, 1975b) and Kaldor (1975a) centred around whether or not Japan, because of its special circumstances, should be regarded as being an outlier in the sample of industrial nations. This points to the possible heterogeneity of countries from a technological point of view. A further proof of this heterogeneity will be given in the final part of this essay, when comparing the estimates of the Verdoorn coefficient for Italy, the European Union, and the United States.

3. While differences between the North and the South of Italy are widely regconized, many studies point to the existence of three or more distinct regions in Italy, characterised by different productive structures. These are mainly tied to the characteristics of the so-called 'industrial districts'. An empirical evaluation of the differences in productivity among Italian regions is provided, even though in the context of conditional convergence, by Bianchi and Menegatti (1997).
4. With reference to the Italian economy, particularly, both the first oil crisis and membership of the EMS produced structural breaks in the fields of industrial behaviour and organisation.
5. This does not mean, of course, that cross-sectional data cannot be tested for the existence of structural breaks, by performing an appropriate test on selected subperiods. However, this procedure implies applying the time-series approach to a cross-sectional framework, by working on the temporal dimension of the original data. Furthermore, the time-series approach enables an endogenous determination of when the structural break occurs, without the necessity of imposing it, a priori. Finally, any test for the existence of structural breaks performed on cross-sectional data must assume the rather strong, and not necessarily realistic, assumption that the break occurs at the same time and is of the same dimension for all the countries or regions in the sample. If this is not the case, spurious and possibly false results might be obtained.
6. Annual data are less subject to a short-run bias, especially when the analysis is conducted, as in this chapter, over a very long time span.
7. Standard labour units are defined as the hypothetical number of people that would be employed if everyone worked a number of hours corresponding to the contractual requirements. The concept, then, is a close substitute for the total number of hours actually worked and is less sensitive to the short-run phenomenon of labour hoarding.
8. This is the longest time span for which homogeneous data exist. In fact, since 1998 the Italian Central Institute of Statistics (ISTAT) has changed the methodological criteria used in the classification and evaluation of the national accounts data, moving from the SEC79 to the SEC95 system. This has produced not only different estimates of value added and standard labour units, but also resulted in a change in the allocation of economic activities to various sectors. The new series are not comparable with the previous ones. All data for the Italian economy used in the calculations have been taken from the national accounts series provided by ISTAT. Data for earlier years (1951–69) have been taken from the reconstruction by Rossi, et al. (1993), when available. Otherwise, they have been reconstructed recursively by applying the annual rates of change of the relevant variables in the old ISTAT national accounts data to the new series. The capital stock series has been taken from Rossi, et al. (1993). In this case data for the most recent years have been computed by adding annual net investments, as defined by ISTAT, to the existing capital stock. An alternative estimate of this same variable is provided by Datastream. The two series are highly correlated (coefficient of determination of 0.993) and can thus be used interchangeably.
9. Data regarding the European Union and the United States have been taken from the OECD National Accounts and Economic Outlook Statistics. In this context, industry refers to manufacturing and labour is defined as civilian employment, rather than standard labour units. Data on the capital stock have been retrieved from Datastream. With reference to Europe, a proxy for the whole Union has

been constructed, corresponding to the capital stock of the five major European countries – France, Germany, Italy, Spain and the United Kingdom – which account for more than 80 percent of total GDP.

10. This is not a necessary condition, since equations (5.1) and (5.2) can be derived from other types of production functions or from different analytical frameworks such as Kaldor's technical progress function (cf., for instance, Dixon and Thirlwall (1975) and Bairam (1987a)). In this essay, however, we shall stick to the traditional Cobb–Douglas interpretation of the law, as endorsed by Verdoorn himself (1949, 1980).
11. Cf., for instance, Bairam (1987a, p. 23, note 10).
12. Comparing equations (5.2) and (5.7) it is easy to check that $1 - b = d - e = (1 - \alpha)/\beta$, so that $1 - b < 1$ implies $\alpha + \beta > 1$. Notice, however, that while the estimate of the coefficient $(d - e)$ allows deriving conclusions about the nature of returns, nothing can be said about their actual size, since the individual values of α and β cannot be ascertained.
13. It can be easily checked that under the assumptions made, we have the following relationship between the parameters: $a = \rho/\beta$; $1 - b = 1/\beta$.
14. The condition is sufficient since $1 - b < 1$ implies that $\beta > 1$ and, a fortiori, $\alpha + \beta > 1$ for any positive α. However it must be noted that the condition is not necessary since it is possible that $1 - b > 1$ and $\alpha + \beta > 1$.
15. Cf. Verdoorn (1949, mathematical appendix), and Thirlwall (1980, p. 307).
16. Indeed $1 - b < 1$ in equation (5.2) only implies that $\alpha f + \beta > 1$. If $f > 1$, this condition may be satisfied even when $\alpha + \beta < 1$.
17. From a purely econometric standpoint, the traditional estimates of Verdoorn's Law using growth rates of the relevant variables are to be preferred to the alternative specifications in levels, because the series are shown to be integrated. As the appropriate test seems to indicate the absence of cointegration, only a specification using first differences is appropriate.
18. The same pattern of behaviour characterises the experience of the construction industry. In this sector, furthermore, value added grows, initially at a very rapid pace, until 1970, but remains practically constant afterwards. As a consequence of this, the estimated Verdoorn equations for the construction industry are never significant.
19. And thus including manufacturing, energy and public utilities.
20. That is the hypothesis that the capital–output ratio is constant or that the capital stock grows at a constant rate through time.
21. This result can be easily understood by considering that fact that the bias in the estimate of $(1 - b)$ is equal to *cov(labour, capital)/var(labour)* × *cov(output, capital)/var(capital)*. Since *cov(output, capital)* is positive, if *cov(labour, capital)* is negative, the coefficient $(1 - b)$ will be underestimated.
22. As Figure 5.2 clearly illustrates, the same evidence characterises the behaviour of the construction sector over the whole sample period and that of industry after 1980.
23. In the case of public services, however, labour productivity data are not quite significant, since sectoral value added is normally defined as incurred costs, quite closely corresponding to paid salaries. In estimating Verdoorn's Law, one might end up with spurious correlations between employment growth and the sum of the same variable plus real wage growth.
24. Of course, a similar partial adjustment model can be easily derived under the alternative assumption of a constant rate of growth of the capital stock.
25. It is clear, from equation (5.17), that $i = (1 - \alpha)/\beta$.

26. Again, from equation (5.17), it is clear that $i/(1 - j)=(1 - \alpha)/\beta$.
27. When an international comparison about the nature of returns is performed, the labour input data are normally defined in terms of civilian employment.
28. The choice of this more limited period is suggested by the opportunity of using less heterogeneous data. The fact that the way in which labour statistics are calculated has been changed several times by ISTAT in the postwar period means that any reconstruction is bound to be arbitrary.
29. In particular, the assumption that the capital–output ratio is constant is not convincing for the Italian economy since, as shown in Figure 5.4 (p.131), its value is highly variable over time and shows a sharp increase after 1960.
30. This critique was firstly proposed by Wolfe (1968).
31. Again, as beforehand, regressions in growth rates are to be preferred to the corresponding regressions in levels because of the problem, outlined above, concerning the absence of cointegration among series.
32. See, for instance, Bairam (1987a, p. 31). An alternative approach to that followed in the paper, as suggested by McCombie and de Ridder (1984), would be to construct a measure of total factor input, corresponding to a weighted average of capital and labour, and to estimate a specification such as equation (5.2), with reference to this new variable. From a theoretical point of view, however, this approach has the drawback of not having a satisfactory theoretical justification for the weights to be given to capital and labour. Moreover, empirically, estimates of equation (5.2) using total factor input within a time-series framework always produce a positive intercept, thus implying an unacceptable negative value of multifactor productivity growth.
33. The weak exogeneity test has been conducted according to the procedure illustrated by Engle and Hendry (1993) – that is, by regressing the growth rate of employment, considered to be the relevant decision variable of the firms, upon the set of instruments consisting of its lagged value, the current and lagged growth rates of capital and, in a truly Kaldorian spirit, the growth rate of exports. Since the residuals of this auxiliary regression, when introduced as an additional independent variable in the main regression, are not significant, the weak exogeneity hypothesis holds and the basic OLS technique can be used.
34. In particular, a Wald test for the null hypothesis of $\alpha + \beta = 1$ is performed.
35. As noted above, labour input data are based on civilian employment figures. With reference to the whole Italian economy, however, the unsatisfactory statistical properties of the series (the definition of numbers of persons employed has been changed several times in the estimation period) make it desirable to use standard labour units instead. An illustration of the differences implied by the use of the two alternative concepts has been provided in the previous section and in Table 5.3.

6
The Verdoorn Law: Some Evidence from Non-Parametric Frontier Analysis

Sergio Destefanis[1]

Introduction

In his inaugural Cambridge lecture, Kaldor (1966) refers to what he terms Verdoorn's Law – the statistical relationship between the rate of growth of labour productivity and the rate of growth of output – as evidence of the pervasive existence in industrial economies of static and dynamic economies of scale. Since this contribution, it has often been suggested that attempts at estimating the law (including, of course, Kaldor's own one) suffer from serious specification problems. As is well expressed by McCombie and Thirlwall (1994, p. 167), 'the debate over the Verdoorn Law would make a good textbook example of the problems that can beset statistical inference!' As can be seen from the surveys in Bairam (1987a) and in McCombie and Thirlwall (1994, ch. 2), problems with estimating the law are related to three major issues.

First, it has been pointed out that if no variable measuring the stock of capital (or its growth) is included in the estimated specification, then no definite conclusion can be made about the nature of returns to scale, unless strong assumptions are made about the evolution of the capital–output ratio. Second, when estimating Verdoorn's Law using OLS, there are problems in positing that either inputs or output are exogenous variables, since most models of economic development imply that neither of them can fulfil this requirement. Third, the statement has often been made that Verdoorn's Law might spuriously arise from some other relationship present in the data. Thus, if different observations experience different rates of growth for exogenous technological progress, and the estimation procedure does not allow for these differences, Verdoorn's Law might just be the spurious result of posing output growth rates *inclusive of exogenous technical progress* against input growth rates. Another problem arises because of the presence of an accounting identity in the data relevant for estimation of the Verdoorn relationship. Since total value added must by definition be equal to the sum of labour and non-labour incomes, the question arises as to whether an estimated relationship between output and (labour and capital) inputs merely reflects this identity or has some behavioural content. Finally, if the law is estimated using time-series data, it is maintained that the positive relationship between the rate of growth of labour productivity and the rate of growth of output might just reflect the existence of labour hoarding in the short run (the so-called Okun's Law).

A further issue is that typically different values for the returns to scale are found when estimating the law in level (static) or rate-of-growth (dynamic) terms. Various explanations have been put forward for this static–dynamic paradox, ranging from the impact of measurement errors to the fact that the correct static model could be a non-linear technical progress function rather than the usually adopted Cobb–Douglas production function (McCombie, 1982a).

In the present work, we show how the nature of economies of scale can be assessed using a set of procedures based on non-parametric frontier analysis.[2] We suggest that this exercise is a useful addition to the existing literature on the law, because these techniques allow a novel approach to the issues of simultaneity and spuriousness. It should also be pointed out immediately that through non-parametric frontier analysis it is possible to characterise qualitatively the nature of returns to scale for each observation, yielding important information on the heterogeneity of observations across both time and space. Indeed, even an approximate quantitative measure of returns to scale can be produced for each observation. By way of application, we assess economies of scale across a sample of 52 countries, taken from the Penn World Table (mark 5.6).

Note that, although in principle non-parametric frontier analysis can deal with variables both in levels and rates of growth, in our opinion the treatment of the latter requires a more complex analysis and shall be taken up in future work. Also, while the empirical procedures here proposed have in our view some strong advantages, it is fair to say at the outset that they also entail drawbacks, which shall be duly outlined. However, these drawbacks are on their way to being resolved in the literature on non-parametric frontier analysis, and it is hoped that the present work might be considered as a useful first attempt, showing the relevance of this literature for the problem at hand, and fostering further analytical developments.

The rest of the work proceeds as follows. In the next section, we expound more fully the specification issues briefly described above. Next, we briefly describe the set of procedures taken from non-parametric frontier analysis which are to be used in the present work, while in the following section we argue in favour of their expediency in the present context. Then, we describe the data utilised in the empirical example and present the empirical results. The final section offers some concluding remarks.

Interpreting and estimating Verdoorn's Law

It is convenient to couch our discussion of the following issues in terms of a simple algebraic representation of the law, which mirrors the formulation given in Dixon and Thirlwall (1975). Let us consider first a linear representation of Kaldor's technical progress function (Kaldor, 1957):

$$r = d + \alpha_0 k \tag{6.1}$$

where r is the rate of growth of output per worker, d is the rate of disembodied technical progress and k is the rate of growth of capital per worker. Now, positing:

$$d = \alpha_1 + \beta_1 q \tag{6.2}$$
$$k = \alpha_2 + \beta_2 q \tag{6.3}$$

where β_1 is a measure of static and dynamic economies of scale,[3] β_2 is an 'accelerator' parameter and q is the rate of growth of output, one can obtain Kaldor's formulation of the Verdoorn Law, by substituting equations (6.2) and (6.3) into equation (6.1):

$$r = \lambda_0 + \lambda_1 q \tag{6.4}$$

where $\lambda_0 = (\alpha_1 + \alpha_0\alpha_2)$, and $\lambda_1 = (\beta_1 + \alpha_0\beta_2)$.

This formulation makes it clear that the Verdoorn relationship exists even in the absence of economies of scale ($\beta_1 = 0$), provided that $\alpha_0\beta_2$ and k differ from zero (the latter condition holds out of steady-state growth). Accordingly, equation (6.4) may be an interesting expression for the modelling of growth and development, but does not allow us to appraise unconditionally the degree of economies of scale. The latter might be assessed in the following expression where only equation (6.2) is substituted in equation (6.1):

$$r = \alpha_1 + \beta_1 q + \alpha_0 k \tag{6.5}$$

The above formulation complements the more usual arguments[4] as to why no definite conclusion can be drawn about the nature of returns to scale, unless explicit allowance is made for the capital stock. This result also suggests some reasons for the lack of parameter stability of equation (6.4). Indeed, it is unlikely that equation (6.3) may satisfactorily represent the determination of k, and hence even if the other behavioural relationships are stable, equation (6.4) – but not equation (6.5) – must show a lack of parameter stability.

In the present work, we take the (not very controversial) view that if Kaldor brought to the fore in his inaugural lecture what he termed Verdoorn's Law, it was mainly because he was interested in favourable evidence for the existence of static and dynamic economies of scale. Hence, it will be equation (6.5), and not equation (6.4), that constitutes the focus of the empirical analysis, and it will be this relation which we will refer to as the Verdoorn Law. This is a fundamental point in the research strategy adopted here, because, as will become clearer in the next section, while non-parametric frontier analysis is likely to yield interesting insights about the degree of economies of scale in equation (6.5), it is rather ill suited to the estimation of equation (6.4).

A point which has often been made in the Verdoorn's Law literature[5] is that in estimating the Verdoorn Law by OLS, there are problems in deciding which are the correct regressors, since most models of economic development imply that r, q or k cannot be exogenous variables. Hence neither equation (6.5), nor its reparameterisation as:

$$n = \alpha'_1 + \beta'_1 q + \alpha'_0 k \tag{6.5a}$$

where n is the rate of growth of the labour input (and there is no risk of spurious correlation between the left- and right-hand side of the equation), are likely to yield unbiased and consistent estimates for their parameters when estimated by OLS.

This is also true of:

$$q = \alpha''_1 + \beta''_1 n + \alpha''_0 k \tag{6.5b}$$

(which is often referred to as the Rowthorn specification). Related to this is the finding that while specifications like equation (6.5a) provide evidence in favour of the existence of economies of scale, equation (6.5b) most often does not.[6] A natural econometric solution to this conundrum is the adoption of instrumental variable techniques, but, by and large, this does not provide any conclusive evidence.[7] Another solution could be the adoption of cointegration analysis, which seems to yield evidence in favour of increasing returns to scale.[8] As the latter analysis is carried out using time-series data, its discussion can be better addressed below.

It has been recalled above that Verdoorn's Law has often been alleged to arise spuriously from some other relationship present in the data. First of all, if different observations experience different rates of growth for exogenous technological progress, the α_1 of equation (6.2), and the estimation procedure does not allow for these differences, Verdoorn's Law might just be the spurious result of regressing productivity growth against output growth rates *inclusive of differing rates of exogenous technical progress.* Consider the case depicted in Figure 6.1.

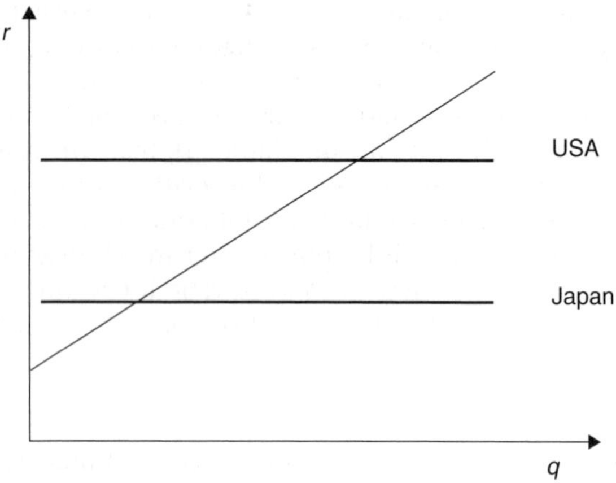

Figure 6.1

By hypothesis, in Figure 6.1 the rate of growth of productivity does not depend on the rate of growth of output in each given country, and the corresponding Verdoorn relationship is given by a horizontal line. Yet, exogenous technical progress may differ across countries, yielding different values for r. A spurious Verdoorn relationship is obtained when r is regressed on q using cross-country data, and the countries with the higher exogenous technical progress also have the higher q, either coincidentally or because α_1 is a source of output growth. Thus, unless the estimation procedure controls for the possibility that α_1 might differ across observations, the Verdoorn relationship has little meaning. A similar argument applies to specifications in levels, where the role of different rates of exogenous technical progress must however be taken by different levels of technology.

Attempts to deal explicitly with this problem include Gomulka (1983) and Bairam (1986), who use dummy variables to model differences in exogenous technical progress. Yet, as acknowledged in Bairam (1987d, p. 26), this procedure is costly in terms of degrees of freedom, which might result in inefficient estimates and the impossibility to choose the appropriate specification. Another possible solution is the use of appropriate data sets. Thus, McCombie and de Ridder (1983, 1984) and Bairam (1987b, 1988c) estimated the law on cross-regional data, under the hypothesis that differences in technology across regions in a given country must be small. This, however, might not always be true (consider for instance, all the references in the Mezzogiorno literature to the technological differences – at least in a broad sense – between Northern and Southern Italy).

It has also been suggested that estimating the law on time-series data for a given country might also circumvent this difficulty. This is only true if exogenous technical progress does not occur through time, which seems a rather large assumption, or, again, if one controls for exogenous technical progress. It is not clear, for instance, whether the time-series works quoted above (Harris and Lau, 1998; Harris and Liu, 1999) are impervious to this critique, since their specifications do not include variables representing exogenous technical progress. Indeed, estimating the law using time-series data might also present other problems. It has often been pointed out that such an exercise incurs the risk of mixing the (long-run) Verdoorn relationship with the so-called Okun's Law, reflecting the existence of labour hoarding in the short run (see on this McCombie and Thirlwall, 1994, pp. 197–200). This would allegedly provide spurious evidence in favour of the law, but, as pointed out in Jefferson (1988), the presence of adjustment costs for other inputs (in particular, for the capital stock) is likely to produce biases with the opposite sign. In any case, all these arguments signal a broad consensus about the need to assess the law on the long-run (low-frequency) component of the data, filtering out other components through appropriate time-series techniques. Again, this argument is just as relevant to specifications in levels as it is to rate-of-growth ones.

Finally, a problem of identification arises because an accounting identity underlies the data relevant for estimation of the Verdoorn relationship (see McCombie and Thirlwall, 1994, pp. 212–16). Since total value added must by definition be equal to the sum of labour and non-labour incomes, the question arises as to whether an estimated relationship between output and (labour and capital) inputs merely reflects this identity or has some behavioural content. Indeed, for any given country (or region), value added is defined by:

$$Q_t = w_t N_t + r_t K_t \tag{6.6}$$

In terms of rates of growth (or of natural logs), the above formula becomes:

$$q_t = a\varphi_t + (1 - a)\phi_t + an_t + (1 - a)k_t \tag{6.7}$$

where φ and ϕ are the rates of growth of real wages and of the real rental price of capital, and it is assumed for simplicity (this is not strictly necessary for the argument, but it simplifies the functional forms considered; see McCombie and Dixon, 1991) that factor shares are constant. Now, consider the following relation (which could be a Cobb–Douglas production function in dynamic terms, or a Rowthorn-like reparameterisation of Verdoorn's Law; for expositional purposes we here assume that there is no loss of generality in doing so):

$$q_t = \lambda + \alpha n_t + \beta k_t \tag{6.8}$$

If the sum $[a\varphi_t + (1 - a)\phi_t]$ can be expressed by a constant, ω (as is often the case, see McCombie and Dixon, 1991), then the estimation of equation (6.8) will just reflect the underlying identity, equation (6.7).

Matters differ to some extent for the usual cross-country (or cross-region) set-up adopted for estimating the law. In this case (always assuming constant factor shares), the underlying identity can be represented by:

$$q_i = a\varphi_i + (1 - a)\phi_i + an_i + (1 - a)k_i \tag{6.9}$$

or, if $\omega_i = [a\varphi_i + (1 - a)\phi_i]$, by:

$$q_i = \omega_i + an_i + (1 - a)k_i \tag{6.9a}$$

On the other hand, Verdoorn's Law can be represented as:

$$q_i = \lambda + \alpha n_i + \beta k_i \tag{6.10}$$

or, if the degree of returns to scale is represented by ν, as:

$$q_i = \lambda + \nu[an_i + (1 - a)k_i] \tag{6.11}$$

Now, across countries it is no longer appropriate to suppose that ω_i is a constant term identical for each country. On the other hand, consider the growth in total factor productivity, $\theta_i = q_i - [an_i + (1 - a)k_i]$. We can write:

$$\theta_i = \omega_i = \lambda + (\nu - 1)[an_i + (1 - a)k_i] \tag{6.11a}$$

$$\theta_i = \omega_i = \lambda/\nu + [(\nu - 1)/\nu]q_i \tag{6.11b}$$

Hence, the accounting identity equation (6.9) underlies the assessment of returns to scale that can be carried out through the estimation of equation (6.10) or equation (6.11). Consequently, what can be ascertained through estimation of the latter is whether a faster weighted growth of real input prices turns out to be associated with a faster growth of output (or with a faster-weighted growth of inputs). This is of interest, but does not allow us to assess the role that increasing returns to scale, exogenous technical progress, or even capital accumulation might have in this correlation. To do so, and in particular to disentangle the role of returns to scale, we require a priori knowledge on the magnitude and bias of technical change, as well as on the determination of income distribution in the economies under examination.

Non-parametric frontier analysis: a brief survey

An overview

A unifying feature of virtually all of the empirical studies carried out so far on the Verdoorn Law is that they have been couched in terms of the econometric estimation of a constant-parameter function (be it considered as a technical progress function or a more traditional production function) fitted to the whole sample. Naturally, this presumes that a constant-parameter function can adequately represent the technology of all productive units being examined, an assumption which has rarely left been unchallenged when put to an empirical test.[9] However, utilising a constant-parameter function is not the only way in which a productive technology can be modelled. A varying-parameter function could be estimated, or, even more fundamentally, some important characteristics of the technology under examination (including the degree of returns to scale) could be assessed without representing this technology through a given functional form. In such a case, mathematical programming techniques are used in order to build a production set which must satisfy some properties (usually strong disposability and convexity). We choose to follow here the second alternative because, as will be argued below, it has some important advantages in the present ambit.

To start with, since these so-called non-parametric methods provide estimates of the upper boundary of a production set (the so-called production frontier) without supposing the existence of a functional relationship between inputs and outputs, they need only a limited number of restrictive assumptions about the production process. Beginning with the seminal contribution of Farrell (1957), these techniques are used to build the frontier of a production set (satisfying some properties which are specified a priori). The frontier is supported by some of the observed producers, which are defined as efficient. It is of paramount importance to stress that non-parametric techniques share the hypothesis that the distance of non-efficient producers from the frontier must be entirely explained by a factor (or a set of factors), traditionally termed inefficiency, which obeys a one-sided statistical distribution.

Non-parametric methods are usually divided between those directly related to Farrell's contribution (usually gathered under the label of Data Envelopment Analysis, or DEA) and those based on the Free Disposal Hull (FDH) approach first proposed in Deprins et al. (1984). In the latter case, the only property imposed on the production set is strong input and output disposability, while in DEA the additional hypothesis of convexity is made.

More formally, in FDH, for a given set of producers Y_0, the reference set[10] $Y(Y_0)$ is characterised, in terms of an observation i, by the following postulate:

$$(\mathbf{X}^i, \mathbf{Y}^i) \text{ observed}, (\mathbf{X}^i + \mathbf{a}, \mathbf{Y}^i - \mathbf{b}) \in Y(Y_0), \qquad \mathbf{a}, \mathbf{b} \geq 0$$

where **a** and **b** are vectors of free disposal of input and output, respectively. In other words, due to the possibility of free input and output disposability, the reference set includes all the producers which are using the same or more inputs and which are producing the same or less output in relation to observation *i*.

Let us take as an example Figure 6.2, where we are considering a technology with one input (*X*) and one output (*Y*). The input–output pairs correspond with a cross-section of producers examined at a given point in time. Beginning with observation B, we define every observation located at its right and/or below it (that is, with more input and the same output, or with less output and the same input; or else with more input and less output, as F) as dominated by B. As for E, it is not dominated by B, because it uses more input but it is also producing more output, but it is dominated by A. On the other hand, C and D are not dominated by either A or B, because they produce less output but are also using less input. Similarly, A is not dominated by any observation, because it uses more input but it is also producing more output. As a matter of fact, A, B, C and D are not dominated by any producer belonging to the reference set.

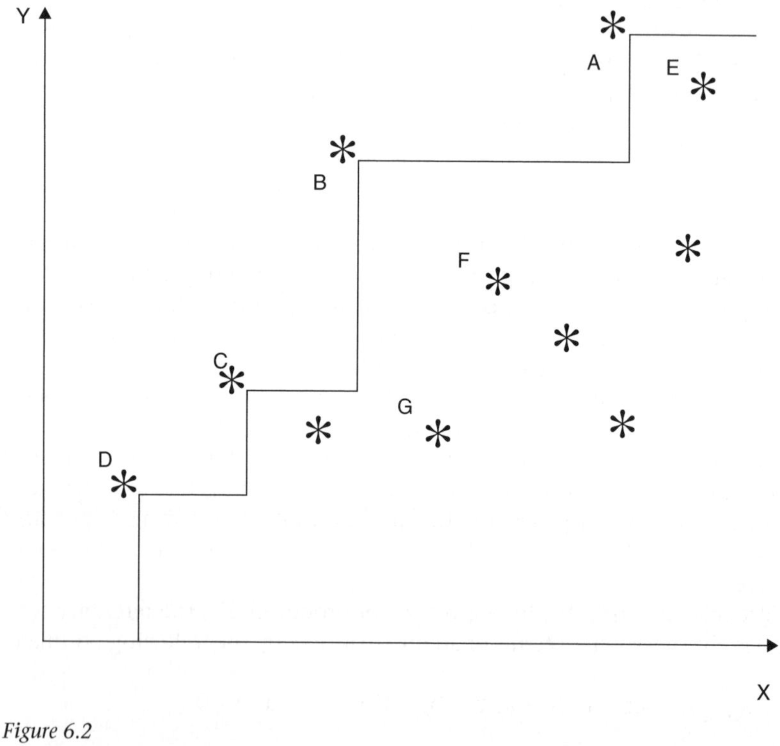

Figure 6.2

In the FDH approach, this procedure of comparison is carried out for every observation, and the observations dominated by other producers are considered as inefficient. Those units which are not dominated by any other observation are considered instead as efficient producers, belonging to the frontier of the reference set.

In DEA, identification of the production frontier is carried out through the construction of a convex hull around the production set, based upon the a priori specification of strong input and output disposability *and convexity* for the production technology. In order to build this convex hull, appropriate linear programming procedures are used. In Figure 6.3, examples of three kinds of convex hulls typical of the application of DEA are shown for a one-input one-output technology. Again, the points on the Y–X planes are input–output pairs corresponding to a cross-section of producers taken at a given point in time. In DEA-CRS, the identification of the convex hull is based on the hypothesis of constant returns to scale, while in DEA-NIRS the (less restrictive) hypothesis adopted is that of non-increasing returns to scale, and, lastly, in DEA-VRS the convex hull is allowed to show a particular type of variable returns to scale (increasing first, and decreasing afterwards).[11]

In both FDH and DEA the distance of producers from the frontier is deemed to give their measures of technical efficiency, or, for short, their efficiency scores. Typically, the (output-oriented or input-oriented) measure of Debreu–Farrell is used. If the measure is output-oriented, technical efficiency is given by the relative output expansion needed to bring a producer on the frontier, for given inputs. A producer who is technically efficient (and who is therefore on the frontier of reference) will not be able to attain such an expansion, achieving an efficiency score equal to one. If the measure of Debreu–Farrell is input-oriented, it is given by the relative input contraction needed to bring a producer on the frontier, for given outputs.[12]

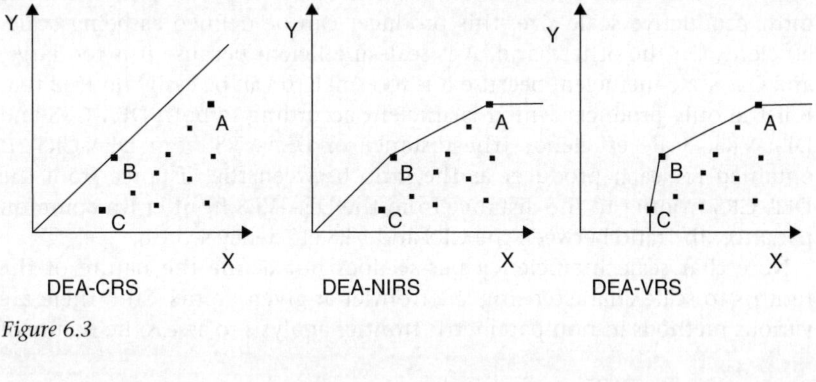

Figure 6.3

Clearly, the adoption of FDH allows us to leave behind the hypothesis of convexity of the production set typical of DEA. This means that the frontier obtained through FDH is likely to fit the data more closely than the one obtained through DEA if the reference set is characterised (at least locally) by the existence of non-convexities. Moreover, it is important to emphasise that, unlike DEA (where the inefficient producers are dominated by virtual observations located on the convex hull of the production set), in FDH an inefficient producer is necessarily dominated by at least another well identified, actually existing producer.

The possibility of building a frontier of the reference set based on actually existing producers, and to make direct comparisons between these and the units dominated by them, can be regarded as one of the major advantages of FDH. For instance, in the context of cross-country comparisons, this allows to identify some 'clubs' of countries constituted by a dominant unit and the relative dominated units, which must share relatively similar technologies. Also, as the frontier of the reference set is made up of actually existing units (rather than by a convex hull), FDH will be less sensitive to the presence in the reference set of outliers (or of erroneously measured values) than DEA. More precisely, the section of the frontier influenced by the presence of the outlier will be smaller with FDH than with DEA.

Yet, a drawback of the definition of reference frontier in the FDH approach is that a producer can belong to it without dominating any other observation. Such a producer (like D in Figure 6.2) could be defined as efficient only because is located in an area of the production set where there are no other observations with which it could be compared.

Non-parametric frontier analysis and returns to scale

The treatment of returns to scale in non-parametric frontier analysis has been first treated for convex technologies like the one depicted in Figure 6.4.

We can see here that, according to the DEA-VRS technology, producers A, B and C are all efficient. However, only B takes advantage of the scale of production consistent with the maximum productivity (or, correspondingly, the minimum average cost). Since the scale of production of B is the most productive scale size, this producer can be defined as being scale-efficient. On the other hand, A is scale-inefficient because it is too large, and C is scale-inefficient because it is too small. It can be easily noticed that B is the only producer which is efficient according to both DEA-CRS and DEA-VRS. Scale efficiency (the distance of DEA-VRS from DEA-CRS) is obtained for each producer as the ratio between the distance from the DEA-CRS frontier to the distance from the DEA-VRS frontier (in common parlance, the ratio between the CRS and VRS efficiency scores).

Note that scale inefficiency per se does not define the nature of the returns to scale characterising the frontier at given points. Still, there are various methods in non-parametric frontier analysis to assess the nature of

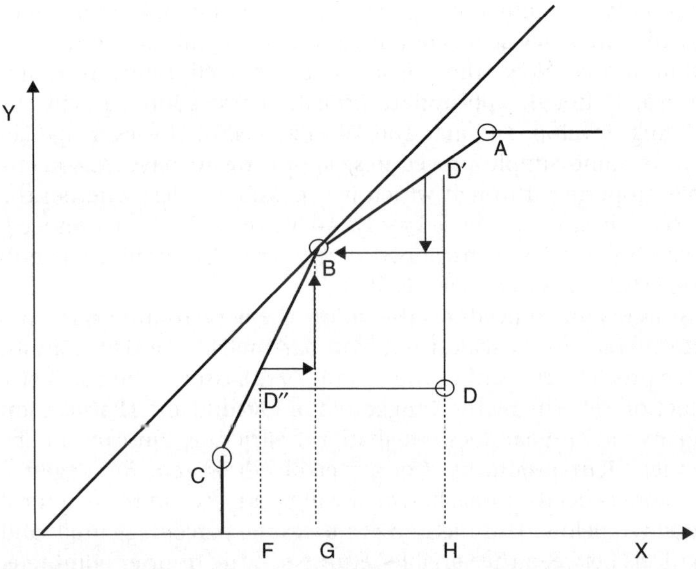

Figure 6.4

returns to scale on the frontier point relevant for any given producer (see the discussions in Førsund, 1996a, or in Kerstens and Vanden Eeckaut, 1999). Basically, one must ascertain whether the frontier point relevant for an inefficient producer according to the variable-returns-to-scale technology must be scaled up or down to obtain the frontier point relevant for an inefficient producer according to the constant-returns-to-scale technology. In the first case, the frontier exhibits increasing returns to scale, while the contrary holds true in the opposite case. If the two frontier points coincide, the frontier exhibits constant returns to scale.

Note that, as a consequence of the hypothesis of variable returns to scale, the frontier point relevant for an inefficient producer might exhibit increasing returns to scale in the sense of input reduction, and decreasing returns to scale in the sense of output expansion. Also, this way to characterise returns to scale implies that at least one producer must exhibit constant returns to scale. But this may not make much sense if all the scale-inefficient units to which this producer can be compared are either larger or smaller than it (that is, in the case in which it might be impossible to define a technically optimal scale of production). These possibilities, as well as their empirical relevance, will be taken up again in what follows.

Naturally, one could also ask whether this qualitative assessment of the nature of returns to scale might depend on statistically insignificant discrepancies between the constant-returns-to-scale and the variable-returns-to-scale technology. Strictly speaking, the answer to this depends on the possibility of constructing, for each observation, confidence intervals for the efficiency scores obtained under the alternative returns-to-scale assumptions. Now, the construction of such intervals is not straightforward, although appropriate bootstrap procedures are in the process of being developed (Simar and Wilson, 2000). However, Banker (1996) suggests some simple procedures, appearing to have reasonable small-sample properties, through which it is possible to test whether the production set is best characterised by DEA-CRS or by DEA-VRS (indeed, DEA-VRS, which is the less constrained model, can also provide the null hypothesis for DEA-NIRS or for DEA-NDRS).

There exist also some procedures that allow the derivation of quantitative measure of returns to scale from non-parametric frontier analysis. Some of these procedures (Banker and Thrall, 1992) assume the convexity of the production set. The method suggested in Førsund and Hjalmarsson (1979) and Førsund (1996a) does not share this stricture, but can only be applied to inefficient producers. Cooper et al. (2000, ch. 5) suggest a simpler and more general approach, which will be adopted in the empirical analysis presented below. This method evaluates the percentage input and output variations between the variable-returns-to-scale frontier point relevant to any given observation and the corresponding most productive scale size. For example, taking observation D in Figure 6.4, one first singles out the variable-returns-to-scale frontier points (*D′* in the output-increasing sense, and *D″* in the input-reducing sense) and the most productive scale size (*B*, in both senses). Then, the output-orientated measure of scale elasticity is found dividing the percentage output variation between *D″* and *B* by the corresponding percentage input variation. Analogously, the input-orientated measure of scale elasticity is found dividing the percentage output variation between *D′* and *B* by the corresponding percentage input variation. Finally, an average measure of scale elasticity is obtained as the weighted average of the input- and output-orientated measures (weights being given by the relative amplitude of the relevant input variations – *FG* and *GH* in this case). When dealing with multi-input multi-output technologies, all the above applies to radial (equiproportional) input and output variations. Naturally, this procedure yields indeterminate results for observations (like *B*) already located at their most productive scale size. This entails no loss of information, as the elasticity of scale of such producers is, by definition, equal to one.

Recently, a class of models has been proposed (Bogetoft, 1996) that preserves most of the flexibility of FDH, while increasing the scope for comparability among producers. These models are of particular interest in the present analysis, because they allow an explicit treatment of returns to scale within non-convex production sets. In line with Kerstens and Vanden Eeckaut (1999), we see these models as refinements of FDH. In FDH-CRS (Figure 6.5) any producer is compared with proportional

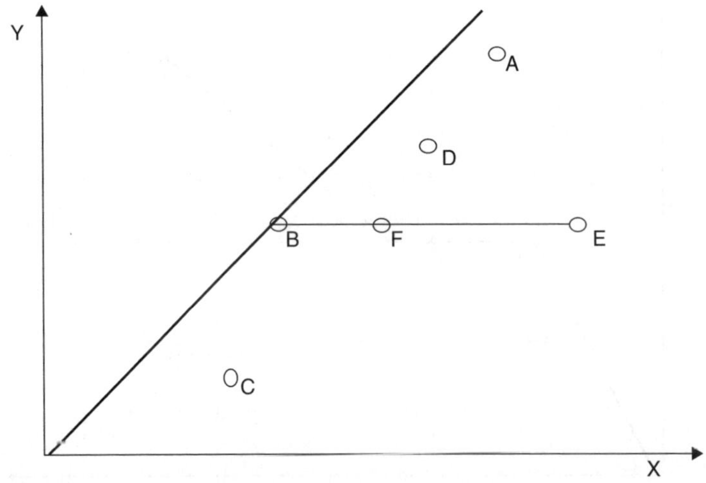

Figure 6.5

rescalings of all other producers (still allowing for non-convexities that can arise from the advantages of specialising in given output- or input-mixes)[13].

In FDH-NIRS (Figure 6.6), any producer is compared with smaller proportional rescalings of all other producers; in FDH-NDRS (Figure 6.7) the opposite is true and producers can only be compared to larger proportional rescalings of other producers.

In this manner, while comparison is no longer restricted to actual producers, any observation is still dominated by a clearly identifiable rescaling of another producer. What is more for present purposes, the assessment of returns to scale can be carried out (along the lines suggested above) in a framework no longer restricted by the assumption of convexity. These considerations suggest the adoption of these models for the empirical application to be presented below, also because, as explained in Kerstens and Vanden Eeckaut (1999), one can define and construct a FDH-VRS model which is constituted by the intersection of the FDH-NIRS and FDH-NDRS models.

Non-parametric frontier analysis and the Verdoorn Law

In our opinion, non-parametric frontier analysis has some distinctive strong points for the assessment of returns to scale. To start with, it seems important to be able to carry out such an assessment without making any assumption about the functional form. Also, the possibility to appraise the nature of returns to scale for each observation yields potentially important information on the heterogeneity of observations across both time and

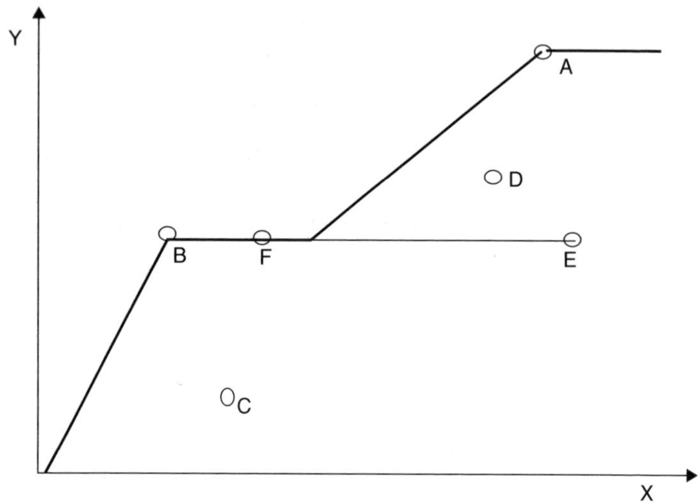

Figure 6.6

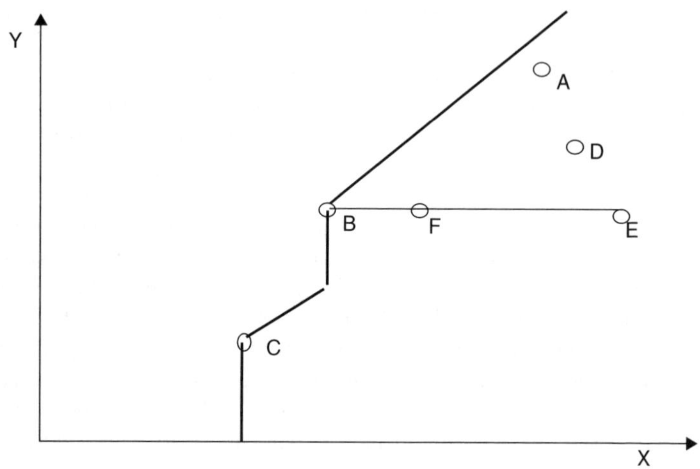

Figure 6.7

space. However, there are other arguments in favour of non-parametric frontier analysis, which are even more closely linked to the empirical debate over the law.

Consider first the (closely related) problems of measurement errors and simultaneity bias. These are very serious issues for econometric analysis, especially in the cross-section set-up so typical for the estimation of the law. Most probably, they also explain why different values are obtained for returns to scale when either inputs or output are taken as dependent variables. In non-parametric analysis these problems are, in some sense, assumed away without great loss for the scope of the analysis. To start with, non-parametric output- or input-orientated estimates must single out the same production frontier.[14] But much more importantly, it has been recently shown[15] that DEA and FDH provide consistent estimators for the production frontier under fairly general conditions. The latter include some typical properties of the production set (strong disposability and, for DEA, convexity) and the assumption that all observed producers reflect feasible choices. In other words, there are no measurement errors, noise, and so on, and the distance of non-efficient producers from the frontier must be entirely explained by a factor (or a set of factors), traditionally termed inefficiency, following a one-sided statistical distribution.

Indeed, this would seem a very stringent condition, and, besides, consistency is an asymptotic property. But recall that we have already argued that in any case the law must be assessed over the long-run component of the data, filtering out other components through appropriate time-series techniques. Now, virtually any filter (ranging from simple moving averages to kernel smoothers) that can be devised in order to take out the cyclical component from the data is also suitable to the extraction of noise, and can do so with usually very little computational cost. As far as small-sample bias is concerned, available evidence suggests that it affects the position (rather than the shape) of the frontier, and that it is not likely to be substantial for a one-output two-input production set like the one traditional for empirical analysis of the law (Park et al., 1997; Kneip et al., 1998; Gijbels et al., 1999). In any case, were this problem thought to be serious, one could devise consistent bootstrap procedures to deal with it (Simar and Wilson, 2000). Finally, as far as the existence of outliers is concerned, it is probably best dealt in any case within non-parametric techniques, due to their flexibility (this is true for FDH in particular).

Consider now the claims that the Verdoorn Law might spuriously arise from some other relationship present in the data. In the previous section, it has been shown that one of the factors behind these claims is the point that most available estimation procedures do not allow to separate in an efficient, data-based, manner producers endowed with different states of technology or with different rates of exogenous technical progress. But in non-parametric analysis the frontier is built by comparing any given producer with other (relatively similar) producers. This is all the more true for FDH, where this comparison is carried out only between any producer and its dominated observations.

To be sure, similarity is only defined in terms of observable inputs and outputs, but, as will be seen in the empirical exercise presented below, *when the production set is specified in terms of input and output levels*, this seems enough to prevent comparisons between producers widely believed to be characterised by different states of technology. Matters are considerably less straightforward when production relationships are specified in terms of rates of growth. Some preliminary estimates did not show in this case any shaping up of comparison groups (constituted by a dominant unit and the relative dominated units) sharing relatively similar technologies. In our opinion, the treatment of rate-of-growth models within non-parametric frontier analysis requires a more complex framework[16] and shall be taken up in future work.

It was also shown above that, since total value added must by definition be equal to the sum of labour and non-labour incomes, the question arises as to whether an estimated relationship between output and (labour and capital) inputs merely reflects this identity or has some behavioural content. But this is only true if one posits the existence of a functional relationship between outputs and inputs. Clearly, this is not the case for non-parametric frontier analysis, which consequently provides means to deal with also this source of spurious relationships.

To sum up, in our view, non-parametric frontier analysis allows us to assess the nature of economies of scale approaching in a novel and promising manner the issues of simultaneity and spuriousness affecting parametric estimates of the law. Also, through this analysis it is possible to characterise qualitatively the nature of returns to scale, and even to produce an approximate quantitative measure of returns to scale, for all producers. Relevant drawbacks of this approach are that fully-fledged statistical inference is not readily obtainable, and that a more complex framework seems to be needed to take care of rate-of-growth specifications of the law. However, taking care of these two issues is not beyond the scope of the non-parametric approach (although this requires a considerable complication of the analysis) and suggests obvious developments of the present essay.

It was already noted that ambiguities might arise in the present framework because the frontier point relevant for an inefficient producer might exhibit increasing returns to scale in the sense of input reduction, and decreasing returns to scale in the sense of output expansion. In principle, these ambiguities can be dealt with through another analytical extension, the adoption of graph efficiency measures, simultaneously allowing for input reduction and output expansion.[17] However, it is also interesting to assess the scope for these ambiguities to arise, and in the present essay we will be content with such an exercise. Finally, recall that the characterisation of returns to scale adopted here implies that at least one producer must exhibit constant returns to scale. This may not make much sense if all the scale-inefficient units to which this producer can be compared are either larger or smaller than it. Indeed, in this case the very definition of a technically optimal scale of production might not make sense. Again, the empirical relevance of this event will be considered in the empirical exercise that follows.

The data

The procedures presented above have been adopted to appraise the nature of returns to scale in 52 countries throughout the 1965–92 period. The data used in this application have been taken from the Penn World Table (mark 5.6). A drawback of the Penn World Table is that it does not contain series for manufacturing or industry, but only data for the whole economy. Yet, we have chosen these data, because:

(a) They are widely available, and they have been used (much as other economy-level data) in empirical research related to the Verdoorn Law. Thus our relatively new analysis can be applied to a rather well-known data set.
(b) These data provide estimates for the stock of capital. As pointed out in the previous sections, we may be confident about the appropriateness of frontier analysis only if it is applied to production relationships, and reduced forms excluding the stock of capital might also depend on other behavioural relationships (for example, an investment function).
(c) Estimates for the stock of capital and GDP are given in PPP terms. The utilisation of a common unit of measurement is indeed crucial to the comparison of different producers needed to build a production frontier.

The Penn World Table data have been elaborated by a group of researchers co-ordinated by Robert Summers and Alan Heston, building on the benchmark studies of the United Nations' International Comparison Program and the national economic accounts of the countries examined. The procedures adopted in constructing the data bank are described in detail in Summers and Heston (1991) and in a file annexed to the table (mark 5.6). The main point, however, is that the series of the expenditure variables are estimated at international prices, expressed in one currency, common to all countries. In this way, it is possible to use these data to carry out quantitative comparisons not only through time, but also across countries.

The data bank contains series on 147 countries throughout the 1950–92 period. However, not all variables are available for all the countries and for the whole period. As a matter of fact, data on the stock of capital are not available before 1965, and they do not exist for all countries. Among those countries for which data on the stock of capital starting from 1965 exist, a further selection has been made according to the following criteria. First of all, we have excluded those countries for which the quality of the data has obtained the minimum score according to the scale of judgement presented in Summers and Heston (1991),[18] because the data of these countries are likely to be biased by important errors of measurement. The only exception to this criterion has been made for Taiwan, owing to the particular analytical importance of this country and because it has been possible to use for it in the Penn World Table (mark 5.6) the (purchasing power parity) national accounting estimates elaborated by Yotopoulos and Lin (1993). Secondly, we have excluded Nepal and Yugoslavia, because for all variables these countries have a high number of missing values at the end of the sample period. Finally, all countries with a population of less than one million inhabitants, as well as Iran, Nigeria and Venezuela (all of them OPEC member countries), have been excluded from the analysis in order to reduce the influence of non-measurable idiosyncratic factors on the estimates for the returns to scale.[19] In the end, the sample used in the empirical analysis includes the 52 countries listed in the first column of Table 6.1.

The output variable that has been used is *Q*, a measure of GDP at 1985 international prices, whereas the input variables are *K*, the capital stock (net of residential construction) at 1985 international prices and *N*, the number of workers in employment. The employment series mostly come from census data (gathered by the ILO) on active population: the data in between the census years have been mainly obtained through interpolation. Indeed, for many countries, the 1991 and 1992 values for this variable were not available from the Penn World Table; however, we utilised simple time-series techniques to extrapolate these values from the existing ones. Finally, in order to estimate the stock of capital, the perpetual inventory method has been applied to the series of gross fixed investments in equipment, machinery and non-residential construction, obtained by multiplying some benchmark estimates for the various countries for the respective growth rates.

In order to consider only the long-run component in these variables, that is to take out the cyclical component and the noise from the data (the latter being a requirement of non-parametric frontier analysis), we take average values over periods not shorter than five years. To maintain some comparability with past empirical works on the law, the periods chosen are 1965–73, 1974–79, 1980–86, 1987–92.

The empirical results

In this section, we provide an application of non-parametric frontier analysis to the data from the Penn World Table. As already stated, we choose to base our empirical exercise on the non-convex models examined in Bogetoft (1996) and in Kerstens and Vanden Eeckaut (1999). More precisely, we define and construct a FDH-VRS model, which, as explained in Kerstens and Vanden Eeckaut (1999), is constituted by the intersection of the FDH-NIRS and FDH-NDRS models.[20] To repeat, in FDH-VRS actual producers are compared not only to actual producers, but also to their rescalings. Hence, the assessment of returns to scale can be carried out in a framework not restricted by the assumption of convexity of the production set.

First of all, we will provide evidence about the relations of dominance in FDH-CRS. The nature of these relations is crucial to understanding whether the assessment of returns to scale is based on comparisons between relatively similar producers. This means that the relations of dominance should not associate producers widely believed to be characterised by different states of technology. Then we present the results relevant for the qualitative assessment of returns to scale, as well as the quantitative approximate measures of returns to scale. Attention will be paid to the possibility that input- and output-orientated estimates might give rise to ambiguous results. In addition, the results will be appraised from the inferential point of view. We close the section comparing the results from non-parametric frontier analysis with some OLS estimates.

In Table 6.1 we provide evidence about the relations of dominance in FDH-CRS. As can be seen, for all of the four periods under consideration these relations do not associate producers too different from each other. Hence, in virtually no case can the assessment of returns to scale be said to rely on the comparison between producers widely believed to be characterised by different states of technology. Table 6.2 spells out the evidence about the qualitative assessment of returns to scale. It can be easily seen that increasing returns to scale are very pervasive, not only among developed countries, for all the four periods. Input- and output-orientated estimates give rise to ambiguous results, but not in very many cases. More precisely, this happens in one case for the period 1965–73, two cases for the period 1974–79, six cases for the period 1980–86 and seven cases for the period 1987–92. While this warrants future research on graph efficiency measures, it does not appear to be enough to weaken the conclusions reached above about the pervasiveness of increasing returns. On the other hand, there are large scale-efficient economies which always dominate smaller economies (the USA and the UK are instances of this). In such a case, perhaps, the very definition of a technically optimal scale of production might be called into question (and these economies characterised by the same kind of returns to scale as the economies they FDH-CRS dominate). However, these considerations must be developed in future work, and they cast no doubt upon the conclusions reached about the other economies.

In Table 6.3 we give some appraisal of the qualitative measures of returns to scale from the inferential point of view. Note that, strictly speaking, the tests of returns to scale proposed in Banker (1996) rely on the assumption of convexity of the production set. We feel, however, that their application in the present context is not arbitrary, as the consistency of non-convex

Table 6.1 The countries in the sample and the relations of dominance in FDH-CRS

Countries	*Dominant observation FDH-CRS 1965–73*	*Dominant observation FDH-CRS 1974–79*	*Dominant observation FDH-CRS 1980–86*	*Dominant observation FDH-CRS 1987–92*
IVORY COAST	PARAGUAY	PARAGUAY	PARAGUAY	PARAGUAY
KENYA	PARAGUAY	PARAGUAY	PARAGUAY	PARAGUAY
MADAGASCAR	MOROCCO	PARAGUAY	PARAGUAY	PARAGUAY
MALAWI	PARAGUAY	PARAGUAY	PARAGUAY	PARAGUAY
MOROCCO	MOROCCO	MOROCCO	PARAGUAY	MOROCCO
SIERRA LEONE	SIERRA LEONE	SIERRA LEONE	SIERRA LEONE	SIERRA LEONE
ZAMBIA	GUATEMALA	GUATEMALA	PARAGUAY	PARAGUAY
ZIMBABWE	ARGENTINA	ARGENTINA	CHILE	GUATEMALA
DOMINICAN REP.	DOMINICAN REP.	GUATEMALA	GUATEMALA	HONG KONG
GUATEMALA	GUATEMALA	GUATEMALA	GUATEMALA	GUATEMALA
HONDURAS	ARGENTINA	GUATEMALA	GUATEMALA	GUATEMALA
JAMAICA	ARGENTINA	ARGENTINA	GUATEMALA	GUATEMALA
MEXICO	SPAIN	UK	UK	HONG KONG
PANAMA	SPAIN	UK	UK	HONG KONG
ARGENTINA	ARGENTINA	ARGENTINA	ARGENTINA	HONG KONG
BOLIVIA	ARGENTINA	ARGENTINA	CHILE	HONG KONG
CHILE	ARGENTINA	ARGENTINA	CHILE	HONG KONG
COLOMBIA	SPAIN	ARGENTINA	ARGENTINA	HONG KONG
ECUADOR	ARGENTINA	ARGENTINA	UK	HONG KONG
PARAGUAY	PARAGUAY	PARAGUAY	PARAGUAY	PARAGUAY
PERU	ARGENTINA	ARGENTINA	HONG KONG	HONG KONG
HONG KONG	SPAIN	ARGENTINA	HONG KONG	HONG KONG
INDIA	PARAGUAY	PARAGUAY	PARAGUAY	MOROCCO
ISRAEL	USA	USA	USA	UK
KOREA, REP.	ARGENTINA	ARGENTINA	HONG KONG	HONG KONG
PHILIPPINES	GUATEMALA	GUATEMALA	GUATEMALA	GUATEMALA
SRI LANKA	ARGENTINA	ARGENTINA	HONG KONG	HONG KONG

Table 6.1 The countries in the sample and the relations of dominance in FDH-CRS *con't*

Countries	*Dominant observation FDH-CRS 1965–73*	*Dominant observation FDH-CRS 1974–79*	*Dominant observation FDH-CRS 1980–86*	*Dominant observation FDH-CRS 1987–92*
SYRIA	SPAIN	ARGENTINA	MEXICO	HONG KONG
TAIWAN	ARGENTINA	ARGENTINA	USA	USA
THAILAND	MOROCCO	GUATEMALA	GUATEMALA	HONG KONG
AUSTRALIA	USA	USA	USA	USA
AUSTRIA	UK	USA	USA	USA
BELGIUM	USA	USA	USA	USA
CANADA	USA	USA	USA	USA
DENMARK	USA	USA	USA	USA
fiNLAND	USA	USA	USA	USA
FRANCE	USA	USA	USA	USA
GERMANY, WEST	USA	USA	USA	USA
GREECE	UK	SPAIN	USA	UK
IRELAND	SPAIN	UK	UK	UK
ITALY	USA	USA	USA	USA
JAPAN	SPAIN	USA	USA	USA
NETHERLANDS	USA	USA	USA	USA
NEW ZEALAND	USA	USA	USA	USA
NORWAY	USA	USA	USA	USA
PORTUGAL	ARGENTINA	ARGENTINA	HONG KONG	HONG KONG
SPAIN	SPAIN	SPAIN	USA	USA
SWEDEN	USA	USA	USA	USA
SWITZERLAND	USA	USA	USA	USA
TURKEY	GUATEMALA	ARGENTINA	CHILE	HONG KONG
UK	UK	UK	UK	UK
USA	USA	USA	USA	USA

Table 6.2 Qualitative assessment of returns to scale

1965–73	*FDH-VRS Output-orientated*		
FDH-VRS Input-orientated	*Decreasing Returns to Scale*	*Constant Returns to Scale*	*Increasing Returns to Scale*
Decreasing Returns to Scale	Ivory Coast, Kenya, Mexico, India, Philippines, Thailand, Japan, Turkey		
Constant Returns to Scale		Morocco, Sierra Leone, Dominican Rep., Guatemala, Argentina, Paraguay, Spain, UK, USA	
Increasing Returns to Scale	Malawi		The other 34 countries
1974–79	*FDH-VRS Output-orientated*		
FDH-VRS Input-orientated	*Decreasing Returns to Scale*	*Constant Returns to Scale*	*Increasing Returns to Scale*
Decreasing Returns to Scale	Ivory Coast, Kenya, Madagascar, India, Philippines, Thailand		
Constant Returns to Scale		Morocco, Sierra Leone, Guatemala, Argentina, Paraguay, Spain, UK, USA	
Increasing Returns to Scale	Malawi, Korea Rep.		The other 36 countries
1980–86	*FDH-VRS Output-orientated*		
FDH-VRS Input-orientated	*Decreasing Returns to Scale*	*Constant Returns to Scale*	*Increasing Returns to Scale*
Decreasing Returns to Scale	Ivory Coast, Kenya, Morocco, India, Korea Rep., Philippines, Thailand, Turkey		
Constant Returns to Scale		Sierra Leone, Guatemala, Argentina Chile, Paraguay, Hong Kong, UK, USA	
Increasing Returns to Scale	Malawi, Madagascar, Zambia, Peru, Sri Lanka, Portugal		The other 30 countries

Table 6.2 Qualitative assessment of returns to scale *con't*

1987–92	*FDH-VRS Output-orientated*		
FDH-VRS Input-orientated	*Decreasing Returns to Scale*	*Constant Returns to Scale*	*Increasing Returns to Scale*
Decreasing Returns to Scale	Ivory Coast, Kenya, Mexico, Argentina, Colombia, India, Korea Rep., Philippines, Thailand, Turkey		
Constant Returns to Scale		Morocco, Sierra Leone, Guatemala, Paraguay, Hong Kong, UK, USA	
Increasing Returns to Scale	Malawi, Madagascar, Zambia, Zimbabwe, Peru, Sri Lanka, Portugal		The other 28 countries

estimators has also been proved in the literature (Korostelev et al., 1995a, 1995b), and as Banker himself (1996, p. 151) vouchsafes for the good small-sample performance of his test when applied to non-convex production sets. Table 6.3 supports the conclusions suggested by Table 6.2. The data favour a FDH-VRS characterisation of the production set (recall that FDH-VRS is obtained as the intersection of FDH-NDRS and FDH-NIRS), and increasing returns to scale rule the roost in dictating the departure of the production set from a situation of constant returns to scale: if FDH-NIRS is tested against FDH-CRS, more often than not the efficiency scores of the two models do not differ significantly.

Both Tables 6.2 and 6.3 suggest that the evidence in favour of increasing returns to scale, although rather strong, is slightly weakened over time. The number of countries characterised by non-increasing returns to scale is higher in the third and fourth periods. Much the same message is conveyed by the quantitative measures of returns to scale given in Table 6.4. Here, in order to ease presentation, countries are divided in four groups: Africa (countries from Ivory Coast to Zimbabwe in Table 6.1), non-OECD America (from the Dominican Republic to Peru), non-OECD Asia (from Hong Kong to Thailand), OECD (from Australia to the United States), and mean values of elasticity of scale per period and group are presented. Also, purely as a descriptive device, a one-sided t-test (with unit elasticity of scale as the null hypothesis) is applied to the period, group and overall mean values of the elasticity of scale. While the mean values of the returns to scale are not too high in terms of the Verdoorn's Law literature (but for non-OECD America),

Table 6.3 Some inference on the qualitative measures of returns to scale

	H1: FDH-VRS		*H1: FDH-NDRS*		*H1: FDH-NIRS*	
	Input-orientated model	*Output-orientated model*	*Input-orientated model*	*Output-orientated model*	*Input-orientated model*	*Output-orientated model*
1965–73	2.55	2.42	1.95	1.61	1.14	1.20
1974–79	2.30	2.21	1.69	1.43	1.18	1.29
1980–86	2.61	2.30	1.51	1.26	1.29	1.50
1987–92	3.24	2.70	1.76	1.36	1.28	1.42

Notes:
The efficiency scores are assumed to follow a half-normal distribution.
The critical values are F (52, 52): *1.43* (10%) *1.59* (5%) *1.92* (1%)
H0 is rejected if the test statistics are larger than the critical values

	H1: FDH-VRS		*H1: FDH-NDRS*		*H1: FDH-NIRS*	
	Input-orientated model	*Output-orientated model*	*Input-orientated model*	*Output-orientated model*	*Input-orientated model*	*Output-orientated model*
1965–73	2.09	1.95	1.73	1.58	1.11	1.14
1974–79	2.01	1.91	1.64	1.51	1.12	1.16
1980–86	1.95	1.83	1.48	1.32	1.20	1.26
1987–92	2.51	2.20	1.72	1.48	1.23	1.28

Notes:
The efficiency scores are assumed to follow an exponential distribution.
The critical values are F (104, 104): *1.29* (10%) *1.38* (5%) *1.58* (1%)
H0 is rejected if the test statistics are larger than the critical values.

Note:
The Banker (1996) Test of Returns to Scale compares (under various distributional assumptions) the efficiency scores from the restricted model (under H0) with the efficiency scores from the unrestricted model (under H1). If the efficiency scores under H0 are significantly lower than the efficiency scores under H1, H0 is rejected. In the above table, the restricted model (H0) is always given by FDH-CRS.

nonetheless they always significantly differ from unity at the 5 per cent significance level when all countries are considered. In fact, the evidence against increasing returns is clearly circumscribed to Africa and non-OECD Asia. On the other hand, the evidence in favour of increasing returns is less decisive in the third and fourth period, consistent with the slight rise in the number of countries characterised by non-increasing returns to scale. While we have no explanation for these phenomena, we believe they highlight the capability of non-parametric analysis of yielding important information on the heterogeneity of observations across both time and space.

Table 6.4 Quantitative measures of returns to scale: a summing-up

	1965–73	*1974–79*	*1980–86*	*1987–92*	***All periods***	*p-value*
Africa	1.13	1.05	0.88	0.95	***1.00***	0.4974
Non-OECD America	1.16	1.24	1.23	1.70	***1.33***	0.0012
Non-OECD Asia	1.07	1.03	1.03	1.18	***1.08***	0.1002
OECD	1.09	1.10	1.06	1.09	***1.08***	0.0000
All Groups	***1.11***	***1.11***	***1.07***	***1.23***	***1.13***	*0.0000*
p-value	0.0016	0.0001	0.0214	0.0174		

Notes: The quantitative measures of returns to scale given in the table above are cell means of the country values calculated as explained in the text.
The p-values relate to one-sided t-tests
(H0: elasticity of scale = 1, H1: elasticity of scale > 1)
carried out on the period, group and overall mean values of these measures.

All the above evidence, pointing to the pervasive existence of increasing returns to scale, contrasts with the results obtained from the OLS estimates of a Cobb–Douglas production function. Here, as is customary, the hypothesis of constant returns to scale can never be rejected (see Table 6.5), when the dependent variable is (the natural log of) output. Relying on the arguments expounded above, we ascribe these differences to problems of simultaneity and spuriousness which are best dealt within non-parametric frontier analysis.

Concluding remarks

In this chapter we have provided estimates of returns to scale for a sample of 52 countries, using a non-parametric frontier approach. In our view, this approach allows a novel and promising treatment of the issues of simultaneity and spuriousness affecting parametric estimates of Verdoorn's Law. Also, through this analysis it is possible to characterise qualitatively the nature of returns to scale, and to produce an approximate measure of elasticity of scale, for each observation. Drawbacks of the present approach are that fully-fledged statistical inference is not readily available, and that a more complex framework seems to be needed to take into account rate-of-growth specifications of the law. However, taking care of these two issues is not beyond the non-parametric approach (although it requires a considerable complication of the analysis) and suggests obvious developments of the present essay.

The results obtained in the present application point to the pervasive existence of increasing returns to scale across developed and developing

Table 6.5 OLS estimates

		Dependent variable : ln Q	
N = 52		*coeff.*	*t-ratio*
1965–73	CONSTANT	4.07	7.55
	ln N	0.44	6.02
	ln K	0.57	11.82
1974–79	CONSTANT	3.93	7.39
	ln N	0.40	5.74
	ln K	0.59	12.79
1980–86	CONSTANT	3.54	7.26
	ln N	0.36	5.69
	ln K	0.63	15.21
1987–92	CONSTANT	3.34	7.01
	ln N	0.36	5.93
	ln K	0.64	16.73

		Dependent variable: ln N	
N = 52		*coeff.*	*t-ratio*
1965–73	CONSTANT	–4.00	–3.88
	ln K	–0.26	–1.96
	ln Q	0.97	6.02
1974–79	CONSTANT	–4.12	–3.85
	ln K	–0.29	–2.00
	ln Q	1.00	5.74
1980–86	CONSTANT	–4.06	–3.73
	ln K	–0.40	–2.43
	ln Q	1.11	5.69
1987–92	CONSTANT	–3.61	–3.30
	ln K	–0.48	–2.88
	ln Q	1.16	5.93

Legend:
ln Q = natural log of GDP (1985 prices)
ln K = natural log of capital stock (1985 prices)
ln N = natural log of employment.

countries, in sharp variance with traditional parametric evidence obtained on the same data set. It is hoped that the present work might be considered as a useful first attempt, showing the relevance of the non-parametric frontier literature to the problem at hand, and fostering further analytical developments.

Notes

1. I would like to thank the editors, an anonymous referee, Finn Førsund, Kris Kerstens and Ute Pieper for useful comments on a previous draft; the usual disclaimer applies. I am also grateful to the MURST, Italy, for financial support.
2. Useful introductions to this body of techniques can be found in Lovell (1993), in the other essays contained in the same book (Fried et al., 1993), and in Cooper et al. (2000).
3. Dixon and Thirlwall refer to this term as a 'learning by doing' coefficient, but there is no reason why it should not also reflect *static* economies of scale.
4. See, for instance, Bairam (1987a, pp. 30–2) or McCombie and Thirlwall (1994, pp. 175–80), who both rely on a dynamic Cobb–Douglas function. The present argument has the advantage of yielding a qualitatively unchanged conclusion even if the technical progress function becomes non-linear.
5. This issue was perhaps first brought out by Rowthorn (1975a).
6. A partial exception to this is found in León-Ledesma (1999b).
7. See, for instance, McCombie (1981, 1985a), Bairam (1986, 1987b, 1988c).
8. Harris and Lau (1998), Harris and Liu (1999).
9. See McCombie and Thirlwall (1994, pp. 171–3). Vaciago (1975) is an early example of non-linear specification of the law, while Pieper (2000) provides estimates based on local regression analysis. Pugno (1996), although not directly concerned with the law, also provides relevant evidence in this respect.
10. This reference set can be indifferently a production set, an input requirement set (for given outputs) or a production possibilities set (for given inputs).
11. Note that a DEA-NDRS model also exists in the literature, but has been very seldom applied. See on this Seiford and Thrall (1990).
12. If the technologies considered have more than one output or one input, then the two measures of Debreu–Farrell are equal to, respectively, the radial (equiproportional) expansion of all outputs needed to bring a producer on the frontier, for given inputs, and to the radial contraction of all inputs needed to bring a producer on the frontier, for given outputs.
13. Clearly, different output-mixes can exist only in the presence of multi-output production sets.
14. To see this, consider that, if constant return to scale are posited, one obtains numerically identical values for output- and input-orientated efficiency scores for any given observation.
15. Banker (1996); Korostelev et al. (1995a, 1995b).
16. Different rates of total factor productivity growth could be measured through a Malmquist index. However, if the production technology does not display constant returns to scale, there is no consensus in the literature on how to account for scale effects (see on this Färe et al.,1994; Färe et al., 1997; Ray and Desli, 1997). In the present context, this means that static and economies of scale may be confused with exogenous technical progress. Førsund (1996b) provides evidence for Norwegian manufacturing establishments suggesting a positive correlation between some Malmquist indices of productivity and output growth. However, no attempt is made in that study to distinguish between exogenous technical progress and scale effects.
17. See on this Färe et al. (1985).

18. This scale of judgement, relative to PWT mark 5, ranges from an A as the highest score to a D as the lowest one.
19. This choice replicates a similar one made in Mankiw et al. (1992).
20. The software for estimating these models was developed and generously made available to me by Antonio Pavone, from ISTAT, Rome.

7
Cumulative Causation and Unemployment

Mark Roberts

Introduction[1]

More than fifty years on, Verdoorn's Law remains significant because it enters as the key 'stylised fact' in the Dixon–Thirlwall (1975) model, a model that has come to be regarded as the 'standard' model of cumulative causation (see McCombie, 2002, this volume). Indeed, it is precisely because of Verdoorn's Law that growth in this model is cumulative. This is because without it there would be no tendency for an initial growth advantage in the model to (positively) feed back into labour productivity growth, which is a necessary prerequisite in the model if an initial growth advantage is to be retained (Dixon and Thirlwall, 1975, pp. 205–6). However, the emphasis in this chapter will not be on the vital role that Verdoorn's Law plays within the Dixon–Thirlwall (1975) model, for this is both obvious and well-known. Rather, we first concentrate on relaxing the model's implicit assumption that workers are passive to the implications of firms' pricing decisions for their real wages. To achieve this relaxation we draw on the NAIRU literature,[2] a literature in which workers only accept the implications of firms' pricing decisions for their real wages if they are consistent with their own aims in the wage bargaining process.[3]

However, despite our extension, our model still shares a key shortcoming with the original Dixon–Thirlwall model. This is that the process of cumulative causation works only through relative price competitiveness. Yet, in reality, it seems that non-price competitiveness has been more important in recent decades in determining success in both international and inter-regional markets (see, inter alios, McCombie and Thirlwall, 1994, 1997a and 1997b; McCombie, 1998a; and Petit, 1999). Given this, this chapter also presents a reformulated version of our extended Dixon–Thirlwall model in which, in contrast to the 'standard' model, the process of cumulative causation works through the relative non-price competitiveness of exports.

The two models that we present not only constitute an advance on the original Dixon–Thirlwall model, but also raise interesting questions about the standard story advanced to explain the levels of OECD unemployment over the last thirty years. First, they suggest that the heterogeneity of unemployment rates across OECD countries may be attributable to more than just differences in wage bargaining institutions and the treatment of the unemployed. Second, they also suggest that the productivity slowdown may be much more closely associated with the general rise in OECD unemployment than the standard story would have us believe. Finally, they suggest that not only may the variety of cross-sectional experience across OECD countries be attributable to more than differences in labour market institutions, but so too may be the phenomenon of unemployment persistence or impure hysteresis.

The structure of the rest of this chapter is as follows. We start by briefly outlining the original Dixon–Thirlwall model. In doing so, we highlight its implicit assumption that workers are passive with respect to the implications of firms' pricing decisions for their level of real wages. We then relax the assumption of worker passivity in order to present an extended Dixon–Thirlwall model. Following this, we present our reformulated version of this model in which cumulative causation works through relative non-price competitiveness. We then discuss the channels through which unemployment may persist in our two models. Finally, we conclude by summarising the implications of our analysis for the standard story of OECD unemployment.

The Dixon–Thirlwall model and worker passivity

The Dixon–Thirlwall model considers a small economy in which growth is export-led. In particular, the small economy competes via prices on international or inter-regional markets in the sale of a diversified range of goods. These goods are priced via the application of a mark-up on unit labour costs and produced according to an increasing returns 'technology'. Following Young (1928) and Kaldor (1966), these increasing returns are viewed as being primarily 'dynamic' in nature. That is to say, they originate in the main from the benefits of a process of increased intra- and inter-industry specialisation made possible only by growth of the economy. These features of the model enter via the following set of four structural equations:

$$y_t = \gamma x_t \tag{7.1}$$
$$x_t = \eta\pi_{h,\,t} + \delta\pi_c + \varepsilon y_c \tag{7.2}$$
$$\pi_{h,\,t} = w_t - r_t + \tau \tag{7.3}$$
$$r_t = r_e + \lambda y_t \tag{7.4}$$

where y denotes the rate of real output growth, x the rate of real export growth,[4] π_h the rate of price inflation of home-produced goods, π_c the rate of price inflation of competitive exports,[5] y_c a measure of the rate of growth of real income in the home economy's main export markets, w the rate of nominal wage inflation, r the rate of labour productivity growth, τ the rate of mark-up growth and r_e the rate of exogenous labour productivity growth.[6] Meanwhile, η represents the own-price elasticity of demand for exports ($\eta < 0$), δ the cross-price elasticity of demand for exports, ε the income elasticity of demand for exports and λ the Verdoorn coefficient.[7] Equation (7.4) is, of course, Verdoorn's Law and it is this that both captures the assumed presence of dynamic increasing returns and makes growth in the model cumulative.

To see the passivity of workers implicit in the Dixon–Thirlwall model, note that equation (7.3), which describes the pricing decisions of domestic firms, can be rearranged to give:

$$w_t - \pi_{h,\,t} = r_t - \tau \qquad (7.5)$$

This tells us that when domestic firms decide how to change the prices of their goods given changes in unit labour costs and in their feasible mark-up, a rate of growth of the real product wage is implied. In terminology reminiscent of the NAIRU literature, and, in particular, of that used by Carlin and Soskice (1990), we may think of this as the price-determined rate of real product wage inflation (PDWI). Given that the model assumes that w_t is exogenously determined it therefore follows that it implicitly assumes that domestic workers passively accept this PDWI regardless of its consequences for their real consumption wages. Thus, for example, if changing competitive conditions in export markets resulted in a faster rate of mark-up growth then the PDWI would decline. In the Dixon–Thirlwall model workers simply accept this decline despite the fact that, ceteris paribus, it also implies a fall in the rate of growth of their real consumption wages.[8,9]

Growth and unemployment in an extended Dixon–Thirlwall model

The set-up of the model

To relax the Dixon–Thirlwall model's implicit assumption of worker passivity it is necessary to endogenise the rate of nominal wage inflation.[10] We choose to do this by first specifying the following two additional structural equations to supplement equations (7.1)–(7.4) of the original model.

$$w_t = a - bu_t + \pi_t^e \qquad (7.6)$$
$$\pi_t^e = \phi\pi_{h,\,t} + (1 - \phi)\pi_c \qquad (7.7)$$

The inspiration for equation (7.6) comes from the NAIRU literature. It states that the negotiated rate of nominal wage inflation in period t is a decreasing linear function of the period's unemployment rate, u_t, and an increasing linear function of both exogenous wage-push factors, captured by a, and the rate of inflation that workers expect for the period for the basket of goods they consume, π_t^e.[11, 12] The negative dependence on u_t can be explained by the fact that the weaker the labour market the less likely workers are to push for increases in their real wages both in the aggregate and relative to one another (see, inter alios, Layard et al., 1991, p. 13 and Rowthorn, 1977, p. 219). Capturing the strength of this negative dependence is the parameter b. We shall return to consider the determinants of this parameter later when we discuss the important role that it plays in both the rest of the NAIRU literature and in our model. Meanwhile, equation (7.7) specifies π_t^e as a weighted average of the actual inflation rates for home-produced goods and imported final consumption goods in period t.[13] The weights, which, for simplicity, are assumed to be exogenously determined, are the respective shares of home-produced goods and of imports in the consumption expenditure of workers. Assuming that w_t is negotiated at the very outset of period t[14], the fact that π_t^e has been specified as a weighted average of *actual* inflation rates means that we have assumed that workers possess rational expectations.

To show that the addition of these two equations to the Dixon–Thirlwall model implies that workers will no longer passively accept the PDWI implied by the pricing decisions of firms we may substitute equation (7.7) into equation (7.6) and subtract $\pi_{h,t}$ from both sides to give:

$$w_t - \pi_{h,\,t} = a - bu_t + (1 - \phi)(\pi_c - \pi_{h,\,t}) \tag{7.8}$$

This shows that not only do the pricing decisions of firms imply a rate of growth of the real product wage, but so too does the bargain struck by workers with their employers in wage negotiations. Using terminology again reminiscent of that from Carlin and Soskice (1990), we may think of this latter implied rate of real product wage growth as the bargained rate of real product wage inflation (BRWI). Clearly, equation (7.8) implies that the BRWI is declining with u_t and increasing with both a and the term $(1 - \phi)(\pi_c - \pi_{h,t})$, which may be thought of as the 'wedge' that exists between the growth rate of the real product wage $(w_t - \pi_{h,t})$ and the (expected) growth rate of the real consumption wage $(w_t - \pi_t^e)$.[15, 16] Equally clearly, in comparing equation (7.8) with equation (7.5), we see that, for any given rate of unemployment, there is no reason why the BRWI need coincide with the PDWI. In other words, workers no longer passively accept what their employers try to impose upon them. Rather, for them to accept the PDWI the unemployment rate must be such as to produce a BRWI that is consistent with the PDWI. Thus, similar to the position found in other NAIRU models, the unemployment rate acts as a disciplining device to overcome the dissatisfaction of workers with the rate of change of the real product wage that firms wish to impose upon them via their pricing decisions. Indeed, given our assumption that workers possess rational expectations the unemployment rate in our extended model will always be such as to ensure the BRWI is consistent with the PDWI. This implies that the unemployment rate in our model, even when the model turns out to be in disequilibrium, is always a NAIRU. In particular, the unemployment rate is always a NAIRU in the sense that with the BRWI always equal to the PDWI inflation is not redistributing income between domestic workers and firms.[17, 18]

In order to complete the endogenisation of the rate of nominal wage inflation in our extended Dixon–Thirlwall model it is necessary to link the unemployment rate in equation (7.6), to the rate of real output growth that appears in equation (7.1). We do this by introducing the following three structural equations:

$$u_t = u_{t-1} + n_t - e_t \tag{7.9}$$
$$e_t = -r_e + (1 - \lambda)y_t \tag{7.10}$$
$$n_t = n_e + \rho(e_t - e_c) - \nu(u_t - u_c) \tag{7.11}$$

Equation (7.9) simply defines the unemployment rate in period t as equal to the unemployment rate in the previous period, u_{t-1}, plus the rate of labour-force growth in period t, n_t, net of the rate of employment growth in period t, e_t.[19] Meanwhile, equation (7.10) specifies e_t as a negative linear function of r_e and a positive linear function of y_t. This equation follows directly from Verdoorn's Law, equation (7.4), and the definition of labour productivity growth as $r_t \equiv y_t - e_t$.[20] It is interesting because it implies that employment growth in our model is quantity-constrained by output growth. Thus, although the unemployment rate in our model is always a NAIRU, all unemployment should nevertheless be thought of as being both involuntary and arising from a deficiency of demand.[21] Finally, equation (7.11) gives the rate of labour-force growth and is taken from Thirlwall (1980b, p. 424; see also McCombie and Thirlwall, 1994, p. 480). In this equation n_e denotes the exogenous rate of labour-force growth in the economy. The fact that n is specified as increasing with e and decreasing with u reflects evidence that increases in perceived employment opportunities are likely to encourage increased labour-force participation, particularly amongst women (see, inter alios, León-Ledesma and Thirlwall, 2002; McCombie and Thirlwall, 1994; McCombie, 1998a, p. 216).[22] Meanwhile, the inclusion of measures of the rate of employment growth, e_c, and the unemployment rate, u_c, in competitor economies is intended to capture the idea that, in a regional setting, it is relative employment opportunities rather than real wages per se that are important in driving migration. Within the context of the national economy it is appropriate to set both e_c and u_c to zero. In such a setting we can do this whilst still maintaining that a buoyant domestic labour market will result in induced immigration and also the possible presence of so-called 'guest workers'.[23]

Equations (7.6)–(7.7) and (7.9)–(7.11) taken together with the four equations, (7.1)–(7.4), of the original model, provide the structural equations of our extended Dixon–Thirlwall model. However, as it stands, the model will lack any interesting transitional dynamics. To introduce such dynamics it is necessary to introduce, in addition to the lag that already exists in equation (7.9), a lag in one or more of the eight structural equations. An outstanding candidate for the inclusion of such a lag is equation (7.2).[24] Quite apart from the recognition and order-delivery lags identified by Hooper and Marquez (1995, p. 109), the reaction to relative price movements typically involves discrete shifts to new suppliers. However, because they are costly, such shifts occur only gradually (Carlin and Soskice, 1990, p. 293; Landesmann and Snell, 1989, p. 4). In view of this, we assume that real export growth reacts to changes in relative prices with a single lag of one period. Assuming one period of logical time in our model to be equivalent to one calendar year, such a specification is reasonably consistent with empirical work (see, in particular, Krugman, 1989; Landesmann and Snell, 1989).[25]

Solution of the model

For empirically plausible ranges of its exogenous variable and parameter values, our extended Dixon–Thirlwall model possesses a stable equilibrium-solution (y^*, u^*) in which both the rate of real output growth and the unemployment rate are strictly positive. This is illustrated in Figure 7.1 using a phase diagram. In this diagram the $\Delta y_t = 0$ schedule shows all combinations of y_t and u_t for which y_t is constant. Its upward slope reflects the fact that a higher rate of unemployment lowers the negotiated rate of nominal wage inflation. This occurs both directly through the negative dependence of w_t on u_t and indirectly via reducing π_t^e, the rate of inflation that workers expect for the basket of goods they consume. Given the use of mark-up pricing by firms, lower nominal wage inflation in turn implies a fall in the rate of inflation of home-produced goods and therefore faster real output growth through increased relative export price competitiveness. Meanwhile, the $\Delta u_t = 0$ schedule shows all combinations of y_t and u_t for which u_t is constant. Its downward slope is a result of the fact that, from equation (7.10), a faster rate of real output growth leads to a faster rate of employment growth which, from equation (7.9), reduces the unemployment rate. From equation (7.11), the faster rate of employment growth and the lower unemployment rate also induce an increased rate of labour-force growth. However, provided $\rho < 1$, the increase in the rate of labour-force growth is not large enough to completely reverse the fall in u_t. We see that the intersection of the $\Delta y_t = 0$ and $\Delta u_t = 0$ schedules defines the equilibrium solution (y^*, u^*) of our model. The arrows in the phase diagram depict the

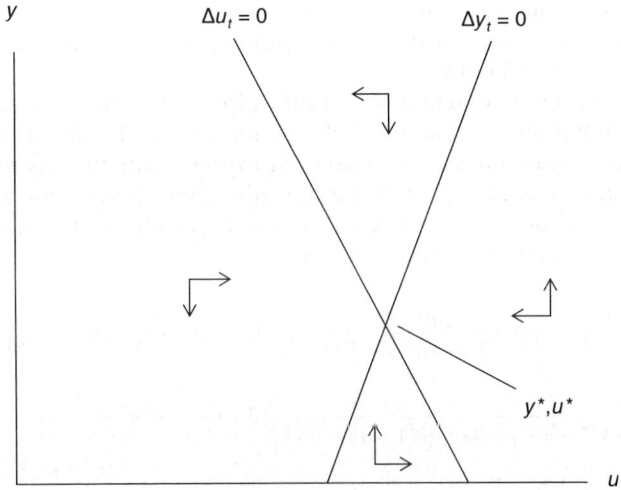

Figure 7.1

dynamics of y_t and u_t. If y_t lies above the $\Delta y_t = 0$ schedule then y_t tends to fall, whilst if y_t lies below the $\Delta y_t = 0$ schedule then y_t tends to increase. Meanwhile, if u_t lies to the right of the $\Delta u_t = 0$ schedule then u_t tends to decline, whereas if u_t lies to the left of this schedule then it tends to rise. Thus, overall, if y_t and u_t are disturbed from their equilibrium values, the system tends to oscillate around (y^*, u^*). As noted in the mathematical appendix, Roberts (2002d) has found that, for ranges of exogenous variable and parameter values that are plausible for the UK, these oscillations are damped and therefore our extended model's equilibrium solution is stable.[26]

As noted earlier, because in extending the Dixon–Thirlwall model we have assumed that workers possess rational expectations, every unemployment rate in our model is a NAIRU in the sense that inflation is not redistributing income between domestic firms and workers. However, despite this, we have just shown our model to possess a unique equilibrium rate of unemployment, u^*, which is also a NAIRU. This may seem confusing, but we can overcome the confusion by thinking of u^* as being a long-run NAIRU which is, obviously, unique, while all other unemployment rates constitute short-run NAIRUs.[27] Therefore, if the economy experiences an unemployment shock that disturbs it from (y^*, u^*) then this shifts it on to a short-run NAIRU that differs from the unique long-run NAIRU. However, over time, the short-run NAIRU changes until it once again coincides with the long-run NAIRU. From this distinction between short-run NAIRUs and the unique long-run NAIRU it follows that unemployment following a shock exhibits what is referred to in the NAIRU literature as persistence, or *im*pure hysteresis. This is a point that we shall return to below.

Whilst our phase diagram is helpful in informing us that a non-trivial stable equilibrium solution exists, it does not tell us what the determinants of the equilibrium rates of real output growth and unemployment are. For this, we need to explicitly state our model's equilibrium solution, which is the particular solution to the linear non-homogenous system given in the mathematical appendix. This is as follows:

$$y^* = \left[\frac{\gamma\eta b}{\nu(1-\phi+\gamma\eta\lambda)-\gamma\eta b(1-\rho)(1-\lambda)}\right]\left[(1-\rho)r_e + n_e - \rho e_c + \nu u_c\right] + \left[\frac{\gamma\nu}{\nu(1-\phi+\gamma\eta\lambda)-\gamma\eta b(1-\rho)(1-\lambda)}\right]\left[(\delta+\eta)(1-\phi)\pi_c + (1-\phi)\varepsilon y_c - \eta(r_e - a - \tau)\right] \tag{7.12}$$

$$u^* = \left[\frac{1-\phi+\gamma\eta\lambda}{\nu(1-\phi+\gamma\eta\lambda)-\gamma\eta b(1-\rho)(1-\lambda)}\right]\left[(1-\rho)r_e + n_e - \rho e_c + \nu u_c\right] - \gamma\left[\frac{(1-\rho)(1-\lambda)}{\nu(1-\phi+\gamma\eta\lambda)-\gamma\eta b(1-\rho)(1-\lambda)}\right]\left[(\delta+\eta)(1-\phi)\pi_c + (1-\phi)\varepsilon y_c - \eta(r_e - a - \tau)\right] \tag{7.13}$$

One point that arises from this explicit statement of our model's equilibrium solution is that if we set the exogenous variables r_e, n_e, e_c, u_c, π_c, y_c, a and τ all equal to zero then $y^* = 0$. Therefore, strictly speaking, growth in our model is exogenous. However, this is *not* to say that government policy cannot influence y^* in our model. In particular, we shall see below that structural reforms that influence such parameters as λ are able to influence y^*. Furthermore, given the presence of Verdoorn's Law in its structural set-up, there is evidently an element of endogeneity about any technological progress that does occur in our model. Another point to emerge is that, similar to the rest of the NAIRU literature, u^* is negatively related to b. We can think of b as measuring workers' degree of real wage growth flexibility.[28] This is because it measures the degree to which the BRWI in equation (7.8) responds to changes in the unemployment rate. In turn, we can expect workers' degree of real wage growth flexibility to vary with wage bargaining institutions and with the search 'effectiveness' of the average unemployed job seeker, which itself can be related to the average duration of unemployment and such determinants of the average duration as the length of entitlement to benefits. More specifically, with regard to wage bargaining institutions, we can expect workers' degree of real wage growth flexibility to be high both for economies in which bargaining is very decentralised and unions are very weak, and for economies where bargaining takes place at the national level between strong unions and strong employers' organisations (Layard et al., 1991). Meanwhile, we can expect a higher average duration of unemployment caused by, amongst other things, a longer duration of benefits to be associated with a lower degree of real wage growth flexibility (Layard et al., 1991). This is because the higher the average duration of unemployment, the lower the search 'effectiveness' of the average unemployed job seeker is likely to be. Indeed, such variations in wage bargaining institutions and the treatment of the unemployed are held by Layard et al. (1991) to be responsible for most of the cross-sectional, if not the time-series, variation in unemployment rates across OECD countries that has existed over the previous twenty to thirty years.[29]

However, our model's explicit equilibrium solution indicates that the heterogeneity in OECD unemployment rates that has been witnessed over recent decades may also be due to factors other than wage bargaining institutions and the treatment of the unemployed. Thus, perhaps most notably, because u^* is decreasing in ε in equation (7.13) our model predicts that OECD countries that have benefitted from higher income elasticities of demand for their exports over recent decades should, ceteris paribus, have experienced lower unemployment rates. This is significant because the main determinant of the income elasticity of demand for a country's exports is its relative level of non-price competitiveness and, as we discuss further below, such competitiveness has become ever more important in determining export success in the post-Second World War period. Our model therefore suggests that the NAIRU literature's emphasis on the heterogeneity of labour market institutions as the cause of OECD unemployment rate disparities may be overstated. However, to assess this claim would require a full empirical analysis, which is beyond the scope of this chapter.[30]

The possibility of a growth–unemployment trade-off

The negative effect of an increase in ε upon u^* implied by our discussion above is hardly surprising given that an increase in ε also has, from equation (7.12), a positive effect on y^*. However, other parameter and exogenous variable changes that increase y^* do not necessarily reduce u^*. In particular, consider an increase in either the Verdoorn coefficient or in the exogenous rate of labour productivity growth. We would expect increases in both of these to result from structural reforms implemented in the economy. In particular, structural reforms that we might expect to affect the Verdoorn coefficient include anything that affects the quality of industrial management or the prevalence of stifling regulations. Thus, for example, we would expect a removal of severe planning restrictions in a regional economy to result in an increase in λ. This is because such restrictions can be expected to inhibit the industrial expansion that is necessary to allow for an increased subdivision of the production process and therefore the full exploitation of dynamic increasing returns. Meanwhile, structural reforms that we might expect to increase r_e include measures that increase an economy's receptiveness to knowledge spillovers from other economies, that enhance the quantity and quality of human capital accumulation, and that improve the spillovers into the economy occurring from government-sponsored research and development.[31, 32]

Anyway, regardless of the precise nature of the structural reform, it follows from equations (7.12) and (7.13) that while an increase in r_e and/or λ will increase y^*, it will only also reduce u^* if the following condition holds:[33]

$$(1 - \rho)(1 + \gamma\eta - \phi) < 0 \tag{7.14}$$

Assuming, for the time being, $\rho < 1$, this condition reduces to $-\gamma\eta + \phi > 1$ (remember, $\eta < 0$). Using the phase diagram in Figure 7.2 we can explain the intuition behind this condition. In particular, the diagram considers structural reform that causes an increase in r_e.[34] We can see that this shifts the $\Delta y_t = 0$ schedule upwards. This is because for every level of u_t a higher r_e implies a lower rate of home price inflation and thus a faster rate of real export and real output growth. The lower rate of home price inflation is both a direct consequence of firms' practice of setting their prices as a mark-up on unit labour costs, and an indirect consequence of the rate of negotiated nominal wage inflation falling as workers revise their expectations of inflation downwards. Consequently, we may attribute the upwards shift in the $\Delta y_t = 0$ schedule to both a *direct price effect* and an *expectations effect*. The higher is $-\gamma\eta$ the stronger is the direct price effect because the greater is the impact of any given fall in $\pi_{h,t}$ on y_t. Meanwhile, the higher is ϕ the greater is the expectations effect because the more does π_t^e fall in response to a given fall in $\pi_{h,t}$.[35] In contrast, the increase in r_e shifts the $\Delta u_t = 0$ schedule outwards. This is because, from equation (7.10), a higher r_e implies a slower rate of employment growth for every level of y_t. We may term this the *Luddite effect* because it provides grounds for worker dissatisfaction. Clearly, only if the direct price and expectations effects outweigh the Luddite effect will the upwards shift in the $\Delta y_t = 0$ schedule be large enough relative to the outwards shift in the $\Delta u_t = 0$ schedule to ensure that the unemployment rate is lower in the new equilibrium. In contrast to Figure 7.2, we see that this is not the case in Figure 7.3.

From the above it is clear that structural reform of an economy designed to work through r_e and/or λ brings with it the possibility of a long-run trade-off between growth and unemployment. Where such a trade-off does exist, it obviously provides policy-makers with a dilemma. Moreover, the oscillatory dynamics of our model, evident from Figure 7.1, are such that even where

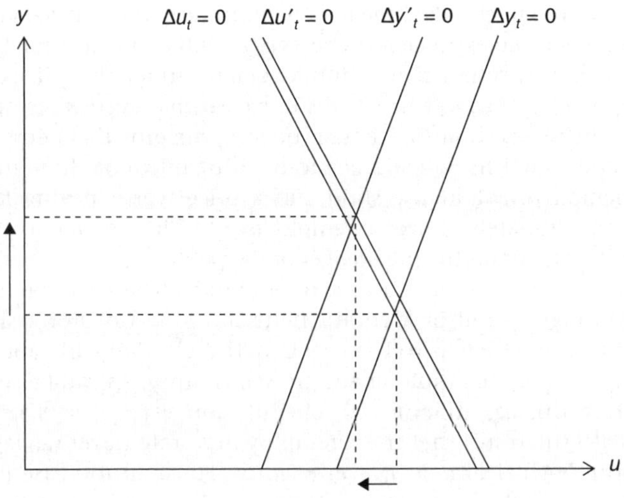

Figure 7.2

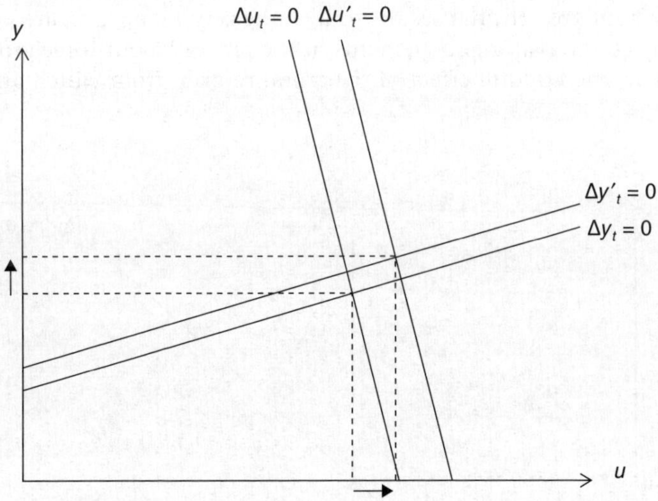

Figure 7.3

such a trade-off does not exist, structural reform that increases r_e and/or λ still entails a short-run trade-off between growth and unemployment. The intuition for this is that whilst, from equation (7.10), the Luddite effect of structural reform comes into immediate effect, the countervailing direct price and expectations effects take time to kick-in. In turn, the delayed kicking-in of the direct price and expectations effects is a result of, in equation (7.2), real export growth only responding to improvements in relative price competitiveness with a lag. Anyway, from this it is clear that even when structural reform that increases r_e and/or λ entails no long-run growth–unemployment trade-off, policy-makers will still be faced with a dilemma. In particular, is higher unemployment in the short run a price worth paying for faster growth and, ultimately, lower unemployment? The answer to this will, obviously, depend upon the preferences of the public.[36, 37]

There is, however, one special case of our model where structural reform working through r_e and/or λ entails neither a long-run nor a short-run trade-off. This is when $\rho = 1$, i.e. when the elasticity of labour-force growth with respect to employment growth is unity. As can be seen from Figure 7.4, in this case the $\Delta u_t = 0$ schedule comes to possess an infinite gradient with the result that the unemployment rate never deviates from the long-run NAIRU of $u^* = (n_e - e_c + \nu u_c)/\nu$. Thus, an increase in r_e that shifts the $\Delta y_t = 0$ schedule upwards increases the equilibrium rate of real output growth, whilst leaving, even during the transition to the new equilibrium, the unemployment rate unchanged. The intuition behind this result is that with $\rho = 1$, both the direct and indirect changes in the rate of employment growth that result from changes in r_e and/or λ are perfectly offset by countervailing movements in the rate of labour-force growth. In particular, the Luddite effect of structural reform, from which arises the

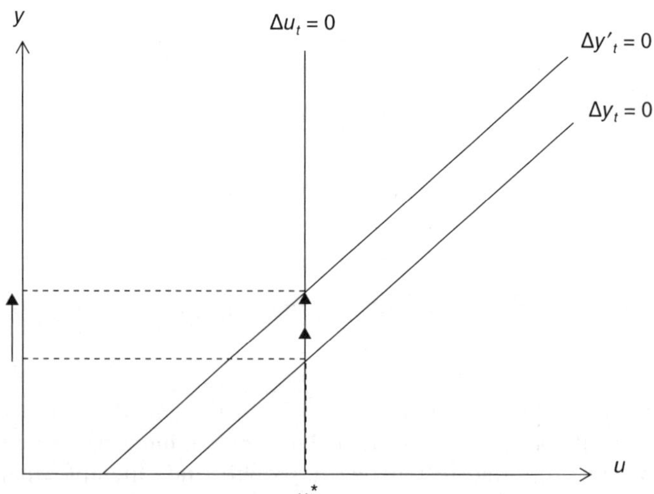

Figure 7.4

possibility of trade-offs between growth and unemployment, is choked-off at source. This being the case, there can be no effect on the unemployment rate.[38, 39]

However, even in this special case of $\rho = 1$, the absence of either a short-run or a long-run trade-off between growth and unemployment may be more apparent than real. This follows from our discussion of the rationale behind equation (7.11). Specifically, that discussion implies that the fall in the rate of labour-force growth that works to immediately choke-off the Luddite effect will be partly attributable to reduced labour-force participation. Consequently, whilst when $\rho = 1$, no increase in the measured rate of unemployment will ever result, a decline in the proportion of working-age people in employment may nevertheless occur.[40, 41]

The above discussion of the effects of changes in r_e and/or λ is interesting not just in its own right, but also because it implies that changes in the rate of labour productivity growth can be associated with changes in our model's long-run NAIRU (that is, with changes in the equilibrium unemployment rate, u^*).[42] This is contrary to the view that dominates the rest of the NAIRU literature. In particular, the standard view is that changes in the rate of labour productivity growth are *not* associated with, and, especially, do not cause, changes in the long-run NAIRU (see, inter alios, Blanchard and Wolfers, 2000, pp. C4–C6; Layard et al., 1991).[43, 44] The origin of this view seems to be the somewhat weaker empirical observation that whilst labour productivity has been trended upwards over the broad sweep of history, the unemployment rate has been untrended (see Blanchard and Katz, 1997, p. 56; Layard et al., 1991, p. 5). To capture this feature of reality standard NAIRU models have found it necessary to assume that workers possess a reservation wage and that this reservation wage adjusts to any changes that occur in the level of labour productivity. However, as a corollary of this assumption, standard NAIRU models produce not only the empirically consistent result that the long-run NAIRU is constant in the face of labour productivity growth, but also the much stronger result that the long-run NAIRU is constant in the face of *changes* in the rate of labour productivity growth.

However, in our model there is no reservation wage that is linked to the level of productivity. If there were, we would expect the rate of labour productivity growth to enter in equation (7.6) as a determinant of the negotiated rate of nominal wage inflation. Yet, despite this, our model still possesses a long-run NAIRU that is constant in the face of labour productivity growth without producing the much stronger result of a long-run NAIRU that is invariant to changes in the rate of labour productivity growth. In particular, whilst productivity growth shocks do not affect the long-run NAIRU,[45] structural changes that influence y^*, and thus, by extension, the equilibrium rate of labour productivity growth, do. Moreover, as the mathematical appendix shows, even if our model is modified to make

w_t dependent upon r_t it still transpires that changes in productivity growth can be associated with changes in the long-run NAIRU. Thus, in this modified model, it is shown that structural reform that leads to an increase in r_e and/or λ not only pushes up y^*, and, hence, the rate of labour productivity growth, but also increases the long-run NAIRU.

The fact that changes in the rate of labour productivity growth can be associated with shifts in the long-run NAIRU in our model has potential implications as to the diagnosis of the causes of the large rises in unemployment that have occurred throughout the OECD, and, in particular, OECD Europe, since the 1960s.[46] Thus, whilst the theoretical conclusion that changes in productivity growth cannot affect the long-run NAIRU has led the NAIRU literature to downplay the productivity slowdown as a direct cause of the large rises in unemployment,[47, 48] our model suggests that this downplaying may be a mistake. Therefore, our extended Dixon–Thirlwall model suggests that the NAIRU literature may have misdiagnosed not only the causes of the cross-sectional variations that have existed in OECD unemployment rates, but also the causes of the general rise in OECD unemployment. If this is indeed the case then the policy implications are profound. In particular, it would suggest that policies to reduce unemployment should focus not just on labour market reform, but also on implementing structural reforms that aim to influence the long-run rate of labour productivity growth. Most notably, from the discussion of this section we know that, provided the condition in equation (7.14) holds, reforms that increase r_e and/or λ will both increase y^* and reduce the long-run NAIRU, whilst from the discussion of the previous section we know that reforms that increase ε will also have the same effect. The latter being the case, we can conclude that perhaps the best route to lower unemployment is not labour market reform, but the implementation of measures that aim to enhance the non-price competitiveness of exports on international markets.[49]

The importance of non-price competitiveness: a reformulation of our extended Dixon-Thirlwall model

As mentioned in the introduction, our extension of the Dixon–Thirlwall model shares the original model's shortcoming that the process of cumulative causation works only through the relative price competitiveness of exports and not also through their relative *non*-price competitiveness. It is a shortcoming because in recent decades relative price competitiveness has declined in significance in determining success on international markets,[50] whilst relative non-price competitiveness has become ever more important. Such competitiveness has several aspects. It refers not only to the 'quality', however that may be measured, of the goods being traded, but also to such features as the ability to keep up with consumers' changing tastes, delivery dates, after-sales follow-up, the effectiveness of marketing, the extent of overseas sales and distribution networks, and the easing of access to finance and communications networks (see, inter alios, Landesmann and Snell, 1989, p. 1; McCombie, 1998a, p. 220; Petit, 1999, p. 159).[51]

In this section we overcome this shortcoming by reformulating our extended Dixon–Thirlwall model. To focus attention on what is novel, we simplify by abstracting completely from relative price competitiveness. This we do by imposing the restriction $\eta = \delta = 0$ on equation (7.2). Meanwhile, relative non-price competitiveness as a channel for cumulative causation is introduced by relaxing the assumption of our original model that the income elasticity of demand for exports is an exogenously determined parameter. Rather, we postulate that the income elasticity of demand is a positive lagged function of the rate of labour productivity growth.[52] In particular, for simplicity, we assume the following linear functional form in which the income elasticity responds to the rate of labour productivity growth with a lag of one period:

$$\varepsilon_t = \alpha r_{t-1} \tag{7.15}$$

where $\alpha > 0$. One justification for the lag follows from the fact that one way in which changes in r_t are likely to affect ε is through their impact on the profits of exporters and, therefore, on their ability to invest in elements of non-price competitiveness. In particular, we might expect a lag between the time at which firms first experience a change in their profit levels and the time at which they respond to this by altering their levels of investment. This is because firms will wish to establish whether any change in profit levels is merely transitory or something more permanent before revising their existing investment plans. Similarly, because investment takes time to bear fruit, we would expect changed investment levels to only impact on relative non-price competitiveness with a lag. An alternative justification is that it may take time for changes in relative non-price competitiveness to alter preferences. This is because there may exist lags both in the recognition of such changes by consumers and, possibly because of brand loyalty, in the response of consumers to them.

Anyway, with the imposition of the restriction $\eta = \delta = 0$ and the introduction of equation (7.15) as an additional structural relationship, the phase diagram for our reformulated model becomes as in Figure 7.5.[53] Once again, the $\Delta u_t = 0$ slopes downwards if $\rho < 1$ and is vertical if $\rho = 1$. The rationale behind the slope is as in our original extension of the Dixon–Thirlwall model. However, in contrast to our original model, the $\Delta y_t = 0$ schedule is horizontal.[54] The intuition behind this is that if relative non-price competitiveness is unimportant in determining success on international, not to mention inter-regional, markets then changes in nominal wage inflation induced by changes in the unemployment rate will have no impact on real export growth and will, therefore, also have no impact on

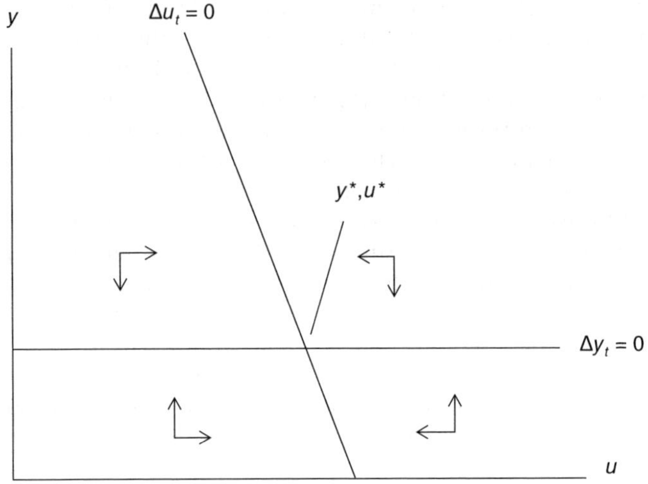

Figure 7.5

real output growth. As for the dynamics, the arrows indicate that these are such that the equilibrium solution (y^*, u^*) associated with the intersection of the $\Delta y_t = 0$ and $\Delta u_t = 0$ schedules is stable.

Turning to the explicit algebraic expressions for the equilibrium rates of real output growth and the unemployment rate (long-run NAIRU) in our reformulated model, these are given by:

$$y^* = \frac{\alpha\gamma y_c r_e}{1 - \alpha\gamma\lambda y_c} \tag{7.16}$$

$$u^* = \frac{1}{\nu}\left[(1-\rho)r_e + n_e - \rho e_c + \nu u_c\right] - \gamma\left[\frac{(1-\rho)(1-\lambda)}{\nu(1-\alpha\gamma\lambda y_c)}\right]\alpha y_c r_e \tag{7.17}$$

From these expressions, we can see that y^* is unambiguously increasing and u^* unambiguously decreasing in γ, α and y_c. With respect to α, this means that the stronger is the cumulative causation effect working through relative non-price competitiveness, the faster is the growth rate of real output in equilibrium and the lower is the long-run NAIRU. Meanwhile, a higher value of y_c results in a higher y^* and lower u^* not only through its obvious direct effect on real export growth, but also by, once again, strengthening the effect of the cumulative causation mechanism working through relative non-price competitiveness. This is because the larger is y_c, the larger will be the increase in the growth rate of real exports that results from a given induced increase in ε_t. As for r_e and λ, an increase in either one of these again has an unambiguous positive effect on y^*. However, just as with our original model, whether or not they also have the impact of reducing the long-run NAIRU is ambiguous. In particular, in this case, the relevant condition for structural reform that results in an increase in r_e and/or λ to both increase y^* and reduce u^* is:

$$(1 - \rho)(1 - \alpha\gamma\gamma_c) < 0 \tag{7.18}$$

The intuition behind this condition is very similar to that behind the equivalent condition, given in equation (7.14), for our original model. Examining Figure 7.6, we again see that, provided $\rho < 1$, an increase in r_e both shifts our model's $\Delta u_t = 0$ schedule outwards and its $\Delta y_t = 0$ schedule upwards. The outwards shift in the $\Delta u_t = 0$ schedule is again explained by a Luddite effect. That is to say, from equations (7.9) and (7.10), an increase in r_e and/or λ automatically tends to increase the unemployment rate by resulting in a lower rate of employment growth for any given rate of real output growth. However, the upwards shift in the $\Delta y_t = 0$ schedule cannot this time be explained by the direct price and expectations effects that appeared in our original model. This is because, as is obvious from our original discussion of them, both of these effects are relative price competitiveness effects. Rather, the upwards shift in the $\Delta y_t = 0$ schedule is attributable to what we may term an *income elasticity of demand effect*.[55] In particular, for any given rate of unemployment, an increase in r_e and/or λ increases the rate of labour productivity growth. From equation (7.15), this faster rate of

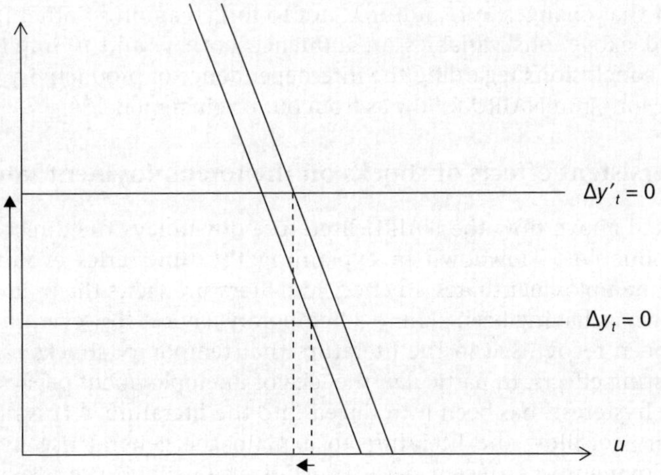

Figure 7.6

labour productivity growth facilitates an improvement in relative non-price competitiveness that feeds through to an increase in ε_t. The increase in ε_t makes, in turn, for faster real export growth, which itself makes for a faster rate of growth of real output. In equation (7.18) we see that the strength of this income elasticity of demand effect is captured by the term $\alpha\gamma y_c$. Thus, the larger are α, y_c and γ the larger is the effect. This is because the larger is α the larger is the increase in ε resulting from any given increase in r_t caused by an increase in r_e and/or λ. Meanwhile, the larger is y_c the larger is the increase in the rate of real export growth resulting from any given increase in ε induced by an increase in r_e and/or λ. Finally, the larger is γ, the larger is the reaction of the rate of real output growth to any such increase in real export growth. Overall, we see that Figure 7.6 has been drawn such that the income elasticity of demand effect outweighs the Luddite effect. Consequently, the condition in equation (7.18) holds and the shifts in the $\Delta y_t = 0$ and $\Delta u_t = 0$ schedules are such that both the equilibrium growth rate increases and the long-run NAIRU falls.

Clearly, had we drawn Figure 7.6 such that the condition in equation (7.18) did not hold then, similar to our original model, we would have observed a long-run trade-off between growth and unemployment. Also similar to our original model, even with the figure drawn as it is, there remains a short-run trade-off between growth and unemployment. Again, this is a result of the staggering of the Luddite effect *vis-à-vis* any offsetting effects: in particular, vis-à-vis the income elasticity of demand effect.[56] As with our original model, the only circumstances in which there is no visible trade-off is when $\rho = 1$. However, the same caveat about the lack of any apparent trade-off being more apparent than real applies as much to our reformulated model here as to our original model. Finally, note that the fact that changes in r_e and/or λ, not to forget, amongst other parameters and exogenous variables, α, influence both y^* and u^* implies that similar conclusions regarding the interdependence of productivity growth and the long-run NAIRU follow as from our original model.[57]

The persistent effects of shocks on the unemployment rate

We noted above how the NAIRU literature downplays the direct role of the productivity slowdown in explaining the time-series evolution of OECD unemployment rates. In effect, the literature views the productivity slowdown as having been akin to a 'temporary' shock. However, that said, it has been recognised in the literature that temporary shocks can have long-lasting effects. In particular, the idea of unemployment persistence or impure hysteresis has been introduced into the literature.[58] This has been necessary to allow the literature to explain the general rise in OECD unemployment over recent decades. Thus, the general rise is explained through postulating that the productivity slowdown and other common 'temporary' negative shocks – such as the commodity price shocks of 1973/74 and 1979/80 – that occurred in the 1970s and early 1980s have had a much more long-lasting impact on unemployment through mechanisms making for unemployment persistence. The mechanisms in question are very closely related to the factors that the NAIRU literature has identified as explaining the cross-sectional component of OECD unemployment – factors that we discussed above. Specifically, the mechanisms are predominantly associated with the working of labour market institutions. Thus, for example, increased long-term unemployment, which, it is argued, would have been far less likely to occur if benefit durations had been shorter, is argued to have been one channel through which persistence has occurred (Layard et al., 1991).[59]

The fact that the mechanisms identified as having made for unemployment persistence in the NAIRU literature are mainly associated with the working of labour market institutions is hardly surprising. This is because the typical model in the literature only really considers the labour market in detail. Thus, it is 'as if' all temporary shocks operate directly on the unemployment rate. However, our models are much more detailed on the side of the goods market. Consequently, not all temporary shocks have to operate directly on the unemployment rate. Rather, some such shocks can operate directly on the rate of real output growth and, through this, *in*directly on the unemployment rate. This being the case, the persistent effects of temporary shocks on unemployment can also be the indirect consequence of the persistent effects of such shocks on real output growth. In turn, this suggests that unemployment persistence may be attributable not only to mechanisms associated with the working of labour market institutions, but also with what are essentially non-labour market institutions.

To make the above points more precisely let us again consider the reformulated version of our extended Dixon–Thirlwall model. In Figure 7.7 we repeat the phase diagram for this model. From this we can see that if we consider a temporary pure unemployment shock then the unemployment rate increases above the equilibrium value u^*. That is to say, we shift from the long-run NAIRU to a higher short-run NAIRU. Following this, we see that the dynamics of our model are such that the unemployment rate begins to fall and the short-run NAIRU starts to shift back towards the long-run NAIRU. This continues until the short-run NAIRU once again coincides with the long-run NAIRU. During the transitional process, the rate of real output growth remains at its equilibrium value y^*. Clearly, we have unemployment persistence here that is the direct result of a temporary shock to the unemployment rate. Precisely how strong the persistence is depends upon the eigenvalues (μ_1, μ_2) of our model, which are given as equations (7.19) and (7.20) below. In particular, because the $\Delta y_t = 0$ schedule is horizontal, the

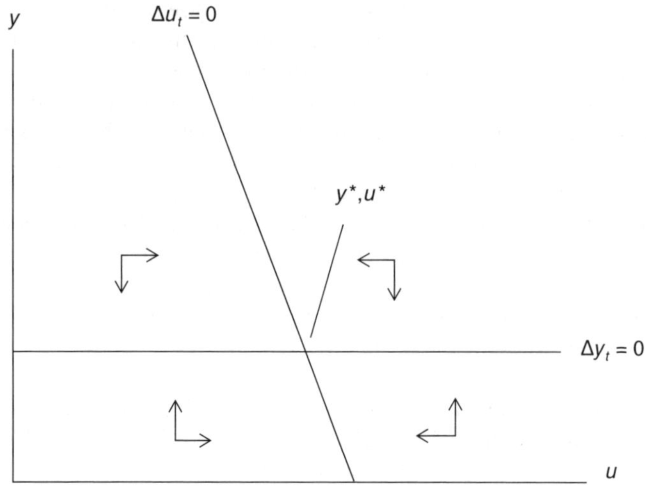

Figure 7.7

extent of persistence is determined solely by the eigenvalue μ_2. Given that this eigenvalue is decreasing in ν, it follows that the extent of persistence is greater the less flexibly does the labour force respond to movements in the rate of unemployment. This we would expect to be affected by labour market institutions and so we have the familiar result that persistence is attributable to mechanisms associated with the working of labour market institutions. However, consider now a temporary negative shock that operates instead directly on the rate of real output growth. From the phase diagram, such a shock initially pushes the rate of real output growth below y^*, whilst leaving the unemployment rate unchanged at the long-run NAIRU. However, the dynamics of our model are such that in the periods following the temporary shock the unemployment rate starts to increase above the long-run NAIRU. That is to say, the temporary negative shock to y_t starts to shift the economy on to short-run NAIRUs that are above the long-run NAIRU. Consequently, we again obtain unemployment persistence, only this time as the indirect result of the temporary negative shock to the rate of real output growth. Moreover, the dynamics of our model are such that this persistence will be increasing not only in the eigenvalue μ_2 but also in the eigenvalue μ_1. From equation (7.19) we can therefore see that unemployment persistence in this case is not only decreasing with ν, but increasing with α, γ, λ and y_c. In other words, unemployment persistence will be greater the stronger is the cumulative causation mechanism that drives real output growth. Although the precise determinants of α, γ and λ are a bit of a black box,[60] it is inconceivable that they do not include non-labour market institutions. Thus, for example, γ will be increasing in the strength of the linkages between the export and non-export sectors of the economy and it does not seem overly speculative to suggest that the strength of these linkages will be influenced by non-labour market institutions.

$$\mu_1 = \alpha\gamma\lambda y_c \tag{7.19}$$

$$\mu_2 = \frac{1}{1+\nu} \tag{7.20}$$

Whilst it would be wrong to deny that labour market institutions are important in the operation of unemployment persistence,[61] the above analysis suggests that the mechanisms through which persistence operates are likely to be more general than those that have thus far been identified. Furthermore, this being the case, non labour market institutions are also likely to be an important determinant of unemployment persistence. This is particularly so when we consider that most temporary shocks that affect the unemployment rate do not tend to be pure shocks to the unemployment rate, but shocks of the sort that we have identified that impact in the first instance on the rate of real output growth. Also note that our models imply, contrary to the rest of the NAIRU literature, that removing unemployment persistence from an economy may actually do more harm than good. This is because in, for example, the reformulated version of our extended Dixon – Thirlwall model we see that not only is unemployment persistence increasing in α, γ, λ and y_c, but so too, from equation (7.16), is the equilibrium growth rate. This is because some of the same factors that influence the extent of unemployment persistence in this model also determine the strength of the cumulative causation mechanism that drives real output growth.

Conclusion

To summarise, the Dixon–Thirlwall model, which is now considered to be the 'standard' model of cumulative causation, implicitly assumes that workers are passive to the implications of firms' pricing decisions for their real wages. In this chapter we have presented two extended versions of the model that, by drawing on the NAIRU literature, relax this assumption. As with the original model, cumulative causation in the first of these extended models works through the relative price competitiveness of exports. However, in the second, cumulative causation works through what is now the more empirically relevant channel of the relative *non*-price competitiveness of exports. Both models are, nevertheless, suggestive of possible shortcomings in the standard story of OECD unemployment over the last thirty years. First, in this standard story the large cross-sectional variations in unemployment rates that have been, and continue to be, observed are explained by the heterogeneity of labour market institutions – in particular, by variations in wage bargaining institutions and the treatment of the unemployed. Our models suggest that other factors – most notably, variations in the income elasticities of demand for exports reflecting variations in relative *non*-price competitiveness – may also have been important in explaining the heterogeneity of experience. The difference between our two models is that in our first such differences are treated as exogenous, whereas in our second they arise endogenously. Second, in the standard story the productivity slowdown is only indirectly associated with the general rise in OECD unemployment.

This is reflected in its reduction to the status of a 'temporary' shock. However, both of our models suggest that this downplaying of the productivity slowdown may have been a mistake. Third, the standard story again sees labour market institutions as the key to explaining the persistent unemployment effects of 'temporary' shocks. Yet our models are suggestive of additional channels through which unemployment persistence may have been working, with the corollary that non-labour market institutions may be more important in the generation of persistence than has hitherto been realised.

However, it is only appropriate to end on a note of caution. This chapter is a theoretical contribution and therefore, as has been emphasised throughout, the above implications of our models are no more than suggestive. To establish the implications as anything more than this will require detailed empirical work that is beyond the scope of this chapter. Nevertheless, it is hoped that this chapter will serve to remind the reader that the standard story of OECD unemployment is not accepted unquestioningly – if only to spur those who espouse the story to continue their efforts to convince those who have their doubts.

Mathematical appendix: the Dixon–Thirlwall (1975) model extended to include unemployment

Through a process of substitution and rearrangement, the structural equations (7.1) – (7.4), (7.6) – (7.7) and (7.9) – (7.11) reduce to the following linear non-homogenous system, where the system is expressed in terms of deviations from the equilibrium (y^*, u^*):

$$\begin{bmatrix} y_t - y^* \\ u_t - u^* \end{bmatrix} = \begin{bmatrix} -\dfrac{\gamma\eta\lambda}{1-\phi} & -\dfrac{\gamma\eta b}{1-\phi} \\ \dfrac{(1-\rho)(1-\lambda)}{1+\nu}\left(\dfrac{\gamma\eta\lambda}{1-\phi}\right) & \dfrac{1-\phi+\gamma\eta b(1-\rho)(1-\lambda)}{(1+\nu)(1-\phi)} \end{bmatrix} \begin{bmatrix} y_{t-1} - y^* \\ u_{t-1} - u^* \end{bmatrix}$$

From this, it is straightforward to show that the system's eigenvalues are given by:

$$\mu = \frac{\gamma\eta b(1-\rho)(1-\lambda)+(1-\phi)-\gamma\eta\lambda(1+\nu)}{2(1-\phi)(1+\nu)} \pm \sqrt{\frac{[\gamma\eta b(1-\rho)(1-\lambda)+(1-\phi)-\gamma\eta\lambda(1+\nu)]^2+4\gamma\eta\lambda(1-\phi)(1+\nu)}{4(1-\phi)^2(1+\nu)^2}}$$

and that the equations for the $\Delta y_t = 0$ and $\Delta u_t = 0$ schedules are given by:

$\Delta y_t = 0$ schedule

$$y = -\left(\frac{\gamma\eta b}{1-\phi+\gamma\eta\lambda}\right)u + \gamma\left[\frac{(\delta+\eta)(1-\phi)\pi_c+(1-\phi)\varepsilon y_c-\eta(r_e-a-\tau)}{1-\phi+\gamma\eta\lambda}\right]$$

$\Delta u_t = 0$ schedule

$$y = \left[\frac{\nu(1-\phi)-\gamma\eta b(1-\rho)(1-\lambda)}{\gamma\eta\lambda(1-\rho)(1-\lambda)}\right]u - \left[\frac{1-\phi}{\gamma\eta\lambda(1-\rho)(1-\lambda)}\right](n_e-\rho e_c+\nu u_c)+ \frac{1}{\eta\lambda}[(\delta+\eta)(1-\phi)+\eta(a+\tau)+(1-\phi)\varepsilon y_c] - \left[\frac{1-\phi+\gamma\eta(1-\lambda)}{\gamma\eta\lambda(1-\lambda)}\right]r_e$$

From these equations it can be seen that the $\Delta u_t = 0$ schedule will be downwards sloping providing $\rho < 1$. If $\rho = 1$ then the schedule is vertical. Meanwhile, the $\Delta y_t = 0$ schedule will be upwards sloping providing $1 - \phi + \gamma\eta\lambda > 0$. Knowing this helps us to draw the following conclusions about the system's dynamic behaviour:

- Case 1: $\rho = 1$ and $1 - \phi + \gamma\eta\lambda > 0$: the system is globally stable.
- Case 2: $\rho < 1$ and $1 - \phi + \gamma\eta\lambda > 0$: the system exhibits oscillating dynamics. Whether or not these oscillating dynamics are stable depends on the system's eigenvalues.
- Case 3: $1 - \phi + \gamma\eta\lambda < 0$: the system is saddle-path stable.

At least for the UK, case 2 seems to be the empirically relevant one. In particular, for the UK $\phi \approx 0.4$, $\eta \approx -0.5$ and $\lambda \approx 0.5$ (see Roberts, forthcoming). The stability of the system therefore depends on the eigenvalues. Unfortunately, the expressions for these eigenvalues are too complex to allow easy generalisations. However, Roberts (forthcoming) simulated the model and found that the oscillating dynamics are stable for combinations of parameter and exogenous variable values that are empirically relevant to the UK.

Extension to allow nominal wage inflation to depend upon productivity growth

The structural equations [3.1]–[3.4], [3.6]–[3.7] and [3.9]–[3.11] remain the same except for equation [3.6], which becomes:

$$w_t = r_t - bu_t + \pi_t^e$$

The system of difference equations, again expressed in terms of deviations from the equilibrium (y*, u*), therefore becomes:

$$\begin{bmatrix} y_t - y^* \\ u_t - u^* \end{bmatrix} = \begin{bmatrix} 0 & -\dfrac{\gamma\eta b}{1-\phi} \\ 0 & \dfrac{1-\phi+\gamma\eta b(1-\rho)(1-\lambda)}{(1+\nu)(1-\phi)} \end{bmatrix} \begin{bmatrix} y_{t-1} - y^* \\ u_{t-1} - u^* \end{bmatrix}$$

and the eigenvalues:

$$\mu_1 = 0$$

$$\mu_2 = \frac{1-\phi+\gamma\eta b(1-\rho)(1-\lambda)}{(1+\nu)(1-\phi)}$$

Meanwhile, the equations of the $\Delta y_t = 0$ and $\Delta u_t = 0$ schedules are given by:

$$\Delta y_t = 0 \text{ schedule} \quad y = -\left(\frac{\gamma\eta b}{1-\phi}\right)u + \gamma\left[\frac{(\delta+\eta)(1-\phi)\pi_c + \eta\tau + (1-\phi)\varepsilon y_c}{1-\phi}\right]$$

$$\Delta u_t = 0 \text{ schedule} \quad u = (1-\phi)\left[\frac{n_e - \rho e_c + \nu u_c + (1-\rho)r_e}{\nu(1-\phi) - \gamma\eta b(1-\rho)(1-\lambda)}\right] - \gamma(1-\rho)(1-\lambda)\left[\frac{(\delta+\eta)(1-\phi)\pi_c + \eta\tau + (1-\phi)\varepsilon y_c}{\nu(1-\phi) - \gamma\eta b(1-\rho)(1-\lambda)}\right]$$

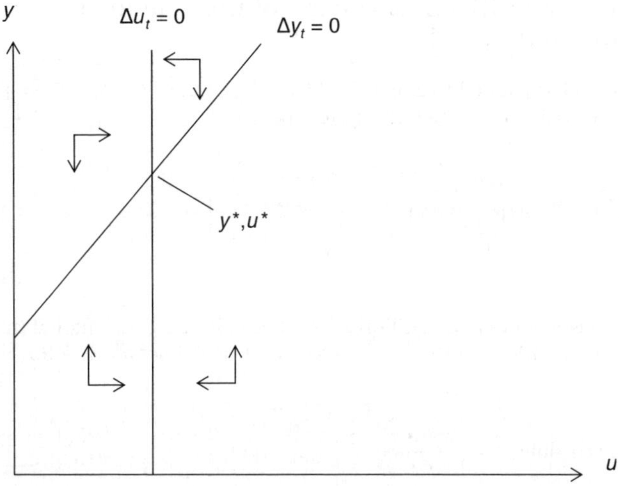

Figure 7.A1

These schedules, along with the associated dynamics of the system, are shown in the phase diagram Figure 7.A1.

The system's equilibrium solution is given by:

$$y^* = \gamma\nu\left[\frac{(\delta+\eta)(1-\phi)\pi_c + \eta\tau + (1-\phi)\varepsilon y_c}{\nu(1-\phi) - \gamma\eta b(1-\rho)(1-\lambda)}\right] - \gamma\eta b\left[\frac{n_e - \rho e_c + \nu u_c + (1-\rho)r_e}{\nu(1-\phi) - \gamma\eta b(1-\rho)(1-\lambda)}\right]$$

$$u^* = (1-\phi)\left[\frac{n_e - pe_c + \nu u_c + (1-\rho)r_e}{\nu(1-\phi) - \gamma\eta b(1-\rho)(1-\lambda)}\right] - \gamma(1-\rho)(1-\lambda)\left[\frac{(\delta+\eta)(1-\phi)\pi_c + \eta\tau + (1-\phi)\varepsilon y_c}{\nu(1-\phi) - \gamma\eta b(1-\rho)(1-\lambda)}\right]$$

From the equations for the $\Delta y_t = 0$ and $\Delta u_t = 0$ schedules it can be seen that structural reform that leads to an increase in r_e and/or λ will, provided $\rho < 1$, shift the $\Delta u_t = 0$ schedule to the right, whilst leaving the position of the $\Delta y_t = 0$ schedule unchanged (NB: for the $\Delta u_t = 0$ schedule, $\delta u/\delta\lambda = (1 - \rho)y^*/[\nu(1 - \phi) - \gamma\eta b(1 - \rho)(1 - \lambda)] > 0$). This increases both y* and u*. Thus, there is an unambiguous trade-off between growth and unemployment.

Non-price competitiveness version of the extended Dixon–Thirlwall model

With equation [3.15] added to equations [3.1]–[3.4], [3.6]–[3.7] and [3.9]–[3.11] and the restriction $\eta = \delta = 0$ imposed, the system becomes:

$$\begin{bmatrix} y_t - y^* \\ u_t - u^* \end{bmatrix} = \begin{bmatrix} \alpha\gamma\lambda y_c & 0 \\ \dfrac{-\alpha\gamma\lambda(1-\rho)(1-\lambda)y_c}{1+\nu} & \dfrac{1}{1+\nu} \end{bmatrix} \begin{bmatrix} y_{t-1} - y^* \\ u_{t-1} - u^* \end{bmatrix}$$

The system's eigenvalues and equilibrium solution (y*, u*) are as quoted in the main text, whilst the equations of the $\Delta y_t = 0$ and $\Delta u_t = 0$ schedules are as follows:

$$\Delta y_t = 0 \text{ schedule} \quad y = \frac{\alpha\gamma y_c r_e}{1 - \alpha\gamma\lambda y_c}$$

$$\Delta u_t = 0 \text{ schedule} \quad y = -\left[\frac{\nu}{\alpha\gamma\lambda(1-\rho)(1-\lambda)y_c}\right]u + \left[\frac{(n_e - \rho e_c + \nu u_c) + (1-\rho)[1 - \gamma(1-\lambda)\alpha y_c]r_e}{\alpha\gamma\lambda(1-\rho)(1-\lambda)y_c}\right]$$

Notes

1. The original version of this paper presented at the conference 'Verdoorn's Law 50 Years After' is available as Roberts (2002b). Comments made by both Geoff Harcourt and John McCombie were extremely useful in the preparation of this original version, whilst the author is grateful to Bernard Fingleton, Maurizo Pugno and participants at the conference and two anonymous referees for comments that helped lead to this (considerably) revised version.
2. NAIRU is an acronym for the non-accelerating inflation rate of unemployment. However, a more appropriate description of the rate of unemployment referred to would be the non-changing inflation rate of unemployment.
3. Hence, our concern is with the New Keynesian imperfect competition literature on unemployment, rather than with the 'natural' rate models of unemployment such as those in Friedman (1968) and Lucas (1972). For an excellent introduction to the New Keynesian imperfect competition literature, see Carlin and Soskice (1990).
4. Equation (7.2), which describes the determinants of x, derives from a multiplicative export demand function (Dixon and Thirlwall, 1975, p. 204). In specifying this equation we have abstracted from movements in the nominal exchange rate. This is entirely natural in the context of a regional economy. Meanwhile, it may be justified for a national economy on the grounds that for movements in the nominal exchange rate to have a permanent effect on real export growth in a multiplicative demand function they must not be one-off but permanently ongoing (Dixon and Thirlwall, 1975, pp. 210–11).

5. That is to say, of exports produced by other economies that compete with home exports in third markets.
6. Variables without a time subscript are assumed to be exogenously determined in our extended Dixon–Thirlwall model of the next section.
7. See the introduction of this book for a definition of the Verdoorn coefficient.
8. According to the NAIRU literature, the *level* of the mark-up in any one industry is: (a) inversely related to the elasticity of demand; (b) directly related to industry concentration and the extent of collusion/co-ordination between firms; and (c) inversely related to the ease of entry into the industry.
9. A further assumption implicit in equation (7.3), which can again best be seen from equation (7.5), is that the PDWI has no direct dependence upon the demand conditions faced by domestic firms in their product markets. Given the work of Carlin and Soskice (1990, see, especially, p. 140), this seems a reasonable assumption.
10. Pugno (1998) also endogenises the rate of nominal wage inflation within a Dixon–Thirlwall-style model. His model also shares other similarities with the model that we present in this section and it can implicitly provide many similar conclusions to those that we draw.
11. Some support for the linear dependence of w_t on u_t comes from David Grubb's finding for the OECD as a whole that 'the average response [of wage inflation] to unemployment is not strongly nonlinear' (Grubb, 1986, p. 72).
12. The reference to π_t^e as an *expected* rate of inflation is in keeping with common use of the word 'expected' in the macroeconomics literature. However, it is actually more appropriate to refer to π_t^e as an *anticipated* rate of inflation. This is because, as Rowthorn (1977, p. 215) argues, 'To *expect* something means simply to believe with greater or less confidence that it will occur, whereas to *anticipate* something means both to expect it and to act upon that expectation.' In equation (7.6) we are clearly assuming that workers act upon their expectations. Interestingly, Rowthorn, in his seminal NAIRU article, assumes that, for workers, expected inflation only becomes anticipated when it passes a certain threshold (see pp. 225–9). This is because '... in an era of slow inflation, expectations about future price changes may not be held with any great certainty and, even if they are, it is not particularly important to act on them. By contrast, in an era of fast inflation, the cost of inactivity may be high and workers must do something to protect themselves against the effects of future price changes.'
13. It is assumed that the same rate of inflation for goods that compete with home exports in third markets is relevant to imports of final consumption goods into the home market.
14. This assumption makes sense because equation (7.3) of the original Dixon–Thirlwall model implicitly assumes that in choosing π_h for period t domestic firms know what w_t will be and therefore do not have to form an expectation of it. In particular, the two assumptions are consistent if domestic firms set $\pi_{h,t}$ immediately after w_t has been set.
15. That the wedge is given by $(1 - \phi)(\pi_c - \pi_{h,t})$ follows from the fact that $w_t - \pi_t^e = w_t - \pi_{h,t} - (1 - \phi)(\pi_c - \pi_{h,t})$. From the rest of the NAIRU literature it may be thought that reducing this wedge must, because it reduces the BRWI, necessarily reduce our model's equilibrium rate of unemployment. However, this is not the case. This is because a fall in $\pi_c - \pi_h$ also leads to a slower rate of increase or faster rate of decline in the relative price competitiveness of home exports. In turn, this feeds through to produce a slower rate of real output growth.

16. Changes in payroll taxes will also drive a wedge between the growth rate of the real product wage and the (expected) growth rate of the real consumption wage. For simplicity, we abstract from such changes.
17. With the BRWI always equal to the PDWI it follows, from equations (7.5) and (7.8), that the unemployment rate at any moment in time is given by $u_t = [(a + \tau) - r_t + (1 - \phi)(\pi_c - \pi_{h,t})]/b$. We could alter the result that the unemployment rate is always a NAIRU by relaxing the assumption that workers possess rational expectations. In particular, if we respecify equation (7.7) as $\pi_t^e = \phi\pi_{h,t}^e + (1 - \phi)\pi_c$, so that workers do not have perfect knowledge of what $\pi_{h,t}$ will be when they enter wage negotiations, then the rate of unemployment at any moment in time will instead be given by $u_t = [(a + \tau) - r_t + (1 - \phi)(\pi_c - \pi_{h,t})]/b - (\phi/b)(\pi_{h,t} - \pi_{h,t}^e)$. This implies that unexpected inflation at any moment in time, $\pi_{h,t} - \pi_{h,t}^e > 0$, will reduce the unemployment rate below the NAIRU currently prevailing. In doing so, it will redistribute income away from workers and towards domestic firms.
18. Given the failure of inflation to redistribute income, we may alternatively think of the unemployment rate in our model as always being what Carlin and Soskice (1990, see especially p. 136) refer to as a 'competing claims equilibrium'.
19. The definition is an approximate one. It is derived from differentiating the exact definition $u_t = 1 - (E_t/N_t)$ where E_t denotes the level of employment in period t and N_t the size of the labour force in period t.
20. Equation (7.10) may be recognised as Kaldor's reformulation of Verdoorn's Law (Kaldor, 1966, p. 12). Also, the rate of employment growth in this equation should be thought of as a net rate. Underlying this, of course, will be considerable microeconomic turbulence.
21. That is to say, unemployment in our model, just as in other NAIRU models (see Carlin and Soskice, 1990; and Layard et al., 1991), should in no way be considered 'natural' in the sense that Friedman (1968) used the term. See also note 3.
22. Equally, reductions in perceived employment opportunities are likely to induce falls in labour-force participation. One particularly important mechanism through which this is likely to occur is early retirement.
23. Balassa (1963, p. 763) suggested that Beckerman's model (Beckerman, 1962), which is a close relation of the Dixon–Thirlwall model, be reformulated to include a (standard) Phillips curve. Not only this, but Balassa hinted that Beckerman's model also be extended to include a labour-force supply function such as that in equation (7.11). Potentially, therefore, Balassa was very close to constructing a model similar in spirit to our own. Beckerman (1962, p. 620) also noted the possibility that 'rising prices in a slow-growing economy might be "imported", via wages, into the faster-growing economy (and vice versa)' and furthermore states that 'In particular, small countries with less diversified economies, and hence more dependence on trade, are likely to import overseas inflation fairly rapidly'. Our equations (7.6) and (7.7) capture these possibilities.
24. Indeed, Dixon and Thirlwall (1975, p. 207) introduce transitional dynamics into their original model by introducing a one-period lag into equation (7.2).
25. Other candidates for the inclusion of lags are equations (7.4), and therefore also equation (7.10), and (7.11) (see Roberts, 2002b). However, including lags in these equations, as well as equation (7.2), would only complicate the analysis without bringing much in the way of additional insight.
26. The $\Delta y_t = 0$ and $\Delta u_t = 0$ schedules derive from the system of two linear non-homogenous difference equations, one for y_t and one for u_t, that follow from substituting and rearranging equations (7.1)–(7.4), (7.6)–(7.7) and

(7.9)–(7.11). Both this system and the equations for the $\Delta y_t = 0$ and $\Delta u_t = 0$ schedules are provided in the mathematical appendix.

27. Layard, et al.(1991) make a similar distinction in their NAIRU work.
28. By the same token, $1/b$ can be thought of as reflecting workers' degree of real wage growth rigidity.
29. These variations have been, and remain, very large. Thus, for example, whilst in the mid-1990s Switzerland's unemployment rate was around 4.0 per cent, Spain's was more than 20 per cent (Blanchard and Wolfers, 2000, p. C1).
30. Another interesting point is that if we set ρ and ν both equal to zero then the expression for y^* becomes $y^* = (n_e + r_e)/(1 - \lambda)$, whilst the expression for u^* becomes $u^* = \{[(\delta + \eta)(1 - \phi)\pi_c + (1 - \phi)\varepsilon y_c - \eta(r_e + a - \tau)]/\eta b\} - [(1 - \phi + \gamma\eta\lambda)/\gamma\eta b][(r_e + n_e)/(1 - \lambda)]$. This corresponds to the case of the pure labour-constrained economy. It is this case that Kaldor believed to be applicable to the UK economy at the time of his 1966 inaugural lecture before subsequently changing his mind (Targetti and Thirlwall, 1989, p. 11; see Roberts (2002b) for more detail on this aspect of our model).
31. This is because it is reasonable to postulate r_e in Verdoorn's Law as being an increasing function of knowledge spillovers from trading-partners, human capital accumulation and government expenditure on research and development. In particular, specification of r_e as dependent upon knowledge spillovers is consistent with recent attempts made in the empirical literature on Verdoorn's Law to control for spatial interdependence (Bernat, 1996; Fingleton and McCombie, 1998; and Roberts, 1998). Meanwhile, *if* the correct underlying specification of Verdoorn's Law is a Cobb–Douglas production function and human capital enters into this production function the law will be misspecified unless the accumulation of such capital is included in it or unless such accumulation has been orthogonal to output growth (Roberts, 1998, p. 10). The empirical work of Mankiw et al. (1992) and Temple (1998) suggests that it is proper to include human capital as an input in any Cobb–Douglas production function. Finally, De Benedictis (1997, p. 255) hypotheses that expenditure on research and development should enter Verdoorn's Law as a determinant of r_e.
32. It is possible that such reforms could also affect other parameters in our model. Thus, for example, an increase in government expenditure on training, especially on the training of the unemployed, that increases the quantity and quality of human capital accumulation may also, from the standard NAIRU literature, be expected to increase b. This is because an increase in such spending can be expected to increase the effective supply of labour, thereby reducing union bargaining power (Carlin and Soskice, 1990, p. 170; Layard et al., 1991). To the extent that this is the case any long-run growth-unemployment trade-off arising from an increase in r_e, the possibility of which is discussed below, will be offset and perhaps even reversed.
33. It is only actually true that an increase in r_e or λ increases y^* if $\nu(1 - \phi + \gamma\eta\lambda) - \gamma\eta b(1 - \rho)(1 - \nu) > 0$ holds. To assume that this condition holds seem reasonable on both empirical grounds (see Roberts, 2002b) and on the grounds that, as shown in the mathematical appendix, only if $(1 - \phi + \gamma\eta\lambda) > 0$ does our model have any chance of being globally stable.
34. Analysing the consequences of an increase in λ using phase diagrams is more difficult. This is because, as can be seen from the mathematical appendix, changes in λ affect not only the intercepts of the $\Delta y_t = 0$ and $\Delta u_t = 0$ schedules,

but also their slopes. However, the intuition as to why the new equilibrium may involve a higher u^* is the same as for an increase in r_e.

35. From this it follows that if we accepted Rowthorn's argument (see note 12) that the inflation that workers expect only becomes anticipated when it passes a certain threshold then, below the threshold, the condition in equation (7.14) would become $(1 - \rho)(1 + \gamma\eta) < 0$. Hence, with expected inflation below the threshold the case illustrated in Figure 7.3 below would be more likely.
36. From note 17 it follows that the creation of unexpected inflation has the potential to ease or even overcome this dilemma.
37. Another exogenous variable in our model that, if it changes, creates the possibility of a long-run and/or short-run trade-off between growth and unemployment is n_e. In particular, assuming $\nu(1 - \phi + \gamma\eta\lambda) - \gamma\eta b(1 - \rho)(1 - \nu) > 0$ (which, from note 33 is reasonable), an increase in n_e will definitely result in an increase in y^*, but will only also result in a decline in u^* if $(1 - \phi + \gamma\eta\lambda) < 0$ holds. Note that this is true even when $\rho = 1$.
38. The absence of a long-run trade-off when $\rho = 1$ is also evident from the condition in equation (7.14).
39. Had we allowed for a lagged reaction of labour-force growth to relative employment growth in equation (7.11) then a short-run trade-off would still exist even with $\rho = 1$.
40. In this chapter we have illustrated the consequences of changes in r_e via the use of phase diagrams. In Roberts (2002b) the consequences are instead illustrated through simulations of the time paths of y_t and u_t following such a change.
41. Note that, both when $\rho < 1$ and $\rho = 1$, in the course of moving from one equilibrium to another, the natural rate of growth is changing in our model. This is because the natural rate of growth is endogenous to the actual rate of growth of real output in our model. This is consistent with the evidence presented by León-Ledesma and Thirlwall (2002) that the natural rate of growth has been responsive to changes in the actual rate of growth in a sample of 15 OECD countries over the period 1961–95.
42. This is because changes in the rate of real output growth produce, via Verdoorn's Law, changes in the rate of labour productivity growth.
43. Blanchard and Katz (1997, pp. 56–7) do note that the theoretical result that the long-run NAIRU is invariant to changes in the rate of labour productivity growth assumes that the productivity growth has been the result of '... a very rarefied form of technological progress, one that affected productivity but did not affect the organization of production in any other way.' However, as is clear from the quote from Blanchard and Wolfers (2000) in note 47 below, the main text provides a fair reflection of Blanchard's, if not necessarily Katz's, actual stance.
44. The dependence of the long-run NAIRU in equation (7.13) of our model on n_e and π_c is also contrary to the conventional wisdom of the NAIRU literature (see Layard, et al., 1991, p. 31; Rowthorn, 1999, p. 414).
45. Thus, if y_t, and, hence, r_t, is perturbed upwards from the equilibrium value y^* in Figure 7.1, the long-run NAIRU remains fixed at u^*.
46. Between 1960–64 and the mid-1990s the overall unemployment rate in OECD-Europe increased from 1.7 % to 11.0 % (Blanchard and Wolfers, 2000, p. C1).
47. To quote Blanchard and Wolfers (2000, pp. C4–C6) on this point, 'There is no question that a slowdown in TFP growth can lead to a higher equilibrium unemployment rate for some time... Can the effects of such a slowdown on unemployment be permanent? Theory suggests that the answer, to a first

approximation, is no… There lies the first puzzle of European unemployment. The initial shock is clearly identified. But, after more than twenty years, it is hard to believe that its effects are not largely gone.' (see also of Blanchard and Katz, 1997, p. 66, on this point). Interestingly, part of the reason Blanchard and Wolfers may find it a puzzle is that they argue that a slowdown in productivity growth affects the unemployment rate by leading to real wage growth in excess of productivity growth. Eventually, workers and firms realise that such excess real wage growth is unsustainable. This leads to real wage growth being reduced to bring it into line with productivity growth. Once this happens, the effect of the productivity slowdown on unemployment disappears (hence, the reason why the long-run NAIRU is unaffected). However, in our model, it is evident from equation (7.5) that, provided we make the reasonable assumption that $\tau = 0$, the PDWI, and, hence, the actual rate of growth of the real product wage, always tracks productivity growth. This being the case there is never any need for expectations to adjust.

48. The use of the adjective 'direct' is important. This is because the NAIRU literature does see the productivity slowdown as having had an important *in*direct role in explaining the time-series evolution of OECD unemployment. We shall return to this point below.
49. Rowthorn (1999) and Daveri and Tabellini (2000) have also questioned the conventional wisdom that changes in the long-run NAIRU have not been associated with changes in the rate of labour productivity growth.
50. Indeed, according to Madsen (1998, p. 859), relative price competitiveness between OECD countries has remained pretty much unchanged over the past two decades. Furthermore, and particularly relevant to our extended Dixon–Thirlwall model, the econometric evidence suggests that the economic significance of such competitiveness in explaining the rise in OECD unemployment (see note 46) has been marginal (Madsen, 1998, p. 859).
51. If it is difficult to argue that relative price competitiveness has been important in determining success on international markets in recent decades then it is near impossible to argue that it has been an important determinant of success on inter-regional markets. This is because, quite aside from the fact that the determinants of success on inter-regional markets are likely to be similar to the determinants of success on international markets, there is much greater scope for arbitrage at the regional than at the national level. The consequence of this is that the prices of most goods traded by regional economies tend to be set at the national level.
52. In doing this we are following Roberts (2002a), who extends the original Dixon–Thirlwall model in this manner in order to reconcile it with the empirical evidence on conditional convergence.
53. The equations for the $\Delta y_t = 0$ and $\Delta u_t = 0$ schedules that appear in the phase diagram, together with the system of linear non-homogenous difference equations from which they derive, are given in the mathematical appendix.
54. In drawing the phase diagram we have assumed $\alpha\gamma\lambda y_c < 1$. This is necessary both to ensure that the $\Delta y_t = 0$ schedule appears in positive y_t space and therefore that there exists an economically meaningful equilibrium solution, and to ensure that the dynamics of the model are stable (see the eigenvalues for the model given as equations (7.19) and (7.20) below).
55. This makes Landesmann and Snell's (1989) finding of an increase in the income elasticity of demand for UK manufacturing exports in the early 1980s and their linking of it to the structural reforms implemented by the Conservative govern-

ment of the period particularly interesting. The same applies for Carlin and Soskice's (1990, p. 264) argument that increased government expenditure on training may be expected to impact upon unemployment by affecting non-price competitiveness.

56. In our original model, an increase in n_e also gave rise to a long-run and/or short-run trade-off. For our reformulated model we obtain a similar result because, even when $\rho = 1$, y^* in equation (7.16) is independent of n_e, whilst u^* in equation (7.17) is increasing in n_e.
57. In attempting to capture the idea of cumulative causation working through relative non-price as opposed to relative price competitiveness, Roberts (2002b) presents an alternative reformulation of our original model. That reformulation has the advantage of being more explicit as to the mechanism through which changes in the rate of labour productivity growth may feed through to changes in relative non-price competitiveness. The downside is that the empirical validity of the postulated mechanism is extremely doubtful (see Roberts, 2002b).
58. This is not to be confused with the idea of *pure* hysteresis (as, for example, appears in Blanchard and Summers, 1987) which the NAIRU literature originally focused more upon. This is the idea that temporary shocks have not just a long-lasting effect on the unemployment rate, but a permanent effect. Amongst other reasons, the literature came down on the side of impure rather than pure hysteresis because pure hysteresis implies that, given a random sequence of temporary shocks, the unemployment rate should eventually hit zero or 100 per cent.
59. Blanchard and Wolfers (2000, pp. C17–C18) provide what they term a 'non-exhaustive' list of mechanisms through which labour market institutions can affect the degree of persistence.
60. Although see the earlier discussion regarding the determinants of λ.
61. As we have seen, our reformulated version of our extended Dixon–Thirlwall model is perfectly consistent with a role for labour market institutions in determining the extent of unemployment hysteresis. To reiterate, this is because v appears in the expression for the eigenvalue μ_2. Moreover, the same is true, even more so, for our original extended Dixon–Thirlwall model. This is because b appears in the eigenvalues for this model (see the mathematical appendix) and, as discussed above, b is determined by labour market institutions.

8

Cumulative Growth and the Catching-Up Debate From a Disequilibrium Standpoint

*Miguel A. León-Ledesma**

Introduction

The economic growth debate of the 1980s and 1990s has opened the door to a greater range of ideas about why and how growth rates differ across countries and regions. The main achievement from a theoretical viewpoint is the construction of models that allow growth rates to be positive in the steady state without the help of any exogenous variable. Growth can be positive in the long run and depends on the investment decisions of individual economic agents. This may seem obvious to the amateur economic growth practitioner. However, this intuitive idea clashes with the complications and constraints that both real data and mathematical models impose for the theoretician of economic growth. How can we explain the continuous growth of output without the generation of an explosion in per capita income that cannot be observed in the data? What factors lie behind this possibility? 'New' growth theory has indeed contributed to specifying growth models in which both questions are addressed. Technical progress, either disembodied or embodied in capital goods, has been placed at the centre of the analysis. National specific non-exogenous factors may now explain why some countries have been more successful than others. Even more, a world of diverging per capita incomes has been more plausibly explained by this more recent analysis.

However, the question must be put forward: to what extent are these results 'new'? And, even more pertinently, do these new theories relax some of the narrower assumptions of the old Solow growth model? The answer to the first question is 'not to a great extent'. The answer to

* The author wishes to thank Tony Thirlwall, Joao R. Faria, Bernard Fingleton, Mark Roberts and all the participants at the conference on 'Verdoorn's Law 50 Years After' held in Genoa, Italy, in September 1999 for helpful comments and suggestions received.

the second is 'not to the extent that the full employment frictionless economy assumption is kept unchanged'. In this essay we will argue that cumulative causation growth models had already produced certain features of the 'endogenous growth' nature of these models. We will also argue that the main difference between cumulative and 'new' growth models lies in the fact that the former does not assume full employment and does not deal with a general equilibrium economy. It may be argued that the most recent contributions to 'new' growth theory – such as Aghion and Howitt (1998) – do allow for the presence of unemployment. However, the unemployment arising in these models is treated as a 'natural' rate related to labour market reallocation when firms face search costs and the skills-mix changes associated with technical progress. No wait or demand-driven unemployment exists because the economy is in general equilibrium and is supply-constrained. In cumulative causation models full employment or the 'natural' rate of growth is never achieved because growth creates the necessary resources for growth itself. In this sense, the nature of the cumulative growth models allows for a 'total' endogeneity of growth to growth itself as a self-reinforcing process. In this context, we will show how a very wide range of dynamics of income distribution across the world is a possible outcome in these models. That is, despite having been ignored by recent debates, cumulative growth models may explain divergence, constant relative differences or catch-up in per capita income levels. This essay will place a particular emphasis on the impact of the Verdoorn effect. Verdoorn's Law has been widely used to justify the existence of diverging patterns of growth. As we will show, the existence of a Verdoorn effect does not necessarily imply divergence or explosive behaviour, although it is the central mechanism that allows for endogenous productivity growth.

Hence, the aim of this chapter is to review important contributions on the cumulative growth literature that emphasise the aforementioned issues. It will also present a model of cumulative causation based on León-Ledesma (2002), in which cumulative growth generates a richer set of dynamics of relative productivities by introducing the effects of catching-up and 'learning by doing', and analyse the role played on these dynamics by Verdoorn's Law.

Our essay will be organised as follows. In the first section we present a brief review of the main cumulative causation models and discuss their strengths and weaknesses. This discussion will help in understanding the model developed in the next section, in which technical progress, technology diffusion and other relevant variables from an empirical point of view are introduced in the canonical cumulative growth model. The dynamic behaviour of the model will be analysed in the following section. In the final section we will extract some relevant conclusions from the arguments put forward.

Cumulative growth: an overview

As a consequence of his *laws of growth,* Kaldor's (1970) paper on the determinants of regional growth disparities entails a definitive adherence of Kaldor with the cumulative causation theories of development in line with Myrdal (1957) and that can be dated back to Veblen's (1915) seminal work. Kaldor's explanation of the differences in growth rates among regions rests on the existence of two interrelated mechanisms: (1) the growth of output is determined by the growth of aggregate demand, concretely by the growth of exports, and this, in turn, is influenced by the degree of competitiveness of the region; (2) productivity growth is a by-product of output growth due to the existence of dynamic increasing returns as a result of the mechanisms underlying Verdoorn's Law. Since prices are set in oligopolistic markets, a mark-up over unit labour costs is the dominant rule of pricing. Growth in productivity stemming from the growth of output would allow for a reduction of unit labour costs and, thus, of prices, increasing the competitiveness of the region (or country). This increased competitiveness allows for further expansions of output through increased exports, and so on. The result is that given an initial advantage, regions will tend, through the circular and cumulative mechanism described above, to maintain it (or even increase it) over time, resulting in uneven development among regions. In this mechanism, Verdoorn's Law plays the crucial role of transforming the growth of output into the growth of demand and, thus, more growth of output.[1] Dynamic increasing returns are a force running against the existence of converging levels of output per capita among regions.

However, the arguments of Kaldor are far from being clearly formalised. It is not clear whether Kaldor was arguing that *growth rates* tend to diverge or whether he was referring simply to the *level of output per capita.* In the first case we would be confronting a rather unstable world with explosive behaviour in some regions and ever-declining behaviour in others, which is not observed in the real world. The canonical Kaldorian model of growth was first formalised by Dixon and Thirlwall (1975). It is worth examining this model in order to extract clear consequences and analyse further extensions that have enriched the possible set of dynamics of Kaldor's verbal arguments. For any given region, the discrete time form of the model can be written as

$$y_t = \gamma x_t \tag{8.1}$$

$$x_t = \eta p_{dt} + \delta p_{ft} + \varepsilon z_t \tag{8.2}$$

$$p_{dt} = w_t - r_t + \tau_t \tag{8.3}$$

$$r_t = r_a + \lambda y_t. \tag{8.4}$$

Equation (8.1) states that the growth of output (y_t) is a linear function of the growth of exports (x_t). Equation (8.2) is a typical export demand function expressed in growth rates, where the growth of exports depends on the growth of domestic prices (p_{dt}), foreign prices (p_{ft}) and the income of the 'rest of the world' (z_t), η, δ and ε being the respective elasticities. Equation (8.3) is the expression for the rate of growth of domestic prices, which is derived from a mark-up pricing equation as $P_{dt} = (W_t/R_t)T_t$, where W_t is the level of money wages, R_t is the average product of labour and T_t is one plus the percentage mark-up over unit labour costs. Finally, equation (8.4) is the expression for the rate of growth of productivity (r_t) derived from Verdoorn's Law relationship, r_a being the autonomous productivity growth. The model is block recursive, and its solution for the equilibrium rate of growth of output is

$$y_t = \gamma \frac{\left\lfloor \eta(w_t - r_a + \tau_t) + \delta p_{ft} + \varepsilon z_t \right\rfloor}{1 + \gamma\eta\lambda}. \tag{8.5}$$

This expression is telling us that the growth rate of a region varies positively[2] with the autonomous rate of productivity growth (r_a), the growth of 'world' income (z), the income elasticity of demand for exports (ε), the rate of growth of foreign prices (p_f) and the Verdoorn coefficient (λ), and negatively with the rates of growth of wages and mark-up (w and τ), the effect of η being ambiguous.

Note that 'it is the Verdoorn relation which makes the model circular and cumulative, and which gives rise to the possibility that once a region obtains a growth advantage, it will keep it' (Dixon and Thirlwall, 1975, p. 205). However, the existence of a Verdoorn relation is not a sufficient condition for the existence of growth rate differences among regions unless the value of λ is different between regions or initially the rest of the parameters of the model differ, so Verdoorn's coefficient serves to exaggerate these differences. Summarising, growth rate differences are determined by the structural characteristics of regions that determine their degree of competitiveness, the rate of induced productivity growth and the extent to which all these characteristics influence the aggregate demand growth. Boyer and Petit (1991) distinguish between productivity and demand *regimes* in order to clarify the double link between productivity growth and aggregate demand growth in this model. The former would reflect the extent to which aggregate demand influences productivity growth, while the latter would determine the effect of productivity growth on aggregate demand growth. For the model to show a stable pattern, the sensitivity of aggregate demand growth to productivity growth must be higher than that of productivity growth to output growth. Otherwise, we would be in the presence of ever-increasing growth rates differences and, as Gordon (1991) states, this is 'too much cumulation'. The stability of the model can be studied by introducing a lag structure in any of the equations (we will use equation (8.2)) and analysing the asymptotic behaviour of the solution. Introducing a lag in equation (8.2) yields a first-order difference equation, the general solution to which is

$$y_t = y_o(-\gamma\eta\lambda)^t + \frac{\gamma\left[\eta(w_{t-1} - r_a + \tau_{t-1}) + \varepsilon z_{t-1} + \delta p_{ft-1}\right]}{1+\gamma\eta\lambda}. \tag{8.6}$$

For the model to be stable $(-\gamma\eta\lambda)$ must be < 1,[3] and growth would converge towards its equilibrium level. If $(-\gamma\eta\lambda) > 1$ the rate of growth of the region would be an increasing function of time, and there would not be a stable solution.[4] If this result holds, divergence *in growth rates* would occur, and the outcome would be that divergence in *per capita incomes* exhibits an explosive behaviour, which is very unlikely to occur given reasonable values for the parameters of the model.[5] The most plausible result is one of sustained equilibrium differences in growth rates between regions.[6]

Setterfield (1997a, 1997b) favours a disequilibrium interpretation of this model that helps to realise the role played by irreversible historical time in determining the growth path. If we assume that the general solution (8.6) has a unit root, that is $(-\gamma\eta\lambda) = 1$, then it is clear that the equilibrium growth will be dependent on the initial conditions. In fact, this is the cumulative nature of the model, in which the starting point of the process determines the rest of the sequences of occurrence. This would also be the case if, even when $(-\gamma\eta\lambda) < 1$, the velocity of convergence towards the determinate equilibrium is too slow in comparison with the changes experienced in the exogenous data determining the equilibrium. In such a case, equation (8.5) would be rendered irrelevant for explaining the long-run growth rate. Thus, the initial condition and the time position of the system would determine the growth rate that, in this case, is said to be *path-dependent* in the sense that it is not independent of the historical shocks. However, Setterfield points out that a more satisfactory explanation of growth would be one in which it depends not only on the initial conditions, but also on all the steps taken towards the actual position. This case is possible if the model shows *hysteresis* with its parameters changing over time depending on the resulting rate of growth. This possibility will be dealt with when we refer to the possible existence of *lock-in* processes, in line with the arguments of Arthur (1989).

The Kaldorian model analysed is advancing the idea of an endogenous determination of the *natural rate of growth*, as discussed and tested in León-Ledesma and Thirlwall (2002). Productivity growth is an endogenous result of the actual rate of growth, and it is assumed that labour adapts automatically to increases in labour demand stemming from increases in aggregate demand. Wages do not play a role in clearing the labour market and, despite the fact that in the canonical model they are exogenously determined, it is possible to introduce a wage and profit bargaining function that determines the distribution of income (see Palley, 1996, 1997; Boyer and Petit, 1991). Thus, the *natural rate of growth* is an endogenous result of the actual rate of growth that, in turn, is determined by the autonomous components of aggregate demand. The endogeneity of growth proposed in this post-Keynesian approach differs substantially from that proposed by the 'new' neoclassical growth theorists represented, among others, by Romer (1986, 1990), Lucas (1988) and Grossman and Helpman (1991b).[7] For this school, the income distribution is determined by the marginal productivity of the factors of production. However, they differ from the 'old' Solovian theories in the assumptions that they make about the returns to capital. New growth theories allow for constant returns to capital[8] and increasing returns to scale, and solve the distribution problem arising from this assumption by treating the excess returns over unity as an externality. In any case, since prices adjust to clear the factor market, the economy is always in equilibrium at full employment. That is, the economy is always on the production possibility frontier and, in this case, and assuming that Say's Law applies, aggregate demand plays no role in determining the growth of output. Although 'new' growth theorists correctly point to technical progress as a source of increasing returns and non-convergent growth, their view is pre-Keynesian in the sense that they only concentrate on the supply side of the economy, and use a general equilibrium approach to model the dynamics of growth. In contrast, cumulative growth models assume that the economy is not at all times in equilibrium at the production possibility frontier. The growth of output moves that frontier and, thus, full employment is not attained and the distribution of income cannot be determined by the slope of the frontier. Growth is endogenous because supply and demand interact in a way determined by the structural parameters of the model. This endogeneity, however, does not depend on the assumptions made about the optimising behaviour of microeconomic agents, and it is thus less restrictive.

The model considered so far does not take account of the possibility that the rate of growth of income generates a rate of growth of imports in excess of that of exports. If this was the case, the country or region would be incurring continuous and sustained balance-of-payments deficits.[9] If one of the policy objectives is the balance-of-payments equilibrium or, simply, monetary constraints related to the balance-of-payments position arise, the growth rate can find a constraint in the balance-of-payments. Thirlwall and Dixon (1979) first introduced this constraint in the model by adding an import growth demand function as

$$m_t = \psi(p_{ft} - p_{dt}) + \pi y_t \quad (8.7)$$

ψ being the price elasticity of imports and π the income elasticity of imports.[10] Starting from an equilibrium balance of payments, the condition for dynamic external equilibrium is $m_t + p_{ft} = p_{dt} + x_t$. Then, the equilibrium rate of growth obtained by satisfying this condition is:

$$y_t = \frac{(1+\eta+\psi)\left[w_t - r_a + \tau_t - p_{ft}\right] + \varepsilon z_t}{\pi + \lambda(1+\eta+\psi)}. \tag{8.8}$$

The interpretation of the equilibrium growth rate is similar to that represented in equation (8.5). The difference rests in the appearance of the income elasticity of demand for imports in the denominator. The higher π, the higher the sensitivity of import growth to the growth of income and the sooner growth will generate balance-of-payments deficits. Since deficits must be corrected, at least in the long run, the higher π the lower will be the equilibrium rate of growth due to the existence of a balance-of-payments constraint. This does not preclude the economy from being export-led, for an increase in the rate of growth of exports will raise the constraint. This shows the two ways in which exports are important: (1) by increasing aggregate demand in an autonomous way – which is the dynamic version of Harrod's foreign trade multiplier – and (2) by relaxing the balance-of-payments and allowing for further increases in the other components of aggregate demand without incurring external deficits – in other words, the Hicks super-multiplier (McCombie, 1985b). This argument helps to explain why macroeconomic performance matters for growth, as pointed out by Fischer (1993), rendering the production function approach to economic growth ill-equipped.

Making the assumption that relative prices do not vary in the long run, the model with a balance-of-payments constraint would collapse to

$$y_t = \frac{\varepsilon}{\pi} z_t \tag{8.9}$$

which is known as *Thirlwall's Law* of growth (Thirlwall, 1979). This shows that the rate of growth of a region or country is determined by the growth of the rest of the world and the ratio between export and import income elasticities. This ratio reflects the degree of non-price competitiveness of the national (regional) products in the international markets and the non-price competitiveness in the domestic market, both determined by the structural specialisation of the region and the degree of product differentiation. *Thirlwall's Law* has generated a vast literature both on empirical and theoretical grounds that, in general, has led to a confirmation of its relevance as an explanation of why growth rates differ.[11]

The equilibrium solution of the canonical model and its extensions, if stable, presents a world in which growth rate differences are steadily maintained over time. If we assume that the initial per capita income of one region A is higher than in region B, and the equilibrium growth rates are $y_t^A > y_t^B$, then the result would be divergence in per capita incomes. If contrawise $y_t^A < y_t^B$, then the result would be initially a catch-up from region B to region A and then region B forging ahead of A. However, this result is not satisfactory when explaining the process of convergence and divergence in the real world. The model rules out the possibility that high growth regions in the past find themselves involved in slow growth processes, and slow growth regions transforming into fast growth. The possible sets of dynamics are limited because they do not make any reference to the influence of the level of income on the rate of growth of income. These models cannot explain why some groups of countries tend to converge to a similar level of per capita income and others tend to diverge. Another problem is that it does not explicitly model the importance of non-price competitiveness and technological progress as another possible source of cumulative tendencies. However, the introduction of a richer set of dynamics has recently been approached in several models (Amable, 1992 and 1993b; Boyer and Petit, 1991; De Benedictis, 1998; Gordon, 1991; Palley, 1997; and Setterfield, 1997a, 1997b). These models point out that, from a Kaldorian model of cumulative causation, the final outcome can be convergence (catch-up), divergence or sustained differences. In all of them, technological factors linked with processes of 'learning by doing', innovation, embodied technical progress and diffusion of technology play a crucial role in the determination of non-price competitiveness of exports (and imports) in the same vein that in the canonical model price competitiveness linked increased productivity with increased aggregate demand. Whether the technological forces favouring convergence (catch-up) are stronger than those favouring divergence (cumulative knowledge) is an empirical question. Two sources of convergence can be pointed out:

(a) *Technological catch-up.* The original idea of Veblen (1915), that backward countries would tend to grow faster than leading countries, was revisited by Gerschenkron (1962), Abramovitz (1986) and Gomulka (1990) among others. The idea is based on the possibility that the technological gap between nations opens up the opportunities for backward countries to access the leader's technology. Higher growth would be attained through the accumulation of new capital embodying more advanced technical characteristics. However, for the catch-up process to take place it is necessary that leaders and followers exhibit some *technological congruence* and that the followers have enough *social capability* to absorb and reward the new technology (Abramovitz, 1986). Catch-up will occur if the technological gap is not 'too big', with groups of countries converging towards similar levels of per capita income and others locked out of the process of development (Baumol, 1986).

Amable (1993b) has introduced catch-up in a Kaldorian cumulative growth model where the technological gap affects the growth of per capita income, the rate of innovation and the rate of school enrolment. Note that the catch-up hypothesis is perfectly compatible with a Kaldorian world in which technology is not freely accessible and countries are not permanently on the production possibility frontier (Pugno, 1991). By introducing a catch-up term in the canonical model the set of possible convergence–divergence outcomes is enriched. It is possible that two countries converge even if there is an underlying cumulative process leading to divergence. Empirical work also suggests that catch-up is an important factor explaining growth (Amable, 1993b; Pugno, 1995; Targetti and Foti, 1997).

(b) *Lock-in*. When analysing the disequilibrium interpretation of the Dixon–Thirlwall Kaldorian model, it was pointed out that if the growth process has a unit root, it will permanently depend on the initial growth conditions. However, Setterfield (1997a, 1997b) points to the possibility that the parameters of the model react endogenously to the rate of growth itself, leading to *path-dependent* processes of growth where the final outcome depends on the initial conditions and all the steps taken towards its equilibrium path position. The cumulative growth characterised by increasing returns leads to increased interrelatedness among components of the production process that, in turn, are inherited from the past (Arthur, 1989).[12] This interrelatedness increases the cost of changing from one specialisation to another, making the growth process more *inflexible*. A certain region or country, thus, can find itself locked into a certain technique of production, into a certain specialisation. If this is the case, the higher the level of development the lower will be the possibilities of realising dynamic increasing returns based on changes of specialisation[13] and, thus, the Verdoorn coefficient λ will fall. Alternatively, since the income elasticities of demand for imports and exports are reflecting the non-price competitiveness, they reflect the ability of a region to adapt to the changing patterns of consumption due to the growth of disposable income. The *lock-in* effect leads to a higher (lower) value of π (ε) because of the higher cost of changes in specialisation due to interrelatedness. Thus, combining increasing returns with *path dependence* can lead to *lock-in* processes that may cause regions with high levels of income to enjoy lower rates of growth. Although empirically *catch-up* and *lock-in* would mean that the rate of growth depends inversely on the level of development, both are different forces leading to converging levels of income.

The existence of these forces does not preclude the possibility that the rate of growth leads to a divergence in per capita incomes. In the Dixon–Thirlwall model with a catch-up term in the productivity growth equation, as in Targetti and Foti (1997), it is still possible that the cumulative forces leading to divergence overwhelm the converging forces of catching-up and the final outcome is divergence. However, it is implausible that price competitiveness is the only link between productivity and export growth causing a cumulative process. If we want to address the importance of cumulative growth some link has to be explicitly considered between technological progress and non-price competitiveness. The fact that the countries gaining more market share in the international markets are not those experiencing a lower growth of relative unit labour costs (RULC) has come to be known as *Kaldor's Paradox* (Kaldor, 1978). This phenomenon reflects the fact that competition in the international markets rests more on technological factors improving the quality and variety of products.

Amable (1992) confronts this problem by introducing a non-price factor in the export equation in a balance-of-payments constrained growth model à la Thirlwall (1979). This factor, reflecting the impact of technical progress on export performance, is the cumulative past production reflecting 'learning by doing'. In the same vein, De Benedictis (1998) introduces the effects of 'learning by doing', national innovation and diffusion of technology as determinants of the national degree of technological innovation that, in turn, affects the export performance. Both models show that the equilibrium rate of growth may be stable given reasonable values of the parameters, and that the possibilities of a laggard economy catching-up with the leader would mainly depend on its ability to generate and adopt innovations faster than the leader. Otherwise, divergence would be the pattern. Palley (1997) uses a model in which productivity growth depends on capital accumulation through capital deepening and embodied technical progress. Though Palley's model is one of a closed economy, it shows the possibility of multiple equilibria in the growth rates and does not rule out the unstable case. Thus, cumulative causation models – that can be initially associated with a description of the world as one in which differences among regions tend to be inevitably increasing – are able to explain a wide set of dynamics without demanding restrictive a priori assumptions as is the case for the old and new neoclassical models.

The richness of these models is also matched with good empirical performance (see, for instance, Atesoglu, 1994; Amable, 1993b; Boyer and Petit, 1991; Targetti and Foti, 1997; Fingleton, 2000; and León-Ledesma, 2002).[14] Empirical testing, though, is still not very generalised. Lack of regional data, lack of long series for variables related with technological factors and the difficulties associated with the interpretation of cross-sectional growth empirics are among the problems of these models when confronting empirical tests. This is, nonetheless, another field of possible extension and understanding of these models, which could easily benefit from what we have learnt from neoclassical growth empirics.[15]

Extending the cumulative growth model

From the discussion in the previous section we conclude that the basic cumulative model can be improved on the basis of two arguments. First, it is a model of growth in which the growth rates differences are constant and, hence, it does not allow for the existence of declining (or increasing) growth rates over time. In other words, no reference is made to the relationship between the rate of growth and the level of per capita income (or productivity) and, thus, any analysis of whether there is convergence or divergence in income or productivity levels is not possible. Secondly, there is no explicit reference to the important role of non-price factors that determine competitiveness. In this regard, the role of innovation and the diffusion of technologies seems of crucial importance (see Fagerberg, 1988). Recent developments in growth theory have emphasised the possible beneficial effects of innovation activities and the role of catching-up as major determinants of the growth performance of countries and regions.

The model we present here, based on León-Ledesma (2002), is an extended version of Dixon and Thirlwall (1975) that introduces technology variables along the lines of Amable (1993b) and De Benedictis (1998). These variables are similar to those emphasised in the 'new growth theory' analysis, but a different interpretation will be given to them. As will be shown below, there are several cumulative forces that may lead to divergent growth rates that interact with the effect that the catching-up – due to the adoption of foreign technologies – has on leading to convergence. Five continuous time equations can describe the relations at work:

$$y = \theta x, \qquad \theta > 0 \tag{8.10}$$

$$x = \eta(p - pf) + \varepsilon z + \zeta K + \delta(I/O), \qquad \eta < 0, \varepsilon > 0, \zeta > 0, \delta > 0 \tag{8.11}$$

$$p = w - r \tag{8.12}$$

$$r = \phi y + \lambda(I/O) + \alpha K + \sigma GAP, \qquad \phi > 0, \lambda > 0, \alpha > 0, \sigma > 0 \tag{8.13}$$

$$K = \gamma y + \beta q + \omega(edu) + \psi GAP, \qquad \gamma > 0, \beta > 0, \omega > 0, \psi < 0 \tag{8.14}$$

The first equation (8.10) states that the growth of output (y) depends on the growth of exports (x), which is equal to equation (8.1) in the Dixon–Thirlwall model. The growth of exports, in turn, depends negatively on the growth of relative prices ($p - pf$), and positively on world income growth (z), the investment–output ratio (I/O) and a technology variable to account for non-price factors (K) reflecting the flow of innovations that affect export performance. The first two variables on the right-hand side of the export equation (8.11) correspond to the usual specification of an export function expressed in rates of growth. The introduction of the investment–output ratio as a proxy for capital accumulation is due to the fact that the capacity of an economy to deliver in international markets depends on the growth of its physical equipment and infrastructure (Fagerberg, 1988). This variable may also capture the effect of embodied technical progress on export performance. Innovation is a key factor affecting the non-price competitiveness of economies. Product differentiation and quality competition characterise modern international trade. These factors determine the national-specific competitiveness and are different from those depending on the product composition of exports (Amable, 1992). The former will be reflected in the innovation variable, while the latter is captured by the income elasticity of demand for exports (ε). A country's ability to differentiate and compete in quality will crucially depend on the degree of innovation of its productive structure, which is reflected in the innovation variable introduced in the export equation (K).

The third equation of the model – equation (8.12) – is equivalent to equation (8.3) assuming that the mark-up over unit labour costs is constant over time. The fourth relation of this model – equation (8.13) – determines the rate of growth of labour productivity (r). One major determinant of productivity growth is the induced effect of output growth – that is, the Verdoorn–Kaldor mechanism. As mentioned earlier, this mechanism is responsible for the circular nature of the growth process in the canonical model. The Verdoorn–Kaldor mechanism reflects the existence of dynamic economies of scale due to increased specialisation (Young, 1928) and embodied technical progress (Kaldor, 1957) and also the existence of static increasing returns.[16] Embodied technical progress is explicitly captured in this model by the introduction of the investment–output ratio (I/O) as a second determinant of productivity growth.[17] The third determinant of productivity growth is innovative activity (K). Innovation not only leads to a higher degree of product differentiation and quality but also promotes process innovation leading to increased productivity. The final determinant of productivity growth is the productivity gap (GAP). The existence of productivity differences between the frontier economy and the followers opens up the opportunity for imitation and diffusion of more advanced technologies generated by the leader. In a simplified version, it implies a positive effect of the productivity gap on the productivity growth of the follower economies, leading to a potential catch-up in productivity levels.[18] The GAP variable, however, may also be thought of as representing the effect of the *lock-in* specialisation discussed in the previous section.

The final set of relationships defining our model – equation (8.14) – is the one determining innovative activity or the flow of new national innovations. This will depend on four factors. First, on the rate of growth of output (y), reflecting the demand-led innovation hypothesis of Schmookler (1966). Secondly, on the rate of growth of the cumulative sum of real output (q) as in Amable (1992) and de Benedictis (1998). This variable is a proxy for the effect of 'learning by doing' originally formulated by Arrow (1962). Both, the new products developed and the new production processes depend crucially on the effect of learning acquired through the accumulated experience of the workers. Thus, the higher the growth of accumulated experience – proxied by cumulative output – the more innovations will be incorporated in the production activities.[19] The third major determinant of the success of an economy to generate innovations is the level of education of its working population (*edu*).[20] The level of education affects the capacity to innovate not only directly but also indirectly because it raises the ability of the economic system to assimilate and understand the new techniques of production. Finally, the productivity gap affects negatively the innovation activity of an economy. With a low level of development few resources are directed to research and development and patenting activities. In other words, the ability to innovate depends on the technological level of the country. Countries with a lower technological level are more likely to rely on the benefits of knowledge created in the leader economies.

We will close the model with the formal definition of both the cumulative output growth (q) and the gap (GAP) variables. Given that $Y(t)$ is the level of output in time t we have:

$$q = \frac{dLog \int_{t=0}^{T} Y(t)dt}{dt} \tag{8.15}$$

The productivity gap is one minus the ratio of productivity between the follower (R) and the leader economy (R^*). The gap will be zero if there is no difference in productivity level and approach unity if productivity in the follower country is very low.

$$GAP = 1 - \frac{R}{R^*} = 1 - G. \tag{8.16}$$

We can, thus, identify several forces in the model, some leading to divergence and others to convergence in productivity. On the one hand, the Verdoorn–Kaldor effect is a cumulative force that reinforces initial growth advantages (and disadvantages). This is also the same for the effect of demand-led innovation that affects both non-price and price competitiveness, and has a similar effect to that of the Verdoorn–Kaldor mechanism. 'Learning by doing' is another force that may make growth cumulative due to the positive effect of cumulative experience on non-price competitiveness and output growth. The final force acting towards a diverging growth pattern is the negative effect of the productivity gap on innovation that tends to perpetuate low levels of technological innovation. On the other hand, the catching-up effect, arising from the flow of technologies from the leader to the follower economies, is the main convergent force of the model. The final outcome will depend on the combination of these multiple effects and their relative power. It will be shown in the next section of this essay that possible outcomes of the model include total catch-up, partial catch-up and divergence from the leader.[21] But, given the cumulative forces at work, can the model generate a stable solution for the rate of growth of output? The relevance of this question lies in the empirical fact that explosive behaviour of the growth of output is not observed in the real world.

The dynamics and stability analysis

As commented on in the introduction to this essay, cumulative growth models are capable of generating a rich set of dynamics relating to convergence issues from the disequilibrium perspective of endogenous growth. In order to describe these dynamics, we solve the model represented by (8.10)–(8.14) for the growth of output (y) and the growth of productivity (r). We obtain the following two equations:

$$y = D - EG + Fq - Hr, \tag{8.17}$$

$$r = J - LG + Mq + Ny, \tag{8.18}$$

where,

$$D = \frac{\theta\zeta\psi}{1-\theta\zeta\gamma} + \frac{\theta\eta}{1-\theta\zeta\gamma}(w - pf) + \frac{\theta\varepsilon}{1-\theta\zeta\gamma}z + \frac{\theta\zeta\omega}{1-\theta\zeta\gamma}edu + \frac{\theta\delta}{1-\theta\zeta\gamma}(I/O),$$

$$E = \frac{\theta\zeta\psi}{1-\theta\zeta\gamma} < 0, \qquad F = \frac{\theta\zeta\beta}{1-\theta\zeta\gamma} > 0, \qquad H = \frac{\theta\eta}{1-\theta\zeta\gamma} < 0,$$

$$J = \sigma + \alpha\psi + \lambda(I/O) + \alpha\omega(edu),$$

$$L = \sigma + \alpha\psi,\ M = \alpha\beta > 0,\ N = \phi + \alpha\gamma > 0$$

Differentiating (8.15) and rearranging we obtain the following expression for the rate of growth of output:[22]

$$y = q + \frac{\dot{q}}{q}. \tag{8.19}$$

From the definition of the gap variable (8.16), we know that the rate of growth of the productivity ratio between the follower and the leader (G) is

$$\frac{\dot{G}}{G} = r - r^{*} \tag{8.20}$$

with r^* being the rate of growth of labour productivity in the leader economy.[23] Substituting (8.19) and (8.20) into (8.17) and (8.18), we have the following system of first-order non-linear differential equations:

$$\dot{q} = q[D - EG + (F - 1)q - Hr], \tag{8.21}$$

$$\dot{G} = G[P - LG + M(q - q^*) + N(y - y^*)], \tag{8.22}$$

where,

$$P = \sigma + \alpha\psi + \lambda[(I/O) - (I/O)^*] + \alpha\omega[edu - edu^*].$$

The stability of the system (8.21)–(8.22) can be analysed through the stability of the system in brackets, ruling out the possibility that q and G are equal to zero (D-stability). In the steady state, $\dot{q} = \dot{G} = 0$, and given (8.19) and (8.20) then $r = r^*$, $y = q$ and $y^* = q^*$. With the steady-state solutions for y^* and r^* given in the Appendix we can obtain the following system representing the equilibrium paths of both G and q:

$$-LG + (M + N)q = -T\,|_{\dot{G}=0}, \tag{8.23}$$

$$-EG + (F - 1)q = -S\,|_{\dot{q}=0}, \tag{8.24}$$

where T and S depend on a set of exogenous variables and the parameters of the model (Θ):

$$T = f(I/O, edu, pf, z, I/O^*, edu^*, w^*, \Theta),$$

$$S = g(I/O, edu, pf, w, z, I/O^*, edu^*, w^*, \Theta)$$

Since all the elements in the off-diagonal of the Jacobian of the system (8.23)–(8.24) are positive, the stability conditions of this model require:

(a) $-L < 0$, thus, $L > 0$ or $\sigma + \alpha\psi > 0$;

(b) $|Jac| > 0$, or $\dfrac{L}{M+N} < \dfrac{E}{F-1}$, which implies that the slope of the phase path line for $\dot{G} = 0$ has to be smaller than the one for $\dot{q} = 0$;

(c) For condition (ii) to hold, it is required that $(F - 1) < 0$.

The steady-state equilibrium point is one where both productivity level differences remain the same and output growth is stable and equal in the leader and the follower economy. If the process of catch-up is strong enough, during the transition output grows faster in the follower than in the leader. Once we approach the equilibrium, both rates of growth equal one another and productivity level differences remain stable. The parameters of the model determine where the follower stops catching-up and, thus, whether this process is absolute or just partial. The existence of per capita income convergence and a tendency for the rates of growth to be equal in the long run for the advanced countries is one of the growth facts reported in Evans (1996) and Temple (1999). Two possible stable cases of equilibrium can arise. These are depicted in Figures 8.1 and 8.2, where the combinations of G and q that make $\dot{q} = 0$ and $\dot{G} = 0$ are represented.

The first one is a stable focus (Figure 8.1), where the path taken towards the equilibrium gap and rate of growth of the cumulative output (and output growth) generates cyclical behaviour.[24] The economy oscillates around the equilibrium point until it is reached. The second case is a stable node (Figure 8.2).[25] In this case, regardless of the initial point, the economy will follow a direct path towards its equilibrium solution, this adjustment being faster than in the former case. In Figure 8.1 we have depicted an equilibrium point where the laggard country catches-up with the leader and even forges ahead of it ($G > 1$). By contrast, Figure 8.2 shows a situation where the equilibrium only allows for a partial catch-up and, thus, differences in levels of productivity would be maintained through time.[26] Of course, it would be possible to find cases of total falling behind ($G = 0$), if both lines do not cross before the q axis. However, this is an implausible case especially for developed and emerging economies. It is also important to note that a positive value of the

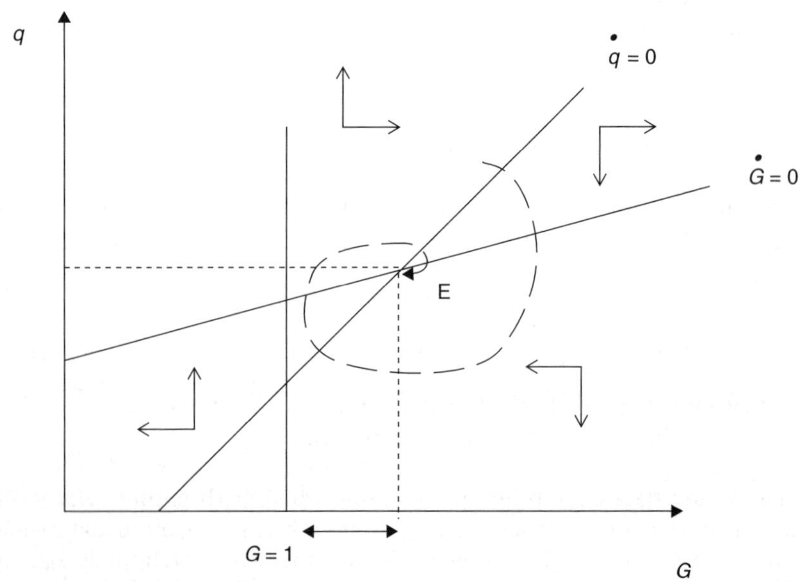

Figure 8.1 Stable focus

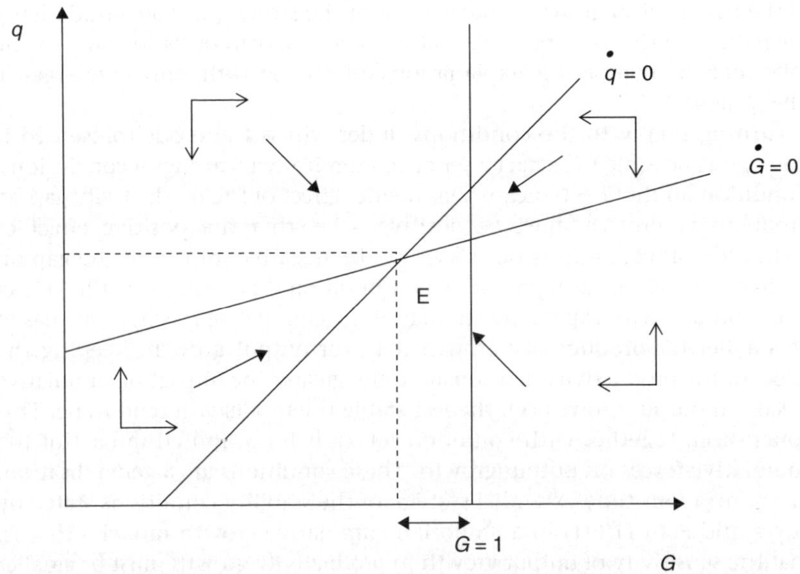

Figure 8.2 Stable node

parameter of the *GAP* variable – or negative value of the parameter of *G* – does not necessarily imply convergence in levels of productivity. The convergence in productivity levels will also depend on the endogenous cumulative mechanism linking the growth of output, 'learning by doing' and innovation with productivity growth and price and non-price competitiveness. Despite the fact that the parameter σ is positive, convergence may not be the outcome if the cumulative forces in the leader economy are stronger than in the follower. Note also that from the system of equations (8.10)–(8.14) we can obtain a reduced form for productivity growth as follows:

$$r = a_1 + a_2G + a_3(edu) + a_4(I/O) + a_5q + a_6(p - pf) + a_7z \quad (8.25)$$

This is similar to those convergence equations used when attempting to test the neoclassical hypothesis of convergence, controlling for the variables that determine the steady-state level of productivity (see Barro and Sala-i-Martín, 1995). From the perspective of the model presented here, a convergence equation that does not include the rate of growth of the determinants of exports would be misspecified. Thirlwall and Sanna (1996) have shown that one of the most robust variables influencing per capita income growth in a convergence equation is the rate of growth of exports. This model gives a plausible theoretical explanation of these results and, on the other hand, shows that the Barro-type convergence equations are not necessarily a test of the neoclassical growth model. A test of the structural model underlying the reduced form convergence equation is necessary in order to compare the relevance of competing explanations of the growth and convergence phenomena.[27]

Turning finally to the conditions under which the model presented is stable, it is possible to extract a set of economically meaningful conclusions. Condition (a) that $L > 0$ means that the net effect of the productivity gap on productivity growth must be positive – i.e. that the positive effect of technological catch-up is not offset by the negative impact of the gap on innovation and, in turn, productivity. Condition (b) is stating that the effect of the productivity gap relative to that of the cumulative mechanisms has to be smaller for productivity growth than for output growth. Keeping the effect of the productivity gap constant, the greater the impact of cumulative forces on output growth (F), the less stable the model will tend to be. This conclusion, together with condition (c), calls for a limited impact of the cumulative forces on output growth. These conditions are a generalisation, in a continuous time extended system, of the stability conditions stated by Boyer and Petit (1991) in a Kaldorian cumulative growth model – that is, that the sensitivity of output growth to productivity growth must be smaller than that of productivity growth to output growth. Otherwise, the model would be unstable, giving as a result a world in which differences in per capita income would reach infinite values in a finite time span.

Regarding the Verdoorn–Kaldor coefficient (ϕ), note that the higher the value of it the more stable the model will tend to be. This is because a high impact of output growth on productivity growth will increase the velocity of convergence towards the steady-state dynamic equilibrium. In other words, it will make the denominator of the left-hand side of condition (b) higher. Thus, contrary to the intuitive idea of a high Verdoorn coefficient leading to unstable growth, it has the effect of accelerating the convergence towards the long-run equilibrium. This convergence towards the steady state does not ensure, however, the existence of catching-up with the leader economy since it only refers to the process of mean reversion. If, nevertheless, the effect of the catching-up variable is strong enough as to lead to an absolute closure of the gap, the Verdoorn coefficient will certainly have the effect of accelerating the process of catching-up. This may explain the results obtained by Fingleton and McCombie (1998) that show how, in the European regions, it is possible to observe a strong and robust Verdoorn effect together with a high velocity of beta (β) convergence.

Conclusions

Throughout this chapter we have presented and discussed some of the most relevant contributions to the cumulative or disequilibrium growth literature. We have argued that cumulative growth models espoused their endogenous nature before and independently of the 'new' growth theories. Furthermore, these models may present dynamic behaviour compatible with the variety of experiences regarding convergence in developed and developing countries. The standpoint of these models departs from the general equilibrium nature of the recent contributions to endogenous growth theory. In this context it is demand that leads growth and the natural rate of growth becomes endogenous to the actual.

In order to show this and to avoid some of the shortcomings of the traditional cumulative growth models we have presented an extended version of the canonical Kaldorian cumulative growth model. The model allows, among other things, for the introduction of technology variables such as innovation and technology gaps that have been stressed as important factors determining the growth performance of modern economies. It allows for the analysis of productivity convergence generating a richer set of dynamics than the traditional cumulative growth models. It has been shown that the model, under some non-restrictive conditions, can generate a stable pattern of growth. Contrary to the popular idea of cumulative growth generating ever-increasing differences in per capita output and productivity levels, a growth process generated by this kind of dynamics is compatible with the existence of catch-up from the followers to the leader economy.

A growth equation similar to those used in recent growth empirical exercises can be derived from the structural form of the model. This fact recommends the estimation of the structural form, in order to avoid second-order identification problems that impede discriminating among competing theories of growth. On the other hand, we have shown how the Verdoorn coefficient can counterintuitively act as a force that increases the velocity of convergence towards the steady state.

Appendix. The dynamics of output growth in the leader economy

For the leader economy $GAP = 0$, for $G = 1$. Thus, re-writing equations (8.13) and (8.14), we obtain,

$$r^* = \phi y + \lambda(I/O)^* + \alpha K^* \tag{8.13'}$$

$$K^* = \gamma y^* + \beta q^* + \omega(edu)^* \tag{8.14'}$$

Solving the new system for the rate of growth of output we obtain:

$$y^* = B + Cq^* \tag{8.A1}$$

where,

$$B = \frac{\theta\eta}{1-\theta[\zeta\gamma-\eta(\phi+\alpha\gamma)]}(w^* - pf) + \frac{\theta\varepsilon}{1-\theta[\zeta\gamma-\eta(\phi+\alpha\gamma)]}z -$$

$$\frac{\theta\eta\lambda}{1-\theta[\zeta\gamma-\eta(\phi+\alpha\gamma)]}(I/O)^* + \frac{\theta\omega(\zeta-\eta\alpha)}{1-\theta[\zeta\gamma-\eta(\phi+\alpha\gamma)]}(edu)^*$$

$$C = \frac{\theta\beta(\zeta-\eta)}{1-\theta[\zeta\gamma-\eta(\phi+\alpha\gamma)]}.$$

From expression (8.19) we have (Amable, 1993b and De Benedictis, 1998),

$$\ddot{q}^* = B\dot{q}^* + (C-1)\dot{q}^{*2}, \tag{8.A2}$$

Only in case that $B > 0$ and $(C–1) < 0$, we have a stable and positive solution for the rate of growth of cumulative output (see Amable, 1993b). Equation (8.A2) is a first-order non-linear differential equation of the Bernoulli form, whose solution path is given by:

$$\dot{q}(t)^* = \frac{1}{\left[\frac{1}{\dot{q}_0^*} + \frac{C-1}{B}\right]e^{-Bt} - \frac{C-1}{B}} \tag{8.A3}$$

Where q_0^* is the initial rate of growth of cumulative output. Given the relationship (8.17) between y and q, we obtain the dynamic solution for the rate of growth of output:

$$y(t)^* = B + \frac{C}{\left[\frac{1}{q_0^*} + \frac{C-1}{B}\right]e^{-Bt} - \frac{C-1}{B}} \tag{8.A4}$$

When $t \to \infty$, $\dot{q}^* = y^* = -B/(C-1)$, and $\dot{q} = 0$. Since the value of $(C-1) < 0$, we have a positive and stable solution for the rate of growth of output, despite the fact that cumulative forces are at work. This solution will depend positively on z, pf, $(I/O)^*$ and edu^*, and negatively on w^*.

Notes

1. See the Introduction and other chapters of this book for an extended and more detailed discussion of Verdoorn's Law.
2. Bearing in mind that $\eta < 0$.
3. Since $\eta < 0$, then the term $(-\gamma\eta\lambda)$ will be > 0.
4. See Guccione and Gillen (1977) and the reply of Dixon and Thirlwall (1978) for a discussion of the stability conditions of the model.
5. See Dixon and Thirlwall (1975, pp. 212–13).

6. See Swales (1983) for the introduction of some non-linearities that enrich the set of possible cases of equilibrium.
7. See Skott and Auerbach (1994) for a critique of the underlying assumptions of new growth theories from a perspective embracing both institutionalist and cumulative causation ideas.
8. Or to the sum of all the reproducible factors as capital, human capital and innovation.
9. Regions do not have a balance of payments in the normal accounting sense but excess imports still need financing. Thus, regions would also be subject to balance-of-payments problems due to monetary constraints. See Thirlwall (1980) for a discussion of this topic.
10. We are assuming that the price elasticity of imports and the cross-price elasticity of imports with respect to the foreign countries are equal. For simplicity we will make the same assumption in equation (8.2) for the export demand function, where η is the relative price elasticity of demand for exports.
11. For recent general overviews on Thirlwall's Law see McCombie and Thirlwall (1994), McCombie and Thirlwall (1999) and the mini-symposium in *Journal of Post Keynesian Economics*, vol. 20, 1997, 311–385.
12. *Interrelatedness* and *roundaboutness* are already mentioned in Young's (1928) verbal exposition of a cumulative growth model.
13. That is to say, the lower the possibilities of achieving a higher growth of productivity arising from the Smith–Young process of division of labour.
14. Notably, Fingleton (2000) introduces spatial effects due to the existence of regional spillovers and externalities that also enriches the dynamics of the model.
15. See Temple (1999).
16. Recent empirical developments in the literature on Verdoorn's Law have stressed its importance at the regional level. See, for instance, Fingleton and McCombie (1998), Harris and Lau (1998) and León-Ledesma (2000), and the review of Pugno in this volume. In an international context, however, it may well be the case that a single equation estimation of the law suffers from a high degree of simultaneity bias.
17. Note that, for simplicity, we treat (I/O) as exogenous.
18. For further qualifications of the concept of catch-up in cumulative growth models see Amable (1993b) and Targetti and Foti (1997).
19. Note that, in this context, innovations do not necessarily mean the creation of new products or production techniques but also the marginal improvements in the existing ones.
20. The level of education (and not its rate of growth) has been introduced in the model due to the fact that the role played by education is wider than a simple human capital variable in a production function. This implies that a constant level of education ensures a constant flow of innovations due to the technical competence and skills of the working population.
21. The model even allows for the case of the follower economies forging ahead from the 'old' leader once the catch-up has taken place.
22. All the variables denoted by a dot represent the time derivative of the variable, i.e. $\dot{x} = dx/dt$.
23. All the variables with the superscript * represent the original variable for the leader economy.
24. This would be the case if the trace of the Jacobian of the system and its determinant are such that $(\text{tr Jac})^2 > 4\cdot|\text{Jac}|$.

25. If $(\text{tr Jac})^2 < 4 \cdot |\text{Jac}|$.
26. Note that the fact that in Figure 8.1 the equilibrium is higher than $G = 1$ and in Figure 8.2 it is lower, does not bear any relationship with the way in which the economy approaches equilibrium.
27. See León-Ledesma (2002) for an estimation of the model represented by equations (8.8)–(8.12) using simultaneous equations techniques.

9

Verdoorn's Law: Some Notes on Output Measurement and the Role of Demand

Giorgio Rampa

Introduction

The issues that I discuss in this chapter, and that appear in the title, might be viewed at being first as independent of one another. In particular, the first one (output measurement) may seem to be quite untheoretical; and the second one might be expected to contribute little to a school of thought, namely the Kaldorian one, which has already, over many decades, stressed the importance of the demand side of the economy. However, I hope to show that coupling some observations drawn from both parts may help in developing a viewpoint about the Verdoorn effect which, although somewhat unconventional, might be useful in interpreting some actual productivity trends that have been observed in the advanced industrial economies.

Output Measurement

Verdoorn's Law can be summarised thus: as (the growth of) output rises, (the growth of) labour productivity increases. The law can be interpreted in more technical or microeconomic terms by invoking the effect of some type of Wright–Hirsch–Alchian progress function, such as seen in the aerospace or the shipbuilding industries.[1] In this case, it is thought that labour productivity grows with output due to a process of 'learning by doing' which takes place *within* single production lines. On the other hand, the law can be interpreted in more aggregative or macroeconomic terms, as seen, for example, in the Young–Stigler–Kaldor approach.[2] These theories suggest that it is increased specialisation among firms, and the birth of new products and processes, that brings about increasing returns. Independently of which of the two viewpoints one prefers, it seems that in both cases what is usually intended is a precise concept. The amount of *physical* output per man (number of ships, quantity of some industrial product, and so on) increases.

Now, apart from some exceptions (a handful of statistical estimations of labour productivity in the building and assembling of large products such as ships, where physical output is used), when facing the problem of empirical analysis, economists use the standard National Accounting concept of output, namely *real GDP* – that is, *constant-price value added*. This procedure seems quite uncontroversial and has been commonly adopted in applied economics. In both the United Nations System of National Accounts and the European System of Accounts, value added is defined as the difference between the value of total production (gross output) and the value of intermediate goods. Thus, of course, one cannot attach any physical meaning to this measure. In fact, given the general input–output interdependence between sectors, any product can be both an output and an input, depending upon which sector we are considering. As a consequence, any change in relative prices might squeeze or inflate the value added of different sectors, even if no real change has occurred. Thus 'real' value added is suggested as a more reliable measure of output. Now, real value added is defined in turn as the difference between the value of production and the value of intermediate inputs, both measured in real terms – that is, in the *constant prices* of some base year. This process is known as 'double deflation', and it is intended to correct the distortions outlined above.

Is real GDP a magnitude which can cope with the required *physical* measure of output? I will argue that this is in general not the case.[3] Of course, I do not deny that GDP might in certain circumstances be a good proxy for some output measure. For instance, when one considers the *whole* economy, value added is also a measure of the value of *final* output. To be precise, this is the case only if the economy is closed. However, if an open economy is considered whose trade balance is not far from equilibrium, value added proxies the value of *domestic* final demand.[4] As a consequence, real value added might be deemed to offer a measure of the ability of this economy to satisfy the needs of the nation (basically, domestic consumption and capital formation). One might, however, wonder why *domestic* final expenditure should be the most meaningful output concept.

Consider, for example, an economy *E* where all prices, employment, wages and gross profits remain unchanged over time. As a consequence, nominal value added equals real value added. Our assumptions imply also that value added per worker is constant; if, in addition, intermediate inputs per unit of output do not change, total production per worker is constant as well. Suppose, however, that the economy becomes increasingly open to international trade. It substitutes imported raw materials for domestic intermediate inputs, in such a way that total intermediate inputs per unit of total production remain constant; and it exports a larger share of its production, in such a way that the trade balance stays in equilibrium. Under these circumstances the ratio of value added to total production does not change, either in nominal or in real terms. However, exports grow relative to total production and to value added. It follows that in our economy final output (including exports) grows *faster* than value added, which is instead equal to domestic final demand. It follows also that productivity growth is different according to whether it is measured in terms of value added or in terms of final output. Thus when studying export performance, a typically Kaldorian mode of analysis, value added might be a biased measure of output even for the aggregated economy.

One might now wonder whether real GDP, which gives an imprecise measure of final output, is a satisfactory measure for *total* output, or (gross) production. To answer this, consider again our hypothetical economy *E*. Everything is as before, except that domestic intermediate inputs are poor substitutes of imported materials,[5] and the quantity of the latter is significantly higher than that of the former per unit of production. Suppose that the price of imported materials decreases in time and that their elasticity of demand is unity. The nominal expenditure for imported inputs per unit of production remains then constant, and that for total intermediate inputs also stays broadly unchanged. Since domestic prices, employment, wages and gross profits are constant, it follows as before that (a) total production per worker is constant, in *both* current and constant prices; (b) the *current-price* ratio of value added to production is constant; and hence (c) *nominal* value added per worker is constant. However, when one computes *constant-price* intermediate inputs per unit of production one finds that they have increased. As a consequence, constant-price value added per unit of production has decreased, and hence the growth of productivity is different when measured in terms of real GDP compared with when it is measured in terms of total production. In the latter case productivity is constant, while, in the former, productivity decreases.

Which notion of output, then, should one prefer? Why not use total production, which is inclusive of intermediate products and is more in accord with the intuitive meaning attached to physical output and productivity?[6] Indeed, if the economy is specialised in producing intermediate goods, as happens in many advanced countries, concentrating only on final products means ignoring a large part of the economy – sectors in which important changes in efficiency and productivity might take place. In addition, as time elapses different products might become more or less oriented to final demand, and simultaneously less, or more, value-added intensive, so that the trend of their production might differ from that of their final output and of their GDP. This observation brings us to sectoral analysis, the level at which Verdoorn's Law is usually tested. From this perspective, value added becomes an ambiguous concept of output. In fact, at the industry level, value added, both nominal and real, is by no means equal to final output. In addition, real GDP might be a bad proxy for physical sectoral production, as the following arguments try to show.

First of all, double deflation, though intended to correct the effects of relative price changes on nominal value added, has long been known[7] to lead to serious inconsistencies[8] including possible negative measurements of real value added. This is due essentially to the role played by changes in the sectoral intensities of intermediate inputs – a fact which will be explored below. Before this, one must ask whether it is in principle possible to attach any physical meaning to real GDP from a theoretical point of view. By itself, real value added measures the income that primary factors would earn in year t, if intermediate-input intensity were that of year t but prices were those of the base year.[9] Of course, this cumbersome notion is not related to any physical quantity.

One might try an alternative route. Suppose that real value added can be thought of as a particular intermediate good, which enters production by co-operating with the other intermediate goods. This particular good, which is produced by capital and labour, can in this case be given a quantity index which depends on capital and labour quantities and prices alone. Viewed in this way, real value added is a well-defined quantity, not of a finished product but of an intermediate one. However, as lucidly explained by Arrow (1974), this procedure makes sense only under two particular assumptions, besides the usual neoclassical one that costs are always at their long period minimum for any quantity produced.[10] These assumptions are (a) constant returns of scale must prevail in the production of both real value added and the finished product, and (b) output and capital must be separable from the other intermediate inputs.[11] The former assumption probably makes it impossible to speak in any satisfactory way of growth and increasing returns as they are observed in practice. The latter assumption is very restrictive, since it does not allow for direct substitution or complementary between capital and intermediate inputs.

Of course, these are empirically refutable assumptions, but one does not expect that they hold in general. In Arrow's words (1974, p. 5), 'Without the separability assumption ... it is hard to assign any definite meaning to real value added, and probably the best thing to say is that the concept should not be used when capital and labour are not separable from materials in production'. This is, indeed, a starkly pessimistic statement.

So we are left with the more prosaic notion of real value added which prevails in national accounting. I now explore the relationship between real value added and physical production. Take a single product, whose quantity produced at date t is Q_t. In the process of production an amount I_t of intermediate inputs is utilised. I do not want to enter into all the intricacies of heterogeneous intermediate goods, so let me assume for the sake of simplicity that intermediate inputs are a bundle of commodities with a fixed composition. Let P_t^Q be the current price of production, and P_t^I the current price of intermediate inputs. Current-price value added (VA_t) is

$$VA_t = P_t^Q Q_t - P_t^I I_t. \tag{9.1}$$

The national accountant estimates the index price in terms of some base year, say 0, of both production and intermediate inputs. This is equivalent to having the price level of Q and I which prevail in the base year, say P_0^Q and P_0^I respectively, so that real value added is

$$RVA_t = P_0^Q Q_t - P_0^I I_t. \tag{9.2}$$

Suppose that from the base year 0 to year t, the production index has grown by the proportion g_Q, so that $Q_t = Q_0(1 + g_Q)$. Similarly, assume that the quantity index of intermediate inputs has grown by the proportion g_I, so that $I_t = I_0\ (1 + g_I)$; define finally $\Delta g_{I/Q} \equiv g_I - g_Q$ the excess-growth of intermediate inputs over production. Thus one can write:

$$\begin{aligned} RVA_t &= P_0^Q Q_0(1 + g_Q) - P_0^I I_0(1 + g_I) \\ &= P_0^Q Q_0(1 + g_Q) - P_0^I I_0(1 + g_Q) - P_0^I I_0(\Delta g_{I/Q}) \\ &= (P_0^Q Q_0 - P_0^I I_0)\cdot(1 + g_Q) - P_0^I I_0(\Delta g_{I/Q}) \\ &= VA_0(1 + g_Q) - P_0^I I_0(\Delta g_{I/Q}) \end{aligned} \tag{9.3}$$

The very first term in the last line of equation (9.3), VA_0, is the current-price value added of the base year, and by definition it is also the *real* value added of that year. Thus, if one wants to compute the index of real value added, $1 + g_{RVA}$, where g_{RVA} is its growth rate, one divides both sides of the last expression by VA_0, thus obtaining:

$$\left(1 + g_{RVA}\right) \equiv \frac{RVA_t}{VA_0} = \left(1 + g_Q\right) - \frac{P_0{}^I I_0}{VA_0}\left(\Delta g_{I/Q}\right), \tag{9.4}$$

or finally:

$$g_{RVA} = g_Q - \frac{P_0{}^I I_0}{VA_0}\left(\Delta g_{I/Q}\right). \tag{9.5}$$

It is apparent that the rate of growth[12] of real value added, or real GDP, diverges from the rate of growth of physical production, *if intermediate inputs have grown at a rate which is different from that of production*, i.e. if $\Delta g_{I/Q}$ is different from zero. When intermediate inputs grow *faster* than production, the growth rate of GDP *under*estimates the growth rate of physical production[13] and vice versa. Notice in addition that this bias is weighted by the ratio between intermediate inputs and value added, both in *current* prices, prevailing in the base year, $P_0^I I_0/VA_0$. Thus *changing the base year modifies the (possible) bias*. It follows that the traditional accounting measure of output growth (namely, the rate of growth of real GDP) might be a bad proxy of the increase of physical production in the economy. Given the rate of growth of employment, this can lead to an over- or underestimation of the Verdoorn coefficient when one regresses output growth on employment growth.

One expects that, given the rate of growth of physical productivity (that is, physical production per worker), the recorded growth rate of GDP per worker might again over- or underestimate the former, depending on $\Delta g_{I/Q}$. However, we should not conclude from this that the bias induced by $\Delta g_{I/Q}$ on productivity growth is the same as the one induced on output growth. If this were the case, one might conclude that a *direct* estimation[14] of Verdoorn's Law, although statistically incorrect, gives the same results independently of which notion of real output one utilises. In fact, call g_E the growth rate of employment. By definition one has $(1 + g_{RVA})/(1 + g_E) = 1 + g_\pi$, where g_π is the rate of growth of standard (GDP) productivity. In a similar manner one has $(1 + g_Q)/(1 + g_E) = 1 + g_\varphi$, where g_φ is the rate of growth of physical productivity, that is physical production per worker. Now, dividing all terms in (9.4) by $(1 + g_E)$, we obtain eventually

$$g_\pi = g_\varphi - \frac{P_0{}^I I_0}{VA_0} \cdot \frac{\Delta g_{I/Q}}{1+g_E}. \tag{9.6}$$

It is clear that if employment does *not* change ($g_E = 0$) then output growth and productivity growth, when measured in terms of real GDP, are biased in exactly the same way with respect to their physical counterparts. In all other cases this will not be the case. In particular, if employment decreases the bias of GDP productivity growth is higher than the bias of GDP growth.

We cannot say to what extent these biases might affect the results of empirical studies. If one takes a long period of time, one might argue that this effect is negligible, since there does not seem to exist a well-defined trend in the I/Q ratio in the long run. If, on the contrary, one takes a single decade, it might be that the effect is not insignificant. Take, for instance, aggregate statistics for the whole economy. There is evidence that the ratio between intermediate inputs and production (in constant prices) decreased in the European economies during the 1950s, while it rose during the 1960s (and again decreased after the oil shocks). This is compatible with a higher recorded overall performance of GDP per worker in the 1950s, and a lower one during the 1960s, as reported in many empirical studies. To this one must add that during the 1960s employment growth was slower than during the 1950s. According to equation (9.6) above, this tends to reinforce the GDP productivity slowdown during the 1960s.

In the case of Italy, according to some estimates[15] the I/Q ratio of the whole economy increased by about 13.5 per cent between 1960 and 1970. The growth rate of this ratio is approximately equal to $\Delta g_{I/Q}$. In addition, total employment decreased by about 5 per cent during that period. finally, in 1960 (a base year for the period) the ratio between current-price intermediate inputs and value added was 0.75. Application of equation (9.6) shows that GDP productivity growth *under*estimates physical productivity growth by about 10 per cent – that is 1 per cent per year. Thus the productivity slowdown of the 1960s, if 'correctly' measured in physical terms, might turn out to be less serious than usually thought. Similar calculations show that the bias is practically nil for the 1970s and the 1990s, while an underestimation of about 0.7 per cent per year occurs again in the 1980s, a period of slow recorded levels of GDP growth. Reconsidering the 1960s, since the ratio of (current-price) intermediate inputs to value added was 0.86 in 1980 –that is, 25 per cent higher than it was in 1960 – a change in the base year from 1960 to 1980 would raise the underestimation of productivity growth to 1.25 per cent, instead of 1 per cent per year.

Of course, things might change if we were to consider not the whole economy but particular sectors, or even single products. We would expect greater variability when passing to a more disaggregated level. However, I do not wish to consider the empirical details here. On the contrary, I prefer to examine three abstract examples which might help in interpreting some productivity puzzles recorded in recent decades.

(i) Suppose that the two products A and B serve similar needs, and that they are classified in the same productive sector S by national accountants. Suppose in addition that, after a proper redefinition of quantity units, *physical* production per worker is the same in both lines of production. Assume for the sake of simplicity that all prices, I/Q ratios, and physical productivity remain constant over time. This implies that (a) current-price valuations are identical to constant-price ones; (b) GDP per worker in each line of production is not biased in the sense of equation (9.5); and (c) conventional GDP productivity stays constant in both productions. However, assume that product A is a *new* one in the base year, and is characterised by a higher ratio of value added to the value of production. It contains more R&D workers, more allowances for capital depreciation, and possibly more profits if less-than-perfect competition initially prevails. Product B, by contrast, is a 'mature' one, and is less value-added intensive. Initial investment costs have been written off completely, no technical consultants nor R&D employees are needed any longer, and profits have been squeezed by a higher degree of competition. It follows that valued added per worker (and, by our assumptions, *real* GDP per worker) is higher in the production of A

than it is in the production of *B*. Suppose finally that over time product *A* becomes more and more important compared with *B*, that is to say its physical production grows faster. Now, if the applied economist reads the national accounts of sector *S*, real GDP per worker will be found to *increase* in time, while aggregate physical productivity will *not*, simply because the internal composition of the sector has changed.

(ii) Imagine that the history of the new product *A* differs from case (i). In the base year it is produced in a rather primitive and frugal manner. But suppose that after some time it becomes more fashionable. Its price rises due to increased demand, assuming weak competition between producers. Given that prices and profits increase, producers do not care to use more, and greater sophisticated, intermediate inputs per unit of production.[16] This in fact does not compress current-price margins. Suppose that each worker keeps producing the same number of items of the product as before. In other words, physical productivity remains constant. However, it is clear that, under double deflation, the production of *A* shows a real GDP growth which is lower than its physical growth, since $\Delta g_{I/Q}$. is positive. As a consequence, GDP productivity decreases while physical productivity does not. If product *B* behaves as in case (i), physical productivity remains constant in sector *S*. On the other hand, since the share of product *A* in sector *S* rises, aggregate GDP productivity might increase or decrease, according to whether the factors of case (i) or the factors of case (ii) prevail.

(iii) Now suppose that the profits earned in the production of *A* are so high in the base year that competition becomes fiercer, and the price falls. As a consequence, producers manage to save on intermediate inputs, so as to avoid a profit squeeze. With respect to case (ii) an opposite process takes place. GDP productivity grows, while physical productivity does not. Even if product *A* is now a mature one, so that its share in sector *S* does no longer increases, aggregate GDP productivity in this sector does increase.[17]

Case (i) shows that a productive sector might show a GDP productivity growth even if physical productivity is constant. One might argue that this is due to the fact that the new product *A* is a 'superior' one, superiority being signalled by a higher value added per worker. Thus when the share of *A* in the economy grows, the economy is seen to become more 'productive'. However, the higher value added per worker of product *A* *cannot* be compared with the older products from any technical viewpoint. It simply means that gross nominal returns are higher in this production line than elsewhere; otherwise no one would undertake this new activity. Monopoly, not competition, is the normal regime in the first phases of the history of a new product. If producers succeed in defending their monopoly power, meaning that there is a large amount of value added per worker, and if the new product's importance grows in time, we can observe an increasing GDP productivity in the economy even though no technical change takes place. In fact under the hypotheses of case (i) if we measured physical output we would find an unchanged productivity performance. One conclusion we can draw from this example is that a sustained GDP productivity growth can be observed more easily in periods when the economy is repeatedly subject to product and process innovations, independently of the trends of physical productivity.

When, on the contrary, the economy experiences phases of 'extensive' growth, during which the product mix stays almost unchanged, we will find a weaker GDP productivity growth. Consequently, the Verdoorn coefficient might depend on the rate of birth of new products. This might to some extent explain the GDP productivity slowdown of the 1960s that was observed in some advanced countries. Notice that this conclusion derives from our reasoning about the meaning of real GDP in national accounts, and not from a model which theorises a link between innovation and physical productivity. Indeed I made no crucial assumption about the latter. Furthermore, one must also ask whether it is meaningful to compare physical productivity in a newly undertaken production process with that in older ones. Since the answer is presumably 'NO', there is no hope to locate the source of increasing physical returns in product innovation per se. Physical productivity changes can be recorded *only* during the life of an already existing good.

Of course, this implication of example (i) holds true if national accountants are able to identify correctly the new products in the base year, and to follow their growth in the subsequent periods. In many circumstances, however, this is not the case, and the expansion of a new monopolised (that is, value-added-intensive) product can be initially mistaken for the relative price increase of an old product. In this case production is over-deflated and productivity underestimated. Take, for instance, the sector of computing machines. In the mid-1970s many statistical offices did not distinguish accurately in their figures between mechanical computing machines and electronic ones, and the quantitative growth of the latter was underestimated. In the early stages, a similar effect might have been induced by initial price increases due to monopoly, as suggested by example (ii) above, or by subsequent price increases due to rapid product innovation. This might account for the well-known complaint of Solow (1987), that 'You can see the computer age everywhere but in the productivity statistics.'

On the contrary, when competition increases and output prices are forced down, as during the 1990s, an opposite trend might prevail, as outlined in example (iii) above. GDP productivity measures start increasing faster than physical productivity. A similar effect takes place if national accountants decide to correct price indexes taking quality into account – that is if the so-called 'hedonic prices' are utilised.[18] If it is believed that consumers have changed their preferences in favour of a given class of products, the price increase of these products is not attributed to purely inflationary trends, and the deflator is reduced accordingly.

As a consequence, the measures of constant-price output and productivity growth are obviously emphasised. Even though the degree of subjectivity of this operation is clearly high, the recorded productivity performance of those economies where it is implemented, like the United States, is increased with respect to other economies.[19] Observe in addition that applying hedonic prices results in a higher growth of constant-price total production, leaving the growth of intermediate inputs roughly unchanged. Thus the recorded ratio of real intermediate inputs to output decreases, and equation (9.5) implies that GDP productivity grows faster than physical productivity.

The previous examples given in (i) to (iii) were motivated by the question of which notion of output one should use to study productivity growth. It turns out that changes in real GDP sometimes do not agree with those in physical production. I do not want to maintain that physical productivity measures are better than GDP productivity ones; but the examples might alert those who favour a strictly physical-technical interpretation of productivity growth, using, however, a concept of output – real GDP – which does not capture only physical phenomena. As we have seen, the problem is particularly serious if the economy is changing in time due to the birth and diffusion of new products, which seems to me the most usual and important source of change.[20] Those who think in terms of production functions, on the contrary, tend to present us with a picture in which a homogeneous output Q lasts unchanged for decades or even centuries, and is produced by homogeneous factors L and K, whose efficiency is augmented by exogenous technical progress or by increases in Q itself. However, in the latter case the sources of increasing returns are seldom spelled out in a convincing way. This picture is, in my opinion, unsatisfactory.

On the other side, those who dislike production functions, and prefer a more 'macroeconomic' perspective, sometimes indulge in a similar ambiguity. They interpret real GDP as a quantity concept, and real GDP per worker as a physical notion of productivity. I do not deny that the trends of GDP per worker can reflect also changes in technical efficiency, as intuitively interpreted. But the arguments of this section show that (a) this measure can be highly imprecise, since it can under- or overestimate physical productivity growth in *existing* production lines; and (b) a possible important source of a sustained growth of GDP-per-worker, as recorded by national accounts, is instead a continuous sequence of successful product *innovations*. As we said, during such a sequence it is meaningless to compare physical productivity across product vintages. On the contrary the recorded growth of GDP-per-worker might signal that producers succeed, as in example (i) above, in selling increasing shares of the new, more value-added-intensive, goods with respect to the mature, less value-added-intensive, ones. Of course, a new product is successful only if the demand for increases. This brings me to the second point of my discussion.

The role of demand

Many interpretations of Verdoorn's Law are basically supply-oriented. Even the most stimulating ones (such as Arrow's 'learning by doing') view the phenomenon as stemming either from workers' increased productivity acquired through repetition, or from the availability of more productive capital goods which in turn depends on cumulated output, often proxied by time. These are important aspects of the story. However, as stated above, it seems that a high growth rate of output and productivity (as conventionally measured) can take place only if new products are introduced successfully in the economy – that is when their demand grows significantly. A Lucas-type interpretation, according to which efficiency is a function of the time spent in training outside the workplace, seems to be unconvincing. Again, if demand does not take off one cannot see how this higher efficiency can be made effective in order to obtain economic miracles.[21]

The Kaldorian tradition of cumulative causation tries to fill this gap. The positive feedback from output to demand is given by the competitiveness gain resulting from higher productivity, which in turn is induced, via Verdoorn's Law, by an output increase.[22] This approach tends to consider the Verdoorn effect as a supply-side phenomenon again, though not a microeconomic one. Increasing returns are derived not from generalised production functions but from endogenous specialisation taking place at the level of the whole manufacturing sector. Demand, however, is considered mostly as a *given* decreasing schedule. If the Verdoorn effect does not take place in production, competitiveness, and hence demand, cannot increase. As argued by Maurizio Pugno in chapter 10 of this volume, this chain of events applies mainly to the mature phases of production, when a product has become well established and well-known to consumers; on the other hand, one expects that Verdoorn's Law declines in importance when newer goods emerge.

In what follows I try to tell the other part of the story, one in which a Verdoorn effect, *as measured by national accounts*, takes place precisely at the point that new production expands. In this sense, my argument is not an alternative, but is complementary, to the more traditional cumulative causation approach. It will be remembered that in the previous section I argued that a GDP productivity growth can be observed in the economy if producers succeed in selling an increasing share of the new, possibly monopolised, products, whose value-added intensity is high with respect to mature ones, without cutting prices. What needs to be explained now is why users should be willing to pay high prices for these new products, that is to buy high quantities of them even if their market price is high, at least initially.

Consider a single new product. The first point to be observed, of course, is that the demand curve for this product *cannot* be well defined (that is, stable) at the start of the story. By definition new products are unknown (or not widely known) to users.[23] This can be expressed by saying that the quality q of the good is uncertain for each user. Assume that quality can be any of the different values belonging to a given set X, and that each user i represents uncertainty by means of a subjective density function $f_i(q)$ defined on X. Thus, opinions differ among users.

If each $f_i(q)$ were given once and for all, one might derive a demand function for the good along the following lines. Let $G_i(q)$ be user i's gain function. It can be a standard utility function, a profit function, or a more general one, defined on q. I assume that users maximise the *expected* gain obtained from acquiring the good, and that a user can buy a single unit of the good at each time. In addition, users are assumed to be risk-averse – that is, $G_i(q)$ is strictly concave. Suppose that quality is measured in such units that the expected gain from buying a unit of the new good measures i's reservation price for that good. The expected gain which i obtains from buying one unit of uncertain quality is then $E_iG_i = \int_{q\in X} G_i(q)f_i(q)dq$, and this is also the price i is willing to pay. Since individual opinions differ from each other, to different market prices there correspond different numbers of buyers, and thus one could observe a stable demand function.

This is not, however, the complete story. Adopting the viewpoint of Bayesian statistical decision theory, $f_i(q)$ must be interpreted as the *prior* subjective distribution of user i. Each user might maintain a prior which is initially to a greater or lesser extent dispersed (or, in equivalent terms, 'precise').[24] As time elapses, users receive some sampling information and by means of this they compute a *posterior* distribution. This latter distribution is used in the subsequent stage to calculate the new expected gain, that is the new reservation price. The posterior distribution after stage $t-1$ can be interpreted as the prior distribution for stage t. In our case, it is reasonable to assume that users collect information if any transactions occur. Actual buyers report to others the quality they experience at each stage. This quality might be higher or lower than expected, given subjective priors and assuming that each unit of the good has a stochastic quality 'shock' attached to it.

All the elements introduced above contribute to the making of a *learning* story. Users start with their subjective prior opinions and make their choices accordingly – that is, they decide whether to be buyers or not. The choices made at each stage affect each other user's posterior opinion, so that the number of buyers, i.e. the extent of the market, changes over time. Without more precise assumptions we cannot forecast the precise evolution of this market. However, we can state some general results. In fact, for a large family of distributions (including the uniform and the normal ones) and under weak assumptions, the following propositions may be derived:[25]

(1) after each stage, the expected value of each user's posterior distribution – that is, the expected posterior quality – is a weighted average of

the prior distribution's expected value and the sample mean which one observes at that stage

(2) the weights of the above average depend, among other things, on the precision of the prior distribution and on the number of cases observed in the sample. The higher the prior precision or the lower the number of cases observed, the higher the weight attached to the prior expected value. In other words, opinion changes slowly if the prior distribution is concentrated or if few users become buyers

(3) the posterior precision is always greater that the prior one, and this increase in precision depends positively, among other things, on the number of cases observed in the sample at each stage.

Proposition (1) above can be a simple explanation in terms of *imitation* phenomena. Given their prior expectations, if users receive a number of positive (negative) reports, their posterior expectations become more (less) optimistic, and the number of buyers increase (decrease) in the subsequent stage. On the other hand, proposition (2) indicates that these changes in opinions are more difficult if users are already self-confident (that is, their prior precision is already high), or if they can observe a limited number of transactions. Taken together, these two aspects imply that an initial situation in which users are on the whole uncertain (that is, their priors are not very precise) is the most conducive to an explosion of adoptions. In fact, in this case the observation of a *few* positive reports can induce a change of mind on the part of *many* potential users. The increased number of buyers in the subsequent stage, in turn, increases still further the number of users who change their mind, and the rate of growth of adoptions increases. This process is clearly path-dependent. If initial reports are by chance negative, the number of those who become more pessimistic is high, given the initial low level confidence about the real quality of the product. Thus, the number of adoptions decreases, making it more difficult to convince a critical mass of potential users to become actual buyers. However, these bifurcation phenomena can only occur in the very first stages of the process. Proposition (3), indeed, means that as time elapses people become more and more self-confident, and then it becomes more and more difficult to change their mind. Notice finally that risk aversion further reinforces a positive cumulative process of the kind we have described. In fact, from proposition (3) it follows that each posterior distribution becomes more and more concentrated in time. If expected quality is not significantly reduced by sample observations, the concavity of $G_i(q)$ implies then an increasing expected *gain*, that is a rising reservation price.[26]

Thus a product might be successful or not depending mainly on the initial opinion on the part of a critical mass of users. It is not the case that only 'good' or 'better' products are successful. Of course, a 'bad' product might have only a temporary success, since after a while many buyers will report mainly a low quality.[27] It might well happen, on the contrary, that a 'good' product does *not* take off due to low initial expectations. At the same time, a product might 'crowd out' a competing one, independently of their intrinsic quality. In other words, learning does not mean 'discovering the truth', but simply becoming satisfied with one's posterior opinion given one's experience. If after a certain number of stages, a user's opinion becomes more 'precise', this user will no longer consider any new information. If the user is firmly convinced that a good is of low quality, a few reports of it being of high quality will not modify this opinion. If there are many such users this situation will be self-reinforcing.

This story gives support to Brian Arthur's contention (1989) that lock-in is a common fact under uncertainty. However, one must observe that in Arthur's model, *objective* increasing returns are *assumed* at the outset. In our case, on the contrary, the change (either an increase or a decrease) in *subjective* expected returns is *endogenous*, since it takes place during the learning process and depends on users' opinions at each stage. It cannot be denied that Arthur-type objective increasing returns (like network externalities or hardware–software positive feedback) are important. I simply suggest that subjective expectations may, under proper conditions, also be an important source of lock-in. As shown by Rothschild (1974), learning lock-in is more probable if a small experimentation cost is present. For instance, it might be the case that people bear some costs in order to collect the reports of others. Under these circumstances, there exists a stage at which users stop their search for better products, and are captured by a product which might be of objective inferior quality. The problem is that they have no incentive to change their choices.

Suppose now that a new product, which is value-added intensive, is introduced in the 'base year' and that it is successful. That is to say, path dependency produces a rapidly increasing number of adoptions. In this case both demand and the demand price increase. One does *not* need a price cut to attract buyers, at least in the initial stages. On the contrary, it is the increased subjectively expected gain that shifts the individual and market demand curves to the right. Of course, one cannot deny that competition might operate in such a way that prices are reduced as time elapses past the base year. In this case, demand grows even still more rapidly. When the national accountants present constant-price data, a rapidly increasing real value added will be recorded, and we will observe an increasing share of this product in the aggregate real value added. These are precisely the conditions we envisaged above in order that an increasing GDP per worker be observable in national accounts at the aggregate level (see example (i)). Even if physical productivity is constant, we will record an increasing share of this value-added-intensive product in the economy – that is, an increase of GDP-per-worker in the aggregate.

In our setting the chain of events which leads to a Verdoorn effect is the following: (1) a new product must be successful in the path-dependent process of learning on the part of users; (2) if this is the case, the share of this product sold in the market increases even without any price cut, so that margins and value added are not squeezed; (3) as a consequence, aggregate national accounts show a rise in real GDP per worker while the share of the new product rises. The Verdoorn effect does take place, since there exists a positive correlation between output growth and productivity growth. However, the productivity increase does not feed back onto demand, being instead simply the observable effect of demand's growth. It is not the Verdoorn effect which stimulates, via price cuts, a higher demand, but it is the increased demand, at given prices, which makes the Verdoorn effect observable in the aggregate.

Self-sustained waves of optimism

One might wonder if this kind of phenomenon can lead to a sustained chain of demand booms – that is, a process which can make the Verdoorn effect clearly observable in macroeconomic terms. Indeed, it is not difficult to understand that the period of increasing demand prices for a single new product *must* come to an end. In fact, the growth rate of adoptions has an upper bound given by the number of potential users and the growth of any individual's reservation price is bounded by the fact that $E_i(G_i(q))$ cannot exceed $G_i(E_i(q))$. Equality is reached when uncertainty has disappeared – that is, subjective precision has become high enough.[28] At this point the market demand curve does not shift any further to the right, and competition is eventually bound to cut prices. It is probably the case that at this point ingenuity on the part of producers will operate in the sense of introducing *marginal* process innovations. Thus, productivity may still increase for a while, but one expects that this happens at a decreasing rate, until it fades out completely. If things stop here the relevance of this process, which involves a single product, is very limited in macroeconomic terms. No story about a cumulative process can be told.

So, one must ask, can we observe periods of massive demand-driven productivity increases? Or is there any possibility that the phenomenon of subjective increasing returns repeats itself in a sustained manner? In my opinion, there is no mechanical law which can be invoked to answer this question either in the affirmative or in the negative. first of all, proposition (3) of the learning process described above, namely monotonically increasing precision, seems to suggest that opinions become more and more rigid. How is it possible to induce users to change further their habits? Secondly, as is apparent from the reasoning offered in the previous section, the whole story is appended to the seemingly *exogenous* constellation of initial prior distributions. If initial opinions are exogenous then there is no hope of construing a self-sustained process. Consider, however, the following brief suggestion.

It is certain that producers, faced with decreasing profits obtained from the mature – though initially successful – product, will try to introduce some newer product, as Schumpeter theorised long ago. The take-off of this product will again be uncertain, being path-dependent, and will be influenced by users' initial opinions. However, it is possible that the success of a previous product will increase the success of a subsequent one. For instance, the reputation gained by the producer of a previously successful good might induce potential users to hold high initial expectations about a new product marketed by this producer. Or it might happen that the new product is similar to a previous very fashionable one, being a more advanced or sophisticated version of the latter – consider the situation with personal computers in the early 1990s, or mobile telephones at the end of the same decade. In these cases, the prior expectations about the quality of the new product cannot be considered to be exogenous. The vague perception of some common factor (either the producer's name, or the good's ability to 'better' satisfy a given need), coupled with the optimistic vein stemming from the old product's success, can bias prior expectations upwards. Thus also the new product can be successful, along the lines described in the previous section; and a third one can be such, giving rise to a self-sustained wave of optimism. Observe that this phenomenon implies both a backward-looking and a forward-looking attitude on the part of users. A number of them become buyers because they have observed many past adoptions of a new good or of its predecessors (*imitation*). Others simply consider more directly that it is worthwhile to become buyers of the good (*expectation*). The latter behaviour is particularly relevant if the very fact of being a buyer of a would-be fashionable good (and possibly being a first-comer) is one of the arguments of the gain function. A status-symbol effect prevails in this case.[29] Of course, the two attitudes feed back on each other in producing a sustained wave.

Not only this – it is also clear that there exists an interplay between users' and producers' expectations. As users are uncertain about the quality of new goods, so producers are uncertain about users' willingness to pay. They will try to forecast how users will perceive the launch of a new product. Obviously, during periods of low demand it does not generally pay to invest resources in new production lines. Thus the probability of introducing a successful new good is reduced during such periods. This effect is further reinforced by the fact that if demand is expected to be low, R&D activity is also perceived to be less attractive. The rate of inventions decreases and so does the probability of undertaking successful innovations. The opposite happens when demand is already high. As a consequence, the choices made by producers can affect users' perceptions and choices in a positive way, and vice versa. This is a further source of cumulative causation on the expectational side of the economy.

Lastly, one must consider the central tenet of Keynes' theory. When demand is high firms and households earn high incomes, and this increases their purchasing power or even their willingness to become indebted. In fact, it is probably the case that increasing incomes positively affect individuals' income expectations. To this one must add the point that not only incomes but also wealth increases during a period of optimistic expectations. Higher expected profits increase prices in the stock market, so that households feel richer and are prone to spend more.

The arguments raised in the previous few paragraphs converge towards the same conclusion. In some historical instances it is expectations, and not simply technology, which might foster an entire swarm of successful innovations and the increasing demand for them. Since expectations tend to be highly self-sustaining, due to the simple facts of cumulative causation that we have explored above, this seems to be a theoretically interesting source of some economic miracles (and misfortunes) we have observed in recent decades. finally, because high expectations imply high demand prices, during these waves of optimism people are willing to spend more on goods which are value-added (that is, income) intensive. Taking the downturn as the 'base year', one is then bound to observe a rapidly increasing GDP-per-worker. In a sense, the perspective on Verdoorn's Law presented here sees it as synonymous with periods of high expectations on the part of consumers in the whole economy. On the other hand, a period of productivity slowdown might be the symptom of an age of diminished expectations.

Conclusion

In this chapter, I have shown that (a) in some cases a growth of real value added per worker can be recorded in national accounts independently of an increase of what is usually understood as physical productivity – namely physical product per worker; (b) one can observe a rising real GDP per worker if the share of new products increases in the economy, and if these new products are more value-added intensive than the mature ones in the base year; (c) as new products are in general more expensive and less known, one needs a 'learning story' on the part of users in order to explain growing demand; (d) learning is a highly cumulative phenomenon, and successful innovations tend to come in swarms (both in time and in space). The last happens when demand is rapidly growing. As a consequence, one observes both increasing demand and production, and an increasing aggregate GDP per worker – that is, one can discern a Verdoorn effect.

Let me conclude with three caveats:

First, I repeat that the view presented here is not to be intended as the only possible explanation of the Verdoorn effect. In many historical instances more objective and technological forces are almost certainly at work. In addition, I want to stress that mine is not a story of product diffusion per se, but mainly a story of the diffusion of value-added-intensive products, so that a Verdoorn effect can be determined from the national accounts. In other words, I do not deny that a standardised product may be successful in some new market as a result of price cuts. This, however, might not lead to a Verdoorn effect if constant-price data are used.

Secondly, although I have tried to offer a particular explanation of cumulative causation booms and slowdowns, it seems difficult to explain the upturn and the downturn of the cycle. As Keynes argued many years ago, their causes are probably to be found in collective psychology.

Thirdly, we know that lock-in is a common phenomenon in economic affairs. As we saw, this means that a successful product is not necessarily an objective improvement. In a similar way, I do not think that a period of rapid output and productivity growth is necessarily Pareto-superior to one exhibiting a slowdown in growth. This is especially the case if in the former exhaustible resources are over-exploited and income distribution is very uneven, provided that in the latter unemployment is not too high. Wearing the spectacles of some growth economists, an already prosperous population may feel unhappy if they cannot become even richer. This is both harmful for the poor and for our grandchildren.

Notes

1. Wright (1936), Hirsch (1952) and (1956), Alchian (1963). See also Arrow (1962) and Fellner (1969).
2. Young (1928), Stigler (1951), Kaldor (1966). For more observations on this point, see McCombie's chapter in this book.
3. This point has already been raised by Heimler and Milana (1984, chapter 6). In this contribution, however, the authors chose a perspective different from the present one, and this particular point was not fully spelled out.
4. I am exploiting the standard accounting identity according to which for an open economy valued added plus imports is equal to *total* final demand (inclusive of exports).
5. Drawing imported inputs on the abscyssa, the isoquants are very flat.
6. The recent revision of the European System of Accounts requires that total production be published yearly in both current and constant prices (see Eurostat, 1996).
7. See Stone and Prais (1952).
8. The actual practice of national accountants might (and in some cases does) diverge from the prescriptions of double deflation. Conider services, whose price is often difficult to define, and whose real output is measured by means of mixtures of quantity or input indexes. In these circumstances the notion of real value added is a hybrid one, and this probably makes the inconsistencies even worse. However, I will not pursue this point.

9. This explains why one can find a negative measure of real value added. Think of a sector which is very energy intensive, and imagine what revenues could have been earned in that sector in the 1960s, when oil was used in very inefficient ways, had the relative oil price been that, say, of the 'base year' 1980.
10. In this case the index of minimum cost is the price index which should be utilised to deflate nominal value added in order to obtain real value added. We are patently far away from national accounting practice.
11. Leontief (1947).
12. I will henceforth use the term 'growth rate' to indicate the growth rate of an index. If for instance one has $Q_t = Q_0 (1 + g_Q)$, then $(1 + g_Q)$ is the index of production, and g_Q will be termed the production growth rate.
13. This is precisely what we observed above in the second example related to the economy *E*, where the intensity of imported inputs increased.
14. That is, a regression of productivity growth on output growth.
15. These estimates come from a database of yearly I–O tables for Italy evaluated in constant prices for the period 1959–97. This database has been obtained according to a methodology described in Rampa (2000). Unfortunately, I–O data for the 1950s are unavailable.
16. Probably the quality of product *A* changes during this process. However, as stated at the beginning of example (i), we assume that the national accountants do not consider this fact.
17. In the three examples we have assumed for simplicity that physical production per worker is constant over time. However, what really matters is the *difference* between GDP productivity and physical productivity growth. Things would be only slightly different if physical productivity were assumed to grow in elementary production lines.
18. 'Hedonic prices' refer to the phenomenon of price increases or decreases due to changing consumers' tastes. In this perspective, if a good becomes more appealing in the consumers' eyes its price rises, but this increase should not be deflated when building constant-price statistics.
19. The effects of the use of 'hedonic prices' on US economic statistics are reviewed by Moulton (2000).
20. If these arguments are important, one should find that a very disaggregated analysis gives poor support to Verdoorn's Law as viewed in purely physical terms. But such an analysis would require being able to follow the life of a *single* homogeneous product, a degree of detail which is quite far from the finest classification available in most empirical studies.
21. See Lucas (1993).
22. See Dixon and Thirlwall (1975).
23. The term 'user' can stand for either producer or consumer, depending on the type of the good we are considering.
24. The 'precision' of a distribution, in Bayesian terms, is an inverse measure of its dispersion. Each different family of distributions admits a different measure of the precision. For example, in the case of a normal distribution its precision is the inverse of its variance.
25. See Groot (1970).
26. The following is a well-known result. If the posterior distribution on quality has the same mean as the prior one, that is, if the change of opinion is 'mean preserving', under the assumption of concavity of the gain function a more concentrated posterior implies a higher posterior expected gain. By continuity, our claim in the text follows.

27. This does not prevent a producer from obtaining profits offering a low quality product, with a 'hit-and-run' policy sustained by high expectations on the part of users.
28. This is a consequence of the result reported in note 26 and of risk aversion, which is defined by the inequality $G_i(E_i(q)) \geq E_i(G_i(q))$.
29. As it appears, our arguments are more forceful in the case of durable or semi-durable goods.

10
Verdoorn's Law and the Analysis of Steady-State Growth: from an Unsatisfactory Marriage to a New Perspective†

Maurizio Pugno

Introduction

This chapter tells a story which has an apparently unfortunate ending. The story concerns a basic, although rather neglected, aspect of Verdoorn's Law – namely its compatibility with steady-state growth. The story appears to be unfortunate, since the attempts to marry Verdoorn's Law to the analysis of steady-state growth produce inconsistencies and weaknesses. This fact seems to prevent Verdoorn's Law from playing a satisfactory role in any long-run analysis. However, as this chapter will briefly show, Verdoorn's Law can still have a useful role in long-run analysis if its role in economic development is explained and made endogenous.

Verdoorn's Law has been conceived as applying to the long run, and not being concerned with short-run relationships because of cyclical variations in the utilisation of resources. Both in the original 1949 article and in Kaldor's reappraisal, the law appears to be a robust statistical relationship. On the theoretical side, steady-state analysis appears to be the most appropriate method for its study. In fact, such analysis has been used by Verdoorn himself to provide foundations for the law. Subsequently, other different theories of economic growth appear to provide foundations for the law. However, as will be argued below, the marriage of Verdoorn's Law with steady-state analysis does not prove to be a satisfactory arrangement, and, moreover, empirical studies have furnished less favourable evidence for the law since the 1960s.

Verdoorn's Law establishes a stable long-run relationship between labour productivity growth and output growth in manufacturing with an elasticity between 0 and 1. The interest in the law stems from this being a true,

† I wish to thank Sergio Destefanis, John McCombie, Giorgio Rampa, and Bruno Soro for comments on a previous draft of this work. The usual disclaimer applies.

rather than a spurious, correlation. It has been tested many times by using different methods, and for many advanced countries and regions over different periods of time. On balance, favourable results have been obtained, but for the most recent decades the law exhibits weaker evidence.

The economic intuition behind the law is still interesting after many decades. It states that larger volumes of output allow a greater division of labour, with the analogous effects in increasing productivity as that occuring from greater mechanisation (Verdoorn 1949, p. 16). This phenomenon has been labelled 'learning by doing' by Arrow (1962), who directly refers to Verdoorn (1949) and to the learning function in Verdoorn (1956, p. 433). In referring to Arrow, Kaldor (1966) remarks that learning is a dynamic and irreversible process, and therefore dismisses the traditional production function with increasing returns to scale as the basis of Verdoorn's Law. Recently, the learning function and the Arrovian externalities have been emphasised by Lucas (1988, 1993) both to provide the foundation for his own endogenous growth model, and to justify the 'miracle' in the growth performance of the NICs.

Verdoorn's Law can be explained by two opposing theoretical approaches: namely, the supply-side (or traditional) theory, and the demand-side (or Keynesian) theory. However, either the restriction to steady-state growth makes the explanation very poor, or the theory cannot sustain steady-state growth, if this is generally defined as a growth in the variables which can be indefinitely prolonged over time without any constraint. Otherwise, if this configuration can be sustained only for a definite period, because a constraint or some feedback emerges, then it must be regarded as a paradoxical analysis of the 'temporary long run'.

Verdoorn's Law remains a useful piece of analysis, however, if the steady-state method is abandoned and a new framework is found for it. This search would be arduous, but an attempt might be made by starting from the original concept underlying the law: the learning function. Since supply- and demand-side theories have used this concept, it is also tempting to combine both kinds of theories within a single framework, and this is possible if the evolution over time of the learning function is considered. In this new perspective of non-linear dynamics, Verdoorn's Law emerges as an endogenously changing relationship.

This chapter is organised as follows: the next section briefly reviews empirical findings on the law. Then we discuss the original supply-side model in Verdoorn (1949) and the second attempt (Verdoorn, 1956) where the learning function is introduced. It is shown that the recent theories of endogenous growth, which appear to substantiate the law using the same concept, are in effect unsatisfactory analyses of steady-state growth. There follows an analysis that shows that demand-side models based on Verdoorn's Law by Kaldor, Thirlwall and their coauthors also exhibit unsatisfactory aspects for steady-state analysis. Next, we argues that the marriage between Verdoorn's

Law and steady-state analysis is not necessary and that Verdoorn's Law could find a better place in a non-steady-state analysis which comprises aspects of both the supply and demand-orientated theories.

The empirical evidence

The volume of empirical literature on Verdoorn's Law is considerable – much larger than the theoretical literature. However, little attention has been paid to whether or not Verdoorn's Law works in condition of steady-state growth.[1]

The focus of many studies has been on testing Verdoorn's Law in the demand-side form:

$$p = a_0 + a_1 q + \varepsilon \tag{10.1}$$

or, equivalently:

$$e = -a_0 + (1 - a_1)q - \varepsilon \tag{10.1'}$$

where p indicates the productivity rate of growth, q the output rate of growth, e the employment rate of growth, a_0 the 'autonomous' technical progress, a_1 the Verdoorn coefficient, and ε the error term. The main test is conducted on the null hypothesis that $a_1 = 0$. The preference for this simple equation implies either that the growth rate of the other main input, that is physical capital, is regarded as constant, and is thus included in a_0, or that it is closely correlated with q, i.e. steady-state growth prevails, so that it can be ignored in the estimation.[2]

Other studies extend equations (10.1) or (10.1′) to include a capital growth variable (k), but the test on the significance of this variable is not usually followed by a test on the correlation between q and k, which is a necessary condition for steady state.

A variety of methods has been used to test for the exogeneity of q. The most widely used method, although it is a fairly weak one, is to convert equations (10.1) or (10.1′) into the so-called 'Rowthorn equations':

$$p = \frac{a_0}{1 - a_1} + \frac{a_1}{1 - a_1} e + \frac{\varepsilon}{1 - a_1} \tag{10.2}$$

$$q = \frac{a_0}{1 - a_1} + \frac{1}{1 - a_1} e + \frac{\varepsilon}{1 - a_1} \tag{10.2'}$$

If q is significant in equations (10.1) or (10.1′), and if e is not significant in equation (10.2) or (10.2′), then q may be regarded as exogenous, but if e is also significant, the question of the exogeneity of q remains unresolved.[3] A preferable method is to use a system of structural and simultaneous equations. Verdoorn (1949) himself suggested a specification of such a system, while Kaldor (1970) suggests an alternative specification. Time-series analysis allows the use of other methods to test causality: the Granger causality test, and the test for 'weak' exogeneity in the multivariate cointegration framework. The application of time series analysis to Verdoorn's Law, however, leads to a number of economic as well as econometric problems.

The data set used varies greatly. It usually refers to manufacturing as a whole or to single industries, to advanced countries or to their regions, but in some cases also to developing and eastern countries. It has been applied over a variety of time spans, although usually to data after the Second World War. Cross-section analysis alternates with time-series analysis, and sometimes with panel analysis.

The Appendix to the Introduction to this volume lists many empirical studies which explicitly refer to Verdoorn's Law. From these studies four main conclusions can be drawn. First, practically all studies find that the Verdoorn coefficient is significantly different from zero, and, moreover, that it is usually less than one. Secondly, the capital growth variable does not play a definite role, since some studies find that capital growth is not significant in explaining productivity, while others, including the cointegration studies, find that it is significant. The correlation between q and k has been found to be significant only in one limiting case.[4] This result hinders understanding the question of any steady-state analysis. Thirdly, the evidence on the exogeneity of q and the endogeneity of p and of e appear to favour the demand-side version of Verdoorn's Law as in the equation (10.1) or (10.1′). In fact, five studies find that e in the 'Rowthorn equation' is not significant, while three studies find that it is significant;[5] two studies find that e is not explained by growth in the labour force, as Verdoorn (1949) would predict;[6] four studies find that q may be endogenous, but only indirectly through the competitive performance of exports, so that cumulative causation takes place.[7] More mixed results emerge from cointegration studies.[8]

As a fourth conclusion, whereas Verdoorn's Law appears to receive fairly strong support from a large body of evidence covering many countries and regions, the evidence for the advanced countries in more recent decades indicates that something has changed. In fact, eight studies find that one or more structural breaks in the estimates of Verdoorn's Law for manufacturing as a whole have occurred after the Second World War: four of these report clear evidence that the Verdoorn coefficient has been reduced, and five clearly report that the importance of the 'autonomous' technical progress has gained in importance as an explanation of productivity.[9] Some authors suggest that the regime has changed from the Fordist regime through the more unstable periods of the 1970s, to the Information Technology regime (Boyer, 1988; Freeman, 1988). If this is true, Verdoorn's Law loses much of its analytical power.[10]

Supply-side theories

Verdoorn's full model

The first formal explanation of the law appeared in the Appendix of the original article (Verdoorn, 1949) as an adaptation of Tinbergen's 1942 model. (See chapters 2 and 3 of this volume.) It consists of five equations:

production function	$Q = Ae^{vt}K^{\alpha}E^{\beta} \quad 0 < \alpha, \beta < 1 \quad \alpha + \beta \geq 1$	(10.3)
labour demand equation	$W = \beta(Q/E)$	(10.4)
labour supply equation	$W = \beta(E/N)^{\rho}$	(10.5)
capital supply equation	$k = \gamma Q/K$	(10.6)
population equation	$N = e^{\eta t}$	(10.7)

where Q is the level of manufacturing output, K is the capital stock with k as its rate of growth, E is the level of employment, α and β their respective elasticities, W is the wage rate, N the total active population growing at the rate η, ρ is the reciprocal of the elasticity of labour supply with respect to the wage rate, and γ is the propensity to invest. Ae^{vt} is the autonomous efficiency index growing at the rate v, which in fact does not appear in the original model.[11] All parameters (Greek letters), including population growth, are positive and exogenous.

Having (temporarily) omitted Ae^{vt} as in the original model, and having differentiated the logarithms of the variables, it is possible to obtain *the elasticity of the labour productivity with respect to output* (V) following Verdoorn's (1949) line of reasoning:

$$V = \frac{(\beta - 1)\rho\eta + \rho\alpha k}{\beta\rho\eta + (1 + \rho)\alpha k} \tag{10.8}$$

Verdoorn's Law claims that V is constant and that $0 < V < 1$. This is true, as Verdoorn (1949, 1980) notes, if all the parameters and k remain constant,[12] and if $\eta < k\alpha/(1 - \beta)$. This result is also maintained in the case of constant returns to scale, i.e. if $\alpha + \beta = 1$.

However, capital growth does not remain constant because, from equation (10.6), it depends on Q/K, which changes because, in turn, output and capital grow at different rates, in general. In fact:

$$q - k = \frac{\beta\rho}{1 - \beta + \rho}\eta - \frac{[1 - (\alpha + \beta) + \rho(1 - \alpha)]}{1 - \beta + \rho}k \tag{10.9}$$

which is generally different from zero.

In order to have a constant V, the usual condition of steady-state growth – that is $q = k$ – must be assumed. In this case one obtains:

$$V = \frac{\alpha + \beta - 1}{\beta} \tag{10.10}$$

This result straightforwardly proves, first, that the Verdoorn elasticity depends on technological parameters only, while in equation (10.8) it also depends on the elasticity of labour supply (ρ), and, secondly, that increasing returns to scale in the production function, i.e. $\alpha + \beta > 1$, is a necessary condition to have $V > 0$.

In Verdoorn's (1980) more general case, autonomous technical progress (Ae^{vt}) is present, so that the generalisation of V, that is V_g, is:

$$V_g = \frac{\rho(\beta - 1)\eta + \rho v + \rho \alpha k}{\rho\beta\eta + (1+\rho)\alpha k + (1+\rho)v} \tag{10.11}$$

which requires $\eta < (k\alpha + n)/(1 - \beta)$ to be positive, and $\alpha k + \rho\eta + v > 0$ to be smaller than 1. The general dynamic is:

$$q - k = \frac{(1+\rho)v + \beta\rho\eta}{1 - \beta + \rho} - \frac{[1 - (\alpha + \beta) + \rho(1 - \alpha)]}{1 - \beta + \rho} k \tag{10.12}$$

This equation suggests the search for the *existence* and for the *dynamic stability* of the (steady-state) solution of the model, where, as later Verdoorn recognised, the 'rigid constancy over time of the productivity–output elasticity is to be expected' (Verdoorn, 1980).

Let us define $X \equiv Q/K$, and observe that its growth rate is $x = q - k$, and that $X = k/\gamma$ from equation (10.6), so that equation (10.12) becomes:

$$\frac{dX}{dt} = \frac{(1+\rho)v + \beta\rho\eta}{1 - \beta + \rho} X - \frac{[1 - (\alpha + \beta) + \rho(1 - \alpha)]}{1 - \beta + \rho} \gamma X^2 \tag{10.13}$$

This is a first-order non-linear differential equation of the Bernoulli type. It admits two steady-state solutions: one trivial solution, $X_0^* = 0$, and the relevant one:

$$X^* = \frac{\rho\beta\eta + (1+\rho)v}{[1 - (\alpha + \beta) + \rho(1 - \alpha)]\gamma} \tag{10.14}$$

so that $q = k = \gamma X^*$, and moreover:

$$e = \frac{\rho(1-\alpha)\eta + v}{1-(\alpha+\beta)+\rho(1-\alpha)} \tag{10.15}$$

$$p = \frac{\rho(\alpha+\beta-1)\eta + \rho v}{1-(\alpha+\beta)+\rho(1-\alpha)} \tag{10.16}$$

$$V_g = \frac{\rho(\alpha+\beta-1)\eta + \rho v}{\rho\beta\eta + (1+\rho)v} \tag{10.17}$$

where e is the growth rate of employment, and p that of labour productivity.[13] However, the non-trivial solution is stable, and the trivial solution is unstable, if the coefficients of the Xs of the equation (10.14) are positive, i.e. if $\alpha < 1$ and $\rho > (\alpha + \beta - 1)/(1 - \alpha)$.[14] This means that ρ must be sufficiently large. In particular, as $\rho \to +\infty$, $dX/dt = (v + \beta\eta)X - (1 - \alpha)\gamma X^2$. These restrictions also guarantee that steady-state solutions for q, e, and p are positive.

From equations (10.14), (10.15) and (10.16) Verdoorn's Law can thus be explained by the following:

$$p = \frac{\alpha+\beta-1}{\beta} q + \frac{v}{\beta} \tag{10.18}$$

However, the same result obtains from the production function (10.3) only, if the steady-state restriction is imposed ($q = k$). In fact, without this restriction equation (10.17) becomes thus:

$$p = \frac{\alpha}{\beta} k - \frac{1-\beta}{\beta} q + \frac{v}{\beta} \tag{10.19}$$

Therefore, four conclusions can be drawn. firstly, despite the assumption of increasing returns to scale, the model is of exogenous growth, since population growth (η) and autonomous technical progress (v) are necessary to determine q, but also e, and p. Secondly, in order to obtain a stable and positive steady-state solution, labour supply must be sufficiently rigid (large ρ), so that η and v can be effective.[15] Thirdly, if the usual production function is maintained, steady-state growth emerges as the natural outcome, where both Verdoorn's elasticity (10.17) is constant and Verdoorn's Law (10.18) is stable over time. Fourthly, strangely enough, η and v do not enter Verdoorn's Law in the steady state, which only depends on the degree of increasing returns to scale, without any reference to ρ. Hence, Verdoorn's Law is independent of the structure of the whole model, except the production function.

A further conclusion, which is the most interesting for us, can also be drawn. Even if output and capital are able to grow at the same rate, employment and population generally grow at different rates. In fact:

$$e - \eta = \frac{(\alpha + \beta - 1)\eta + v}{1 - (\alpha + \beta) + \rho(1 - \alpha)} \tag{10.20}$$

which is greater than zero, since $\rho > (\alpha + \beta - 1)/(1 - \alpha)$, as required. This is an uncomfortable result for steady-state analysis, since the level of employment in other sectors and of the unemployment will reach zero at some point of time, and $e - \eta$ can no longer remain positive. This implies a structural change of the model, which is not, however, studied.

This problem is not usually raised in either the Solow-type models or endogenous growth theory, because of the assumption that labour supply is inelastic, i.e. $\rho \to +\infty$ so that $e - \eta \to 0$. Solow may have been aware of this problem when he wrote the famous article in 1956, because he includes a section in which labour supply is assumed positively elastic with respect to wages. However, he also assumes no autonomous technical progress in the same section, thereby skirting round the problem once again. In fact, if $\rho \to +\infty$ and $v > 0$, then $e - \eta \to 0$ from equation (10.20). But if $0 < \rho < +\infty$ and $v > 0$, then $e - \eta = v/(\rho - \rho\alpha) > 0$, under constant returns to scale, as Solow (1956) still assumes, and the problem remains.

Verdoorn's alternative explanation

The first attempt to explain Verdoorn's Law by Verdoorn himself can thus be regarded as unsuccessful, but the second attempt, that is, Verdoorn (1956), seems more promising, though it is not developed into a full model. It can be simply rewritten as follows:

$$A = \psi\left[\int_{-\infty}^{t} Q dt\right]^{\xi} \text{ with } \psi, \xi > 0 \tag{10.21}$$

This is a generalisation of Hirsch's (1952) 'progress function' apparently prevailing in important manufacturing sectors. If it is combined with Verdoorn's (1980) production function, which is equal to equation (10.3) but with $\alpha + \beta = 1$, then the two equations give, after some manipulations, the following steady-state relationship:

$$p = \frac{\xi}{\beta} q + \frac{v}{\beta} \tag{10.22}$$

where ξ can be interpreted as exactly the excess over the constant returns of equation (10.18).

Therefore, this attempt is far less confusing than the first one, since the labour market constraint does not appear, and an interesting concept is introduced (cf. McCombie, 1982a; Soro, 1983), that is, equation (10.21), which interprets the law as a process of learning, rather than as an allocation over time, as suggested by the use of the production function alone. This hint, however, is not further developed in Verdoorn (1956).

Endogenous growth theory and Verdoorn's Law

The assumption of increasing returns to scale and the underlying justification of learning as a widespread macroeconomic phenomenon can also be found in the recent theory of endogenous growth, which has modified the famous Solow (1956) model. It seems thus possible to explain Verdoorn's Law along different lines.

Romer (1986) proposes a model, which is based on the positive externalities in accumulating physical capital, as in Arrow (1962). The essence of his model can be captured by the following equations:

$$\text{production function} \qquad Q = Ae^{vt}K^{\alpha}E^{\beta} \quad \text{with } \alpha + \beta = 1 \tag{10.23}$$

$$\text{learning function} \qquad A = \left[\int_{-\infty}^{t} Idt\right]^{\varphi} = K^{\varphi} \quad \text{with } \varphi > 0 \tag{10.24}$$

where φ measures the degree of capital externalities which determines the degree of overall technical efficiency, and I is investment in non-depreciating physical capital. In growth terms equations (10.23) and (10.24) yield:

$$q = v + (\alpha + \varphi)k + \beta\eta \tag{10.25}$$

where e equals η.

The steady-state condition implies the following:

$$p = \frac{\varphi}{\beta}q + \frac{v}{\beta} \tag{10.26}$$

$$V = \frac{\varphi\eta + v}{\beta\eta + v} \tag{10.27}$$

which are not greatly different from the results already obtained, since equation (10.26) is similar to equations (10.18) and (10.22), with φ being the excess over constant returns, and equation (10.27) is similar to equation (10.10) for $v = 0$.

In order to show that growth is endogenously sustained, let us assume that $v = 0$ and $\eta = 0$. Hence:

$$q = p = \gamma Q/K = \gamma K^{\alpha + \varphi - 1} E^{\beta} \tag{10.28}$$

Both output growth and productivity growth depend on the economy's size – that is, on the number employed. But the endogenous steady-state solution further requires: $\alpha + \varphi = 1$. As employment is fixed, growth is constant.

However, all these restrictions are far from innocuous. They imply not only that the degree of externality, population growth and autonomous technical progress take certain empirical values and not others, but also, that they take exactly those values, and not approximately, if steady state is to be guaranteed. Obviously, these conditions are not warranted.[16] Moreover, since $\varphi = \beta$, then $q = p + v/\beta$ and $V = 1$.

Therefore, Romer (1986) represents very little improvement over Verdoorn (1949). Instead of some positive growth in population and autonomous technical progress, a zero growth of them is required, while all these conditions do not affect the Verdoorn Law as such.

The other major work on the theory of endogenous growth – Lucas (1988) – is interesting because it pays particular attention to the learning function.

The well-known model includes the following key functions:

production function	$Q = AK^{\alpha}(uHE)^{\beta}H^{\theta}$	(10.29)
learning function	$dH = H^{\zeta}\delta(1 - u)$	(10.30)

where u indicates the portion of time devoted to current production, and H is the human capital measured as the workers' skill level. The production function exhibits increasing returns to scale, since $\alpha + \beta > 1$ and $\theta > 0$, which measures the degree of externalities. Having assumed an inelastic labour supply ($e = \eta$), steady-state growth is then obtained as follows:

$$q = k = (1 + \theta/\beta)h + \eta \tag{10.31}$$

where h is the growth rate of H. Equation (10.30) is a learning function, which, if similar to Verdoorn (1956) and Arrow (1962), would exhibit decreasing returns. However, here it exhibits constant returns, since Lucas assumes that $\zeta = 1$, while u is proved to be constant in steady-state growth,[17] so that $h = \bar{h} = \delta(1-u)$. He justifies the constant returns assumption of learning on the basis that the accumulation of human capital is a social activity, formally pursued by the typically infinitely-lived family, rather than the typical finitely-lived individual. In his words: 'one needs to assume both that each individual's capital follows this equation [i.e. eq.(30)

with $\zeta = 1$] and that the initial level each new member begins with is proportional to the level already attained by older members of the family' (Lucas, 1988,p. 19). The assumption that $\zeta = 1$ is crucial for an endogenous explanation of steady-state growth, that is, independently of autonomous technical progress and of η. In fact, if $\zeta < 1$, then:

$$q = (1 + \theta/\beta)H^{\zeta - 1}\delta(1 - u) + \eta \tag{10.32}$$

and, for $t \to +\infty$, the possibility of endogenous growth vanishes, since $q \to \eta$.

As the steady-state growth of labour productivity is:

$$p = (1 + \theta/\beta)\bar{h} \tag{10.33}$$

it can be calculated that:

$$V = \frac{(\beta + \theta)\bar{h}}{(\beta + \theta)\bar{h} + \beta\eta} \tag{10.34}$$

which is between 0 and 1. However, population growth assumes a crucial role in determining V. In particular, if $\eta = 0$, then $V = 1$.

Therefore, although the Lucas model exhibits increasing returns to scale, includes a learning function, yields $0 < V \leq 1$ and endogenous steady-state growth, it does not provide an interesting basis for the explanation of Verdoorn's Law. Firstly, V does not provide useful information since it crucially depends on population growth, and, secondly, constant returns in the learning function must be assumed. This restriction is very severe, because the justification of a sequence of individual learning functions with decreasing returns to form a social learning function with constant returns requires the additional condition that the sequence is a progressive and smooth process.

Therefore, steady-state analysis requires the imposition of severe restrictions on both Lucas' and Romer's models. These restrictions refer to the exact and peculiar specifications of knowledge externality, labour growth, and human capital accumulation.[18] These are necessary because they refer to the supply-side determinants of long-run growth.

Demand-side theories

Kaldor's analysis

Several authors emphasise that demand-side theory may offer a better explaination of Verdoorn's Law. The learning function itself suggests that productivity depends on the size of the market, and it represents an irreversible process, while the neoclassical production function instead represents the static allocation set of choices. The 'better' Verdoorn would be thus Verdoorn (1956).

The leading proponent of the demand-side interpretation of Verdoorn's Law is undoubtedly Kaldor, as shown in McCombie's chapter 4 in this volume. Kaldor states that output growth responds to the exogenous growth of effective demand, while both productivity growth and employment growth are endogenous. He extends the justification of Verdoorn's Law from the 'learning-by-doing' process to the increased specialisation among sectors, and to the endogenous process of increasing mechanisation (Kaldor, 1966). Verdoorn's Law thus properly applies only to manufacturing as a whole, according to Kaldor, but he does not provide formal explanations for his different justifications. Hence, the Verdoorn elasticity is a technological relationship and is a good indicator of relative growth performance among economies, but Kaldor's explanations for Verdoorn's Law are only verbal.

Kaldor estimates Verdoorn's Law for some advanced countries and for the period 1953–64, as specified in equations (10.1) and (10.1′). Kaldor (1967) also includes the investment/output ratio in the relationship, and finds that it does not significantly affect the estimates – it merely explains the residuals. This suggests that Kaldor is not much interested in the stability of the whole of Verdoorn's Law, nor even in the elasticity V, but only in the Verdoorn coefficient (a_1 in equation (10.1)). Kaldor's explanation of economic growth is thus not a steady-state one.

However, as observed earlier, subsequent studies have revealed that capital may have some significant role to play, and that the Verdoorn coefficient decreases, while 'autonomous' technical progress increases. These facts raise the problem of changes in the theoretical explanation of Verdoorn's Law, and this would require a wider growth model.

A second problem arises in Kaldor's treatment of the labour market, since he (Kaldor, 1968) assumes the existence of surplus labour, or more rigorously that $\rho = 0$. In the long run, the transfer of labour from low-productivity sectors and immigration may make η irrelevant or endogenous. But the labour market is heterogeneous in specialisation and location of the labour force, and changes in sectoral specialisation may encounter bottlenecks in hiring labour. Are these bottlenecks irrelevant in the long run?

A third problem regards exogeneity of demand, as proxied by q. Higher productivity growth undoubtedly has some effect on q through prices. Kaldor admits this, but only as a 'far less regular and systematic' relationship (Kaldor, 1975b).

Dixon and Thirlwall's cumulative causation model

A more promising approach to the simultaneity problem is the extended model for Verdoorn's Law suggested by Kaldor himself and formalised by Dixon and Thirlwall (1975). Since this model is well known (see, e.g.,

Roberts' or León-Ledesma's chapters in this volume), the presentation is extremely short here. The essential model is the following:

Verdoorn's Law	$p = a_0 + a_1 q$	(10.35)
mark-up pricing	$\pi = w - p$	(10.36)
export function	$x = b_0(\pi_f - \pi) + b_1 q_f$	(10.37)
output function	$q = c_0 x$	(10.38)

where π denotes price inflation, w nominal wages, and x export growth, while f is attached to the exogenous variables of the rest of the world, and in particular π_f is adjusted for exchange rate changes.[19] The solutions for q, p and for V are:

$$q = \frac{1}{1 - b_0 c_0 a_1} c_0 \left[b_0 \left(\pi_f - w + u_0 \right) + b_1 q_f \right] \tag{10.39}$$

$$p = \frac{a_0 + a_1 c_0 \left[b_0 \left(\pi_f - w \right) + b_1 q_f \right]}{1 - b_0 c_0 a_1} \tag{10.40}$$

$$V = \frac{a_0 + a_1 c_0 \left[b_0 \left(\pi_f - w \right) + b_1 q_f \right]}{c_0 \left[b_0 \left(\pi_f - w + a_0 \right) + b_1 q_f \right]} \tag{10.41}$$

For realistic values of c_0 (not larger than 1), b_0 (smaller than 2), and a_1 (smaller than 0.5), so that $c_0 b_0 a_1 < 1$, Dixon and Thirlwall also show the stability of the (steady-state) solution given by the equation (10.39). The model thus seems able to explain productivity growth and to determine a constant V, as long as the exogenous variables π_f, q_f and w remain constant.

Moreover, Verdoorn's Law can rely on the learning function without incurring the restriction usually imposed by the theory of endogenous growth. In fact, equation (10.35) can be derived by a learning function similar to equation (10.21), which does not have a binding restriction on ξ. A persistent growth is ensured by the maintenance of competition abroad, i.e. b_0 and b_1, whereas in the endogenous growth theory (see Romer, 1986, and Lucas, 1988, above) a persistent growth requires a sufficient degree of learning over a given initial condition.

However, problems about the steady-state concept are present in this model as well. In fact, the solution of the model (10.35)–(10.38) yields meaningful results from an economic point of view, when adequate initial conditions are given – in particular, when exports are less than output, and the unemployment rate is positive. However, these conditions hold for a finite period only, if $c_0 < 1$, and if $e > \eta$, so that a meaningless steady-state growth eventually takes place. Moreover, in order to model a meaningful steady-state growth it is desirable to specify the accumulation function, and, since the economy is open, the import function. A further uncomfortable feature for the sustainability of a steady-state growth is the unceased divergence between domestic prices and foreign prices as implied in the solution of the model. Therefore, the model is able to sustain a steady-state growth for a finite period only, and this leads one to expect a structural change in the parameters, which, however, is left unexplained.

Thirlwall's external constraint model

McCombie and Thirlwall (1994) further extend and modify the model to take the external constraint, as given by the balance between exports and imports, into account, thus avoiding one of the shortcomings. They add an import equation:

$$m = d_0(\pi - \pi_f) + d_1 q \tag{10.42}$$

the condition for the external equilibrium:

$$x + \pi = m + \pi_f \tag{10.43}$$

and they drop equation (10.38). Equations (10.37), (10.42), and (10.43) give the famous Thirlwall formula of the external constraint growth rate:

$$q_T = \frac{b_1 q_f + (\pi - \pi_f)(1 - b_0 - d_0)}{d_1} = \frac{b_1 q_f}{d_1} \tag{10.44}$$

under the restriction $\pi - \pi_f = 0$. In order to justify the restriction, which is comforted by the evidence, McCombie and Thirlwall refer to the arguments of the wage resistance, and of price rigidity.[20] However, if this is the case exports do not grow as output, and the steady state cannot be sustained indefinitely (a coefficient for c_0 as the equation (10.38) is reintroduced).

If one considers the full model, which includes the Verdoorn's Law (and the mark-up pricing), but without the restriction $\pi - \pi_f = 0$, one obtains:

$$q = \frac{b_1 q_f + (w - a_0 - \pi_f)(1 - b_0 - d_0)}{d_1 + q_1(1 - b_0 - d_0)} \tag{10.45}$$

In this case Verdoorn's Law has some role to play. In fact, if growth is high, that is $q > (w - a - \pi_f)/a_1$, then cumulative causation dampens price inflation so that $\pi_f > \pi$, if growth is low, i.e. $q < (w - a_0 - \pi_f)/a_1$, then $\pi_f < \pi$.

Therefore, this model, while extending consideration to the external equilibrium, also maintains the problems already encountered in Dixon and Thirlwall's model. Moreover, it reduces the role of Verdoorn's Law in the growth process, because, under the restriction $\pi = \pi_f$, Verdoorn's Law affects the dynamics of real wages but not those of output growth.

Setterfield's analysis

The problem of stability of Verdoorn's Law and of the steady-state growth in the demand-side theory has been investigated by Setterfield (1997a). He finds it unsatisfactory that Dixon and Thirlwall's model predicts divergence in output between economies (or regions) which is dependent on initial conditions only, and which is unbound. He thus proposes that the Verdoorn coefficient (a_1 in equation (10.35)) is negatively affected by past dynamics of output growth.[21] The justification is that 'an initial period of high relative growth may ... impair the ability of a region to realise dynamic increasing returns based on changes in technique' (Setterfield, 1997a, p. 372). In this way, the recent pattern of economic growth in the UK can be captured.

Setterfield's analysis undoubtedly takes a step forward in dealing with the problem of Verdoorn's Law and of the steady state, since it recognises the necessity to study the changes in Verdoorn's Law, and to endogenise them. However, this endogenisation has a very low explanatory content. The link between past growth and the Verdoorn coefficient has no structure, the verbal justification is not formalised. It thus appears rather 'ad hoc'. Moreover, the problems raised before for Dixon and Thirlwall's model are not answered by Setterfield.

The steady-state analysis

The history of Verdoorn's Law is paradoxical. Having been conceived as a stable long-run relationship in the industrial countries, it has been subsequently explained within a steady-state analysis by different growth models. However, they encounter serious problems, if the long run is conceived as an indefinite long period of time, because structural change in the model becomes necessary, but has not been studied. The above analysis has shown why this failure occurs in both the supply- and demand-side models. But one may wonder why steady-state analysis is used. To answer this question, it is useful to briefly remind oneself of its origins.

In 1958, Kaldor listed some 'stylised facts' about the growth of the advanced countries; namely, a constant growth of output and labour productivity, a constant capital–output ratio, constant profit–income and investment–output shares, and different trends of economic growth. The attempts to explain these facts in formal models, apart from the last one, are the well-known Kaldor (1961) and Solow (1956; cf 1970, ch.1) models, which provided the foundation for the study of the steady-state growth of models. Hence, their aim is not to explain the rate of economic growth per se, but rather (although from different viewponts) the conditions for a constant growth rate to occur for an indefinite period of time, with an unchanging economic structure.

Unfortunately, after two decades of prolonged growth, since the 1970s the advanced countries have once again experienced large fluctuations and stagnation, while they have been caught up by rapidly growing NICs. Economic theory has thus moved to a detailed consideration of the business cycle. Real business cycle theory is perhaps the most important example from the supply side, while demand-side theory has paid more attention to non-linear dynamics. One would expect steady-state analysis to cease to attract interest from economists. Yet, especially in the mid-1980s and 1990s, steady-state analysis has attracted a new interest both by reformulating the Solow model with an infinite horizon of consumption preferences, and by proposing models of endogenous steady-state growth and convergence to the steady state. The aim of the analysis has thus shifted from the steady-state growth to the causes of growth, but the method has not changed. The reasons for using steady-state analysis have changed from explaining stylised facts to mathematical tractability, especially when microfoundations are specified. Therefore, steady-state growth has become less the outcome of the models, but is rather assumed through proper specifications of the parameters.[22]

The consequences of these shifts cannot be dealt with here. The point of interest is rather that steady-state analysis emerges as a possible, rather than a necessary, method of analysis, and that its application to Verdoorn's Law may be due to an inertia in the methods used.

Verdoorn's Law in a new perspective

Earlier sections have shown that Verdoorn's Law offers an unsatisfactory explanation within the context of a steady-state analysis. We may also seem to have confirmed that Verdoorn's Law does not remain valid for a prolonged period of time, because it diminishes in empirical importance in advanced countries. One could also observe that manufacturing is now a declining sector in these countries, while the service sector, which does not exhibit increasing returns to scale, according to Kaldor (1966, 1967), is generally expanding. However, as shown in the original paper and in other subsequent studies (see note 2 above), Verdoorn's Law can be also applied to single industries, where the justification of the learning function is more appropriate. Hence, the search for a new analytical framework in which Verdoorn's Law can find a satisfactory explanation may start from the learning function in individual industries, and from their interaction with the rest of the economy. This would be a formidable research undertaking, however, which would have to deal with all the analytical contributions from both the supply and the demand side, as reviewed above. Therefore, only a brief theoretical sketch is provided in this final section.

The sectoral pattern of the learning curve, as generally observed, is one of diminishing returns.[23] To solve the problem of explaining prolonged growth by means of the learning curve, an aggregation of a rapid succession of them has been suggested, so that, as shown above in Lucas' case, the aggregate returns can become constant. However, this aggregation hides not only interesting dynamics, but also the interaction between the supply side and the demand side.

The learning curve itself synthesises the supply-side aspect of the changes in production practices over time, and the demand-side aspect of their adoption, which converts the curve from being a potential to an actual outcome. This distinction is usually implicitly neglected by supply-side economists, who simply assume that demand is always sufficient to absorb production. However, from the perspective of macroeconomic growth with many sectoral learning curves, products are numerous both at any moment of time and through time. The assumption of homothetic preferences is not tenable, but the assumption of 'love of variety'[24] also appears too restrictive to maintain in the presence of changes in the composition, quality and also prices of the product basket. Therefore, the study of the demand side becomes important. In this regard, Utterback (1979) recognises that incremental innovation is specifically pursued by firms to reduce costs and enlarge market shares when production becomes 'mature', and that this emerges as a mixed process together with organisational 'learning by doing'. Furthermore the dissemination of this process is largely a demand-driven phenomenon, as observed by the literature on technological diffusion (see, for example, Stoneman, 1983). These facts make the price elasticity of demand particularly relevant in explaining the realisation of the learning curves.

Empirical research on this point would offer extremely useful guidance for theoretical analysis, although one stylised fact is already available for this purpose – namely, the Engel curve. According to this, the consumption of a specific good depends on the level of real income, and this gives rise to the shapes of the familiar curves. Pasinetti (1981, pp. 73–4) suggests that demand for that good also depends significantly on price just before the saturation phase, while both at low and at very high levels of income, the price elasticity of the good is inelastic. In fact, the basket of consumption goods is particularly varied among middle-income consumers. Pasinetti (1981, pp. 75–6) also stresses the importance of learning on the demand side. If this is regarded as a social activity through imitation, rather than an individual activity, then the Engel curves become relevant for the supply side. To retard market saturation, firms strive to increase efficiency and reduce prices. Hence, one can deduce that demand can convert the (supply) learning curve to an actual outcome both in the initial stages when productivity is low, but the characteristics of the good are new, through a high income elasticity, and afterwards when productivity is high, but the characteristics are old, through a high price elasticity.

Learning and imitation on the demand side has another important macroeconomic implication: the positive effects on employment, which tend to decline as the saturation point is approached. This fact is stylised by Verdoorn's Law for the case of manufacturing as a whole, as noted by Kaldor in the mid-1960s. This phase can be regarded as the mature phase of this composite type of product. Kaldor (1966, 1967) also observes that the rise in manufacturing employment has two effects on agriculture: it reduces the labour employed in that sector, and it also increases its productivity. This suggests that the nearly-mature type of production, such as agricultural production, 'receives' increases in productivity from other, newer sectors of the economy. This could also be the case for manufacturing in the recent decades, when in fact 'autonomous' technical progress rises, due to the R&D sector and other producers' services. This generalisation should not be taken too far, but an application of Verdoorn's Law to more narrow lines of production of both manufacturing and services would be fruitful.[25] In this case, it would not only prove to be typical for the mature phase of production, but would also be expected to decline in importance, when newer productions expand.

In this demand-driven part of the story, the supply side plays a constraining but important role. It not only shapes the potential learning curves, together with possibilities for incremental innovations, but also determines whether production of a good moves abroad before being substituted by new goods. This may occur if, during a prolonged expansion, the demand for labour encounters a bottleneck, thus raising wages and pushing the location of production out of the domestic market.[26] Therefore, the constraint of the labour market can be regarded as neither absent, nor completely or partially fixed.

The supply-driven part of the story should explain how a new product or collection of products can be launched. Some studies of the theory of endogenous growth provide a neat answer to this question. Lucas (1993), Young (1993) and Grossman and Helpman (1991a) suggest that the development of new production process can only occur sequentially, because each one is constrained by the necessity of an increase in the stock of technical knowledge, or else it would incur fixed costs that are too high. Hence, the past increase in knowledge and productivity becomes a necessary condition for a new type of production.[27]

In conclusion, the supply-side aspects are expected to prevail in the initial phase of production, since the latter largely depends on the availability of resources, and demand-side aspects are expected to prevail in the mature phase, which depends on the realisation of the learning curve. The two sides are complementary, but their sequentiality allows them to maintain a distinct role and to act as necessary conditions for each other.

Verdoorn's Law can thus depict a phase in this development for distinct learning curves, but it changes over time as the phase changes. More precisely, it can be endogenised as a changing relationship. It thus becomes possible to divorce Verdoorn's Law from the steady-state growth analysis, and to explain it within a more promising, albeit more complex, analytical framework.

Notes

1. For extensive surveys on Verdoorn's Law see Bairam (1987a), McCombie and Thirlwall (1994, ch. 2), Vaglio (1990).
2. The third possibility for ignoring capital growth in the estimation of (10.1) and (10.1′), is that it is orthogonal to output, but this is very unlikely. These assumptions should more generally regard other inputs growth rates, like human capital.
3. For a more detailed analysis on this point, see McCombie in chapter 4 of this volume.
4. This is McCombie and Thirlwall (1994, p. 557n), who regress q on k, but only for a period before 1973. By contrast, Michl (1985, p. 485n) finds a very low correlation between q and k. These results appear as inconclusive, maybe because k is misspecified and includes measurement errors. Note, moreover, that the alternative specification of (10.1), i.e.: $f = a_0' + a_1'q + \varepsilon'$, where $f = \lambda e + (1 - \lambda)k$, which has been sometimes used and which tests for endogeneity of k, does not guarantee that $q = k$.
5. The five studies are: Chatterji and Wickens (1983), Chen (1979), Hildreth (1988–89), Rayment (1981) and Stoneman (1979). The three studies are: Cripps and Tarling (1973), León-Ledesma (1999), and McCombie and de Ridder (1984).
6. These are Bairam (1990), McCombie (1986).
7. These are Boyer and Petit (1981), Parikh (1978), Pugno (1995), and Targetti and Foti (1997).
8. See Fase and van den Heuvel (1988), Hamalainen and Pehkonen (1995), Mohammadi and Ram (1990).
9. The four studies are Boyer and Petit (1988), McCombie (1986), Metcalfe and Hall (1983), Stavrinos (1987). The five studies are Boyer and Petit (1981), Michl (1985), Ranci and Samek (1982), Rayment (1981), and Stavrinos (1987).
10. Two studies suggest that this is not always the case: Targetti and Foti (1997), who show that Verdoorn's Law does not weaken in the developing countries, and Harris and Liu (1999), who do not find temporal breaks in Verdoorn's Law applied to the total GDP of a sample of 62 countries.
11. The second difference with respect to the original model is that the exogenous growth term in the wage supplied is dropped, which is here uninteresting.
12. Or if their changes exactly offset one another. But this is a very special case.
13. This proof shows more clearly the dynamic stability than that implicit in Vries's (1980) asymptotic solution of the model.
14. Note that if the restriction $\rho > (\alpha + \beta - 1)/(1 - \alpha)$ is true, then also the restriction $1 - \beta + \rho > 0$ is true.

15. If $\rho = 0$, then η does not affect q, e, and p, while v does not affect p.
16. These criticisms are also raised by Solow (2000).
17. u is a choice variable by the usual maximising agent.
18. It is interesting to note that some recent models attempt to avoid the scale effects, as implicit in equation (10.28), which apparently contrasts with the evidence, by relaxing some of these restrictions, thus reverting to exogenous growth (Jones, 1999, calls this 'semi-endogenous growth').
19. This specification of the export function, where, in particular, price competitiveness is due to different growth rates of prices, and not to different levels of prices, allows McCombie and Thirlwall (1994, p. 426) to obtain a steady-state solution.
20. For a full discussion on this point, and on the related point of the conditions for dynamic stability of the Thirlwall's solution, see Pugno (1998).
21. He also considers an analogous relationship for export elasticity to income (b_1 in equation (10.37)).
22. See, for example, the recent literature on the relationship between unemployment and economic growth, such as Pissarides (1990) or Aghion and Howitt (1994).
23. See the famous 'Horndal effect', which has been cited by Arrow (1962), or the 'Liberty ship' case, as reported by Lucas (1993).
24. It states that consumers' utility rises as variety of goods increases within an additively separable functional form (Dixit and Stiglitz, 1977).
25. Unfortunately, productivity growth in service production is very hard to measure, but the phenomenon is too important to be neglected.
26. These dynamics are studied in particular by the literature on the international product cycle (from Vernon, 1966 to Krugman, 1979). The models of this literature, however, show not fluctuations, but rather a trend of growth.

    An alternative interesting outcome from rising wages is to induce labour saving innovations, which, through demand for investment, may generate a new wave of production (Pugno, 1996b).
27. On this point see also other authors from other schools of thought from the 'cumulative' character of innovations by Rosenberg (1969), through the technological conditions for 'major product innovations' by Utterback (1979), to the 'natural trajectory' of technological advance by Nelson and Winter (1977).

Bibliography

Abramovitz, M. (1986) 'Catching-up, Forging Ahead and Falling Behind', *Journal of Economic History*, vol. 46, 385–406.

Aghion, P., and Howitt, P. (1994) 'Growth and Unemployment', *Review of Economic Studies*, vol. 61, 477–94.

Aghion, P. and Howitt, P. (1998) *Endogenous Growth Theory*, Cambridge, MA: MIT Press.

Alchian, A. (1963) 'Reliability of Progress Curves in Airframe Production', *Econometrica*, vol. 31, 679–93.

Amable, B. (1992) 'Effets d'apprentissage, compétitivité hors-prix et croissance cumulative', *Economie Appliqueé*, vol. 45, 5–31.

Amable, B. (1993a) 'Apprentissage et macro-dynamique Kaldorienne', *Economie et Société*, vol. 27, 197–216.

Amable, B. (1993b) 'Catch-Up and Convergence in a Model of Cumulative Growth', *International Review of Applied Economics*, vol. 7, 1–25. Reprinted in E.N. Wolff (ed.) (1997), *The Economics of Productivity*, vol. II, Cheltenham: Edward Elgar.

Anderson, P.S. (1993) 'The 45°-Rule Revisited', *Applied Economics*, vol. 25, 1279–84.

Archibugi, D. and Michie, J. (1998) 'Technical Change, Growth and Trade: New Departures in Institutional Economics', *Journal of Economic Surveys*, vol. 12, 313–32.

Armstrong, H. and Taylor, J. (1993) *Regional Economics and Policy*, Hemel Hempstead: Prentice Hall/Harvester Wheatsheaf (third edition, Oxford: Blackwell, 2000).

Arrow, K.J. (1962) 'The Economic Implications of Learning by Doing', *Review of Economic Studies*, vol. 29, 155–73.

Arrow, K.J. (1974) 'The Measurement of Real Value Added', in P.A. David and M.W. Reder (eds), *Nations and Households in Economic Growth*, New York: Academic Press.

Arrow, K.J. (1994) 'The Production and Distribution of Knowledge', in G. Silverberg and L. Soete (eds), *The Economics of Growth and Technical Change*, Aldershot: Edward Elgar.

Arthur, W.B. (1989) 'Competing Technologies, Increasing Returns and Lock-in by Historical Events', *Economic Journal*, vol. 99, 116–31.

Arthur, W.B. (1994) *Increasing Returns and Path Dependence in the Economy*, Ann Arbor, MI: University of Michigan Press.

Atesoglu, H.S. (1993) 'Manufacturing and Economic Growth in the United States', *Applied Economics*, vol. 25, 67–9.

Atesoglu, H.S. (1994) 'An Application of a Kaldorian Export-led Model of Growth to the United States', *Applied Economics*, vol. 26, 479–83.

Bairam, E.I. (1986) 'Returns to Scale, Technical Progress and Output Growth in Branches of Industry: the Case of Eastern Europe and the USSR, 1961–75', *Keio Economic Studies*, vol. 23, 63–78.

Bairam, E.I. (1987a) 'The Verdoorn Law, Returns to Scale and Industrial Growth: a Review of the Literature', *Australian Economic Papers*, vol. 26, 20–42.

Bairam, E.I. (1987b) 'Returns to Scale, Technical Progress and Output Growth in Branches of Industry: the Case of Soviet Republics, 1962–74', *Scottish Journal of Political Economy*, vol. 24, 249–66.

Bairam, E.I. (1988a) *Technical Progress and Industrial Growth in the USSR and Eastern Europe: an Empirical Study, 1961–75*, Aldershot: Avebury.

Bairam, E.I. (1988b) 'Verdoorn's Law Once Again: its Specification and Interpretation', *Indian Economic Journal*, vol. 35, 30–8.

Bairam, E.I. (1988c) 'Technical Progress, Elasticity of Substitution and Returns to Scale in Branches of Soviet Industry: Some New Evidence Using Soviet Republic Data, 1961–74', *The Manchester School*, vol. 54, 103–17.

Bairam, E.I. (1988d) 'Balance of Payments, the Harrod Foreign Trade Multiplier and Economic Growth: the European and North American Experience, 1970–85', *Applied Economics*, vol. 20, 1635–42.

Bairam, E.I. (1990) 'Verdoorn's Original Model and the Verdoorn Law Controversy: Some New Empirical Evidence Using the Australian Manufacturing Data', *Australian Economic Papers*, vol. 30, 107–12.

Bairam, E.I. (1991) 'Economic Growth and Kaldor's Law: the Case of Turkey, 1925–78', *Applied Economics*, vol. 23, 1277–80.

Bairam, E.I. (1993) 'Static Versus Dynamic Specifications and the Harrod Foreign Trade Multiplier', *Applied Economics*, vol. 25, pp. 739–42.

Bairam, E.I. (1994) *Homogeneous and Nonhomogeneous Production Functions*, Aldershot: Avebury.

Bairam, E.I. (1995) 'Kaldor's Technical Progress Function Revisited', *Applied Economics Letters*, vol. 2, 302–4.

Balassa, B. (1963) 'Some Observations on Mr Beckerman's "Export-Propelled" Growth Model', *Economic Journal*, vol. 62, 781–5.

Banker, R. (1996) 'Hypothesis Tests using Data Envelopment Analysis', *Journal of Productivity Analysis*, vol. 7, 139–59.

Banker, R.D., and Thrall, R.M. (1992) 'Estimation of Returns to Scale Using Data Envelopment Analysis', *European Journal of Operational Research*, vol. 62, 74–84.

Barro, R.J. and Sala-i-Martín, X. (1995) *Economic Growth*, New York: McGraw-Hill.

Baumol, W.J. (1986) 'Productivity Growth, Convergence and Welfare: What the Long-run Data Show', *American Economic Review*, vol. 78, 1155–9.

Bean, C.R. (1994) 'European Unemployment: a Survey', *Journal of Economic Literature*, vol. 32, pp. 573–619.

Bean, C.R., Layard, P.R.G. and Nickell, S.J. (1986) 'The Rise in Unemployment: a Multi-Country Study', *Economica*, supplement, vol. 53, S1–S22.

Beckerman, W. (1962) 'Projecting Europe's Growth', *Economic Journal*, vol. 61, 912–25.

Bernat, G.A. (1996) 'Does Manufacturing Matter? A Spatial Econometric View of Kaldor's Laws', *Journal of Regional Science*, vol. 36, 463–77.

Bertola, G. (1993) 'Models of Economic Integration and Localised Growth', in F. Torrens and F. Giavazzi (eds), *Adjustment and Growth in the EMU*, Cambridge: Cambridge University Press.

Bianchi, C. (1985) 'Crescita, produttività e occupazione in una analisi dinamica. Prospettive e proposte per l'economia Italiana nel prossimo decennio', *Economia e Politica Industriale*, vol. 48, 37–58.

Bianchi, C. and Menegatti, M. (1997) 'Differenziali regionali di produttività e crescita economica: un riesame della convergenza in Italia nel periodo 1970–94', *Studi Economici*, vol. 63, 15–42.

Black, J. (1962) 'The Technical Progress Function and the Production Function', *Economica*, vol. 29, 166–70.

Blanchard, O.J. (1999) 'European Unemployment: the Role of Shocks and Institutions', presented at the 1999 Royal Economic Society Conference, Nottingham University, downloadable from: http://web.mit.edu/blanchar/.

Blanchard, O.J., and Katz, L.F. (1997) 'What We Know and Do Not Know About the Natural Rate of Unemployment', *Journal of Economic Perspectives*, vol. 11, 51–72.

Blanchard, O.J., and Summers, L.H. (1987) 'Hysteresis in Unemployment', *European Economic Review*, vol. 31, 288–95.

Blanchard, O.J., and Wolfers, J. (2000) 'The Role of Shocks and Institutions in the Rise of European Unemployment: the Aggregate Evidence', *Economic Journal*, vol. 110, C1–C33.

Blitch, C.P. (1990) 'Kaldor's Lecture Notes from Allyn Young's London School of Economics Class, 1928–29', *History of Political Economy*, vol. 22, 443–64.

Bochove, C.A. van, Eijk C.J. van, Siebrand, J.C., Vries, A.S.W. de, and Zwan, A. van der (eds) (1977) *Modeling for Government and Business: Essays in Honor of Prof. Dr. P.J. Verdoorn*, Leiden: Martinus Nijhoff Social Sciences Division.

Bogetoft, P. (1996) 'DEA on Relaxed Convexity Assumptions', *Management Science*, vol. 42, 457–65.

Boggio, L. (1974) *Crescita e specializzazione produttiva in un' economia aperta*, Milano: Vita e Pensiero.

Boggio, L. (1996) 'Growth and International Competitiveness, In a "Kaldorian" Perspective', *Structural Change and Economic Dynamics*, vol. 7, 299–320.

Bougrine, H. (1994) 'Capital Accumulation, Output Growth and Disparities in Labour Productivity Among Canadian Regions', *International Review of Applied Economics*, vol. 8, 283–90.

Boulier, B.L. (1984) 'What Lies Behind Verdoorn's Law?', *Oxford Economic Papers*, vol. 36, 259–67.

Boyer, R. (1988) 'Formalising Growth Régimes', in G. Dosi et al. (eds), *Technological Change and Economic Theory*, London: Pinter.

Boyer, R., and Petit, P. (1981a) 'Progrès technique, croissance et emploi: un modèle d'inspiration Kaldorienne pour six industries Éuropéennes', *Revue Economique*, vol. 32, 1113–53.

Boyer, R., and Petit, P. (1981b) 'Employment and Productivity in the EEC', *Cambridge Journal of Economics*, vol. 5, 47–58.

Boyer R and Petit, P. (1988) 'The Cumulative Growth Model Revisited', *Political Economy*, vol. 4, 23–43.

Boyer, R. and Petit, P. (1991) 'Kaldor's Growth Theories: Past, Present and Prospects for the Future', in E.J. Nell and W. Semmler (eds), *Nicholas Kaldor and Mainstream Economics*, London: Macmillan.

Boylan, T.A., and O'Gorman, P. (1999) 'Kaldor on Method: a Challenge to Contemporary Methodology', *Cambridge Journal of Economics*, vol. 21, pp. 503–17.

Bradley, J., and Prendergast, C. (1986) 'Verdoorn's Law: a Retrospective View', *Economic and Social Review*, vol. 17, 75–85.

Burridge, P. and Gordon, I. (1981) 'Unemployment in the British Metropolitan Labour Areas', *Oxford Economic Papers*, vol. 33, 274–97.

Carlin, W., and Soskice, D. (1990) *Macroeconomics and the Wage Bargain: a Modern Approach to Employment, Inflation and the Exchange Rate*, Oxford: Oxford University Press.

Casetti, E. (1984) 'Verdoorn's Law and the Components of Manufacturing Productivity Growth', in A.E. Anderson, W. Isard, and T. Puu (eds), *Regional and Industrial Development Theory: Models and Empirical Evidence*, Studies in Regional Sciences and Urban Economics Series, vol. 11, Amsterdam: North Holland.

Chatterji, M. and Wickens, M.R. (1981) 'Verdoorn's Law – the Externalities Hypothesis and Economic Growth in the UK', in D. Currie, R. Nobay and D. Peel (eds), *Macroeconomic Analysis*, London: Croom Helm.

Chatterji, M. and Wickens, M.R. (1982) 'Productivity, Factor Transfer and Economic Growth in the UK', *Economica*, vol. 49, 21–38.

Chatterji, M. and Wickens, M.R. (1983) 'Verdoorn's Law and Kaldor's Law: a Revisionist Interpretation?', *Journal of Post Keynesian Economics*, vol. 5, 397–414.

Chen, E.K.Y. (1979) 'Kaldor's Law and the Developing Countries: an Empirical Study', *Rivista Internazionale di Scienze Economiche e Commerciali*, vol. 26, 274–85.

Clapham, J.H. (1922) 'Of Empty Boxes', *Economic Journal*, vol. 32, 305–14.

Clark, C. (1957) *The Conditions of Economic Progress* (third edition), London: Macmillan (second edition, 1951).

Clark, C. (1962) (in collaboration with H. Frankel and with the assistance of L. Moore), *British Trade in the Common Market*, London: Stevens & Sons Ltd.

Clark, J. (1983) 'Employment Projections and Structural Change', in D.L. Bosworth (ed.), *The Employment Consequences of Technological Change*, London: Macmillan.

Conlisk, J. (1968) 'Non-Constant Returns to Scale in a Neoclassical Model', *International Economic Review*, vol. 9, 369–73.

Conti, V., and Filosa, R. (1975) 'Produzione, occupazione e produttività nel settore industriale', *Rivista Internazionale di Scienze Sociali*, vol. 83, 490–519.

Cooper, W.W., Seiford, L.M., and Tone, K. (2000) *Data Envelopment Analysis*, Boston: Kluwer.

Cornwall, J. (1976) 'Diffusion, Convergence and Kaldor's Law', *Economic Journal*, vol. 86, 307–14.

Cornwall, J. (1977) *Modern Capitalism: its Growth and Transformation*, London: Martin Robertson.

Cripps, T.F., and Tarling, R.J. (1973) *Growth in Advanced Capitalist Economies 1950–70*, Cambridge: Cambridge University Press.

Daveri, F. and Tabellini, G. (2000) 'Unemployment and Taxes: Do Taxes Affect the Rate of Unemployment?', *Economic Policy*, vol. 15, 47–104.

De Benedictis, L. (1998) 'Cumulative Causation, Harrod's Trade Multiplier and Kaldor's Paradox: the Foundations of Post-Keynesian Theory of Growth Differentials', in G. Rampa, L. Stella and A.P. Thirlwall (eds), *Economic Dynamics, Trade and Growth: Essays on Harrodian Themes*, Basingstoke: Macmillan – now Palgrave Macmillan.

Denison, E.F. (1962) *The Sources of Economic Growth in the United States and the Alternatives Before Us*, New York: Committee for Economic Development.

Denison, E.F. (1991) 'Scott's "A New View of Economic Growth": a Review Article', *Oxford Economic Papers*, vol. 43, 224–37.

Deprins, D., Simar, L., and Tulkens, H. (1984) 'Measuring Labor-Efficiency in Post Offices', in M. Marchand, P. Pestieau and H. Tulkens (eds), *The Performance of Public Enterprises: Concepts and Measurement*, Amsterdam: North Holland.

Dixit, A., and Stiglitz, J. (1977) 'Monopolistic Competition and Optimum Product Diversity', *American Economic Review*, vol. 67, 297–308.

Dixon, R.J., and Thirlwall, A.P. (1975) 'A Model of Regional Growth Rate Differences on Kaldorian Lines', *Oxford Economic Papers*, vol. 27, 201–14.

Dixon, R.J., and Thirlwall, A.P. (1978) 'Growth Rate Stability in the Kaldorian Regional Model', *Scottish Journal of Political Economy*, vol. 25, 201–14.

Domar, E.D. (1946) 'Capital Expansion, Rate of Growth and Employment', *Econometrica*, vol. 14, 137–47.

Dormont, B. (1984) 'Productivité-croissance. Quelle relation a moyen-long terme? un rapprochement des modèles de Brechling et de Kaldor-Verdoorn', *Revue Economique*, vol. 3, 447–78.

Dosi, G. (1982) 'La circolarità tra progresso tecnico e crescita. Alcune osservazioni sulla "Legge di Verdoorn–Kaldor"', *L'Industria*, n.s., vol. 3, 233–45.

Drakopoulos, S.A., and Theodossiou, I. (1991) 'Kaldorian Approach to Greek Economic Growth', *Applied Economics*, vol. 23, 1683–9.

Driver, R. and Wren-Lewis, S. (1999) 'New Trade Theory and Aggregate Export Equations: an Application of Panel Cointegration', University of Exeter Discussion Paper, April.

Eijk, C.J. van (1977) 'Professor Dr P.J. Verdoorn', in C.A. Bochove et al. (eds), *Modeling for Government and Business: Essays in Honor of P.J. Verdoorn*, Leiden: Martinus Nijhoff Social Sciences Division.

Engle, R.F., and Hendry, D.F. (1993) 'Testing Superexogeneity and Invariance in Regression Models', *Journal of Econometrics*, vol. 56, 119–39.

Eurostat (1996) *European System of Accounts: ESA 1995*, Luxembourg: Eurostat.

Evans, P. (1996) 'Using Cross-Country Variances to Evaluate Growth Theories', *Journal of Economic Dynamics and Control*, vol. 20, 1027–49.

Fabricant, S. (1942) *Employment in Manufacturing 1899–1939*, New York: National Bureau of Economic Research.

Fagerberg, J. (1988) 'International Competitiveness', *Economic Journal*, vol. 98, 355–74.

Faini, R. (1984) 'Increasing Returns, Non-traded Inputs and Regional Development', *Economic Journal*, vol. 94, 308–23.

Färe, R., Grosskopf, S., and Lovell, C.A.K. (1985) *The Measurement of Efficiency of Production*, Boston: Kluwer.

Färe, R., Grosskopf, S., Norris, S., and Zhang, Z. (1994) 'Productivity Growth, Technical Progress and Efficiency Change in Industrial Countries', *American Economic Review*, vol. 84, 66–83.

Färe, R., Grosskopf, S., and Norris, M. (1997) 'Productivity Growth, Technical Progress and Efficiency Change in Industrial Countries: Reply', *American Economic Review*, vol. 87, 1040–3.

Farrell, M.J. (1957) 'The Measurement of Productive Efficiency', *Journal of the Royal Statistical Society*, Series A, Part III, vol. 70, 253–81.

Farrell, M.J. (1967) 'The Convexity Assumption in the Theory of Competitive Markets', *Journal of Political Economy*, vol. 87, 377–91.

Fase, M.M.G., and Heuvel, P.J. van den (1988) 'Productivity and Growth: Verdoorn's Law Revisited', *Economic Letters*, vol. 28, 135–9.

Felli, E. (1981) 'Produttività del lavoro, rendimenti di scala e accumulazione di capitale nell'industria manifatturiera italiana (1954–78)', *Rivista di Politica Economica*, vol. 71, 279–327.

Fellner, W. (1969) 'Specific Interpretation of Learning by Doing', *Journal of Economic Theory*, vol. 1, 119–40.

Ferber, R and Verdoorn, P.J. (1962) *Research Methods in Economics & Business*, New York: Macmillan.

Fingleton, B. (2000) 'International Economic Growth: Simultaneous Equation Models Incorporating Regional Effects', *International Review of Applied Economics*, vol. 14, 283–305.

Fingleton, B., and McCombie, J.S.L. (1998) 'Increasing Returns and Economic Growth: Some New Evidence from Manufacturing from the European Union Regions', *Oxford Economic Papers*, vol. 50, 89–105.

Fischer, S. (1993) 'The Role of Macroeconomic Factors in Growth', *Journal of Monetary Economics*, vol. 32, 485–511.

Fleck, F.H. and Linotte, D. (1985) 'The Law of Verdoorn: Some Critical Remarks and Empirical Findings for the Socialist Countries of Eastern Europe', University of Fribourg: Institute for Economics and Social Sciences, Working Papers, vol. 71.

Førsund, F. (1996a) 'On the Calculation of Scale Elasticity in DEA Models', *Journal of Productivity Analysis*, vol. 7, 283–302.

Førsund, F. (1996b) 'Productivity of Norwegian Establishments: a Malmquist Index Approach', in D.G. Mayes (ed.), *Sources of Productivity Growth*, Cambridge: Cambridge University Press.

Førsund, F., and Hjalmarsson, L. (1979) 'Generalised Farrell Measures of Efficiency: an Application to Milk Processing in Swedish Dairy Plants', *Economic Journal*, vol. 89, 294–315.

Freeman, C. (1988) 'New Technologies and the Pattern of Structural Change in the World Economy', in G. Dosi et al. (eds), *Technical Change and Economic Theory*, London: Pinter.

Friedman, M. (1968) 'The Role of Monetary Policy', *American Economic Review*, vol. 58, 1–17.

Fumagalli, A. (1991) 'Attività innovativa, produttività ed occupazione industriale: un'analisi teorica', *L'Industria*, n.s., vol. 12, 103–26.

Gerschenkron, A. (1962) *Economic Backwardness in Historical Perspective*, Cambridge, MA: Harvard University Press.

Ghosh, D., and Banerjee, A.K. (1993) 'Production Function Underlying Kaldor's Technical Progress Function', *Economic Notes*, vol. 22, 478–86.

Gijbels, I., Mammen, E., Park, B.U., and Simar, L. (1999) 'On Estimation of Monotone and Concave Frontier functions', *Journal of the American Statistical Association*, vol. 94, 220–8.

Gomulka, S. (1971) *Inventive Activity, Diffusion, and the Stages of Economic Growth*, Aarhus: University of Aarhus.

Gomulka, S. (1983) 'Industrialisation and the Rate of Growth: Eastern Europe, 1955–75', *Journal of Post Keynesian Economics*, vol. 5, 388–96.

Gomulka, S. (1990) *The Theory of Technological Change and Economic Growth*, London: Routledge.

Gordon, D.M. (1991) 'Kaldor's Macro System: Too Much Cumulation, Too Few Contradictions', in E.J. Nell and W. Semmler (eds), *Nicholas Kaldor and Mainstream Economics: Confrontation or Convergence?*, Basingstoke: Macmillan – now Palgrave Macmillan.

Grossman, G.M., and Helpman, E. (1991a) 'Quality and Product Cycles', *Quarterly Journal of Economics*, vol. 106, 557–86.

Grossman, G.M., and Helpman, E. (1991b) *Innovation and Growth in the Global Economy*, Cambridge, MA: MIT Press.

Groot, M.H. de (1970) *Optimal Statistical Decision*, New York: McGraw Hill.

Grubb, D. (1986) 'Topics in the OECD Phillips Curve', *Economic Journal*, vol. 96, 55–79.

Guccione, A., and Gillen, W.J. (1977) 'Growth Rate Stability in the Kaldorian Regional Model', *Scottish Journal of Political Economy*, vol. 24, 175–6.

Hahn, F.H. (1973), *On the Notion of Equilibrium in Economics: an Inaugural Lecture*, Cambridge: Cambridge University Press.

Hahn, F.H. (1989) 'Kaldor on Growth', *Cambridge Journal of Economics*, vol. 13, 47–57.

Haitovsky, Y., and Verdoorn, P.J. (1972) 'A Note on the Efficiency of the First Difference Least Square Estimators', Jerusalem: Hebrew University of Jerusalem, Department of Economics, Research Report no. 42.

Hamalainen, K., and Pehkonen, J. (1995) 'Verdoorn's Law in the Multivariate Context', *Economic Notes*, vol. 24, 175–86.

Hansen, J.D., and Zhang, J. (1996) 'A Kaldorian Approach to Regional Economic Growth in China', *Applied Economics*, vol. 28, 679–85.

Harris, R.I.D., and Lau, E. (1998) 'Verdoorn's Law and Increasing Returns to Scale in the UK Regions, 1968–91: Some New Estimates Based on the Cointegration Approach', *Oxford Economic Papers*, vol. 50, 201–19.

Harris, R.I.D., and Liu, A. (1999) 'Verdoorn's Law and Increasing Returns to Scale: Country Estimates Based on the Cointegration Approach', *Applied Economics Letters*, vol. 6, 29–33.

Heimler, A., and Milana, C. (1984) *Prezzi relativi, ristrutturazione e produttività. Le trasformazioni dell'industria italiana*, Bologna: Il Mulino.

Heyndels, B., and Vuchlen, J. (1990) 'Verdoorn's and Kaldor's Law in Tax Administration: an International Analysis', *Applied Economics*, vol. 22, 529–37.

Hicks, J.R. (1939) *Value and Capital*, Oxford: Oxford University Press.

Hicks, J.R. (1989) 'The Assumption of Constant Returns to Scale', in A. Lawson, J.G. Palma and J. Sender (eds), *Kaldor's Political Economy*, London: Academic Press.

Hildreth, A. (1988–89) 'The Ambiguity of Verdoorn's Law: a Case Study of the British Regions', *Journal of Post Keynesian Economics*, vol. 11, 279–94.

Hirsch, W.Z. (1952) 'Manufacturing Progress Function', *Review of Economics and Statistics*, 34, 143–55.

Hirsch, W.Z. (1956) 'Firm Progress Ratios', *Econometrica*, vol. 24, 136–43.

Hooper, P., and Marquez, J. (1995) 'Exchange Rates, Prices and External Adjustment in the United States and Japan', in P.B. Kenen (ed.), *Understanding Interdependence: the Macroeconomics of the Open Economy*, Princeton: Princeton University Press.

Houthakker, H.S., and Magee, S.P. (1969) 'Income and Price Elasticities in World Trade', *Review of Economics and Statistics*, vol. 51, 111–25.

Huang, C.J., and Crooke, P.S. (1997) *Mathematics and Mathematica for Economists*, Oxford: Blackwell.

Jefferson, G.H. (1988) 'The Aggregate Production Function and Productivity Growth: Verdoorn's Law Revisited', *Oxford Economic Papers*, vol. 40, 671–91.

Jones, C.I. (1998) *Introduction to Economic Growth*, New York: Norton.

Jones, C.I. (1999) 'Growth: With or Without Scale Effects?', *American Economic Review, Papers and Proceedings*, vol. 89, 139–44.

Journal of Post Keynesian Economics (1997) 'Minisymposium on Thirlwall's Law and Economic Growth in an Open-economy Context', vol. 20, 311–85.

Kaldor, N. (1955–56) 'Alternate Theories of Distribution', *Review of Economic Studies*, vol. XXIII, 82–100.

Kaldor, N. (1957) 'A Model of Economic Growth', *Economic Journal*, vol. 67, 591–624.

Kaldor, N. (1961) 'Capital Accumulation and Economic Growth', in F.A. Lutz and D.C. Hague (eds), *The Theory of Capital*, London: Macmillan.

Kaldor, N. (1966) *Causes of the Slow Rate of Economic Growth of the United Kingdom: an Inaugural Lecture*, Cambridge: Cambridge University Press. Reprinted in N. Kaldor (1978), *Further Essays on Economic Theory*, London: Duckworth.

Kaldor, N. (1967) *Strategic Factors in Economic Development*, New York: Cornell University Press.

Kaldor, N. (1968) 'Productivity and Growth in Manufacturing Industry: a Reply', *Economica*, vol. 75, 385–90.

Kaldor, N. (1970) 'The Case for Regional Policies', *Scottish Journal of Political Economy*, vol. 17, 337–48.

Kaldor, N. (1971) 'Conflicts in National Economic Objectives', *Economic Journal*, vol. 81, 1–16.

Kaldor, N. (1972) 'The Irrelevance of Equilibrium Economics', *Economic Journal*, vol. 82, 1237–55.

Kaldor, N. (1975a) 'Economic Growth and the Verdoorn's Law – A Comment on Mr. Rowthorn's Article', *Economic Journal*, vol. 85, 891–6.

Kaldor, N. (1975b) 'What is Wrong with Economic Theory', *Quarterly Journal of Economics*, vol. 89, 347–57.
Kaldor, N. (1976) 'Inflation and Recession in the World Economy', *Economic Journal*, vol. 86, 891–6.
Kaldor, N. (1977) 'Capitalism and Industrial Development: Some Lessons from Britain's Experience', *Cambridge Journal of Economics*, vol. 1, 193–204.
Kaldor, N. (1978a) 'Introduction', in N. Kaldor, *Further Essays on Economic Theory*, London: Duckworth.
Kaldor, N. (1978b) 'The Effect of Devaluations on Trade in Manufactures', in N. Kaldor, *Further Essays on Applied Economics*, London: Duckworth.
Kaldor, N. (1979) 'Equilibrium Theory and Growth Theory', in M. Boskin (ed.), *Economics and Human Welfare: Essays in Honor of Tibor Scitovsky*, New York and London: Academic Press.
Kaldor, N. (1986) 'Recollections of an Economist', *Banca Nazionale del Lavoro Quarterly Review*, vol. 156, 3–26.
Kaldor, N., and Mirrlees, J. (1962) 'A New Model of Economic Growth', *Review of Economic Studies*, vol. 29, 174–92.
Karanassou, M. and Snower, D.J. (1998) 'How Labour Market Flexibility Affects Unemployment: Long-Term Implications of the Chain Reaction Theory', *Economic Journal*, vol. 108, 832–49.
Katz, J. (1968) 'Verdoorn Effect, Returns to Scale, and Elasticity of Factor Substitution', *Oxford Economic Papers*, vol. 20, 342–52.
Kennedy, C., and Thirlwall, A.P. (1972) 'Technical Progress: a Survey', *Economic Journal*, vol. 82, 12–72.
Kennedy, K.A. (1971) *Productivity and Industrial Growth: the Irish Experience*, Oxford: Clarendon Press.
Kennedy, K.A., and Foley, A. (1978) *Industrial Development*, Dublin: Economic and Social Research Institute.
Kerstens, K., and Vanden Eeckaut, P. (1999) 'Estimating Returns to Scale Using Non-Parametric Deterministic Technologies: a New Method Based on Goodness-of-Fit', *European Journal of Operational Research*, vol. 113, 206–14.
Kie, C. (1997) *The Effects of Flexible Manufacturing Contexts: Geographical Patterns in Labour Productivity Impact of Output Growth. Studies on Industrial Productivity*, New York and London: Garland.
Klundert, T. van de, and Schaik, A. van (1993) 'On the Historical Continuity of the Process of Economic Growth', in B. van Ark and N. Crafts (eds), *Quantitative Aspects of Post-War European Economic Growth*, Cambridge: Cambridge University Press.
Kneip, A., Park, B.U., and Simar, L. (1998) 'A Note on the Convergence of Non Parametric DEA Estimators for Production Efficiency Scores, *Econometric Theory*, vol. 14, 783–93.
Korostelev, A., Simar, L. and Tsybakov, A. (1995a) 'Efficient Estimation of Monotone Boundaries', *Annals of Statistics*, vol. 23, 476–89.
Korosteler, A., Simar, L., and Tsybakov, A. (1995b) 'On Estimation of Monotone and Convex Boundaries', *Publications de l'Institut de Statistique, Université de Paris*, vol. 1, 3–18.
Krugman, P.R. (1979) 'A Model of Innovation, Technology Transfer, and World Distribution of Income', *Journal of Political Economy*, vol. 87, 253–66.
Krugman, P.R. (1989) 'Differences in Income Elasticities and Trends in Real Exchange Rates', *European Economic Review*, vol. 33, 1031–54.
Krugman, P.R. (1991) *Geography and Trade*, Cambridge, MA: MIT Press.

Landesmann, M., and Snell, A. (1989) 'The Consequences of Mrs Thatcher for UK Manufacturing Exports', *Economic Journal*, vol. 99, 1–27.

Layard, R., Nickell, S.J., and Jackman, R. (1991) *Unemployment: Macroeconomic Performance and the Labour Market*, Oxford: Oxford University Press.

Le Bas, C. (1988) 'Formules de productivité, progrès tecnique et rendements croissants', *Économie Appliquée*, vol. 41, 633–48.

Lenderink, R.S.G., and Siebrand, J.C. (1977) 'Employment and Production in the Dutch Empirical Tradition', in C.A. van Bochove, C.J. van Eijk,, J.C. Siebrand, A.S.W. de Vries, and A. van der Zwan (eds), *Modeling for Government and Business: Essays in Honor of Prof. Dr. P.J. Verdoorn*, Leiden: Martinus Nijhoff Social Sciences Division.

León-Ledesma, M.A. (1999) 'Verdoorn's Law and Increasing Returns: an Empirical Analysis of the Spanish Regions', *Applied Economics Letters*, vol. 6, 373–6.

León-Ledesma, M.A. (2000) 'Economic Growth and Verdoorn's Law in the Spanish Regions, 1962–91', *International Review of Applied Economics*, vol. 14, 55–69.

León-Ledesma, M.A. (2002) 'Accumulation, Innovation and Catching-up: an Extended Cumulative Growth Model', *Cambridge Journal of Economics* (forthcoming). Also available as WP 1999/06, Department of Economics, University of Kent.

León-Ledesma, M., and Thirlwall, A.P. (2002) 'The Endogeneity of the Natural Rate of Growth', *Cambridge Journal of Economics*, vol. 26, 441–59.

Leontief, W.W. (1947) 'Introduction to a Theory of the Internal Structure of Functional Relationships', *Econometrica*, vol. 15, 361–73.

Li Chol-Won (1999) 'Endogenous vs. Semi-endogenous Growth in a Two-R&D-Sector Model', *University of Glasgow Discussion Paper in Economics*, no. 9901, January.

Lovell, C.A.K. (1993) 'Production Frontiers and Productive Efficiency', in H. Fried, C.A.K. Lovell and S. Schmidt (eds), *The Measurement of Productive Efficiency: Techniques and Applications*, Oxford: Oxford University Press.

Lucas, R.E. (1970) 'Capacity, Overtime, and Empirical Production Functions', *American Economic Review, Papers and Proceedings*, vol. 60, 23–7.

Lucas, R.E. (1972) 'Expectations and the Neutrality of Money', *Journal of Economic Theory*, vol. 4, 103–24.

Lucas, R.E. (1988) 'On the Mechanics of Economic Development', *Journal of Monetary Economics*, vol. 22, 3–42.

Lucas, R.E. (1993) 'Making a Miracle', *Econometrica*, vol. 61, 251–72.

McCombie, J.S.L. (1980) 'On The Quantitative Importance of Kaldor's Laws', *Bulletin of Economic Research*, vol. 32, 103–12.

McCombie, J.S.L. (1981) 'What Still Remains of Kaldor's Laws?', *Economic Journal*, vol. 91, 206–16.

McCombie, J.S.L. (1982a) 'Economic Growth, Kaldor's Laws and the Static–Dynamic Verdoorn Law Paradox', *Applied Economics*, vol. 14, 279–94.

McCombie, J.S.L. (1982b) 'How Important is the Spatial Diffusion of Innovation in Explaining Regional Growth Rate Disparities?', *Urban Studies*, vol. 19, 377–82.

McCombie, J.S.L. (1983) 'Kaldor's Laws in Retrospect', *Journal of Post Keynesian Economics*, vol. 5, 414–30.

McCombie, J.S.L. (1985a) 'Increasing Returns and the Manufacturing Industries: Some Empirical Issues', *Manchester School*, vol. 53, 55–75.

McCombie, J.S.L. (1985b) 'Economic Growth, the Harrod Foreign Trade Multiplier and the Hicks Super-multiplier,' *Applied Economics*, vol. 17, 55–72.

McCombie, J.S.L. (1985–86) 'Why Cutting Real Wages will not Necessarily Reduce Unemployment – Keynes and the "Postulates of the Classical Economics"', *Journal of Post Keynesian Economics*, vol. 8, 233–48.

McCombie, J.S.L. (1986) 'On Some Interpretations of the Relationship Between Productivity and Output Growth', *Applied Economics*, vol. 18, 1215–25.

McCombie, J.S.L. (1987) 'Verdoorn's Law', in J. Eatwell, M. Milgate, and P. Newman (eds), *The New Palgrave: a Dictionary of Economics*, London: Macmillan – now Palgrave Macmillan, vol. 4, 804–6.

McCombie, J.S.L. (1987–88) 'Keynes and the Nature of Involuntary Unemployment', *Journal of Post Keynesian Economics*, vol. 10, 202–15.

McCombie, J.S.L. (1988) 'A Synoptic View of Regional Growth and Unemployment: I – Neoclassical Theory', *Urban Studies*, vol. 25, 267–81.

McCombie, J.S.L. (1991) 'The Productivity Growth Slowdown of the Advanced Countries and the Inter-sectoral Reallocation of Labour', *Australian Economic Papers*, vol. 21, 70–85.

McCombie, J.S.L. (1998a) 'Harrod, Economic Growth and International Trade', in G. Rampa, L. Stella and A.P. Thirlwall (eds), *Economic Dynamics, Trade and Growth: Essays on Harrodian Themes*, London: Macmillan.

McCombie, J.S.L. (1998b) 'Are There Laws of Production?: an Assessment of the Early Criticism of Cobb–Douglas Production Function', *Review of Political Economy*, vol. 10, 141–73.

McCombie, J.S.L. (1998–99) 'In Defense of Kaldor: a Comment on Casillas's "Kaldor versus Prebisch on Employment and Industrialization"', *Journal of Post Keynesian Economics*, vol. 21, 353–61.

McCombie, J.S.L. (2002) 'Increasing Returns and the Verdoorn Law from a Kaldorian Perspective', chapter 4, this volume.

McCombie, J.S.L., and Dixon, R.J. (1991) 'Estimating Technical Change in Aggregate Production Functions: a Critique', *International Review of Applied Economics*, vol. 5, 24–46.

McCombie, J.S.L., and. Ridder, J.R. de (1983) 'Increasing Returns, Productivity, and Output Growth: the Case of the United States', *Journal of Post Keynesian Economics*, vol. 5, 373–88.

McCombie, J.S.L., and Ridder, J.R. de (1984) 'The Verdoorn's Law Controversy: Some New Empirical Evidence using US States Data', *Oxford Economic Papers*, vol. 36, 268–84.

McCombie, J.S.L. and Roberts, M. (2002) 'The Role of the Balance of Payments in Economic Growth', in M. Setterfield (ed.), *The Economics of Demand-Led Growth*, Cheltenham: Edward Eigar.

McCombie, J.S.L., and Thirlwall, A.P. (1994) *Economic Growth and the Balance-of-Payments Constraint*, Basingstoke: Macmillan – now Palgrave Macmillan.

McCombie, J.S.L., and Thirlwall, A.P. (1997a) 'The Dynamic Harrod Foreign Trade Multiplier and the Demand-Orientated Approach to Economic Growth: an Evaluation', *International Review of Applied Economics*, vol. 11, 5–26.

McCombie, J.S.L., and Thirlwall, A.P. (1997b) 'Economic Growth and the Balance-of-Payments Constraint Revisited', in P. Arestis, G. Palma, and M. Sawyer (eds), *Markets, Unemployment and Economic Policy: Essays in Honour of Geoff Harcourt, Volume Two*, London: Routledge.

McCombie, J.S.L., and Thirlwall, A.P. (1999) 'Growth in an International Context: a Post Keynesian View', in J. Deprez and J.T. Harvey (eds), *Foundations of International Economics: Post Keynesian Perspectives*, London: Routledge.

Madsen, J.B. (1998) 'General Equilibrium Macroeconomic Models of Unemployment: Can They Explain the Unemployment Path in the OECD?', *Economic Journal*, vol. 108, 850–67.

Mankiw, N.G., Romer, D., and Weil, D.N. (1992) 'A Contribution to the Empirics of Economic Growth', *Quarterly Journal of Economics*, vol. 107, 407–38.

Marshall, A. (1890) *Principles of Economics*, London: Macmillan.

Metcalfe, J.S. (1994) 'Competition, Fisher's Principle and Increasing Returns in the Selection Process', *Journal of Evolutionary Economics*, vol. 4, 327–46.

Metcalfe, J.S., and Hall, P.H. (1983) 'The Verdoorn Law and the Salter Mechanism: a Note on Australian Manufacturing Industry', *Australian Economic Papers*, vol. 12, 364–73.

Michl, T.R. (1985) 'International Comparisons of Productivity Growth: Verdoorn's Law Revisited', *Journal of Post Keynesian Economics*, vol. 7, 474–92.

Mohammadi, H., and Ram, R. (1990) 'Manufacturing Output and Labour Productivity: Further Evidence for the United States', *Economic Letters*, vol. 32, 221–4.

Mortenson, D.T., and Pissarides, C.A. (1995) 'Technological Progress, Job Creation and Job Destruction', *CEP Discussion Paper*, no. 264, September.

Moulton, B. (2000) 'Improved Estimates of the National Income and Product Accounts for 1929–99: Results of the Comprehensive Revision', *Survey of Current Business*, vol. 80, 11–6.

Myrdal, G. (1957) *Economic Theory and Underdeveloped Regions*, London: Duckworth.

Nadiri, I. (1970) 'Some Approaches to the Theory and Measurement of Total Factor Productivity: a Survey', *Journal of Economic Literature*, vol. 85, 1137–77.

Nelson, R.R. (1956) 'A Theory of the Low-Level Equilibrium Trap in Underdeveloped Economies', *American Economic Review*, vol. 46, 894–908.

Nelson, R.R. (1998) 'The Agenda for Growth: a Different Point of View', *Cambridge Journal of Economics*, vol. 22, 497–520.

Nelson, R.R. and Winter, S. (1977) 'In Search of a Useful Theory of Innovation', *Research Policy*, vol. 6, 36–76.

Newell, A., and Symons, J.S.V. (1987) 'Corporatism, Laissez-Faire and the Rise in Unemployment', *European Economic Review*, vol. 33, 567–614.

Nickell, S.J. (1998) 'Unemployment: Questions and Some Answers', *Economic Journal*, vol. 108, 802–16.

Office Statistique des Communautée Européennes (1960) 'Méthodes de Prévision du Développement à Long Terme', *Informations Statistiques*, vol. 6, 566–70.

Ofria, F. (1997) 'Una verifica empirica della legge di Verdoorn per il Centro-Nord e il Mezzogiorno (anni 1951–92)', *Rivista Economica del Mezzogiorno*, vol. 11, 497–518.

Olson, M. (1982) *The Rise and Decline of Nations: Economic Growth, Stagnation and Social Rigidities*, New Haven, CT: Yale University Press.

Oulton, N. (1995) 'Depreciation, Obsolescence and the Role of the Growth of Capital in Growth Accounting', *Bulletin of Economic Research*, vol. 47, 21–34.

Palley, T.I. (1996) 'Growth Theory in a Keynesian Mode: Some Keynesian Foundations for New Endogenous Growth Theory', *Journal of Post Keynesian Economics*, vol. 19, 113–36.

Palley, T.I. (1997) 'Aggregate Demand and Endogenous Growth: a Generalized Keynes–Kaldor Model of Economic Growth', *Metroeconomica*, vol. 48, 161–76.

Palmerio, G. (1969) 'Economie di scala e progresso tecnico incorporato nel settore industriale in Italia nel periodo 1951–65', *L'Industria*, n.s., vol. 3, 316–46.

Panas, E.E. (1980) 'The Simple and True Verdoorn Coefficient for Greek Manufacturing Industries', *Rivista Internazionale di Scienze Economiche*, vol. 4, 341–57.

Parikh, A. (1978) 'Differences in Growth Rates and Kaldor's Laws', *Economica*, vol. 45, 83–91.

Park, B.U., Simar, L. and Weiner, C. (2000) 'The FDH Estimator for Productivity Efficiency Scores: Asymptotic Properties', *Econometric Theory*, vol. 16, 855–77.

Pasinetti, L.L. (1981) *Structural Change and Economic Growth*, Cambridge: Cambridge University Press.

Pasinetti, L.L. (ed.) (1992) *Italian Economic Papers*, vol. I, Oxford: Oxford University Press.

Pasinetti, L.L. (ed.) (1993) *Italian Economic Papers*, vol. II, Oxford: Oxford University Press.

Petit, P. (1999) 'Integration and Convergence in the European Union', in M. Setterfield (ed.), *Growth, Employment and Inflation*, Basingstoke: Macmillan – now Palgrave Macmillan.

Pieper, U. (2000) 'Sectoral Regularities of Productivity Growth in Developing Countries: a Kaldorian Interpretation', MERIT, November, mimeo, 1–31.

Pigliaru, F. (1983) 'Legge di Verdoorn e *Cumulative Causation* nel modello a due settori di Kaldor: una nota', *Quaderni Sardi di Economia*, vol. 1/2, 73–82.

Pigliaru, F. (1987) 'The Performance of the Mezzogiorno's Indigenous Manufacturing Sector, 1951–70: a Discussion on Graziani's Effect and the Cumulative Causation Hypothesis', *Studi Economici*, vol. 33, 3–40.

Pini, P. (1996) 'An Integrated Model of Cumulative Growth: Empirical Evidence for Nine OECD Countries, 1960–1990', *Labour*, vol. 10, 93–150.

Pissarides, C.A. (1990) *Equilibrium Unemployment Theory*, Oxford: Blackwell.

Posner, M.V. and Steer, A. (1979) 'Price Competitiveness and the Performance of Manufacturing Industry', in F. Blackaby (ed.), *De-Industrialisation*, National Institute of Economic and Social Research, Economic Policy Papers 2, London: Heinemann.

Pugno, M. (1991) '"Catching up" in the (Old and New) Theories of Economic Growth', *Annali Scientifici del Dipartimento di Economia dell'Università di Trento*, vol. 4, 113–44.

Pugno, M. (1995) 'On Competing Theories of Economic Growth: Cross-country Evidence', *International Review of Applied Economics*, vol. 9, 249–74.

Pugno, M. (1996a) 'Structural Stability in a Cross-Country Neoclassical Growth Model', *Applied Economics*, vol. 28, 1555–66.

Pugno, M. (1996b) 'A Kaldorian Model of Economic Growth with Labour Shortage and Major Technical Changes', *Structural Change and Economic Dynamics*, vol. 7, 429–49.

Pugno, M. (1998) 'The Stability of Thirlwall's Model of Economic Growth and the Balance-of-Payments Constraint', *Journal of Post Keynesian Economics*, vol. 20, 559–81.

Rampa, G. (2000) 'Squaring Circles: I–O Table Deflation and the Constrained LS Approach', mimeo, University of Genoa.

Ranci, P., and Samek, M. (1982) 'La crescita industriale negli anni dell'inflazione', *L'Industria*, n.s., vol. 2, 201–32.

Ray, S., and Desli, E. (1997) 'Productivity Growth, Technical Progress and Efficiency Change in Industrial Countries: Comment', *American Economic Review*, vol. 87, 1033–9.

Rayment, P.B.W. (1981) 'Structural Change in Manufacturing Industry and the Stability of the Verdoorn Law', *Economia Internazionale*, vol. 34, 105–23.

Reid, G.C. (1989) *Classical Economic Growth: an Analysis in the Tradition of Adam Smith*, Oxford: Basil Blackwell.

Roberts, M. (1998) 'The MRW Model and Verdoorn's Law: Some Preliminary Results for the UK Counties, 1981–1991', Department of Land Economy, University of Cambridge, mimeo.

Roberts, M. (2002a) 'Essays in Cumulative Causation', unpublished PhD dissertation, University of Cambridge.

Roberts, M. (2002b) 'Growth and Unemployment: Does a Trade-off Exist?', Department of Land Economy, University of Cambridge, Discussion Paper.

Romer, P.M. (1986) 'Increasing Returns and Long-Run Growth', *Journal of Political Economy*, vol. 94, 1002–37.

Romer, P.M. (1987) 'Growth Based on Increasing Returns Due to Specialization', *American Economic Review*, vol. 77, 56–62.

Romer, P.M. (1989) 'Capital Accumulation in the Theory of Long-Run Growth', in R.J. Barro (ed.), *Modern Cycle Theory*, Cambridge, MA: Harvard University Press.

Romer, P.M. (1990) 'Endogenous Technological Change', *Journal of Political Economy*, vol. 98, 71–102.

Rosenberg, N. (1969) 'The Direction of Technological Change: Induced Mechanisms and Focusing Devices', *Economic Development and Cultural Change*, vol. 18, 1–24.

Rossi, N., Sorgato, A., and Toniolo, G. (1993) 'I conti economici italiani: una ricostruzione statistica, 1890–1990', *Rivista di Storia Economica*, Nuova Serie, vol. X, 1–47.

Rothschild, M. (1974) 'A Two-Armed Bandit Theory of Market Pricing', *Journal of Economic Theory*, vol. 9, 185–202.

Rowthorn, R.E. (1975a) 'What Remains of Kaldor's Law?', *Economic Journal*, vol. 85, 10–19.

Rowthorn, R.E. (1975b) 'A Reply to Lord Kaldor's Comment', *Economic Journal*, vol. 85, 897–901.

Rowthorn, R.E. (1977) 'Conflict, Inflation and Money', *Cambridge Journal of Economics*, vol. 1, 215–39.

Rowthorn, R.E. (1979) 'A Note on Verdoorn's Law', *Economic Journal*, vol. 89, 131–3.

Rowthorn, R.E. (1999) 'Unemployment, Wage Bargaining and Capital–Labour Substitution', *Cambridge Journal of Economics*, vol. 23, 413–25.

Salter, W.E.G. (1966) *Productivity and Technical Change* (with an addendum by W.B. Reddaway), second edition, Cambridge: Cambridge University Press.

Sandilands, R.J. (ed.) (1990) 'Nicholas Kaldor's Notes on Allyn Young's LSE Lectures, 1927–29', *Journal of Economic Studies*, vol. 17, 18–115.

Sangha, K.S. (1992) 'Production, Productivity, and the Verdoorn Law', *Indian Economic Journal*, vol. 40, 45–8.

Schmookler, J. (1966) *Invention and Economic Growth*, Cambridge, MA: Harvard University Press.

Scitovsky, T. (1954) 'Two Concepts of External Economies', *Journal of Political Economy*, vol. 62, 141–51.

Scott, M. FG. (1989) *A New View of Economic Growth*, Oxford: Clarendon Press.

Scott, M. FG. (1991) *A New View of Economic Growth. Four Lectures*, World Bank Discussion Papers, no. 131.

Seiford, L., and Thrall, R. (1990) 'Recent Developments in DEA: the Mathematical Programming Approach to Frontier Analysis', *Journal of Econometrics*, vol. 46, 7–38.

Setterfield, M. (1997a) 'History Versus Equilibrium and the Theory of Economic Growth', *Cambridge Journal of Economics*, vol. 21, 365–78.

Setterfield, M. (1997b) *Rapid Growth and Relative Decline: Modelling Macroeconomic Dynamics with Hysteresis*, Basingstoke: Macmillan – now Palgrave Macmillan.

Setterfield, M. (1998) 'Demand Shocks and Long-Run Growth', Economie Appliquée, vol. 51, 7–27.

Setterfield, M. (ed.) (1999) *Growth, Employment and Inflation: Essays in Honour of John Cornwall*, Basingstoke: Macmillan – now Palgrave Macmillan.

Simar, L., and Wilson, P.W. (2000) 'Statistical Inference in Nonparametric Frontier Models: the State of the Art', *Journal of Productivity Analysis*, vol. 13, 49–78.

Skott, P. (1999) 'Kaldor's Growth Laws and the Principle of Cumulative Causation', in M. Setterfield (ed.), *Growth, Employment and Inflation: Essays in Honour of John Cornwall*, Basingstoke: Macmillan – now Palgrave Macmillan.

Skott, P. and Auerbach, P. (1994) 'Cumulative Causation and the "New" Theories of Economic Growth', *Journal of Post Keynesian Economics*, vol. 17, 381–402.

Smith, A. (1776) *An Inquiry into the Nature and Causes of the Wealth of Nations*, edited by A. Skinner, Harmondsworth: Penguin Books, 1973.

Solow, R.M. (1956) 'A Contribution to the Theory of Economic Growth', *Quarterly Journal of Economics*, vol. 70, 65–95.

Solow, R.M. (1957) 'Technical Change and the Aggregate Production Function', *Review of Economics and Statistics*, vol. 39, 312–20.

Solow, R.M. (1970) *Growth Theory: an Exposition*, Oxford: Oxford University Press (second edition, 2000).

Solow, R.M. (1987) 'We'd Better Watch Out', *New York Times Review of Books*, July.

Solow, R.M. (1994) 'Perspectives on Growth Theory', *Journal of Economic Perspectives*, vol. 8, 45–54.

Soro, B. (1983) 'Una nota sulla ripresa del dibattito attorno alla "Legge di Verdoorn"', *Ricerche Economiche*, vol. 3, 580–91.

Soro, B. (1985) 'Crescita regionale a tassi differenziati: possibilità e limiti di applicazione di uno schema analitico kaldoriano', *Economia e Politica Industriale*, vol. 45, 85–107.

Soro, B. (1986) 'Crescita della produttività, dell'occupazione e della produzione manifatturiera nell'esperienza regionale italiana', in R. Camagni and R. Malfi (a cura di), *Innovazione e Sviluppo Nelle Regioni Mature*, Milano: Angeli.

Soro, B. (1997) 'Una nota su Kaldor e l'economia dell'imposta selettiva sull'occupazione', in *Studi in Onore di Victor Uckmar*, Padova: CEDAM.

Sraffa, P. (1926) 'The Laws of Return under Competitive Conditions', *Economic Journal*, vol. 36, 535–50.

Stavrinos, V.G. (1987) 'The Intertemporal Stability of Kaldor's First and Second Growth Laws in the UK', *Applied Economics*, vol. 19, 1201–9.

Stigler, G.J. (1951) 'The Division of Labour is Limited by the Extent of the Market', *Journal of Political Economy*, vol. 59, 185–93.

Stone, J.R.N. and Prais, S.J. (1952) 'Systems of Aggregative Index Numbers and their Incompatibility', *Economic Journal*, vol. 62, 565–83.

Stoneman, P. (1979) 'Kaldor's Laws and British Economic Growth: 1800–1970', *Applied Economics*, vol. 11, 309–19.

Stoneman, P. (1983) *The Economic Analysis of Technological Change*, Oxford: Oxford University Press.

Summers, L., and Heston, A. (1991) 'The Penn World Table (Mark 5): an Expanded Set of International Comparisons, 1950–1988', *Quarterly Journal of Economics*, vol. 106, 327–67.

Swales, J.K. (1983) 'A Kaldorian Model of Cumulative Causation: Regional Growth with Induced Technical Change', in A. Gillespie (ed.), *Technical Change and Regional Development*, Leeds: University of Leeds.

Swan, T.W. (1956) 'Economic Growth and Capital Accumulation', *Economic Record*, vol. 32, 334–61.

Sylos Labini, P. (1983–84) 'Factors Affecting Changes in Productivity', *Journal of Post Keynesian Economics*, vol. 84, 161–79.

Targetti, F. (1985) 'Growth and the Terms of Trade: a Kaldorian Two Sector Model', *Metroeconomica*, vol. 37, 79–96.

Targetti, F. (1988) *Nicholas Kaldor. Teoria e politica economica di un capitalismo in mutamento*, Bologna: Il Mulino.

Targetti, F., and Foti, A. (1997) 'Growth and Productivity: a Model of Cumulative Growth and Catching-Up', *Cambridge Journal of Economics*, vol. 21, 27–43.

Targetti, F., and Thirlwall, A.P. (1989) *The Essential Kaldor*, London: Duckworth.

Temple, J. (1998) 'Equipment Investment and the Solow Model', *Oxford Economic Papers*, vol. 50, 39–62.

Temple, J. (1999) 'The New Growth Evidence', *Journal of Economic Literature*, vol. 37, 112–56.

Thirlwall, A.P. (1979) 'The Balance of Payments Constraint as an Explanation of International Growth Rate Differences', *Banca Nazionale del Lavoro Quarterly Review*, vol. 32, 45–53.

Thirlwall, A.P. (1980a) 'Rowthorn's Interpretation of Verdoorn's Law', *Economic Journal*, vol. 90, 386–8.

Thirlwall, A.P. (1980b) 'Regional Problems are "Balance-of-Payments" Problems', *Regional Studies*, vol. 14, 419–25.

Thirlwall, A.P. (ed.) (1983a) Symposium on Kaldor's Laws, *Journal of Post Keynesian Economics*, vol. 5, 341–429.

Thirlwall, A.P. (1983b) 'A Plain Man's Guide to Kaldor's Growth Laws', *Journal of Post Keynesian Economics*, vol. 5, 341–4.

Thirlwall, A.P. (1986) 'A General Model of Growth and Development on Kaldorian Lines', *Oxford Economic Papers*, vol. 38, 199–219.

Thirlwall, A.P. (1987) *Nicholas Kaldor*, Brighton: Wheatsheaf Books.

Thirlwall, A.P. and Dixon, R. (1979) 'A Model of Export-led Growth with a Balance of Payments Constraint', in J.K. Bowers (ed.), *Inflation, Development and Integration: Essays in Honour of A.J. Brown*, Leeds: Leeds University Press.

Thirlwall, A.P., and Sanna, G. (1996) 'The Macro Determinants of Growth and "New" Growth Theory: an Evaluation and Further Evidence', in P. Arestis (ed.), *Employment, Economic Growth and the Tyranny of the Market: Essays in Honour of Paul Davidson*, Aldershot: Edward Elgar.

Timmer, M.P., and Szirmai, A. (2000) 'Productivity Growth in Asian Manufacturing: the Structural Bonus Hypothesis Examined', *Structural Change and Economic Dynamics*, vol. 11, 371–92.

Tinbergen, J. (1942) 'Zur Theorie der Langfriestigen Wirtschaftsentwicklung', *Welwirtschaftliches Archiv*, vol. 55, 511–49. English translation, 'On the Theory of Trend Movements', in L.H. Klaassen, L.M. Kayck and H.J. Witteveen (eds) (1959), *Jan Tinbergen: Selected Papers*, Amsterdam: North Holland.

Toner, P. (1999) *Main Currents in Cumulative Causation: the Dynamics of Growth and Development*. Basingstoke: Macmillan – now Palgrave Macmillan.

Turner, R.E. (1983) 'A Re-examination of Verdoorn's Law and its Application to Manufacturing Industries of the UK, West Germany and the USA', *European Economic Review*, vol. 23, 141–8.

UNECE (1977) *Structure and Change in European Industry*, New York: UNECE.

Utterback, J.M. (1979) 'The Dynamics of Product and Process Innovation in Industry', in J.M. Utterback and F. Hill (eds), *Technological Innovation for a Dynamic Economy*, New York: Pergamon.

Vaciago, G. (1968) 'Sviluppo della produttività e Legge di Verdoorn nell'economia italiana', *Moneta e Credito*, vol. 83, 326–43.

Vaciago, G. (1974) 'Rendimenti crescenti e "residuo" nello sviluppo europeo (1950–1970)', *Moneta e Credito*, vol. 108, 395–420.

Vaciago, G. (1975) 'Increasing Returns and Growth in Advanced Economies: a Re-evaluation', *Oxford Economic Papers*, vol. 27, 232–9.

Vaglio, A. (1988) 'Static and Dynamic Economies of Scale in Export-Led Growth', *Economic Notes*, vol. 2, 61–81.

Vaglio, A. (1990) 'Fatti stilizzati ed interpretazione teorica: il caso della Legge di Verdoorn', *L'Industria*, n.s., vol. 11, 143–72.

Valcamonici, R. (1977) 'Struttura di mercato, accumulazione e produttività del lavoro nell'industria manifatturiera italiana 1951–71', in G. Carli (ed.), *Sviluppo economico e strutture finanziarie in Italia*, Bologna: Il Mulino.

Valdés, B. (1999) *Economic Growth: Theory, Empirics and Policy*, Cheltenham: Edward Elgar.

Veblen, T. (1915) *Imperial Germany and the Industrial Revolution*, London: Macmillan.

Verdoorn, P.J. See chapter 3, Appendix II, this volume, for the bibliography of Verdoorn's articles in Dutch and English.

Verdoorn, P.J. (1949) 'Fattori che regolano lo sviluppo della produttività del lavoro', *L'Industria*, vol. 1, 3–10 (reprinted as chapter 2, this volume).

Verdoorn, P.J. (1956) 'Complementarity and Long-range Projections', *Econometrica*, vol. 24, 429–50.

Verdoorn, P.J. (1980) 'Verdoorn's Law in Retrospect: a Comment', *Economic Journal*, vol. 90, 382–5.

Vernon, R. (1966) 'International Investment and International Trade', *Quarterly Journal of Economics*, vol. 80, 190–207.

Vries, A.S.W. de (1980) 'The Verdoorn Law Revisited: a Note', *European Economic Review*, vol. 14, 271–7.

Wee, H. van der (1987) *Prosperity and Upheaval: the World Economy, 1945–80*, Harmondsworth: Penguin Books.

Whiteman, J.L. (1987) 'Productivity and Growth in Australian Manufacturing Industry', *Journal of Post Keynesian Economics*, vol. 9, 576–92.

Winters, A.L. (1981) *An Econometric Model of the Export Sector: UK Visible Exports and Their Prices, 1955–73*, Cambridge: Cambridge University Press.

Wold, H. and Faxer, R. (1957) 'On the Specification Error in Regression Analysis', *Annals of Mathematical Statistics*, vol. 28, 265–7.

Wolfe, J.N. (1968) 'Productivity and Growth in Manufacturing Industry: Some Reflections on Professor Kaldor's Inaugural Lecture', *Economica*, vol. 35, 117–26.

Wright, T.P. (1936) 'Factors Affecting the Cost of Airplanes', *Journal of Aeronautical Sciences*, vol. 3, 122–8.

Wulwick, N.J. (1991) 'Did the Verdoorn's Law Hang on Japan?', *Eastern Economic Journal*, vol. 17, 15–20.

Wulwick, N.J. (1993) 'What Remains of the Growth Controversy', *Review of Political Economy*, vol. 5, 321–43.

Yotopoulos, P.A., and Lin, J.Y. (1993) 'Purchasing Power Parities for Taiwan: the Basic Data for 1985 and International Comparisons', *Journal of Economic Development (Korea)*, no. 1, 177–212.

Young, A. (1928) 'Increasing Returns and Economic Progress', *Economic Journal*, vol. 38, 527–42.

Young, A.A. (1993) 'Invention and Bounded Learning by Doing', *Journal of Political Economy*, vol. 101, 443–71.

Index